THE MARCH OF SOCIALISM

THE MARCH OF SOCIALISM

J. ALVAREZ DEL VAYO

Translated by

JOSEPH M. BERNSTEIN

 HILL AND WANG   New York

A division of Farrar, Straus and Giroux

Translation copyright © 1974 by Farrar, Straus and Giroux, Inc.
All rights reserved
First printing, 1974

Library of Congress catalog card number: 73-80221

ISBN: 0-8090-6746-3

Published simultaneously in Canada
by Doubleday Canada Ltd., Toronto
Printed in the United States of America

1 2 3 4 5 6 7 8 9 0

Designed by Gustave Niles

CONTENTS

36222

THE MARCH OF SOCIALISM

INTRODUCTION

This is not a history book. Its author is not a historian—neither by temperament nor by training. It is, rather, a political action, undertaken by a Socialist who believes in socialism. As you will see in the following pages, there have been far too many Socialists to whom socialism was nothing but a label or a mere party card.

Here the term "socialism" is used in its broadest sense. The utopian socialism of the forerunners. Scientific socialism since Karl Marx. The socialism of the Russian Revolution of October, 1917, the fiftieth anniversary of which coincided with the beginning of the writing of this book. The socialism of the Chinese Revolution.

These events are here either studied in depth or personally lived through. Whenever a movement of revolt, whether two thousand years old or unfolding before our very eyes, reveals Socialist stirrings, I have pointed to its existence. It does not matter how vague or rudimentary these stirrings have been: the gamut runs from the first revolts against man's exploitation of man to the current guerrilla struggles in Latin America and elsewhere. Of course, I could not cover everything in a few hundred pages of a book. But I have sought to include the most representative episodes in humanity's long struggle for socialism.

Every genuine movement of revolt, every revolution with even the faintest and feeblest social content, is linked with all others across time. The long intervals between them, occurring for a multitude of reasons, have never succeeded in stifling or crushing the revolution-ary impulse.

Wherever there is a human being or a group of human beings undaunted by obstacles and determined to crush slavery in its ancient and modern forms, a new step forward is taken in the ceaseless march toward socialism—arousing the people and guaran-teeing them victory over privilege and exploitation.

The scripts vary; the characters range from a leader of the enslaved masses in the ancient world to a contemporary Marxist thinker opposed to opportunistic sacrifice of principles in this heyday of the atomic age.

This is not, therefore, a standard history of world socialism comparable to the useful works by G. D. H. Cole, Max Beer, and other well-known historians of socialism. It is rather a highly personal, selective history which omits entirely much material that would be included in a conventional text. On the other hand, it offers data that academic and even Socialist scholars rarely, if ever, mention—for example, the precursor role of the early-eighteenth-century French revolutionary priest Jean Meslier; and the special fight for women's rights that has occurred in all the modern revolutions commencing with the French Revolution of 1789. In some instances—notably the case of the Spanish *Comunidades* (communes) of Castile in the early sixteenth century—I discern pre-Socialist stirrings in a social movement about which scholars, even Socialist scholars, are still sharply divided.

In a general way, of course, I have presented a chronological history of socialism—of both the forerunner movements and modern socialism as first formulated by Karl Marx and Friedrich Engels in the mid-nineteenth century. But here too the reader will find some overlapping, intertwining, foreshortening, and telescoping of events. It should come as no surprise if here and there I have omitted specific events, doctrines, or individuals that are usually associated with the development of socialism. As the story comes closer to us in time, the chronology naturally becomes more clearly defined; and this is above all true of the march of socialism in our own lifetime.

In the course of my life I have been fortunate to have personally known virtually every important Socialist and Communist leader in the world, beginning with Lenin and Rosa Luxemburg and extending to the current leaders on the world scene. Because I believe that individuals *do* play a role in history—or, as Marx put it: "Man makes his own history but not out of whole cloth"—I have seen fit to include descriptions and evaluations of many of these Socialist personalities as I have known them.

Too often books about socialism, despite lip service to internationalism, deal largely or only with countries and movements in the Northern Hemisphere. But in our twentieth century the march of socialism has become a truly world-wide phenomenon, embracing all the seven continents on earth. That is why I have devoted lengthy chapters to socialism in Asia, Africa, and Latin America; indeed, Socialist breakthroughs in the historically "backward" nations contain significant and profound lessons for the technologically powerful and "advanced" nations of the West. In the final analysis, what we are witnessing is a constant process of interaction and cross-fertilization in the march of world socialism.

The story begins with Spartacus.

1

FORERUNNERS

SPARTACUS

The revolt of Spartacus in 73–71 B.C. was the third and last of its kind in a span of seventy years in ancient Rome. Yet in scope and duration as well as in the remarkable personality of its leader, Spartacus, it has remained a landmark in human history. What was behind the uprising? The concentration of land in the hands of a minority of landowners; but, above all, the self-bestowed right of the power elite of that time to treat great numbers of human beings as mere objects.

Slavery was not a unique institution in the first century before the Christian era. All the nations of antiquity had had slaves. But the conditions of the slaves worsened as the Roman upper classes indulged in increasingly riotous living, especially as the disintegration and fall of the Roman Empire drew near. There was an element of class struggle in the way the Roman nobility used—or, more accurately, abused—their slaves. For slavery made it possible for the privileged caste to live in great luxury and ostentation, by exploiting human beings bought and sold at will, reduced to the level of "things."

Thus the Roman citizen of good taste with sufficient means to satisfy his every whim could not only obtain unlimited domestic help but could also press into service the outstanding talents of the day.

All he had to do was to go into the marketplace to select the architects, sculptors, poets, and even philosophers who would lend luster to his house and brilliantly adorn his feasts. The highborn Romans competed for these talents, creating a veritable industry of hired professionals. Youths of sound body and handsome features were trained as expert craftsmen or artists, exclusively serving their masters.

Slaves had no political and social rights. They were not even permitted to bear weapons to defend themselves against wild animals. They were simply heads to be counted on the vast estates of the large landowners.

This huge mass of harshly exploited human beings broke out in numerous but futile slave revolts—until it found its leader: Spartacus. He was a man born free, but imbued with deep sympathy for the downtrodden slaves and moved by an irrepressible spirit of rebellion. Michelangelo has immortalized him in his sculpture "Slave in Chains."

Born free in Thrace but then taken prisoner by the Roman army and sold as a slave, Spartacus impressed his captors with his physical prowess. So he was sent to a training school for gladiators at Capua. But the role of gladiator, in which slaves killed one another, did not appeal to him. He preferred to strike at tyranny. And he soon found that he could awaken a yearning for freedom in other slaves, inspiring them to fight for it even at the cost of their lives. They in turn, sensing the direction in which the social winds were blowing, made him their leader in the impending revolt. His magnanimity equaled his physical power.

The first battles took place at the foot of Mount Vesuvius in 73 B.C. The Roman authorities were confident that on that terrain they could easily surround the rebels and crush them, especially the insolent professional gladiator who had turned revolutionary. Under Spartacus' command the slaves held out for an entire winter. The ranks of the insurgents were continually swelled with new recruits, for Spartacus was able to persuade as well as command. Attacks on rich country estates brought new supporters and supplies. The irons with which the slaves had been shackled were used as weapons. Oxhides and sheepskins proved admirably suitable for combat uniforms. Here for the first time in history the principle of expropriation without indemnification—recognized many centuries later by scientific socialism—was introduced.

The insurrection had its ups and downs. Yet even in moments of greatest adversity Spartacus held firm and succeeded in turning temporary setbacks into new victories over the Roman Consuls. The revolt, treated at first by the Roman nobility with ridicule and disdain, lasted three years, from 73 to 71 B.C. By this time there was no great desire to tangle with Spartacus, now revered by his forces and demonstrating each day increasing mastery of the art of warfare. But the proconsul M. Licinius Crassus, overweeningly ambitious, offered personally to lead the forces of repression. A large landowner himself, Crassus spoke for the ruling class of his era, and the thought of wiping out the man who had dared to challenge property rights gave him particular pleasure.

Spartacus fought off the new punitive expeditions without risking more of his army than was necessary. Husbanding his forces, he retreated skillfully. But Crassus, crucifying thousands of captured slaves en route along the Appian Way, thought that now he had Spartacus surrounded and would finish him off. By this time, the fight had become increasingly unequal. Harried on every hand, betrayed by the Sicilian pirates who, had they not turned against him, would have enabled him to reach the sea, and thence the islands where he could have reorganized his exhausted army after its grueling march across Italy, Spartacus fought battle after battle in the final stage of the uprising. Heroically he sought to break the blockade and find an escape route for his men.

At last, the armies met face to face. The decisive battle took place in 71 B.C. in Luamia, near the Silarus River. Spartacus was in the front line until wounded by the blow of a spear. Despite his wounds, he fought on. Then, finally, he became just another corpse on the mounds of slaves' corpses, unidentifiable, indistinguishable from the mass of those from whom he had emerged and with whom he had been a brother in suffering and revolt. Yet when the Roman legions entered Spartacus' camp after his death, they found three thousand Roman prisoners unharmed.

Spartacus fell under the banner of "equality among men." From that day, his name has been honored, a symbol of humanity's epic struggle for freedom.

THE COMMUNES OF CASTILE

The rebellion of Castile against the Holy Roman Emperor Charles V in the early sixteenth century shows some well-defined aspects of class struggle. It represented the clash of feudal forces, agrarian and pastoral, with the nascent urban bourgeoisie; and indeed one of its results was to delay the consolidation of the Spanish bourgeoisie for a long period of time.

The *Comunidades* of Castile—the English equivalent would be "communes" or "municipalities"—have been the subject of vigorous controversy for over a hundred years. The central point at issue has been: Was the *Comunidades* movement revolutionary or reactionary? In a closely reasoned study, Manuel Azaña, who in the 1930's became President of the Spanish Republic, disputed the thesis held by many Spanish intellectuals that the uprising of the *comuneros* was simply a feudal exercise in sound and fury. These intellectuals looked upon the communal leaders as the representatives of a backward, medieval Castile, clinging to their privileges against Charles V, the "European," the wielder of absolute royal power, who seemed to them the symbol of the nation's progress and unification.

The theory concerning the reactionary character of the *comuneros'* revolt is based chiefly on the nature of the leadership of the movement. Its leaders, the claim runs, were the outstanding gentry and noblemen of their time: they bore such names as Don Pedro Girón, the Count of Salvatierra, the Bishop of Zamora, Juan de Padilla, Juan Bravo, and Francisco Maldonado. But this interpretation glosses over the presence of popular elements among the *comuneros*. Thus in Avila the community leader was a mechanic, in Medina a foundry worker, in Salamanca a harness-maker, in Burgos a locksmith.

On the surface, the *comuneros* fought to safeguard the traditional rights of the municipality, which had been challenged by the centralizing activity of the Crown. In reality, they were fighting to free their institutions of the threat to their historical evolution—and the key to this was an independent municipality. The *comuneros* may not have been liberals; they were certainly liberators. Their struggle for liberation was against the all-encompassing, centralizing, imperial despotism of Charles V. The rebellion brought to power local authorities whose political program was not always to the liking of the nobility. Proof of this is the fact that a number of noblemen soon abandoned the cause of the *Comunidades* and went over to the Emperor's camp.

Our main attention should be focused on the socio-economic aspects of the uprising. While a revolutionary document such as the *Capítulos de Tordesillas* stressed constitutional aspects of the problem, other petitions of the *comuneros* sought to protect the wool-trading cities, such as Segovia, and those who worked in them. Moreover, the principle of equal taxation, especially in the *alcabala*, or sales tax, the most unpopular of all the levies, was defended with a vehemence that angered the nobility. The development of the *Comunidad* gave rise to a decidedly anti-aristocratic movement just as soon as antagonistic class interests clashed.

Over-all, this movement signified—politically, socially, and economically—the defense of freedom in medieval Spain against the authoritarianism of the new sovereign. The monarchy remained feudal; but with its Cortes, or parliament, and its own *ayuntamientos*, or municipal councils, it was reluctant to be transformed into an absolute monarchy. By crushing the municipality of Villalar, Charles V struck a blow at Castile's representative government, substituting for it despotic rule.

The rising urban middle classes were repressed. The same hand that struck at the *comuneros* later turned against the Jews and the Marranos, who were for the most part merchants and artisans. And thus the Inquisition was given a powerful stimulus.

In the events of 1519–1521 we even see some of the *comuneros* advance the idea of free association, by which Castile would become a federation of free cities, on the order of the North Italian communes of the thirteenth century. Is that a reactionary trait? Eyewitnesses of the period, partisans of the Emperor, accused the Spanish *comuneros* of seeking to achieve "rights and freedoms," just like the citizens of Venice, Genoa, Florence, and Siena. The one thing about the Italian cities that most attracted the *comuneros* was that, as communes, they were not subject to any prince. They chose their own government. The governing body of the Italian commune was able to ward off tyranny because it called on the combined efforts of all its citizens. To achieve this end, it had to have institutions of self-government. If it did not have them, it would always be at the mercy of a prince's whims. The expression *ciudadanos*—citizens—appears a number of times in the documents of the *Comunidades* of Castile. For, in the final analysis, what is community if not self-government based on the will of the mass of the citizenry?

The list of demands submitted to the King by the Junta of Tordesillas stresses constitutional questions, and the petition expresses perhaps better than any other document of the time the thinking and the political program of the *comuneros*. The General Junta demanded—and, in fact, exercised—the right to name and dismiss officials, to regulate taxation, and to control the military. It insisted on dealing with the King as equal to equal.

The "Oath of Tordesillas" reflected the *comuneros*' protest against the excesses of royal power. The Emperor was put on notice that there were five reasons that had impelled the people to rebel: violation of the prerogatives of the Parliament of La Coruña, a disturbing indication of the threat to the principle of representation; increases in the sales taxes; too much money being taken out of the country; too many public offices being given to non-Spaniards; appointment of foreigners as governor.

It was general welfare, not merely narrow local selfishness, that motivated the *comuneros*. Proof of this is in the Valladolid petition to the attorneys for the Crown, in which the citizens seek the higher, "universal interests of these realms." Segovia asks "that we remain united in seeking remedies for Spain." The Junta's writings show a tendency to speak increasingly in the name of the kingdom as a whole. This attitude, couched in prudent and responsible terms, is reflected in the Junta's concrete recommendations for reforms and other social measures; and it was this that made the *Comunidades* so popular throughout Castile.

As the revolutionary process developed, political ideas spread and grew stronger, going well beyond the limits of the cities. The leaders of the revolt, particularly Juan de Padilla, sought their instructions from the Junta and asserted that they would not undertake anything without the Junta's approval. Legalistic at the outset, insisting that it opposed certain decisions of the King and his counselors only because it sought to re-establish the laws of the kingdom, the *Comunidades* movement quickly moved to higher ground, demanding what today we would call structural reforms.

In the course of the rebellion, opposition to unfair taxes intensified. It was this appearance of "the social and economic factor" that alienated many of those who at the outset had sympathized with the *comuneros'* cause. This grew more and more apparent as the movement became increasingly radicalized. The Junta vigorously defended the right of resistance, invoking the doctrines of St. Thomas Aquinas which justify even the use of violence in getting rid of intolerable tyranny. With the participation of the Third Estate, "by whose labor and industry we are all maintained," to quote a document of the period, the *comuneros'* uprising acquired revolutionary political content.

If on the political level the *Comunidades* sought to limit the powers of the King, on the social level their movement marked the coming of age of the Third Estate, with clear-cut examples of class struggle. The presence of working-class elements in the movement— the first faint outlines of a proletariat, despite all the limitations and restrictions of the period—frightened the high nobility and made them withdraw their initial support of the revolt. This shift in positions is especially noticeable in cities such as Madrid, Sigüenza, and Guadalajara, where, under pressure from the popular forces, the nobles were barred from public office. At critical moments in the revolt the numerical weight of the common people made itself felt. Hence charges by the dissident nobles that "the subversives are seeking to take government away from the gentry and place it in the hands of the plebeians, the working mechanics."

To back up their democratic demands by military force, the *comuneros* sought urgently to obtain the means to resist Charles V's armies. Military needs took precedence over all others. Hence the Junta of Tordesillas did not have much time to introduce the legislation that would have given juridical form to their state. Nevertheless, their outline of a *"Ley Perpetua"* (Perpetual Law) was of considerable significance. This draft, running to about a hundred articles, was put forward with the aim of submitting it to the King in Flanders, who would then accept it and swear to uphold it. The Junta was in no mood to beg the Crown for concessions. They anticipated the King's refusal to accept the law and were therefore determined to impose it by force of arms.

Running through the paragraphs of the draft Perpetual Law is a theme vigorously reiterated: opposition to the granting of important posts, such as the command of fortresses, to foreigners. But the law does not stop at assailing the privileges of Charles V's men, who had been brought to Spain from abroad so as to consolidate the centralist power against the liberation movement of the cities. It defends with equal vigor the equal rights of citizens, of qualified Spaniards, to hold government posts and offices. Though at times the *comuneros* give the superficial analyst the impression of having been primarily interested in perpetuating the past—the stagnant medieval past of the Spanish cities—in reality they fought to guarantee that the rising bourgeois class in the Castilian cities would have its say in the nation's future evolution. The projected Perpetual Law is concrete evidence of this interest. But in a general way this fact is confirmed by all the incidents preceding the decisive battle of Villalar in April, 1521. The King simultaneously attacked the two bulwarks of Spanish freedom, the Cortes and the municipal councils; the *comuneros* defended those institutions.

They defended them with popular passion and fury, throughout the entire country, identifying the uprising as a mass action. In Burgos, there was violence. In Medina, Bobadilla the cloth-shearer took the town hall by storm. In Toledo, those who regretted the radicalization of the movement complained that it was attracting only "the rabble and vagabonds."

The hero of the revolt was the body of *comuneros* as a whole. As for individual leaders, the one name that towers above all others is that of Juan de Padilla. For centuries after his execution, the military leader of the rebellion has been acclaimed for his courage and sacrifice in the defense of freedom and the struggle for national independence. Others were beheaded with Padilla at Villalar: among them, Juan Bravo and Francisco Maldonado, but to the ordinary Spaniard, Padilla has remained the symbol of heroism. And his fame has been celebrated in Spanish song and story.

2

PEASANT REVOLTS

Peasant revolts, some of them approaching the dimensions of a genuine revolution, have occurred periodically from the Middle Ages on. Until the appearance of the industrial working class as the vanguard of the Socialist movement, peasants were in many instances the precursors of socialism in their mass uprisings in the countryside against the large landowners. The medieval countryside exhibited all the signs of exploitation of one class by another. There the class struggle remained in a latent state until peasant anger exploded. Slavery as it had existed in the time of Spartacus was disappearing; in its place, serfdom became the general rule.

Food shortages and animal diseases combined to make poverty endemic. Abrupt changes in the price of grain were devastating to the people in the countryside. They profited little from steep drops in the prices of commodities; but they suffered greatly from sharp rises. Thus at the beginning of the fourteenth century, wheat rose rapidly in price, causing widespread starvation in southern France and many other places.

By the fourteenth century, then, bread had become a luxury item in many countries. The poor had to do without it, especially the rural poor who had grown the wheat from which it was made. Either they ate something else, or they died of starvation. Hence in the language of the people peasant revolts have often been called "bread revolts." Down through the centuries hunger was an ever-present affliction.

Around 1750 the French writer Voltaire wrote: "The country, sated with poems, tragedies, comedies, operas, novels, sentimental stories, moral reflections, and theological arguments, is finally beginning to think about wheat." By then France had intermittently experienced four hundred years of peasant uprisings, some of them extremely violent, followed by periods of apparent calm.

The most significant of these, apart from those immediately preceding the Great Revolution of 1789, was the "Jacquerie" of 1358. The word "Jacquerie" is derived from Jacques Bonhomme (Good-man James), the name the nobles derisively applied to the French peasant. The Jacquerie was an explosion of rage that had accumulated for centuries in the peasants' hearts—rage against the overlords, their "bloodsuckers." It was a fundamental challenge to feudal power.

Every feudal community has three characteristics in common: (1) The people live in an agricultural system; (2) it is a warrior's society based on the principle that being armed is the safest way of maintaining the established order; (3) it is an aristocratic society, with unequal classes: the few who enjoy the privileges and the many who are exploited.

The aristocratic class owns the land and has a monopoly on fighting arms. In that way it is in a position to dominate and oppress the peasant as it pleases. In feudal society cultivation of the land constitutes virtually the only source of wealth—for the owner, not for those who work the soil. It is through landownership that the right to rule over other human beings is acquired. Lands in which the relationship of lord to vassal was fixed were called "fiefs," and the term "feudal" characterized the entire system.

Under feudalism landownership represented an intermediate stage between the system of collective property prevailing in primitive societies and the system of unrestricted property in modern societies. But the feudal lord's authority was not limited to the domain of work where he could punish the serf as he pleased without any law to restrain him. Moreover, under feudalism the serf's entire family was forced to toil on the land to ward off starvation. Women and children were objects of the cruelest exploitation. In the fourteenth and fifteenth centuries French children working in the fields were paid twenty francs—at times as little as twelve francs—per year.

For the peasant the fact that he had no say in his destiny was even more humiliating than his wretched conditions of work. He was treated in every respect like a beast of burden, stripped of the most elementary rights essential to a free existence. The feudal lord had an army, a court of justice, and a governing council. The serfs were bound by his decisions—with no right of appeal whatever. They could be bought, sold, exchanged at will. They could not marry without their lord's consent, or in any way dispose of whatever few possessions they owned—either by selling or by bequeathing them.

Feudal justice was not only an attribute of the all-powerful master but also an instrument of profit. It included the right to coin money and decree its use. All the serfs—men and women alike—had to buy things made in the lord's workshops and at prices fixed by him. The lord could impose taxes and levies at will; he held a monopoly on the sale of salt, and had the right to tax marketplaces as well as collect all bridge tolls. In the light of such abuses and such highhanded rule by the landowning class, it is easy to see why in France, England, Germany, Russia, Spain, and China, peasant uprisings were often unusually violent, regardless of nationality or geography.

The Jacquerie of 1358 had from its inception a first-rate leader, a peasant from Meaux named Guillaume Karle (or Cale), sturdy, courageous, and imaginative. Having been a soldier, Karle had a rudimentary knowledge of the art of war. Instead of scattered little bands of men, he formed a genuine small army that numbered some six thousand under his command. Had Karle been able to capture a single city—Beauvais, for example—and consolidate his position there, the Jacquerie might have turned out differently. But he failed to do so. Lured to the Navarrese camp on the pretext of a truce, he was taken prisoner. No one in his movement could take his place. The ensuing repression was fierce.

The *Jacques* had destroyed castles; so the nobles burned the peasants' farms. The human slaughter was frightful. In his play, *La Jacquerie, scènes féodales,* the nineteenth-century French writer Prosper Mérimée underlined the historical significance of the events. Prior to 1358 there had been uprisings in France similar to the Jacqueries, but none of such scope and militancy. There were more to come. In some instances the peasants acted on their own; in others they took advantage of a general feeling of discontent to put forward their specific demands. Taxes in all shapes and forms, falling most heavily on the peasants, played a big part in these revolts. Direct taxation rose sharply in the period of Richelieu and Mazarin, more than doubling in the years between 1620 and 1660. One way of maintaining the armed forces was to make the peasants foot the bill. Regiments would enter a village, pillage it, and seize everything of value in it. The farmers were forced to eat grass to keep alive. But not always did they give in. In 1630 thousands of peasants led by women, armed with halberds and farm implements, attacked the city of Poitiers, forcing the authorities to flee. They then proceeded to storm the bakeries and flour mills in protest at the exorbitant price of bread. Five years later, in 1635, a new salt tax, or *gabelle*, falling most heavily on the vineyard workers, caused disturbances in the Bordeaux area. Manor houses were burned and there was "veritable madness" in the fields, according to the Duc d'Épernon, who assembled all the cavalrymen he could, to put down the revolt. In 1636 at Blanzac, in southwestern France, repeated attempts by the King to augment the wine taxes led to disorders. Feeling ran high against His Majesty's tax collectors; it was summed up in a general demand by the peasants that Cardinal Richelieu's functionaries and advisers stop behaving despotically. Peasant "communes" were organized in every parish in the region. Inhabitants were required to obtain arms, gunpowder, and bullets. As these uprisings developed across the years, the peasants grew more and more conscious of the fact that victory for their cause depended on their ability to wage armed struggle. "With mere sermons alone one cannot win"—such sayings became increasingly popular in the French countryside. The poor did gather to discuss and debate, but at the same time they collected as many muskets and pikes as they could. The sound of the "tocsin" became the quickest and surest way of assembling the people in arms. Along with a readiness to do battle went a willingness to sabotage the arbitrary system of taxation. In practice the *taille*—a personal tax—was not paid.

When this 1636 insurrection of *Les Croquants*—the clodhoppers—was finally overcome, the nobility was on the side of the state. In a solemn declaration the nobles affirmed that they were "creatures of our sovereigns" and "grateful for the privileges and authority granted them by His Majesty." Thus was nourished among the peasants a feeling of hatred for the aristocracy which at long last exploded violently during the Revolution of 1789.

But just one year later, in 1637, the *Croquants* of Périgord undertook to continue the fight. The peasants, reinforced by former soldiers, again rebelled against the *tailles* and other taxes: in their complaint to the King they declared they had had enough of being wounded in their sense of human dignity. The abuses of the tax collectors were compounded by the scandalous behavior of the King's troops, who robbed the peasants, raped their wives and daughters, and behaved as if they were in enemy territory.

Asserting repeatedly and with suspicious emphasis that he was the King's most loyal and obedient servant, La Mothe, head of the Périgord communes, was not the man to lead the peasants to victory. He lacked genuine militancy, and at the first sign of defeat sought out the nobles of the province to ask them to effect a reconciliation with the Royal Court. A doctor in Périgueux, Magot, accused La Mothe of treason and assumed leadership of the *Croquants*, who refused to surrender in their fortress of Bergerac. It was too late. A hopeless struggle ensued. The surviving peasants fled to the woods. The revolt was over.

In 1670 there was a revolt at Vivarais, in which, as in the uprising in the 1630's, peasants were allied with urban artisans. Worsening economic conditions continued to be the main source of dissatisfaction. Increases in taxation were growing unbearable for the peasantry. The main direct tax, the *taille*, quadrupled in amount from the beginning to the middle of the sixteenth century. The state was forced to take the sternest measures to overcome peasant resistance to payment of taxes. The "finance officials" of the Crown, hated and despised by the peasantry, added to the state's fiscal burdens by greedily pocketing large commissions.

The peasants in revolt found support and allies in the most unlikely quarters. Under Louis XIV a priest named Meslier—Curé Meslier, atheist, communist, and revolutionary, according to Maurice Dommangent—joined with the peasants. Meslier's vigorous criticism of the institutions of the *ancien régime,* beginning with the doctrine of the divine right of kings, made him a "premature" Jacobin, a precursor of the Revolution of 1789, more than a century before it occurred.

Peasant revolts continued all during Louis XIV's reign and in the subsequent period known as *La Fronde*, in which the ultra-conservative feudal nobility fought the centralizing monarchy. In 1675 there was an uprising in Brittany, popularly known as the "stamped paper" revolt, in protest against a system that gave the feudal lords the unchallenged right to administer justice for their own ends. This right was invoked whenever the first signs of discontent appeared among the peasants, victimized by hunger and disease and often forced to live with their families in crowded one-room huts. In April, 1674, a royal decree had been issued, making obligatory throughout the kingdom the use of official stamped paper for all court and notary transactions. The Breton population was indignant. Their anger mounted when that same year the profits of the tobacco monopoly were reserved exclusively for the King. The peasants saw in all these measures an intolerable abuse of power. The tobacco monopoly virtually forced the poorer among them to stop smoking. As a result, government tobacco shops were attacked and looted, with artisans and small shopkeepers joining the peasants in the assaults.

The people directed their fire at the nobility, who were held accountable for this system of exploitation. Bread was scarce, and the authorities did nothing to alleviate the situation. As one document of the time says: "There are the well-known epidemics and the epidemic of the tax collectors." In lower Brittany châteaux were pillaged. In many instances the peasants first invaded the wine cellars and then, fortified by the heady wine, went into action. Along with these attacks, delegates from fourteen parishes drew up a "Peasant Code" to submit to the government, listing their demands and proposals. But when this movement proceeded from violent direct action to a formulation of its demands, it lacked the political substance and maturity of Father Meslier, who clearly saw that the only way to destroy the power base of the nobility was by radically changing the political and social structure of his day.

Jean Meslier (1664–1729) seems to have been one of the most extraordinary men in France during the reign of Louis XIV—as is shown in his written *Testament*. He was a precursor of the priests who, in Spain and Brazil in the 1960's, brought about the so-called "cassock revolt"—indeed, Meslier was much more radical than his modern counterparts. Serving a tiny parish, Meslier became the faithful interpreter of the deep dissatisfaction of the masses of the peasantry and bravely fought for their demands, in defiance of all the Church and secular authorities. Thinkers such as Voltaire esteemed him highly. Branded an "atheist, rebel, and Communist priest" by his contemporaries, Meslier was not intimidated by the designation; in fact, he took pride in it. A Communist priest in the reign of Louis XIV—that is really something!

Born in Mazerny, a hamlet in the duchy of Rethel, in Champagne, Meslier served in the parish of Etrépagny, where he was in close contact with his peasant parishioners and in constant conflict with the lords of the region. He read widely and thought much. He soon rejected the ideas of feudalism, which, in his opinion, were outdated, and spread libertarian ideas of his own. He based his position on three main elements: socialism, revolution, and materialism. In his *Testament* he does not shrink from praising tyrannicide and expresses the desire to have enough strength to be able to joyfully "destroy with pleasure" all enemies of the people. He trades insults with the local overlord, Monsieur de Toully, ignoring the warnings and threats of his archbishop. Let the archbishop support the exploiter of the peasants if he so chooses; he, Meslier, will not tire of exposing him and of urging the peasants to resist him, if necessary by violence. He denounces the hypocrisy of those who condemn violence when it is practiced by the poor in their despair yet who accept it as a divine gift when the violence is exercised from above on behalf of the rich and the pillars of social order. In Meslier's words: "There is no order in social injustice. The order the hierarchies seek to defend is that of the right to oppress the peasant so that the lord can live a life of luxury and extravagance. Against such an order, revolution is justified." He continues: "Let the priests and preachers who serve the lords and all the propagators of lies to keep the people in a state of submission and resignation, treat me as an infidel, an apostate, a blasphemer and atheist; let them heap upon me all the maledictions they wish. While social injustice remains, all such curses leave me indifferent. The only thing that would disturb me would be the contempt of the peasant masses. It is to them the truth belongs."

It was in his Socialist work, unique in his time, that Father Meslier attained full greatness. It was not and could not be scientific socialism; on the other hand, it was not utopian socialism, since he intended to utilize the anger of the masses and direct it someday against survivals of the feudal regime. Meslier insists from the outset on "the inequality of conditions." Here was foreshadowed, almost two centuries ahead of time, the Marxist concept of class struggle. "All men are equal by nature; hence they all have the right to live and walk on earth, to equally enjoy their natural freedom and share in the good things of the earth, working usefully with one another." However, this right is denied the majority by a minority that considers itself above natural rights and feels itself entitled to practice its domination indefinitely in the name of the inviolability of institutions. The only inviolable right is the right to eat.

Father Meslier talks more about oppression than possession. The origin of possession is often unfair plunder. His criticism of the tax system that grinds down and impoverishes the peasantry is sharp, surprisingly similar in its analysis to that of a post-Marxian Socialist. Above all he attacks the *taille,* the most important of the direct taxes; and he assails "those kings who impose heavy taxes so as to make a profit from everything bought and sold, and cause the prices of wine and meat to rise. The kings may feel happy when they see their treasury increase, but the man of the people is the one who suffers from such enslavement." He lashes out at class justice: "Those who fasten on the slightest misdemeanor of the poor gloss over the vices and hateful excesses of the kings and princes." Alongside the anti-monarchist "crime of *lèse-majesté*"—insult to royalty—Father Meslier points to "the crime of *lèse*-injustice," as practiced daily against the poor. He does not accept the theory of divine right on which the absolute monarchy was based; nor does he spare Louis XIV himself in his criticism.

At the very center of Meslier's political philosophy is the peasantry: "The peasants who deserve a fate other than that of being deprived of the very bread they have sown." "The food that nourishes all these proud nations," writes Father Meslier, "the great riches and vast wealth extorted every day from the painful work of your hands, peasants and humble folk—this system of exploitation will one day have to end, but only by revolt."

In Father Meslier's writings one finds a defense of strikes as well as a rejection of blind obedience. The exploiter does not have to be obeyed. The philosophy of obedience and of the defense of the social order serves the interests of the oppressors by helping them to oppress the oppressed even more. Against such a system the refusal to work—that is, the strike—is a legitimate weapon.

Meslier was a partisan of direct action, an expounder of violence, a precursor of the Russian Narodniks (Populists) and the early Spanish and Italian anarchists. In his eyes, "men are cowards to allow the tyrant to live so long." He regretted that "just men do not rise up as in the time of Spartacus." His socialism was revolutionary, not reformist. To him a people's revolution was beneficial and necessary.

On more than one occasion during the peasant revolts in France the masses were ahead of their leaders. A Father Meslier was rare. Uprisings lacking political guidance, based solely on the discontents of the moment, were bound to fail; whereas more sustained actions might at least have forced the wealthy classes and the government to grant concessions. Consider, for example, the attack on the château of Kergoat in July, 1675. With thick stone walls and enough interior space to quarter an army of several thousand men, the castle rose up like an unassailable fortress of feudalism. But the peasants of the region, fully aware of what they were up against, refused to draw back. For two days they awaited the order to attack. Every one of them had obtained some kind of primitive weapon. They were not frightened at the prospect that the Duc de Chaulnes had at his disposal a host of horsemen and heavy pieces of cannon, in anticipation of popular uprisings. The castle was surrounded and taken. The cannon were dismounted. Legal deeds and parchments were burned in a bonfire of celebration. So impressive was this capture of Kergoat castle that a veritable pre-revolutionary situation arose. In some places the peasants proclaimed: "Our hour of absolute rule has struck, and we laugh at the King and his edicts." They spoke of a "new social order." But the outstanding leader of this 1675 revolt, Le Balp, let himself be swayed by rumors spread by the aristocrats concerning significant troop movements, and so ordered the peasants to retreat. A commentary from the above-mentioned Duc de Chaulnes may give an idea of the prevailing attitude of the nobles: "The rebels have been executed in Quimper, one of the most subversive districts, and the trees are beginning to bend with the weight of the hanged men."

In England, exploitation of the peasantry proceeded, but with "good manners," until the patience of the hard-working population wore thin and the masters replaced their paternalist attitude with the whip and club. By the time of Henry II (reigned 1154–1189), new social forces were at work in England, hastening the breakdown of the manorial system in the English countryside and leading to the freeing of the villeins (literally, peasants or rustics). The "manor" may be described in brief as an extent of land owned by a lord and occupied by a community of peasants in various categories, but all of them engaged in enriching their master. The first group in order of importance was the villeins, originally free, then after the middle of the twelfth century serfs. Below them were the "cottagers" whose living conditions were inferior to those of the villeins. Above both groups was the lord of the manor.

The years of the Black Death (1348–1349, 1361–1362, and 1368–1369), crucial for the social evolution of England, brought in their wake a multitude of woes. The country suffered an economic catastrophe of major proportions, fanning discontent and imbuing many of the peasants with a passion to do away with the oppressive system of feudalism. Two leaders of the people stand out: John Ball and Wat Tyler, both of whom died in 1381, the year of the "Great Revolt of 1381." Both were revolutionaries with advanced social views. Here, for example, is a passage from the French historian Froissart which sums up John Ball's social views: "My good people— Things cannot go well in England, nor ever will, until all goods are held in common, and until there will be neither serfs nor gentlemen, and we shall all be equal" (M. Beer, *History of British Socialism*, p. 28).

Once again, in 1413, the peasants moved against the feudal lords. This time monasteries did not escape the people's anger, for the monasteries too had been busily acquiring land and had become big landlords. There were intervals of relative tranquillity, followed by new explosions. Thus in 1449, under Henry VI, peasants of Kent rose up, led by Jack Cade; barely half a century later, the Cornish peasants revolted. Throughout the sixteenth century peasant revolts and insurrections multiplied. Under Henry VIII the rebellions against royal authorities found their readiest recruits among the landless peasants. Nor were social disturbances absent during the reign of Queen Elizabeth. It was therefore no accident that when Sir Thomas More wrote his utopian-communist work, *Utopia*, in 1516, it was against this background of social and political strife.

The Protestant Reformation that erupted in Germany at the start of the sixteenth century was not in its origins an exclusively religious revolt. It also bore within itself the seeds of a social movement. When the leaders of the Reformation broke with Catholicism, they were supported by the great mass of the discontented. As a matter of fact, at that moment in history no social class, except the clergy, was really satisfied with its status. It is not too much to say that the sixteenth-century Reformation anticipated in spirit the Socialist movement several centuries later. When on December 15, 1520, before the gates of Wittenberg, Martin Luther solemnly burned the papal bull of excommunication that had been issued against him, he gave the initial signal for the social agitation that was to convulse Germany for decades to come.

The peasants—particularly those in Swabia and Franconia—greeted the Reformation not so much because of their opposition to the dogmas of Rome but because of their hostility to the clergy, the bulwark of a system they hated and sought to destroy. For over thirty years in Germany peasant uprisings against the clergy and the big landowners had been occurring with increasing frequency. By refusing to serve in the army, the peasants expressed their antagonism toward the feudal lords and toward a system of justice that had become a grim joke to the dispossessed classes. From year to year the peasant outbreaks intensified in violence. The first uprising in 1476 in the archbishopric of Würzburg, led by a shepherd named Hans Boeheim, also called "Hans the Piper," demanded the abolition of discriminatory taxes, the removal from office of all lay and ecclesiastic authorities, and the establishment of a regime of equality. Another broke out in 1491 in the abbey of Kempten in upper Swabia; an even more violent one, in 1505, at Bruchsal, in the Rhineland-Palatinate, in which seven thousand men and four hundred women took up arms. By the early 1500's the movement had spread to "the windy marshes," the provinces of Carinthia, Styria, and Carniola of latter-day Austria. The peasants stormed castles, killed their owners, and attacked monasteries.

The social disorders engendered by the Reformation brought forth an outstanding leader, Thomas Münzer, a disciple of Luther who displayed far more revolutionary ardor and understanding than his erstwhile master. He preached reforms in manners and customs, denouncing luxury and advocating simple dress and the ascetic life; at the same time he demanded the elimination of Church tithes and taxes and the complete abolition of personal serfdom. In his demand for social justice Münzer went far beyond Luther, and eventually turned against him. Aware of the revolutionary potential of the printing press, Münzer established one in Nuremberg. From it emerged a series of radical books and pamphlets. Chroniclers of the period tell how in 1525 the subversive pamphlets were read in the taverns, which were focal points of the insurrection. In some cities the bourgeoisie and even, occasionally, the petty nobility, hoping to profit from the uprising by acquiring Church lands, made common cause with the rebels. Thus the peasants gained the cooperation of persons trained in the use of arms.

The peasant revolt in Germany in the years 1524–1525, in the southern and central areas of the country, was, as we have said, touched off by the Reformation. But as early as the fourteenth century there had been disturbances in the German countryside. The uprising in 1524 was led by Joss Fritz, its symbol the *Bundschuh* (Union Shoe). The agitation began in Swabia. There, on April 2, 1525, the peasants drew up "The Twelve Articles," a constitution in embryo, in which they submitted their demands, the most important of which were: election of clergymen by the communities; the right to remove priests; the abolition of the *Zehnten,* or small tithe, and the use of the large tithe for public purposes; and release from serfdom.

In 1525 the revolt spread to Thuringia, Switzerland, and Austria. Under the leadership of Florian Geyer, a Franconian knight, they demanded a new government for the German Reich and made preparations for a peasant parliament to meet in Heilbronn. In the Tyrol, Michael Geismaier went much further and advocated a genuine peasant state.

In Thuringia, Thomas Münzer gave the *Bundschuh* movement a tone of religious radicalism. But the causes of the uprising were not merely theological quarrels. Underlying these was the wretched condition of the countryfolk. The peasant was in poverty while in the cities wanton luxury prevailed. The nobles outdid one another in ostentation and, whenever they fell into debt, levied new taxes on the peasants. So now the peasantry refused to allow itself to be exploited any longer. In the region of the Landgrave of Stuhlinger they fought against the Counts of Lupfen. The whole Black Forest area was aroused by the anathemas pronounced by the most impassioned preachers of the *Bundschuh*. In many places the rebels demanded that the clergy renounce their privileges, including the right to levy taxes, in which they vied with the nobility.

At first the peasants displayed far more enthusiasm than organizational ability. But eventually they realized the need for discipline and military skill, and elected as their leader the very popular Goetz von Berlichingen. Initially Emperor Charles V took little note of events in Germany, and for a while the authorities reacted feebly. But as the violence increased they grew harsher. At Weinsberg the defenders of the "established order," Dietrich von Weiler and his followers, were rounded up by the peasants in the local church and hurled from the belfry to the pavement below.

The energy of the masses frightened Luther and the Church hierarchy. With the support of the clergy, therefore, the authorities proceeded to hunt down the peasants at will. On both sides the Peasants' War caused heavy casualties—the exact count will never be known. In his study of this massive peasant revolt, August Bebel, the outstanding German Socialist leader at the end of the nineteenth century, demonstrated that the peasantry were not passive and resigned in the face of landlord abuses; on the contrary, they responded to the Socialist appeal—whether primitive or modern—to do away with human exploitation.

At the start of the sixteenth century the atmosphere in Germany was so charged that a call for social justice of a new type was bound to attract a large number of the dissatisfied. It was the Reformation, as we have seen, that offered this appeal. To the German peasant in the 1520's the preacher condemning the lack of generosity of the rich was an ally and a guide. So in the summer of 1524 the first outbreak in the Black Forest was the precursor of a violent revolt in which elements of a social and religious character were mingled; but class struggle was the underpinning of the movement. In every region, from the Tyrol to the Rhine, groups of peasants elected their leaders. He might be a modest innkeeper such as Georg Metzler; or a nobleman such as Florian Geyer. Armed with pikes, the peasants, although fragmented and disorganized at the outset, turned into a disciplined force able to impose their will in the cities, where they obtained the support of the artisans—the proletariat of that era.

Gradually the rebellious peasants realized the need for a single, unified command. To that end they named the knight Goetz von Berlichingen their leader. He was an aristocrat whose clashes with the reactionary Church hierarchy had won him widespread sympathy. Now a great panic seized the princes, the nobility, and the landowning class in general. They moved quickly to organize the forces of repression. In May, 1525, these forces combined to defeat Thomas Münzer at Frankenhausen, taking him prisoner and executing him. In all, some one hundred thousand human beings died in this Peasants' War. The memory of these dead hung over all future "bread revolts."

To be sure, in many of these bread rebellions, in Germany as elsewhere, motives were mixed. It was not only grinding poverty; it was also a protest against the abuses of royal power, against the highhandedness of the nobles and the magistrates. But in the majority of instances the movements arose out of peasant anger. The peasants sought to form their "communes." It is a curious but significant fact—which seems to have escaped most of those who have written about the Chinese Revolution—that the idea of the commune, which in China has taken the form of people's communes, has a historical background that goes far back into the past, assuming different forms in different epochs and places.

In the final analysis the peasants' revolt in Germany was a reaction against the state. The same was true in France, in Russia, and in China.

In few countries was the peasants' lot more wretched than in Czarist Russia. Hence the story of their insurgency is one of the most dramatic and memorable ever recorded. The process developed parallel to the consolidation of the Russian state—a process fascinating in itself. On the broad plains from the Vistula to the Dnieper, and the Oder to the Warte, up to the heart of Central Europe, where strong Germanic elements of culture were soon absorbed by the Slavic tide, as well as from the Danube and the Adriatic Sea to the Alps, peacetime activities replaced warlike exploits and began to threaten the established feudal order. Cattle breeding, farm cultivation, and fishing quickly absorbed the energies of these simple folk. The election of heads of family to the town councils and town meetings of the local population marked a beginning of the disintegration of feudalism and a first step toward the revolt of the serfs. The masses were beginning to challenge the old established order.

In their way the builders of the Russian state in the ninth and tenth centuries also contributed to this break with the past. The princes persuaded their subjects to settle in Novgorod, not far from the Baltic coast, whence the founders of a powerful dynasty extended their vast rule toward the south and east, embracing ever larger zones of influence. The princes, adopting the languages and customs of the peoples they ruled, soon moved southward and established their residence on the great river route of Kiev. Thus they drew menacingly close to the feeble Byzantine Empire. Discovering affinities with the Greek dynasty, they embraced, under Vladimir the Great, Christianity in its Greek Orthodox rite. This was another way of asserting their rule.

Influenced by European culture, the Great Prince Varaeger, of the Rurik dynasty, consolidated the country, which now extended from the Dnieper to the shores of the Baltic, Lake Ladoga, and the Duna River. But when land distribution was attempted, the princes quarreled greedily among themselves and left the new state without inner cohesion. What resulted was a weak federation, instead of a firmly consolidated central government.

In any case, the princes were too feeble to resist the invasion by the Mongol conqueror Genghis Khan, whose fierce cavalry struck wherever there were weak spots. His original name, Temuchin, means "better steel" in Mongolian; the one he later adopted, Genghis Khan, means "mighty lord." This came after he had conquered most of Central Asia. At its height his empire was one of the greatest of all time, extending from Tibet to the upper limits of Siberia and from the Danube to Korea. His Mongol hordes "destroyed even the grass through which they passed," according to one contemporary account. In the course of this destructiveness, Batum was taken by storm and the leader of the Golden Horde advanced as far as the Black Sea, slaughtering and pillaging at will. For a time he put an end to the recently founded Russian principality.

Only at the Oder River was the onslaught of the Golden Horde checked. But for two centuries the brutal effects of the invasion were felt throughout Russia, imposing an unbearable burden on the population, making the peasants' lot even harsher, and cutting off all contacts with outside cultures. In this desperate situation the peoples of Russia began to see the need for a unified and centralized nation. Now the great principality of Moscow—as well as Novgorod and Kiev—became the focus of efforts to create a new state.

Exhibiting shrewd diplomacy, the most adroit of the princes played on the rivalries that had arisen between Batum, the pivotal point of Mongol influence, and local leaders. The Tartar khans preferred to deal with a single prince who had genuine power. Thanks to his gifts of leadership and suppleness, the Grand Duke of Moscow was acknowledged as the most effective mediator among the various forces that contended for control of Russia. The boyars, a group of large landowners, pledged allegiance to the Muscovite prince and in exchange were exempted from taxation. Thus the entire tax burden was shifted onto the peasants.

Then came the moment in the late fifteenth century when Ivan Vasilievich, called Ivan the Great, who ruled in Moscow, dared to challenge the Mongols' authority. By 1480 he had liberated the land from their yoke and driven foreign exploiters from Russian soil. His activities went much further. As a result of several victorious wars, he laid the foundations of the Russian nation. In the centuries to come, that nation, vast in area and rich in human resources, would play a powerful role in Europe's history.

Unfortunately, the central government was strengthened along authoritarian lines and at the expense of the peasant masses. Then, however, the Cossacks, descendants of Russian and Ukrainian serfs, entered upon the scene. Although they later became the symbol of the repressive policies of the Czars, at their origin they bore the germs of rebellion. Cossack formations, aided by a rich farmer named Stroganov, undertook legendary expeditions as far as the Siberian steppes, in some cases with as few as eight hundred men. Their energy brought quick results. With lightning rapidity they expelled the Mongolian hordes and acquired vast territories for the Russians. These lands were soon colonized and, before long, the Pacific coast was reached. Another Cossack chieftain, Deiniov, completed this work of colonization. In the Dnieper region the Cossacks built an independent community. Masters of their destiny and led by freely elected authorities, they confronted their neighbors, the Poles, Mongols, and other peoples.

In the Don Basin too and on the borders of the Caucasus the Cossacks organized themselves in free communities until Ivan the Great and his successors temporarily succeeded in depriving them of their liberties and at the same time ended the autonomy of the commercially important free state of Novgorod. Nevertheless, they could not stifle the feeling of freedom in the hearts of the masses. This feeling triggered the great uprisings that exploded from time to time within the absolutist Russian state.

A people capable of such immense achievements as the exploration and colonization of Siberia could not remain permanently enslaved. Nothing in Russian history, neither at its origins nor in its subsequent growth, could enshrine the arbitrary despotism of a handful of overlords who believed in the immutable nature of their privileges. In time, the imagination and political genius of the Russian people made such a condition of despotic power historically untenable.

After the death of Ivan the Terrible (1584), the Russian Empire, like many other European nations, passed through a dangerous government crisis. With the death of Ivan's son, the Rurik dynasty was extinct. In the ensuing period of disintegration a strong figure emerged: the boyar Boris Godunov, who became head of state. His regime consolidated the economic situation of the large landowners. Farm production markedly increased. The nomadic phase of existence ended for the rural population. But at the same time inhuman restrictions were placed on the peasants' freedom.

Godunov, the creator of this system, was not destined to enjoy its fruits. He left no legitimate heir to the throne after him. Ivan the Terrible had murdered his older son with his own hands; his second-born, Dimitri, was imprisoned by Boris Godunov in a monastery and was one day found there assassinated. The swarm of pretenders claiming succession to the throne, particularly the false Dimitri, throws a weird light on the turbulent atmosphere of the times—and the theme later became a favorite with such world-famous writers as Lope de Vega, Schiller, and Pushkin.

The lot of the peasants was wretched indeed. Rotation of the crops three times a year demanded hard labor; yet it left the peasants, after all taxes had been paid, with an insignificant return. They paid most of the taxes and had to supply soldiers for the Czar's army. By the end of the sixteenth century their conditions had decidedly worsened. To survive, the peasant had to supplement his work in the fields with bee cultivation, hunting, fishing, and handicrafts. The monasteries and the well-born of all classes, on the other hand, became rich from the revenues of their respective landholdings. So the harassed peasants fled toward virgin lands. This large-scale emigration was halted by a decision in the year 1580 prohibiting peasants from leaving their place of residence without the Czar's permission. Peasant discontent, repressed, ever latent, accumulated from year to year and czar to czar.

The land fell into indescribable chaos. But it was the patriotic feeling of the common people—not that of the feudal lords or boyars—that saved the nation from the abyss. The attempt by King Sigismund of Poland to take advantage of the chaotic situation failed, owing to the people's resistance. A kind of parliament, or popular assembly, the *Zemsky Sobor,* was formed and took charge of public affairs. A newly created militia attacked the enemy in their fortified positions and forced them to retreat. Then they proceeded to elect a new czar, the son of a boyar, Michael Romanov, who was proclaimed emperor in 1613.

One episode among many—which later furnished the theme for Glinka's opera *Ivan Susanin*—gives a good idea of how national sentiment coexisted with the sentiment of revolt in the Russian peasant of that day. The hero of *Ivan Susanin* was a peasant of that name who succeeded in thwarting the plans of the Poles and gave his life for his motherland.

Dynasties had succeeded one another; but one of them felt obliged to repay the peasant for his loyalty to the nation or at least do something to improve his lot. When the new dynasty, the Romanovs, ascended the throne, its first aim was to free the country of foreign invaders and extend its frontiers toward the south. A new era now began for the Russian Empire. The people, for their part, did not give up their aspirations for freedom. (It is really a cruel and unjust irony of etymology that the word "Slav" seems so closely related to the word "slave.")

One of the prevailing conditions of that period was popular election of the czar. Thus the first Romanovs had to consult the *Zemsky Sobor.* The example of the free Cossack republics of the Dnieper also influenced the turn of events.

The uprising of the Don Cossacks was violent and far-reaching in its consequences. Under the first Romanov the Don Cossacks had acknowledged Moscow's supremacy but without giving up their own way of life. In the hetman Stenka Razin, these *golytba* (propertyless Cossacks) had a leader of extraordinary qualities, a man of superhuman energy, courageous, resolute, undaunted by adversity. By dint of his personal magnetism he touched off a widespread peasant revolt. The uprising was directed not so much against the Czar's despotism as against the wealthy families who were the Czar's favorites and who fed their greed by exploiting the peasants.

In the Russia of that day I. N. Romanov, uncle of the Czar, may serve as the prototype of the large landowner. Romanov had received as a gift more than sixteen thousand rural estates, containing tens of thousands of serfs. Not only could he make them work under oppressive conditions; he could also dispose of them at will, selling them either with the land or independently of it. Then there were "the servants of the state," high up in the social hierarchy, who also profited from the total exploitation of the peasantry. Many of these large landowners, such as the wealthy boyar Morozov, were favorites of the Czar. This was class struggle in a primitive state but no less intense for all that.

So it was against this order of things that Stenka Razin rose up in armed struggle in 1667. But it was not until 1670 that the peasant uprising led by Razin changed from a mere uprising into a genuine revolution. The revolt was not against the Czar but against his evil advisers, the nobility, the "servants of the state," the parasites and bureaucrats who hid behind the Czar's prestige.

Stenka Razin's advance was triumphal. The people saw in him a wizard, invulnerable to enemy sabers and bullets. With a few comrades he struck first on the Volga, seizing a boat loaded with large quantities of food and routing a contingent of Muscovite troops. He next attacked the shores of the Caspian Sea and Persia. Then he returned with his booty to Astrakhan, where he divided it among the poor.

His forces quickly increased until they constituted an actual army corps. Then he declared that the moment had come to march against the boyars in Moscow. Some of the soldiers sent to block his advance went over to his side. At the entrance to every important town he conquered, the priests and local authorities met him and offered him bread and salt, as well as allegiance and friendship. Disdaining their collaboration, Stenka Razin set up his own institutions, a Cossack republic of an egalitarian type. There was an element of embryonic socialism in his measures.

His call for equal possession of the land incited the peasants to proceed on their own to destroy the feudal power. Everywhere they invaded the manor houses, killed the lords if they resisted, and seized all the arms they could find. Then they hastened to enroll in Razin's army under the slogan of "absolute equality." In one of his appeals to the peasants, the dynamic leader told them: "I do not seek to be your czar. I want to live among you like a brother." Stenka Razin occupied the city of Tsaritsyn, renamed Stalingrad several centuries later (and after Stalin's demise renamed Volgograd). He conquered Samara and Saratov and wherever he set foot, after killing off the nobles, left behind a Cossack government. All southeastern Russia was in ferment, one uprising following another. Then Razin sent an official declaration to Moscow, announcing his determination to abolish privileges from one end of the country to the other and to end class differences by instituting an egalitarian regime in Russia.

Simbirsk—where Lenin was born two hundred years later— marked a turning point for the Cossack revolutionary Stenka Razin. The feudal power, feeling itself threatened, sent strong forces from Moscow, armed with the best weapons available. Their orders were to take Razin alive and bring him back to the capital. Wounded in a battle, Razin was forced to retreat with his partisans south of the Volga. He finally reached the Don Basin, where the burghers betrayed him and handed him over to the Moscow authorities. In

Moscow, Stenka Razin was tortured atrociously and then executed. Thus ended the epic struggle in which the Russian peasants and Cossacks, both closely tied to their native soil and striving for freedom, joined forces under the leadership of Stenka Razin to write some of the most striking pages in Russia's long history.

Russia, as we have said, was a land in which peasant revolts assumed such far-flung proportions because its peasants lived under such wretched conditions. The nobility owned "souls," the name given to the serfs. "Souls" were the personal property of their owner just as much as livestock. Their bodies too belonged to the lord. He could dispose of them at will, making them farm workers, household servants, or artists for his rustic picnics. He could dispose of his serfs in any way, especially if they were attractive. Let us cite one unusual, perhaps unique, case. In the 1760's Count Cheremetev fell in love with a peasant girl who had shown acting talent in plays presented at his private theater. He married her. But in general the lords simply took young women away from their husbands or parents, used them sexually for six months or a year, and then forgot the whole thing. If an indignant husband or father made a fuss about offended honor, he was horsewhipped. Honor was the exclusive privilege of the nobility.

The big landowner sold his peasants the way he sold his cattle or furniture. Newspapers of that day carried advertisements reading: "For sale: a peasant barber and a few pieces of furniture"; or "For sale: a young woman of eighteen, of good character, and a carriage scarcely used." Here is another advertisement, which appealed to a certain class of purchasers: "For sale: a young woman of sixteen, knows how to sew, iron, and dress her mistress; with a pretty face and a fine figure." Prices varied: 300 to 500 rubles for a male, 50 to 200 rubles for a female.

Serfdom was legal and general in Russia. Even Catherine the Great, the empress of "enlightenment" who corresponded with Voltaire and Diderot, an extraordinarily intelligent and capable person, failed to understand the seriousness of the peasant problem, its poignancy, and its revolutionary potential in Russia. From time to time Catherine appealed to "the kind sentiments" of the nobility and exhorted them to treat their serfs well. But she did nothing to put an effective end to the system of serfdom. In her reign the big landlords continued to view these "souls" as their absolute property, as much a source of wealth as their landed estates.

Exploitation of the Russian peasant was not the only evil in the regime of serfdom. There was also administrative corruption at all levels, which the great nineteenth-century writer Gogol satirized so effectively in his play *Revizor* (*The Inspector-General*). In his edict of March 17, 1772, Peter the Great acknowledged the futility of issuing laws that were simply ignored or flouted by the civil servants, so easily bought off by the serf-owners. While he was Grand Duke, Alexander I wrote on May 10, 1796, to Count, later Prince, Kotschubey: "Our affairs of state are in incredible disarray; they are stealing on all sides; all the government departments are administered disastrously." An eyewitness of the period adds, "Considering the evil incurable, Emperor Alexander I yielded with gentle resignation." The same observer continues: If the peasant, generally loyal to the Crown, had only had to pay for the *Obrok*, local taxes, road repairs, transportation costs, and the billeting of troops, he might just have got by. But the abusive demands government bureaucrats made on the hapless peasants worsened their lot beyond repair; they found themselves cheated and robbed without recourse.

The campaign for the freeing of the serfs in Russia was met with the counter-argument of: Watch out! You'll create a proletariat! But it was this kind of thinking that laid the basis for the revolution in the countryside.

Revolutionaries with anarchist inclinations, such as Mikhail Bakunin, saw in Stenka Razin their precursor. Russian Marxist historians have analyzed the reasons why Stenka Razin's revolt failed; yet some of them properly link the uprising with later events. It was the forerunner of revolutions to come. It was the first attempt to free the working people to the cry of "the land to those who work on it," and it was a clear-cut denunciation of the identity of interests of the exploiting class: in this instance, the large landowners, the "servants of the state," and the earliest primitive representatives of finance capital—merchant monopolists and moneylenders.

Soon there appeared on the Russian scene a powerful innovator, Czar Peter I, son of Alexis. Peter the Great combined despotic tendencies with a constructive genius unprecedented in the Slavic world. He took Russia out of backwardness and turned it into a modern and awakened nation. The philosopher Leibniz, who met him, later described Peter the Great as a revolutionary cloaked beneath the mantle of emperor. Traveling as a minor official under the assumed name of Preobajensky, Peter the Great visited the principal cities of Germany, Holland, England, and Italy. With ax in hand he learned the techniques of naval construction. In Holland, as a carpenter he learned cabinetmaking. He mingled with the masses yet at the same time negotiated with kings, generals, and scholars. On his return to Russia he firmly grasped the reins of government.

His gaze was concentrated on the sea. He realized how vital it was for Russia to have outlets to the Baltic Sea. Soon he collided with a powerful rival, Charles XII, King of Sweden and an aggressive military leader. Organizing a modern army, Peter conquered the Baltic countries and founded St. Petersburg on the Neva River. Conqueror of the Swedes, he delivered a historic address to his armies in which he imbued them with the zeal to fight for the aggrandizement of Russia. The battle of Poltava (1709), subject of a beautiful poem by Pushkin, marked the rise of Russia to the rank of a major power and the decline of Sweden as a military factor capable of ruling beyond its own borders. The sea remained Peter's obsession.

Peter the Great revolutionized the government apparatus from top to bottom. He put an end to the old hierarchies of power and laid the foundations for an absolutist state at the head of which stood the Czar. He ended the traditional patriarchate of the Orthodox Church and replaced it with a synod named by himself. In 1705 the first Russian newspaper appeared in Moscow. He saw with unerring clarity that Russia could emerge from her backwardness only by modernizing, by developing her cultural and industrial resources. Supported by the "Westerners," assailed by the Slavophiles, Peter determinedly pursued his path of reform. The social structure, on the other hand, was scarcely touched. The system of serfdom continued. Class differences among the Russian people remained unchanged. But the impetus given to technology, professional training, and economic progress led inevitably to the birth of a working class—the basis of the victorious revolution of the future.

Following Peter the Great there was a period that might be called the German era in Russian history, with a series of women of

German origin on the throne: Catherine I, Anna Ivanovna, Anna Leopoldovna, and Catherine II (the Great), Elizabeth being the only Russian exception. The reign of Catherine the Great was enlightened and Western-oriented. Arts and letters flourished with the poet Derzhavin, the playwright Fonvizin, and the publicists Radishchev and Novikov. Nevertheless, absolutism and the system of class inequalities remained intact, intensifying popular discontent. There was much talk about the urgent need to end serfdom, yet that oppressive system continued in force. There was a moment when Catherine the Great planned a kind of agrarian reform that would satisfy the demands of the peasants. But the reform amounted to nothing but a redistribution of estates to her favorites and courtiers, as a reward for their various services rendered.

The number of "souls" owned by a landowner varied: rich proprietors had as many as tens of thousands, modest ones possessed a few hundred. As land was transferred, the serfs went with it. Take the Orlovs, for example, the family that helped Catherine the Great ascend the throne. One of them, Gregory, was her lover; another, Alexis, assassinated her husband, Peter III. Once in power, Catherine gave them titles of nobility as well as huge estates, with a corresponding number of "souls."

The peasants performed all sorts of duties: they were servants, artists, craftsmen, forced to work at any hour of the day or night, at the bidding and whim of their master. Count Razumovsky, brother of Empress Elizabeth Petrovna's favorite—she was as beautiful as she was prodigal in bestowing her favors on any male who attracted her—employed his peasants in a vast project of diverting the waters of a stream so that he could invite his friends to hear the nightingales sing at the moment of the river's rising. Other landowners had the peasants build roads and work as masons or roofers, thus creating a class of workers who foreshadowed the revolutionary proletariat of Lenin's day.

Between 1765 and 1773, peasant discontent manifested itself in various ways. These included the curious "resurrection" of Peter III, Catherine's husband, who was assassinated a few months after succeeding Elizabeth, Peter the Great's daughter. Peter Feodorovich had been one of the most unpopular monarchs in Russian history because of his pro-German zeal and his devotion to Frederick the

Great, the exemplar of German military aggression. In death his "ghost" stalked the countryside and created the legend that he was a true friend of the poor. A Cossack who resembled him physically, Emelyan Pugachev, posed as the dead Emperor amid insistent rumors that Peter III had escaped death at the hands of Alexis Orlov's conspirators.

Thus arose the social rebellion known as "Pugachev's revolt." Wherever he went, Pugachev electrified the peasant masses. Village after village joined his movement. Catherine derided the rebel leader, referring to him as "the marquis of Pugachev"; and his detractors accused him of being a rank impostor parading as a dead emperor. But the serfs looked upon him as a redeemer. Undoubtedly the myth that he was Peter III who had miraculously escaped a death plot played a part in his popularity. But the desire of the serfs to be treated as human beings played an even bigger part.

General Bibikov, appointed by Catherine in 1773 to crush the uprising, showed better judgment and deeper insight when he wrote: "What is important is not Pugachev but the general discontent." Catherine viewed the situation differently. She preferred to believe that in reality the peasants were resigned to their lot and not as badly off as they claimed. One has only to read her *Memoirs* to confirm this. In 1774 she wrote to Diderot, who, keenly aware of the wretched conditions of the Russian peasantry, had warned the Empress that the patience of the exploited masses had limits: "The bread that feeds the people, the religion that consoles them—those are their ideas. These ideas will always be as simple as they are natural. The prosperity of the state, centuries, generations—these are terms that do not enter their heads. In that immense space that constitutes the future, the people—the peasants—see only tomorrow."

The despotic Empress Catherine had contradictory impulses. On the one hand, she yearned for progress, seeking in a sense to continue the work of Peter the Great. But she was a German princess by birth, placing order and discipline above all else, and a staunch believer in private property; hence she shut her eyes to the peasant question. Meanwhile Pugachev's followers increased to formidable proportions and his army, fifteen thousand strong, advanced to less than 125 miles from pleasure-loving and undefended Moscow. Catherine's advisers had to work strenuously to dissuade her from undertaking personally the defense of the city. The revolt spread like a prairie fire. It was a guerrilla war and a war of vengeance. The nobles most notorious for mistreating their peasants were hung from trees on their own estates. The whole system of serfdom was shaken by the violence of the insurrection.

The peasants made their strength felt. For that reason alone Pugachev's revolt was of historic significance. The fact that at a given moment the peasant masses had paralyzed much of the Russian economy was something future generations would never forget. Over a large section of the territory won by Pugachev and his followers, crops were neither planted nor harvested. Suvorov, the general who had conquered the Turks, had to employ the full force of his army to get the better of the armed guerrillas, Cossacks, and peasants, and end the revolt. He was aided by a group of traitors who betrayed Pugachev in return for their own safety and substantial money payments.

The repression was savage. Enclosed in an iron cage in which he could barely move, Pugachev was exhibited throughout the provinces he had won over to his side at the height of his influence. When he appeared before his judges in Moscow he was virtually a dead man. Because of his shattered physical condition he could not die laughing and singing, like his great predecessor Stenka Razin. Writing to Voltaire in October, 1774, Catherine the Great pointed out that, although he could neither read nor write, Pugachev was "an extremely hard and resolute man" and that he "had not been the instrument of any foreign power." She added that she would have pardoned him, in view of his personal courage, had it not been a question "of the interests of the Empire and the laws."

The army took charge of the repression. But it also allowed the big landlords themselves to wreak personal revenge. Every village had a scaffold raised in its central square. At that time the death penalty was prohibited in the cities and for noblemen, but peasants could be slaughtered like wild beasts. "Peace for many centuries," commented one of Catherine's advisers. Before two centuries had passed the October Revolution of 1917 had occurred and triumphed.

Chinese historians give the title of hero to the rebel leaders that led peasant revolts, some of them so powerful that they resulted in the foundation of new dynasties. Among these was the Ming dynasty (1368–1644), one of the most famous of all, renowned for its art, its porcelains, and its literature. That dynasty was born of a peasant and former Buddhist monk, Chu Yüan-chang, who became "son of heaven." Affiliated with the White Lotus sect, the most important of the period, Chu took Nanking in 1356, then Peking, and proclaimed himself emperor—the first emperor of the Ming dynasty.

In China, peasant revolts have arisen as a result of ever-present misery, with empty granaries and natural catastrophes ravaging the land, the worst of all being the Yellow River floods. Hence there also arose a popular belief in the justness of rebellion. If the peasants revolted, it was because the monarch had failed in his duties as a prince and had therefore fallen in disfavor with the Creator of the Universe. So when they rose up in arms, the rebels were only obeying the will of heaven.

In traditional Chinese society, scholars, chosen by a system of competitive examinations, formed a very important part of the elite. They held the public offices, maintained the Confucian temples, and distributed aid during great hunger crises. But since landed property was the surest way of being able to pay for one's studies and join the scholars' ranks, the rise of this group could not occur without an element of peasant exploitation.

Succeeding dynasties inherited the never-ending problem of peasant poverty in a country that was predominantly agricultural. Even under the Tangs, in the seventh century, when the country enjoyed a period of prosperity, with great emperors such as Hsüan Tsung, the peasants' lot remained essentially unchanged. Dissatisfaction was always just below the surface. Li Po, the great literary figure of that dynasty and the most renowned Chinese poet in the East for a thousand years, fascinated by the beauty of Yang Kuei-fei, the preferred mistress of Emperor Hsüan and the cause of his downfall, sang magnificently of the green mountains and the flowering peach trees. Yet he never forgot the unfortunate peasant, "for whom the unworthy and perverse men of the court do not have a compassionate glance."

Undoubtedly the Ming dynasty witnessed the longest and most violent peasant uprisings. The revolts generally originated in Shensi province, in northern China, where the peasants' lot had deteriorated around the middle of the seventeenth century. Prices soared, that of rice tripling between 1616 and 1642. The Shensi peasants, heavily in debt, beggared, were easily won over to rebellion. But in other parts of China conditions in the countryside were scarcely any better. Despite the fact that in the Yangtze Valley the climate permitted three rice crops a year and the introduction of American plants such as corn and sweet potatoes improved the food outlook, misery prevailed and popular uprisings broke out in rapid succession.

On a national scale, the most popular leaders, Li Tzu-ch'eng and Chang Hsien-chung, attracted great numbers of peasants and army deserters. They replaced the right of petitioning the Emperor with demands that bypassed the offices of the influential Court eunuchs and the Great Secretariat, and backed up their demands by violence. These uprisings were extraordinarily violent and occurred amid the ravages of drought and floods.

The hunger of those below combined with the spectacle of corruption on high to intensify the revolutionary ferment. The peasant had to pay for the weaknesses of the emperors, the avarice of the eunuchs, and the whims of the empresses and imperial concubines. The eunuchs got hold of private lands, turning them into state property. But in fact these estates remained their own property or that of their allies in the government or at Court. Bribes were freely proffered to consolidate their power. The eunuchs held sway. At times this assumed such proportions that in 1619 a young Emperor, sixteen years old when he mounted the throne, ruled under the total influence of the eunuch Wei Chong-hien, who had dominated him from childhood. The Emperor remained a puppet on his throne, while the all-powerful eunuch settled all problems and created such animosity throughout the country that when the Emperor died no one dared enter the temples built for the worship of his remains. The eunuch, for his part, was forced to commit suicide by hanging.

In 1630 a terrible drought in Honan unleashed a new peasant rebellion. The forces of the two above-mentioned rebel leaders, Li and Chang, grew until they constituted genuine armies. Li Tzu-ch'eng's fame arose from his reputation for shunning wealth, for not robbing individuals for his personal gain, and for redistributing the land fairly among all.

Fourteen emperors of the Ming dynasty succeeded one another on the throne. They attained notable successes in the fields of government, law, literature, and fine arts; but they did little to resolve the agrarian question. Thus commenced the decline and fall of that dynasty.

Several centuries later, around the middle of the nineteenth century, "the Heavenly Kingdom of Great Peace" experienced one of the most significant peasant revolts in the revolutionary history of China, the Taiping Rebellion (1850–1864). Its leader, Hung Hsiu-ch'üan, born of a poor peasant family, was a combination of mystic and warrior. Hung gathered a large-sized army of rebels and, making Nanking his headquarters, defeated the Manchu Emperor's troops. Nanking was renamed T'ien-king, the capital of heaven. Hung led a highly disciplined, organized, and austere rebel army. Opium, prostitution, and witchcraft were strictly prohibited. Full equality between men and women was proclaimed. The land-reform program—a kind of primitive Communism—called for common ownership of property and the participation of all in the harvests. Land was divided into equal parts and rigorously fair standards of equality were maintained with respect to grains, fowl, livestock, and other resources. Calendar and literary reforms were instituted, with a view to giving more emphasis to the spoken and colloquial language of the people.

The rebellion had so weakened the Manchus that the foreign powers, alarmed, went to the Emperor's aid. An Anglo-French expedition was formed to intensify pressure on the Taipings. Defeated, and seriously ill, Hung committed suicide on June 1, 1864. The rebellion, with all its ups and downs, had lasted for fifteen years and spread to fifteen provinces.

The Manchu repression was brutal. British and French soldiers cut off the heads of Taiping men, women, and children and engaged in general looting. Temple idols were bayoneted so that the precious gems they contained could be pillaged. Yet in the British House of Commons, Lord Palmerston described the expedition as eminently civilizing. All documents and publications of the Taipings were banned by decree. The few items that survived found their way to the libraries of Europe and the United States, forcing later Chinese historians to travel abroad to do research on their own history of the period.

Although defeated, the Taiping Rebellion affirmed once and for all the truth that only with the liberated peasant masses could a strong, independent, and progressive China be built. Eighty-five years later, with irresistible momentum, this China came into being.

3

THE
FRENCH REVOLUTION

Intellectuals were the pioneers of the French Revolution—its heralds and spiritual leaders, especially in its first stages. The masses of workers and peasants constituted its shock troops. They entered the historic conflict and risked their lives—but actually for the cause of the bourgeoisie, not that of the working class. Without these proletarians of town and country, humanity would not have known the great liberal upsurge of the nineteenth century that reached out from France and extended in all directions.

The arbitrary and wasteful policies of the monarchy had left staggering problems for France. Indebtedness reached the figure of billions of livres. Gold and silver spiraled in price, and yielded to paper money which constantly fell in value. Taxes weighed especially hard on the poor. As in all such situations, official corruption knew virtually no bounds. Favors of every kind and description could be bought, from titles of nobility to government posts. Tens of thousands quit the countryside and wandered to Paris in search of a better life, some of them falling into even more abject poverty. Early in the eighteenth century the writer-prelate Fénelon wrote: "We have only one winter ahead of us before the deluge."

Under Louis XIV's successors, the Regent Philippe of Orléans and Louis XV, conditions had not improved. On the contrary, government outlays as well as the state debt increased markedly. Under Louis XV, France lost her position as the dominant colonial power in

North America. Her military renown suffered eclipse. As France's "grandeur" declined in the growing national crisis, the support of traditional institutions by those classes that had previously been the firmest pillar of the monarchy weakened. The middle classes realized that, along with the peasantry, they would bear the brunt of heavier taxation, whereas for the nobility and high clergy taxes virtually did not exist.

The hardest hit was the peasantry. The *dîme* (tithe) appears to have been expressly devised to victimize the peasants. On top of that came the crushing tax on land and property, the *taille*, the *vigésime* or head tax and house tax, and the *gabelle* or salt tax. The "money-grabbers," as a popular ballad of the time dubbed them, were not lacking in imagination when it came to giving each new extortion a new name.

As the misery of the masses increased, the rich indulged in shocking displays of luxury—an old, familiar story in history. In the decade before the Revolution the wealthy spent money with wanton abandon. A fourth of the country's income was accounted for between the royal palace and the approximately four thousand noble families who took part in the court pageantry. Church revenue reached 120,000,000 livres annually, about the same figure as the income from the grain harvest. Clergy and aristocracy grew rich. A courtier in the palace at Versailles was considered poor if his income was not above 100,000 livres yearly. That of the Polignac family exceeded 700,000. At the same time, life in Versailles consumed even the largest fortunes. Between balls, hunting parties, gambling, upkeep of carriages and horses, banquets, and receptions, huge sums of money were squandered.

At a lower level, government officials and administrators lived well beyond their means. The only way they could manage was by stealing from the nobility. It was a regime of debts and deceit. The largest landowner in France, the Duc d'Orléans, owed 74,000,000 livres yet he continued his extravagant life style, while the Comte de Clermont went bankrupt twice.

The economic breakdown affected all strata of society and invaded every level of public administration. Similar chaos prevailed in the law courts, where sentences could be lessened or rendered invalid by the use of "persuasive" arguments: that is, if one were prepared to pay the sums required to influence judges' verdicts. A corrupt administration gave concessions to the segment of the bourgeoisie interested in stimulating industry and trade. Some fortunes disappeared; others were born in the wake of official favoritism and protection. Despite far-reaching corruption, France possessed enough inner resources to remain second only to England in world trade. France enjoyed a virtual monopoly in food production, its sugar trade being quite important. The silk industry in Lyons employed 65,000 workers, an impressive figure for that period. In the fashion, clothing, and furniture industries, France led the world.

The rise of the French bourgeoisie was the outstanding feature of the epoch, contrasting with the decline of the nobility. In large measure the Revolution rose out of the antagonism and clash of these two classes. Gaining more and more self-confidence, the bourgeoisie began to break the feudal bonds that hampered its freedom of movement. Undoubtedly the bourgeoisie by itself was not yet powerful enough to confront the Court. As in ancient Greek tragedy, it needed a chorus to make its voice heard. The chorus was the masses of the people. The latter had the revolutionary instinct, but as yet no clear class-consciousness. Day laborers, workers, and peasants marched behind the enlightened bourgeoisie but were nonetheless the driving force of the movement. Without the common people the bourgeoisie would have been defeated. Almost a century later the proletariat, in 1789 not yet aware of its identity as the genuinely rising class in society, waged its own fight in the Paris Commune of 1871—and in the great Socialist revolutions of the following century. Meanwhile it gave its enthusiasm and its blood to put an end to feudal power, even though others benefited from its generosity and subsequently betrayed it.

For a short time some of the liberals pinned their hopes on the new King, Louis XVI. They felt that the change in monarchs would bring about a change in the regime. This was a failure to understand the basic elements that in every concrete situation shape the course of events. It was a distorted view, typical of a situation in rapid flux. But on this occasion the hopes pinned on Louis XVI went beyond the ordinary bounds of politics and sought to make of him a savior—when there was nothing to save in a system rotten to the core.

A fat monarch more interested in good eating and hunting than in affairs of state, Louis XVI got so bored that he often fell asleep at meetings of the state council over which he presided. He could not have chosen a better mate for his parasitic life than the Austrian Marie Antoinette. She was beautiful, flirtatious, easily flattered, and she proved a favorite target for the satirical poets and artists in the pre-revolutionary period, all of whom had one thing in common: their hatred and contempt for everything related to the Court at Versailles. The scandal of the notorious Queen's necklace in which a worldly amorous priest played the chief role overshadowed other juicy tidbits that made the rounds in the palace surroundings. The "little people" doted on this gossip; it confirmed the image they already had of a dissolute queen. Louis XVI was not only the prisoner of Marie Antoinette's whims; he also fell under her ultra-conservative influence in politics. She had brought with her from the absolutist and reactionary Austrian Court a special taste for repressive measures. Her advice always pointed in the direction of authoritarianism; she refused adamantly to heed the state of mind of the people, much less satisfy it. She would not hear of a change in policy that might entail more bread and less taxes for the people.

France was passing through a period of peasant disturbances. From 1774, when Louis XVI mounted the throne, to 1783, uprisings large and small occurred in the countryside. The causes were twofold: shortage of bread and unbearable feudal levies. After a brief respite the uprisings resumed in 1786 on a wider scale. Gradually the peasants went beyond simple economic demands. They were increasingly attracted by the political slogans of equality and fraternity advanced by the intellectual forerunners of the Revolution. The ideology of what could be called the progressive bourgeoisie went far beyond the urban literary groups and penetrated the villages. And conditions in the villages went from bad to worse. But as the poorer peasants sank into deeper destitution, the rich peasants—the type that in the Russian Revolution of 1917 earned the name "kulak"— got richer. This added fuel to the flames of rural discontent.

Dimly aware that things were going awry but uncertain as to what was wrong, Louis XVI felt he had to do something to avert the threatened bankruptcy of the regime. He had appointed to his government two persons of distinction: Turgot, the theorist of the Physiocrats, and Malesherbes. Turgot was named Controller General of Finance. Backed by Malesherbes, he urged an immediate and total reform of the government, designed not only to cut out the waste but also to eliminate highhanded police methods epitomized in the notorious *"lettres de cachet"* (arbitrary orders for imprisonment).

On the initiative of the two ministers, some reforms were instituted: free trade in grain was proclaimed in 1774; corporal punishment was suspended; and serfs on the royal estates were freed in 1779. These measures nourished exaggerated hopes among the people and quickly drew a reaction from the nobility and privileged classes. There was even talk of representative government. As a matter of fact, Turgot was working on a reform plan calling for popular participation in the provincial assemblies, with the eventual aim of setting up a genuine parliament. The then existing Supreme Tribunal, dominated by the nobility, bore little resemblance to a true parliament. The aristocracy and high clergy intensified their intrigues against Turgot, and the King got rid of him. The only immediate show of solidarity for the deposed minister came from Voltaire, who wrote his "Letter to a Man" (*Epître à un homme*).

To avoid giving the impression that the experiment in reform had been completely given up, Turgot was replaced by the Geneva banker Jacques Necker, father of Madame de Staël. A study of the situation in France brought Necker close to Turgot's viewpoint; indeed, he emphasized to the King that not much time was left to put national affairs in order. He proposed that the monarch serve as a mediator among the classes. Louis XVI's response was: "My authority is not to mediate but to command."

The ultra-reactionary Court circles were hostile to any reform; but in Necker's case this was doubly aggravated by the fact that he came from the bourgeoisie and was a Protestant. The publication by the new minister of a blunt and honest report on the financial situation earned him new hostility. He felt himself so isolated and hated that in 1781 he asked to be relieved of his post. His departure intensified the financial disorder. The road to reform, if it had ever been open, was now closed once and for all. There remained a single alternative: revolution.

In 1782–1783, new bread riots broke out, with mounting intensity. In Lyons in 1786 there was a genuine uprising; and two years later uprisings in Brittany and other provinces. In October, 1788, a royal decree whereby the population was forced to register so that they could be more closely watched met with organized resistance in several districts of Paris. There were clashes with soldiers, and blood flowed.

In Calonne the King had found a compliant and irresponsible Minister of the Treasury. He winked an eye at all the extravagances of the princes and courtiers. But the lightheaded Finance Minister soon found himself at the end of his tether, with the vaults of the exchequer half empty. To avoid facing the impending catastrophe alone, he favored the creation of an Assembly of Notables—composed of clergy, nobility, and high government officials. Their first act was to discover a state debt of 1,646,000,000 livres and an annual deficit of 140,000,000. There was no prospect of covering it, for Calonne's proposal for an emergency tax levied on the clergy and nobility was rejected by both groups. From the streets rose the cry that the States-General be summoned. Even in the parliament—that is, the Supreme Tribunal—voices were raised, like that of Duval d'Eprémesnil, calling into question some of the prerogatives the Crown had enjoyed from the time of Richelieu. The groundswell of dissatisfaction rose on all sides.

It was undoubtedly from the countryside that the fiercest winds of revolt arose. In 1789 the French peasant was not legally a serf. Serfdom had been formally abolished in the laws. But in some places justice continued to be administered by the local lord. The peasant had to pay a tax to the landowner to marry off his daughter and to baptize and bury members of his family.

The winter of 1788 was a severe one, and was followed by a bad harvest. Economic conditions called for recourse to action. The following year the peasants were not satisfied with merely swapping tales of their woes. With shovels and carving knives they forced some of the landlords to lower the price of grain or to share the supply with them. Granaries were looted and flour was handed over to the bakers so that they could bake a minimum of loaves for the hungry people. From time to time the cry of "Bread, bread!" mingled with that of "Long live freedom!"

A pre-revolutionary situation was developing. It was hastened by a budgetary crisis, the state's need of funds, and, as in the English Revolution, a financial collapse that for the time being left the few wealthy families unaffected but that finally forced the King to yield and agree to call the States-General. It was the first time since 1614 that that body had been summoned. The States-General was no longer the one that had sat in the Middle Ages. It reflected the deep-seated changes in France's social structure and bore some resemblance to a modern parliament. Its representatives, who had gathered for debate, did not speak for merely one aspect of national life—a specific class or corporation—but for the entire French people. This became obvious immediately in the debate on the procedures for voting. The Third Estate, representing the mass of the people, won out over the recalcitrant Notables.

A new power element, the Third Estate, was now on the scene. In the Abbé Sieyès it found a vigorous and brilliant spokesman. In answer to the question "What is the Third Estate?" he replied: "The Third Estate is and must be the nation itself, in all its sovereignty and authority." With this definition the Revolution already had its program. From a state built upon its apex, France had now moved toward a state with its own base: the people. One hears the voice of Jean-Jacques Rousseau in this new doctrine.

Of course, the preparatory work of the intellectual forerunners of the Revolution, however valuable, would not have come to fruition without the backing of the masses. On April 27, 1789, there was a revolutionary outburst in Paris, known afterward as the "Réveillon affair." Angered by the provocative attitude of the owner of the Réveillon wallpaper factory in the Faubourg Saint-Antoine, who had insulted workers propagandizing on behalf of the new voting system, a crowd gathered on the public square and hung his effigy. Réveillon's factory was attacked. Troops intervened to protect private property, and a street battle broke out. Twelve soldiers were dead and eighty wounded; on the side of the people, estimates ran as high as two hundred dead and three hundred wounded. Several days later the Bicêtre prison was stormed. A new element appeared now, destined to decide the course of history for a long time to come: *Le Peuple*, the common people.

Each one of these skirmishes was a prologue to the great epic at hand. Each one of them had repercussions throughout France. The slogans on the streets of Paris aroused the villages. A new literature came into being, with pamphlets and song sheets snatched from the street vendors as soon as they appeared. The Revolution was creating its own organs of information by means of anecdotes and satires. Rumors helped in the psychological warfare—to use an expression made popular a hundred and fifty years later. One rumor, for example, had it that the nobles had spontaneously given up their privileges. It was patently untrue; but, as a result, many people vowed they would no longer pay their taxes.

At the beginning of May the States-General met in Versailles. The various representatives could be identified by their different dress: the nobles were in black trimmed with gold and lace braid, with plumed hats. The bourgeois were in plain black without trimmings, hats without feathers or buttons. There was an initial skirmish over the matter of approving the delegates' credentials. Meanwhile clubs sprang up in Paris, the most active being the one in the Palais Royal in whose sessions everyone present was allowed to participate.

The representatives of the city districts, deputies of the Third Estate caught up in the excitement of the street throngs, initiated several steps that were decisive in the development of the Revolution. In agreement with the presidents they had just elected, the astronomer Bailly and the Comte de Mirabeau, they voted for Abbé Sieyès' motion by which the States-General was transformed into the National Assembly.

It was an act of defiance vis-à-vis the privileged classes, who would thus have their privileges automatically annulled. A similar challenge was the support for the people's cause given by Honoré Gabriel Victor Riquetti, Comte de Mirabeau. He had already broken with his class and flouted the canons of high society when he fled to Holland with the young wife of a fellow aristocrat. Condemned to death, he had been arrested and imprisoned in the Vincennes prison on orders of his own father. Yet a year later he was a free man and published his essay "On Despotism." A voluntary exile in England and Germany, Mirabeau returned to France when popular agitation spread. As a candidate of the Third Estate—which signified a clean break with the nobility—Mirabeau led the first attacks in the National Assembly against the Court and the privileged classes. A combination of revolutionary and bohemian, he made a brilliant start as orator and polemicist. But he later became involved in shady compromises and, constantly in debt, ended as a corrupted oppositionist without prestige or authority. But as a figure of transition he undoubtedly played an important part.

The deputies of the Third Estate invited the other classes to follow them in their fight for the rights of the Assembly; one part of the lower clergy joined with them. Their proposals and decisions lent the debate an increasingly radical tone. Thus they asserted that in the future no tax would be legal unless approved by the Assembly. And the Assembly sent a message to the King to this effect. Louis XVI rejected it, as he did all other decisions implying a lessening of his prerogatives. An absolute monarch by the grace of God, he took as his model the British kings James I and Charles I, whose fate filled him with a blend of enthusiasm and terror. The royal princes, d'Artois, Condé, and Conti, advocated a "hard line" policy. In secret they prepared for a royal session that would put the Assembly "in its place"—that is, silence its debates and bring it to an abrupt end.

When they learned of the conspiracy, the deputies met in another part of the palace, the royal tennis court, while a huge throng led by Bailly marched along the streets of Versailles. It was the day of the famous "oath of the tennis court"—June 20, 1789. With only one dissenting voice, the deputies took a solemn oath not to disband until they had given France a constitution. When the Master of Ceremonies, on direct orders of the King, commanded the deputies to adjourn and leave the palace, the nobles and high clergy obeyed. But not the Third Estate. In their name Mirabeau uttered his famous words: "We have heard the orders. . . . Who is it that gives these orders, and dictates these laws? We are the representatives of the nation. The nation gives orders, but does not receive them. Go and tell those who sent you that we shall not budge from our places here except at the point of bayonet." The King's first reaction was: "Very well, let them stay." But the conspiracy continued, under a different guise. In the ensuing days the royal plotters continued their plans for a counterblow, with the support of the Court. Louis XVI himself, more vacillating than ever, did nothing to stop them. But July 14 was only a few days away.

As the weakness in the King's position became increasingly clear, a section of the Church hierarchy, led by several well-known archbishops, went over to the camp of the bourgeoisie. As we have stated above, the French Revolution was fundamentally a bourgeois revolution, although some elements of a proletarian and Socialist nature did appear in it. In that revolution the bourgeoisie took the lead in the general assault on privilege. To be a bourgeois in the twentieth century means, in most cases, to be conservative and reactionary; but in 1789, when it was a question of toppling Louis XVI from power, being a bourgeois meant being a revolutionary and ushering in a period of history in which the demands of the people came to the fore. In the final analysis all subsequent revolutions—the Russian Revolution of 1917, the Chinese Revolution, the Cuban Revolution, and the social upheavals in Asia, Africa, and Latin America—had their origins in the French Revolution.

Among the high churchmen who joined with the bourgeoisie to confront the King were Talleyrand-Périgord, Bishop of Autun, and Henri Grégoire, Bishop of Blois. Their attitude helped weaken royal authority in a country that was predominantly Catholic. It also gave added impetus to the French people as they approached the decisive events of July 14, 1789.

The King began to mistrust everybody. Realizing that even his household troops (*garde du corps*) sympathized with the bourgeoisie and heeding the advice of the palace clique, he brought all the German regiments and all the Swiss troops that could be mobilized to Versailles for his personal protection. They were placed under the command of Marshal de Broglie. The National Assembly protested against this measure as an insult to national feeling. But the palace refused to yield, thus adding another explosive element to the situation. Members of the National Assembly, especially Mirabeau and the Duc d'Orléans, spread word among the masses that foreign troops were being brought to Versailles. The bourgeoisie, which on the one hand used the masses on behalf of its own interests and on the other hand feared lest the masses one day acquire class-consciousness and become a formidable rival for power, understood that on this occasion it needed the people in its struggle with the Crown. The Court made ready to resist. Left to itself, the bourgeoisie was powerless vis-à-vis the King. There was no margin for further vacillations or compromises. So the bourgeoisie decided to run the risk of arming the people. At the same time, it armed itself for that future day when it would have to fight, not against the King, but against those same masses of the people. The bourgeoisie was prompted by a powerful motive that continued to feed its aggressiveness and belligerency all during the nineteenth and twentieth centuries: the defense of money and the principles of free enterprise and private property.

One group of bourgeois deputies, more resolute than the others, founded the Club Breton in Versailles as an information center for what was happening at the Court. Among the founders were such deputies from Brittany as Le Chapelier, Mirabeau, Sieyès, the Duc d'Aiguillon, Abbé Grégoire, and Robespierre. Paralleling the activities of the Club Breton, the Palais-Royal, formerly the town house of the Duc d'Orléans, attracted a growing number of anti-royalists. The cafés and taverns of the Palais-Royal were like a branch of the parliament. Subversive pamphlets circulated freely there; revolutionary poems and satirical couplets were recited, a favorite theme being Marie Antoinette's frivolous love life.

On July 11, Necker was summarily dismissed. As he was on his way to a meeting of the Council of Ministers, he was stopped and told to get ready to leave Paris. The following day, a Sunday, the news began to spread throughout the city. Crowds swarmed toward the Palais-Royal. Leaving the Café Foy, a sword in one hand and a pistol in the other, Camille Desmoulins shouted to the throng: "Citizens, I have just come from Versailles. Monsieur Necker has been dismissed from his post. His dismissal is the signal for a St. Bartholomew massacre of patriots. This afternoon all the German and Swiss battalions will march from the Champs de Mars to butcher us. We have only one way out—to take up arms." Soon a procession formed, with likenesses of Necker, now transformed into a popular hero, and the Duc d'Orléans, concerning whom there was a rumor of impending exile. The procession moved along the Rue Richelieu toward the Place Louis XVI, today the Place de la Concorde, where the German and Swiss soldiers had taken up positions. Swords flashed, a few shots rang out; but the people of Paris, veterans of many uprisings, were not intimidated by the first troop movements. They surrounded the soldiers and forced them to retreat. Church bells pealed violently. From every section of the city new crowds joined in the tumult. The agitation continued throughout most of the night and July 13 dawned menacingly. Victory in the streets drew near.

The bourgeoisie itself began to feel threatened. It hastened to arm itself before the common people got arms. The big words "equality, fraternity!" hid its fear of the working class, still a small minority and an embryonic group. The bourgeoisie took the initiative in creating its own militia, which was to number twelve thousand men under the command of the shopkeepers' committee. Its commanding officer was an aristocrat, the Marquis de La Salle. Louis Blanc, the nineteenth-century French Socialist, characterized this militia as "a pretorian guard." Sparks of the class struggle were visible, revealing momentary signs of disagreement in the Third Estate.

But events rushed toward a climax. When July 14 dawned, nothing could hold back the upsurge of the masses. The previous night a few shots had been exchanged between roving bands and the guards of the Bastille, the prison that was both symbol and reality of oppression. The Arsenal of the Bastille, commanded by the Marquis de Launey, had been reinforced a few days before. But the masses on that July 14 advancing with shouts of "Storm the Bastille!" were stronger. The crowds were made up of various elements: bourgeois carried away by popular emotion, artisans, and workers, including a number of those who were later called "Lumpenproletarians."

Barricades were hastily erected. The problem of obtaining weapons was urgent. It was solved in a way that became the rule in all subsequent revolutions: capture them from the enemy. The decision was made to attack the Hôtel des Invalides, where large amounts of arms were kept. At first there was an effort to win over the guards on duty at the Invalides. Negotiations were short-lived and fruitless. Then, like an irresistible wave, some seven to eight thousand men and women forced the entrance to the building. Much gunpowder was found. The night before, there had been a similar attack on a convoy bound for Rouen, and large quantities of much-needed gunpowder had been seized. It was a classic example of the possibilities at hand when a mass of people decides to take action, not stopping to examine with an overcritical eye the lack of means, but concentrating all their efforts on using whatever means are available. The people quickly gained confidence in themselves. Soon they numbered approximately 300,000 aroused human beings. A crowd of this size made such an impression on the troops sent to break up the first scattered groups that the officers decided not to intervene for the time being. When they later decided to step in, it was too late.

The bourgeoisie tried to prevent the masses from playing the key role in solving the situation. As soon as the Municipal Council realized how many tens of thousands had taken to the streets, it began negotiations with the Marquis de Launey, so that he in turn might negotiate with the leaders of the people and thus avert the storming of the Bastille. One of the envoys, the lawyer Thuriot, obtained from de Launey the promise not to shoot at the people provided they did not try to storm the prison. But the revolutionary élan of the people of Paris was more powerful than the adroitness of the advocates of compromise. In fact, compromise was no longer possible. It was open struggle, with no turning back. Now that they had arms, the masses felt able to confront de Launey and his German and Swiss regiments. No one could hold them back.

At this point a dramatic incident occurred which even today remains insufficiently understood. Historians of the French Revolution analyze it in various ways, depending on their own political orientation. Despite the official promise not to fire on the crowd, there were shots and even a few discharges of cannon. At this, the people were so enraged that they determined to take the offensive. They opened fire with one of the cannons captured at the Hôtel des Invalides. The fight lasted three hours, the people suffering more than eighty dead and many wounded. Between four and five o'clock in the afternoon, the prison commandant, acknowledging defeat, raised a white flag. There was, however, one condition: that the troops be allowed to leave the fortress with their weapons. The people refused categorically: they demanded unconditional surrender. Overcoming all remaining resistance, the people seized de Launey and brought him to the Municipal Council. For his vacillation and double-dealing he had to pay with his life. Hué, commandant of the Swiss Guards, remained alive thanks to his public statement that he placed himself completely at the service of the city and the nation.

When the people stormed into the Bastille, they searched every corner of the fortress. They rushed into cells and underground dungeons, liberating prisoners who at first were unable to walk because they were so unaccustomed to daylight. These men were then triumphantly hoisted on the shoulders of the crowd amid shouts of frenzied jubilation. It was a day of delirious joy and triumph. Victory over those who were preparing a reactionary coup against the incipient revolution was won, not by negotiations with the enemy, not by diplomacy, but by moving into action. Victory was achieved at the price of the people's blood, in a generous outpouring of heroic determination. It was a victory of what might be termed the lower classes, the embryonic proletariat, portent of things to come.

Masses are drawn into a struggle because of an idea. Those who stormed the Bastille on July 14, 1789, embodied an idea: the deep-seated human duty of fighting against social injustice, and of not being sidetracked by hollow phrases about the theoretical equality of all human beings. As Karl Marx wrote in his *Class Struggles in France*: "A class in which the revolutionary interests of society are concentrated, so soon as it has risen up, finds directly in its own situation the content and the material of its revolutionary activity: foes to be laid low, measures, dictated by the needs of the struggle, to be taken; the consequences of its own deeds drive it on. It makes no theoretical inquiries into its own task."

Henceforth the Third Estate had a new ally—but also a new enemy. The road to the future would be based on this dual orientation: immediate demands of the moment and the final goal of socialism.

The palace was the only place that ignored the lesson of July 14—which subsequently became, and remains, the French national holiday. As the Bastille fell, festivities went on at the Court without interruption. Confident of his ability to control the situation with the support of his soldiers, Louis XVI seemed contemptuously indifferent to the disturbances, looking upon them as ephemeral. The King had only one moment of uneasiness when the Duc de Liancourt, coming from Paris, gave him a detailed account of what had transpired there. The King then went before the National Assembly and informed it of his decision to withdraw the troops. But even at that moment he did not appear to be in a mood for bigger concessions.

Bailly had been named Mayor of Paris by the Municipal Council, and Lafayette, who, as friend and comrade-in-arms of George

Washington, enjoyed considerable popularity among the French, took command of the National Guard. The Church hierarchy quickly adapted itself to the new situation: the Archbishop of Paris offered a Te Deum service in Notre-Dame Cathedral in honor of the seizure of the Bastille.

The royal princes advised Louis XVI to move to Metz, whence he could lead an army to bring Paris "to its senses." But the two men capable of commanding the army—Marshal de Broglie and the Comte de Provence—opposed the idea. The King himself was not enthusiastic, for he feared that in his absence the Duc d'Orléans would seize the throne. So he had no choice but to yield and recall Necker, something he would have adamantly refused just a few days before.

It was not enough. Louis XVI had to appear before the Paris Town Council in the company of Bailly and put the new tricolor hat on his head, a gesture that implied approval of what had occurred during the previous few days. Alarmed by the turn of events and by the King's weakness and cowardice, to use the language that soon became commonplace among the palace clique, the Comte d'Artois, the Prince de Condé, and the Duc de Polignac fled abroad with their entourage of aristocrats. They were the forerunners of the many counter-revolutionary émigrés who placed their skill at intrigue, their military talents, and their money in the service of a lost cause.

Henceforth the King had at his side two powers that rapidly destroyed his own power: the National Assembly and the sovereign people. The ideas of the Encyclopedists blossomed forth. "From this moment," wrote the English ambassador, the Duke of Dorset, "we may consider France a free country."

The revolutionary movement extended from Paris into the provinces. The peasantry was won over to the Revolution—and this was decisive. The bases of the feudal state were shaken to their very foundations; and there emerged a conscious mass of peasants, aroused, militant, and deeply imbued with the new ideology of the Revolution. As the principles of absolute monarchy were shattered, the new republican principles showed the incompatibility between the hereditary monarchy and the ideals of equality and fraternity. This is what gave the French Revolution a depth that was lacking in the Puritan Revolution of the previous century in England. The

Levelers cannot be compared with the stormers of the Bastille, or with the French peasants who challenged the very concept of private property that remained sacrosanct to the English.

Economically, the British aristocracy emerged stronger, not weaker, from the Puritan Revolution. The Enclosure Act did not liberate the English peasants from their bondage. To the contrary, it increased their servitude even more and "proletarianized" a good many of them. That was why the English example and the English constitution proved so attractive to the French bourgeoisie at the end of the eighteenth century. They wanted the political revolution, but *not* the social revolution. However, their desire to keep the demands of the masses within limits—within limits they themselves set—was doomed. It encountered a stronger will, that of the people, moving with the tide of history, refusing to stop in midstream.

The big battles took place more in the streets than in the parliament. When news of the storming of the Bastille spread throughout France, the cities experienced rising popular pressure against the unjust tax system and the increases in the price of bread. Bread played a very important part in local demonstrations of dissatisfaction. In many places crowds invaded the town hall and set up their own committees to deal with immediate problems. This municipal revolution influenced Paris in turn, where the Commune took over more and more of the functions of parliament and tackled emergency problems on its own initiative. Paris took the lead in the municipal revolution, naming its own Town Council and mayor and setting up its own National Guard. The city was organized into sixty districts, each of which functioned independently. There was even discussion of creating a system of law courts free of feudal influences and the arbitrary highhandedness of the nobility. In many respects it was a liberation movement of great vitality. The fight was not only for immediate improvement in living conditions but also for civil liberties and political rights, particularly the equal right to vote.

This was also the period of *la grande peur* (the great fear). The phrase recurs in political writings and popular songs of the time, and refers to the panic that gripped the nobility and a section of the bourgeoisie. Bands of peasants armed with primitive weapons began to invade the cities and attack the grain warehouses. A loose alliance was formed between the profiteering merchants and big landlords.

Fearing lest the peasants and soldiers make common cause against the rich, they set up an army of private guards. In all this, the element of class struggle was clearly in evidence. In fact, the privileged classes to some extent exploited "the great fear." They heightened and exaggerated it so as to isolate the more revolutionary forces and then crush them. (This phenomenon occurred again a hundred and thirty years later in Germany in 1919, when the reactionaries deliberately exaggerated the danger of an attempt to set up a dictatorship of the proletariat. So they mobilized against the German working class all those who felt their property—even though it consisted only of scanty savings subject to constant devaluation—jeopardized by the strikes and uprisings. Thus a counter-revolutionary front was formed; by successfully crushing the most militant section of the working class it prepared the way for the rise of Hitler.)

The mounting pressure of the French people was felt in the National Assembly, which, a few days after the taking of the Bastille, drafted a Declaration of the Rights of Man. The Declaration was watered down somewhat: thus, there was no mention of the right of association, and the principle of indemnification in the event of future confiscations was overemphasized, showing how the majority of the Assembly members were still imbued with the concept of private property. In some respects the document departed from Abbé Sieyès' thinking, summarized in the phrase: "When men are not equal in means, wealth, culture, or strength, they will not be equal in rights." Yet with all its limitations the Declaration marked a big step forward.

Now the Third Estate was confronted with the specter of the "Fourth Estate"—the peasantry. Every day the peasants grew surer of themselves and more determined to substitute action for the delays and vacillations of an Assembly governed by contradictory impulses—seeking on the one hand to spur the revolt against despotism and on the other to limit the action of the masses. Voices were raised in the Assembly advocating stern repression of the peasant uprisings in the provinces. It would lead us too far afield to study in detail the passionate debates on this matter. But it is at least of interest to point out that some of the liberal-minded nobles, such as the Viscount de Noailles, Lafayette's brother-in-law, and the Duc d'Aiguillon, showed a more generous attitude than a number of representatives of the Third Estate. Thus the liberal nobles boldly proposed radical reforms in taxation and the abolition of all feudal charges such as "seigneurial levies," indemnification, and *mainmorte* (by which the possessions of a serf who died childless went to the lord). But bourgeois deputies such as Salomon, alarmed by the violence in the countryside, proposed measures that would have led to a reinforcement of royal power.

So we arrive at the night of August 4, 1789, a memorable date in the history of the Revolution. On that night some of the people's most important demands received legal sanction. This was but a declaration of purpose; there was still a long way to go before it became a reality. But the peasants took the declaration literally and began to refuse to pay the feudal taxes. When the lords resisted, in many places the peasants attacked and set fire to their châteaux. The Assembly reacted by retreating from its generous mood of the night of August 4. At bottom, its feeling for private property prevailed. This respect for property led it to introduce certain restrictions on the resolutions it had previously passed. Such an attitude, however, far from causing the peasants to retreat, spurred them to new revolts. Class positions in the Third Estate as well as the aristocracy hardened. The peasants were labeled "bandits." (A century and a half later, when the Russian and Chinese Revolutions erupted and threatened the basic underpinnings of world capitalism, the code word became "vandalism.")

Now there was even a movement to rally around the King again. Louis XVI was aware of this, as is shown in his letter to the Archbishop of Arles in which he makes clear his intention of gaining time and of waiting until revolutionary passions had subsided. When the Declaration of the Rights of Man was presented to him for his official signature, the King uttered a few superficial remarks designed to give him "a period of reflection." If under the stress of the events of July 14 the monarch seemed for a moment to move toward complete liberalization, the spread of the peasant uprisings throughout the country impelled him to take the reins of power arbitrarily into his own hands. The Court and, above all, the Queen encouraged him in this hardened attitude. But this was a two-edged weapon: for any new outbreak of authoritarianism on the King's part could only radicalize a National Assembly that was showing signs of yielding. A thoroughgoing debate ensued regarding the King's power of absolute veto. Eventually the Assembly rejected this power of the King, even though it was defended momentarily even by Mirabeau. Instead of an absolute veto, the Assembly accepted a kind of delaying veto. In the place of a two-chamber parliament favored by the more conservative deputies, attracted as always by England's example, the Assembly voted for a single chamber with the prerogative of initiating legislation—a right previously reserved exclusively to the Crown.

In his heart Louis XVI had never given up the hope of reversing the situation. Avidly he read accounts of Charles I of England—not to draw lessons from that monarch's fate and thus avoid the mistakes that had led to his downfall, but to devise all sorts of maneuvers and intrigues against the Assembly. Again the King thought of fleeing to nearby Rambouillet or Orléans, whence he could lead his troops against Paris and force the Assembly to its knees. But the old fear that the Duc d'Orléans or "Messieurs"—Louis XVI's brothers— would profit by his absence to seek the throne themselves, and some misgivings regarding the loyalty of his troops, forced the King to defer the plan from one day to the next.

The truce was short-lived. As the moderate Girondists in the Assembly sought with increasing effort to slow down the forward thrust of their opponents, the more radical faction known as "the Mountain" prepared for new clashes. The first fight occurred in the Jacobin Club, to which many Girondists still belonged. The powerful voices of Chabot, Fabre d'Eglantine, and Billaud-Varenne could be heard. In the course of the violent controversy, one Girondist fell. Brissot, who enjoyed the favor of Minister Roland and especially of Madame Roland, was expelled from membership in the club when he refused to explain certain maneuvers he had made against the leaders of the opposing faction. The Girondists withdrew from the club, which henceforth was controlled by the Mountain.

They withdrew from the club to meet elsewhere and pursue their political intrigues. At times it was in the circle around Madame Dodun, wife of the wealthy head of the Compagnie des Indes; at other times in the drawing room of Madame Roland, at the Ministry of Interior. Many of the leaders of the moderates—including

Vergniaud and Condorcet—frequented these drawing rooms. They gathered not only to dine, flirt, and amuse themselves; they also conspired. They drew up lists of candidates for the most important government posts; and lists of those who in due course would have to be disposed of.

When the Constitutional Committee was named, and seven of its nine members turned out to be habitués of Madame Roland's salon, with Abbé Sieyès (very close to that group) and Danton completing the list, public opinion turned against such a scandalous show of favoritism. As one poem aimed at Madame Roland put it: it was "a policy dictated by women's skirts." Was the fate of the Revolution to be decided in society drawing rooms?

Georges Couthon, hitherto on the moderate side, rose up in the National Convention, which had replaced the National Assembly, and became the mouthpiece of popular indignation. "What has just happened," he cried, "has opened my eyes. It is that faction [i.e., the Girondists] which wants liberty only for itself that we must closely watch." The Girondists were not only friendly to the aristocracy, Couthon asserted; they wanted to consolidate their own influence. Not content with retaining all the levers of command, they also sought to destroy the opposition so that then they could proceed more easily to build and consolidate their bourgeois state. Their prime task was to behead the opposition by discrediting its most redoubtable leaders. The one enemy above all to be silenced was Robespierre. His consistency, his integrity, his hold on the masses made the Girondists hate him. By destroying him they would utterly crush the Mountain.

Debates grew more and more bitter. Without naming names, Pastor Lassource had attacked the men who, he claimed, were trying to sow anarchy and disorder. Rebequi, the young deputy from Marseilles, interrupted him: "The party you are referring to is the party of Robespierre." Fearful of being similarly accused, Danton spoke up. He adopted a middle position, demonstratively dissociating himself from Marat. He proposed that anyone who sought to set up a dictatorship or a triumvirate, or to dismember France on the altar of impermissible federalism, should be given the death sentence.

The main thrust of the Girondist attack was directed against the

Commune. But now Marat came to the fore with a sensational speech. Resolutely joining Robespierre's party, Marat asserted that he did not care if he drew all the hatred of the moderate faction. Ironically he accused himself of having defended the same ideas as Robespierre the Incorruptible; of having thought of a dictatorship and a triumvirate in order to crush the intriguers and traitors. It was a courageous, forthright speech that made a profound impression. Especially when at the end of a bitter exchange of charges and countercharges between Vergniaud and Robespierre, Marat's latest article was cited as proof of Robespierre's hankerings for a dictatorship. At that moment Marat took a pistol out of his pocket, aimed it at his head, and said: "If the charge had been leveled at me, I would have blown my brains out at the foot of this podium. Is that the fruit of three years of torture to save the country? Very well, I remain among you, to confront your frenzy." The effect was instantaneous. Attacks against Robespierre stopped—at least for the time being.

Roland emerged seriously compromised from all these clashes. But he was determined to drag down Danton with him as well. He had not forgiven Danton for having ridiculed him in the Assembly, accusing him of being tied to Madame Roland's skirts and of having allowed his wife to run the Ministry of Interior, while she protected all those who paid court to her. Roland publicly voiced doubts about Danton's honesty in managing the state finances. Danton had to justify his actions. He gave a credible account of his use of the ordinary funds of the Ministry, but he was far less convincing in the matter of the secret funds amounting to 200,000 livres. When he indulged in contradictory and evasive answers, ill-suited to his aggressive, dynamic character, the Assembly turned against him. His critics brought up his relations with dubious speculators such as Abbé Espagnac. This time all his gifts of oratory failed him; nor could his best friends save him.

As in the case of Mirabeau, the fall of Danton, one of the most impressive figures of the Revolution, exposed the fatal weakness of some great individuals who succumb to the temptations of money, luxury, and pleasures. From the viewpoint of the Revolution, his fall was tragic because it emboldened his enemies, all those interested in saving the King. Reaction now took the offensive. There were attacks on the Vigilance Committee of the Commune; attempts were made to undermine the authority of the extraordinary tribunal that tried traitors and those implicated in plots on behalf of Louis XVI.

In some French *départements* and even some sections of Paris, songs began to circulate demanding the heads of Marat and Robespierre. Intermingled with these were cries of "No trial for Louis XVI!" Rumors were rife of an impending coup to free him; and indeed some questionable armed units were concentrated in Paris. In a noteworthy speech to the National Guard, Robespierre exhorted his listeners to do their duty toward the nation and at the same time to remain patient and not let themselves be provoked. Marat personally visited the headquarters of the Marseilles Guard, dealt with all their complaints concerning their barracks, distributed food, and even sat down to eat with several men of the Guard.

The trial of the King was at hand. The relationship of forces in the National Convention had altered to the disadvantage of the advocates of delay. The Girondists had lost the chairmanship, which was now held by Abbé Grégoire, a man of strong convictions and a consistent foe of the monarchy. At this time too, in one of the walls of the Tuileries gardens an iron chest was uncovered containing letters and documents that proved the King and his Court were maintaining contact with Austria and the émigrés. There were also plans based on the corruptibility of people like Mirabeau; lists of newspapers and journalists that could be bought; and the strategy to be followed in revising the constitution. The evidence was more than sufficient for the Republicans to demand that the King be tried immediately. Now commenced a test of strength between advocates of an immediate trial and those who sought to postpone it until the revolutionary spirit of the masses was spent. The fight centered on procedural questions. The bourgeoisie feared the consequences of still another confrontation with the people. For there had been much discussion of how the trial should be held, including the direct participation of representatives of the people. To what extent would they constitute an element of undue pressure? By the end of October the lawyer Mailhe, considered close to the Mountain, was named mediator of the dispute.

The Girondists counterattacked by proposing Dufriche-Valazé, who was considered receptive to compromise and who was inclined to justify Louis XVI's behavior on the grounds of bad advisers and the like. In any case, Valazé had proved quite "understanding" in his dealings with foreign banking circles. Mailhe, realizing that it was a race against time, hastened to present his report. Accusing the King of open violation of the constitution, he proposed that the Convention appoint three commissioners who would collect all evidence of guilt and then present a true bill of indictment. A brilliant speech by Saint-Just put an end to all delaying tactics. The man whom his enemies later named "the exterminating angel" cut through all the fine-spun legalisms and raised the debate to its genuinely political level. The King, said Saint-Just, is not an accused person but an enemy. The King had fought against the people and had been defeated. Consequently, he had to be considered a prisoner of war. No foreigner had done so much harm to France as that man.

The major piece of evidence was the iron chest found in the Tuileries, which Louis XVI had given to the locksmith Gamain so that it could be covered with a thick protective covering before being hidden in the wall. Roland had it opened, but not in the presence of witnesses. But the compromising letters of Mirabeau, the Bishop of Clermont, Lafayette, and Talleyrand could not be lightly wished away. A few minor arrests were made. The leading culprits had enough influence to escape for the time being. But the discovery of the coffer meant that the King's trial could no longer be put off. Agitation increased in the various sections of Paris and there were demonstrations in front of the Convention against any more delaying maneuvers. In a powerful speech Robespierre supported Saint-Just's point of view. Confronting the Girondists, he accused them of obstructing the holding of the trial: "What other means will they resort to, to restore royalty?" On a motion by Marat the Convention decided that henceforth it would vote openly and by roll call on all circumstances regarding the trial.

The revolutionary government was based on a coalition. Consequently, the various opposing forces found it difficult to adopt a clear and consistent political line. Yet that was imperative if they were to make a clean break with the old order of things. The contradiction between the masses of the people and the petty bourgeoisie, the two elements that governed France at that decisive period in its history, operated frequently in a negative sense. And within the masses themselves, including most of the small-handicrafts workers, sentiment was divided: as producers they favored economic freedom; as consumers they required some degree of economic regulation so as to halt the rise in prices.

As in other revolutions and wars marked by revolutionary fervor, it was easier to unite when in opposition than when in power. Outside the government it was the easiest thing in the world to fight it from a revolutionary viewpoint, demanding a series of measures more attainable on paper and in words than in reality. To accuse a revolutionary government of a lack of revolutionary élan is always a tempting attitude when one does not have the responsibilities of governing. Then, and sometimes when it is too late, this same opposition group acknowledges that it would have been better to be on the side of the government than to undermine its authority. Thus Babeuf, the first "Communist," rejoiced at the fall of Robespierre on the day after 9 Thermidor (July 27, 1794); but several months later he regretted it. He also had the courage to admit that, of the two of them, Robespierre had been right. This was a case of genuine and spontaneous self-criticism—rarely encountered in history.

Although Robespierre was the head of the revolutionary government in a bourgeois revolution—as we have frequently emphasized —his unshakable loyalty to the cause for which he had been elevated to power led him to conclude that the broad masses, not the bourgeoisie, possessed the power to safeguard the Revolution. They were the ones who had stormed the Bastille, marched on Versailles, responded to every appeal to crush the émigrés' plots and counteract the propaganda of the defeatists.

Robespierre needed the active support of the masses for his policy of *salut public* (public safety) in the summer of 1793 that encountered so much resistance among the middle classes. The people of Paris saw to it that the soldiers urgently needed for national defense were recruited. Again, the people of Paris, realizing how the enemies inside and outside the country were fomenting counter-revolution, took an indispensable weapon in their hands—the weapon of Terror. Power through Terror! Defense of the Fatherland through Terror! The people understood that that was the only way to save the Revolution and the nation.

The Year 2 of the First Republic, lasting from September, 1793, to September, 1794, encompassed the period in which Robespierre's dynamism inspired the Committee of Public Safety. Robespierre sought and won the cooperation of the broad masses; but his profound sense of the relationship of forces led him to a policy of equilibrium in which he never forgot the bourgeois origins of the Revolution. Marx has pointed out that at every concrete moment in history "humanity never raises more problems than it can solve." To Robespierre the main problem was that of saving a revolution whose lineaments remained bourgeois to the very end.

What happened afterward has been a frequent occurrence. In defeat the leaders of yesterday are assailed by the very ones who shortly before had praised them to the skies. The revolutionary bourgeoisie that during the grim period of 1793 had supported Robespierre in his most radical measures and even encouraged him to take them, asserted after his fall that it had all been Robespierre's fault, that he had been responsible for the Terror. On one point Robespierre's opponents after the Thermidorean reaction, and conservative historians ever since, have joined in distorting the truth. In his *Almanach de la Révolution Française*, Jean Massin has cited some carefully authenticated figures: From April 6, 1793, to 9 Thermidor (that is, July 27, 1794), a period of sixteen months, the revolutionary tribunal sentenced 2,627 persons to death in Paris. The number of military death sentences in all France, over the same period, was 16,594. Moreover, 71 per cent of the death sentences occurred in regions where the civil war was waged most violently: in La Vendée, the West, and the Southeast. Historians tell us how much blood of the aristocrats was spilled, but not of the killings carried out by the counter-revolutionaries, and the blood of revolutionaries and patriots spilled out of devotion to the idea of freedom.

After August 10, 1792, the powers of the executive had to be reorganized. First they passed to the Assembly, after the King was placed under arrest. Since only a third of the deputies were present, the rest staying away for fear of the people's wrath, government posts were allotted to various groupings then considered to be on the left. Danton, enormously popular at that moment because of a series of impressive speeches in the various Paris districts, was named Minister of Justice by a big majority. Roland took the Interior ministry; Clavière, Finance; and Servan, War. Monge, the great mathematician, was elected Minister of the Navy, and Lebrun was chosen Minister of Foreign Affairs. Three bodies shared power: (1) the Assembly, combining in itself the legislative and executive branches; (2) the Provisional Executive Council, with dictatorial powers to enforce agreements; (3) the Revolutionary Commune of Paris, recognized by the Assembly and, after elections held in the Jacobin sections, led by Robespierre, Billaud-Varenne, and Chaumette. The Commune exercised administrative functions. It also took measures against counter-revolutionary activities, confiscated reactionary publications and transferred them to adherents of the Revolution, expropriated monasteries, and guarded against maneuvers and intrigues of the upper clergy.

The people did not rest on their laurels. Government departments were subjected to critical scrutiny. Marat complained in his diary that as yet nothing had been accomplished. To him, demolishing the statues of previous kings, including that of Henri IV, and ardently singing the "Marseillaise" and the "Carmagnole" did not mean much. He denounced the intrigues of priests in the provinces against the Revolution.

The Revolution was also menaced from abroad. Alarming rumors were rife that the Prussians were marching on Verdun. The Girondist ministers, in a panic, wanted to move from Paris to Blois. But Danton remained cool and exerted all his energy to convince the government to remain in Paris. The Assembly, enthusiastically supported by the Commune, decided to recruit 30,000 soldiers. Young people rushed en masse to enlist under the banner of the Revolution.

The bourgeoisie, with arms at its disposal, sought to use them against the Left mainly as an instrument of pressure, for it had little desire for a direct confrontation with the masses gathered around the Commune. It preferred intrigue, in which the Girondists had shown themselves past masters.

The King's trial was a test of strength between the moderates and the radicals. Danton addressed the judges and told them that only if they proved effective would the people's courts be unnecessary. Robespierre was in favor of a special court (*tribunal extraordinaire*). Eventually his motion won out.

Danton's finest hour was during the debate of August 28, 1792.

Telling the Assembly he was going to speak to them as a revolutionary minister, he denounced the fact that hitherto they had waged a make-believe war against Lafayette and the counter-revolutionaries. Notorious plotters, such as the former ministers Montmorin and Dossonville, had been cleared. Danton demanded a harsher struggle against the royalist agents. He called upon the people to rise en masse against their enemies. Anything that harmed the nation had to be swept aside. It was one of his greatest speeches. At the same time, however, maneuvers against the Commune continued. On the night of August 30, the Assembly discussed a proposal whereby the Commune would be dissolved and re-formed. Robespierre spoke against the motion. He lauded the work of the Commune—if it had to be reconstituted, this should be done by a direct appeal to the people for a new mandate. The Commune decided to remain in office, and elected Marat to its Vigilance Committee.

Events abroad developed along parallel lines with those on the home front. On September 2 a rumor spread in Paris that Verdun, the last fortified position between the border and Paris, could hold out for only a few days longer. The Prussian uhlans were marching on Châlons. Now the Commune moved into action. Countering the defeatism of the aristocratic officers whom the government had supinely left at their posts in the army, the Commune asserted it would fight on two fronts, at home and abroad. Addressing an appeal to the masses, it immediately raised a people's army of 60,000. It was new proof of what a people could do when convinced of a cause. The military units were formed with a speed that impressed even the moderates in the Assembly, although it did not exactly make them feel happy. All modes of transport, beginning with horses, were commandeered. Commissars and delegates of the Commune toured the city districts exhorting the masses to be on the alert for any show of surrender. Again, Danton was imbued with the patriotic élan of the people of Paris and uttered his famous phrase: "Paris has deserved well of the whole nation." And he went on: "The bugle that is about to sound is not an alarm signal; it is a summons to attack the enemies of the country. To defeat them, we need boldness, more boldness, and still more boldness! That is how France will be saved!"

The masses were furious when the monarchists' intrigues—their plottings with the émigrés and the invading troops—were made public. Their anger expressed itself in a series of violent outbreaks, for which reactionary historians later held Danton and the Commune responsible, as if they had organized the outbursts. But they were spontaneous explosions and of such fury that the Commune itself felt it necessary to take steps to protect the Temple and its prisoners, including the Queen's ladies-in-waiting. On the night of September 2–3, the Commune ordered the popular Santerre of the National Guard to prevent excesses and killings. One of the July fighters, Maillard, was said on reliable evidence to have personally saved forty-six persons from slaughter.

On one point there was total agreement among the Girondists and the revolutionary Left—the Mountain, the Jacobins, and the Commune: their policy toward the Church. The change-over from a France that for centuries had been clerical and ultramontane into a secular France occurred with startling swiftness. The buildings housing the religious orders—*les maisons des Ordres*—were ordered by the decree of October 1 to be vacated and sold. Another big step toward secularization was the treatment of recalcitrant priests: they had to leave the country or face internment. Some 25,000 ecclesiastics fled abroad. Spain eyed them with suspicion; England, on the other hand, received them warmly. Nevertheless, many priests remained in France, especially those who because of their advancing years were exempted from the general decree.

The elections for the Constitutional Committee in October, 1792, intensified the differences between the Mountain and the Girondists. The Girondists indulged in all sorts of maneuvers as the electoral lists were being drawn up. Under the impact of the street demonstrations, all the outstanding figures in the Assembly gave verbal allegiance to the Republic. But this did not prevent them on occasion from joining with the foes of the new institutions. In some circles opportunism was the order of the day. Danton voted for an electoral list that included the Duc d'Orléans, who now bore the democratic name "Philippe Egalité." Language became more democratic too. The word *citoyen* (citizen) supplanted *monsieur*. Monarchist newspapers were suppressed; the calendar was changed. On August 22, 1792, the Year I of the Revolutionary Calendar began. It was hailed as the commencement of a new era. But the fight between the halfhearted and full-blown revolutionaries—in the final analysis, an aspect of the class struggle—sharpened with each passing day.

Participation in the elections was generally light because both the monarchists and the advocates of compromise stayed home. The working class was barely represented: out of 750 deputies there were only two workers, a blacksmith and a wool-comber. In Paris all the elected deputies belonged to the Commune and were followers of its leader, Robespierre. Antagonisms became more acute. Madame Roland, the minister's witty wife, made no bones about her hatred for Danton, even though he had saved her husband from arrest. But this was trifling compared with the hatred Robespierre inspired among the moderate deputies and the bourgeois leaders who had accepted the Republic against their will. Reactionaries of every stripe realized that now the Revolution had found a man to lead the people in a principled way, to struggle and, if need be, die for them. Robespierre was that man.

Lenin used to say that the Bolsheviks were the Jacobins of the twentieth century, so great was the esteem in which he held the leading Jacobins, especially Saint-Just and Robespierre. The social forces they represented were quite different, and separated by a hundred and twenty-five years of history. Robespierre had the support of the middle bourgeoisie and artisans: a typical example was Duplay, in whose house on the Rue Saint-Honoré Robespierre lived like a member of the family. As Jean Jaurès wrote in his epic *Histoire Socialiste de la Révolution Française*, these were not the upper but the middle bourgeoisie, enjoying close ties with the artisans and small shopkeepers. They brought with them the lower strata who were not yet clearly conscious of their own interests but who shared, with persons like Duplay, a hatred of tyranny and a passion for freedom.

Robespierre's charisma exerted a strong pull on all these groupings. Between 1793 and 1794 he became a national figure, epitomizing, as no other individual, the forward march of the Revolution. Robespierre the man of action was also a man of ideas, representing the ideology of Jean-Jacques Rousseau more faithfully than any of the other great leaders. He led the Jacobins, and they in turn were the only political force organized on a national scale. The Jacobin Club, parliamentary in origin, was the oldest of the clubs and the one in which revolutionary policy was discussed and at times decided, whereas the Cordeliers Club was strictly Parisian, its strength residing in the fact that it was more democratically open to the people and hence able to play a very active part as the Revolution developed. Undoubtedly Robespierre's weakness lay in his lack of personal contact with the masses, who, nevertheless, instinctively saw in him the unchallenged leader of all genuine patriots. But he was essentially a man of the study, of the Jacobin Club, of parliamentary sessions and committees, not a man of the street.

Robespierre's rise to power marked a new stage. He brought to the Committee of Public Safety not only his personal qualities of courage, composure, and integrity but, more important, a clear and consistent political line. He was a poor speaker and lacked organizing ability. Yet from the time the Constituent Assembly was formed, Robespierre was the most popular revolutionary leader among the artisans and the "little people," who had complete faith in him. He was the undisputed head of the *sans-culottes*. Robespierre did not enter the Committee alone. He brought with him the most militant members of the clubs who, in the words of the historian Albert Mathiez, "had no alternative but to win, or die." His accession to power came in the midst of a near-chaotic political situation. The government was being attacked from both the Right and the Left. In many areas the people were on the brink of starvation. The war against foreign invaders spurred the various foes to unite in a common front. To deal with such a crisis situation required a person with the moral and political stature of Robespierre "the Incorruptible."

His action was limited by the social reality in which he operated. The economic institutions were still, for the most part, based on private, individual economy. To build a rational economy, with radical economic changes corresponding to the political changes, many essential factors were lacking. Above all, there was no heavy industry employing a working class conscious of its strength and its class interests. Class struggle, as we have stated above, appeared in embryonic fashion during the French Revolution. But these were fleeting moments, hinting at a social revolution but without solid substance. They pointed to a far-off perspective rather than an immediate possibility of ending the bases of human exploitation. All the best minds of the Revolution—Marat, Robespierre, Saint-Just—spoke out against exploitation, but they differed in their views as to the ways and means of achieving this. At the outset Robespierre seemed the most moderate, probably because he did not want to jeopardize the future of the Revolution with demands he found more rhetorical and emotional than based on a cool examination of the real correlation of forces. From the beginning of the struggle, however, Marat fought for social equality and against wealth, with such passion that he became a kind of "premature Communist" a half-century before the *Communist Manifesto*.

But Robespierre was not inflexible. At the start he inveighed harshly against the *Enragés*, the ultra-lefts, and sought to solve poverty with measures of a police-state nature. But as the counter-revolutionaries grew bolder, he became the spokesman of the Left. His initially "centrist" position in the Mountain, prompted by his desire to act as intermediary between the National Assembly and the street, evolved leftward step by step as the dangers threatening the Revolution took concrete shape.

We must also bear in mind that for a time even the advanced sector of the Revolution was beset by contradictions, frequently paralyzing its activity. Robespierre sought to make an objective estimate of the strength of those who claimed to be his adherents. Even the radicalism of the Jacobin Club, he felt, should not be exaggerated. In terms of the political vocabulary of today, his was originally a bourgeois radicalism; but in moments of urgent danger, with war or famine threatening, he rose to the occasion and got rid of all his vacillations. In the course of events, the Jacobin Club hardened its position and Robespierre could count more confidently on its support. This was particularly true after the Cordeliers brought their revolutionary ardor to the club, preparing it for the decisive days that lay ahead.

For the Revolution not only had enemies within. On the outside it confronted monarchist Europe. After the events of August 10, England abruptly recalled its ambassador in a manner that bordered on blatant interference. Catherine of Russia did likewise. Hesse, Austria, and Prussia dragged France into war. Switzerland mobilized several regiments. The Spanish ambassador demanded his passport, and the Dutch ambassador left Paris. Only Sweden and Denmark maintained a correct attitude.

The Mountain and the Commune were not intimidated by this threat of foreign intervention. But the Girondists, who had helped to create this situation, grew fearful. Influenced by his Cabinet colleagues, Danton proposed negotiations and concessions. He sent secret emissaries to London to win Prime Minister Pitt over to a policy of neutrality. Pitt would not even receive them. Similar overtures were made to Prussia and Austria, with the same negative result. The Girondists pinned too much hope on their appeals to the other peoples of Europe, believing them equally disposed to get rid of their ultra-conservative and despotic regimes. They even attempted "intellectual alliances." On the initiative of the poet Marie Joseph de Chénier, a list of foreign writers noted for their criticism of tyrannical regimes was drawn up: it included such names as Joseph Priestley, Jeremy Bentham, Thomas Clarkson, and William Wilberforce (the antislavery crusader), Alexander Hamilton, Tom Paine, Schiller, Klopstock, Anacharsis Cloots, and Pestalozzi. Priestley, Cloots, and Paine were among those elected to the Convention. The first-named declined; the other two accepted.

The political generals were busy sabotaging the defense of the Revolution. With their intrigues and deliberate slowdowns they gave the enemy time to elaborate its plan to strike at key points. The Austrian-Prussian army commanded by the Duke of Brunswick crossed Lorraine on its way to Champagne. Frederick William II, who shared command of his army with his two sons, called for all-out war against the revolutionaries to avenge "humiliated Majesty" and restore it with full powers to the throne. They were confident of bringing the campaign to a victorious close by the beginning of October.

On the revolutionary side, serious mistakes were committed. Lafayette, who had gone over to the counter-revolutionary camp, was replaced as army head by a German, Nicolas Luckner, not much more trustworthy than his predecessor. Two delegates of the Council of Ministers, Billaud-Varenne and Laclos, were entrusted with the task of keeping him under surveillance. They quickly became convinced of his lack of ability and questionable loyalty. He was replaced by François Christophe Kellermann, a capable and reliable general.

On September 12 the Duke of Brunswick went on the offensive, forcing General Dumouriez, who was moving north, to retreat. The road to Paris lay open. Never for a moment did the King of Prussia dream that the *sans-culottes*—"the rabble"—who constituted the backbone of revolutionary resistance could give equal battle with the highly organized army under his command. It simply did not enter into his calculations. Moreover, he did not understand the decisive role of morale in warfare: the strength a people draws in the fight for its own destiny and for a higher ideal. Despite its disorganization and lack of resources, the revolutionary force defeated Frederick William's highly trained and disciplined army. Exhorting his men with the cry of *Vive la Nation!* Kellermann wrested the initiative from the Prussians. At the battle of Valmy revolutionary fervor won out over the overconfident monarchist general staffs. For a brief time Goethe's eyes were opened; he altered his hitherto rather disdainful attitude toward events in France. And at Valmy, on September 20, 1792, Goethe, who was at the side of his patron, the Duke of Brunswick, burst out spontaneously: "At this place and on this day a new era in world history has begun, and you can say that you were there!"

After long and difficult negotiations with Dumouriez, the Prussians, utterly demoralized, began to retreat toward Verdun and gave up captured French territory. En route they were also harried by French peasants who shared in the victory.

Elections to the Convention had been a success for the Girondists, and the victory at Valmy strengthened their position. The Mountain had to yield to this reality. Meanwhile Maillard, who had been among the stormers of the Bastille, led a huge Paris street crowd to shouts of "Bread, bread!" and "To Versailles!" That afternoon they reached Versailles.

The worsening situation and the threat of foreign invasion organized by monarchist agents produced a movement toward unity in the revolutionaries' ranks. At the Jacobin Club, Robespierre made peace with Brissot. The Girondists followed suit. One of their great orators, Vergniaud, whose stentorian voice rivaled that of Danton, uttered a harsh diatribe against the King: "A king capable of placing himself at the head of troops against the nation, or who incites them to that, has lost the right to the Crown." This eloquence on the part of the Girondists did not convince those who were resolved to put an end to the monarchy. Its aim was to slow down rather than to accelerate the Revolution. Robespierre spoke out against any such tactics of compromise and half measures. Unmoved by the intervention of the Minister of Justice, who demanded that he be prosecuted in court as an inciter to violence, Robespierre spoke repeatedly in the ensuing debate and called for the King's abdication. He denounced a new plot by Lafayette that seemed timed with the appeasement tactics of the Girondists; and he drew increasing support from the most militant section of the Jacobins. To frustrate the various intrigues that sought to change the course of the Revolution and hold back the mass upsurge, Robespierre proposed the establishment of a secret committee. It would meet at the home of the carpenter Duplay, where, as we have seen, Robespierre himself and Arthoine, another reliable revolutionary, now lived. Thenceforth he had a clear line: to fight against the defeatists and to fight against the King's agents who were conspiring to save them. He wanted to replace the Legislative Assembly, paralyzed by internal dissensions, with a *Convent*—a Convention charged with drawing up a new constitution. Here we begin to see a leveling tendency on his part, a growing alignment with the exploited, who later became the working class. Thenceforth Robespierre, the most interesting and important leader of the French Revolution, was increasingly attuned to social motives: he turned more and more to the common people for support, calling upon them to be his allies against the bourgeoisie.

State funds—many of them secret—flowed freely. Many leaders, unlike the "Incorruptible," were bribed. Lafayette claimed that Danton had received 50,000 gold crowns from the secret funds. In less than a month the Minister of the Interior had dispensed sums amounting to about a million livres. With the government people chiefly interested in getting rich, the King felt safe. Nevertheless, he deemed it wise to double the palace guard. Vacillating between occasional mock-heroic gestures and pretenses of yielding to popular sentiment, Louis XVI finished by seeking protection in the Assembly. But then came the fateful August 10, the people's attack on the Tuileries, and the dethronement of the King. As soon as Louis XVI quit his palace, a majority of the National Guard went over to the insurgents. A bloody battle ensued nonetheless, with heavy losses on both sides and in the course of which the Swiss guards were virtually wiped out.

Now the Assembly had no choice: they were confronted with a condition, not a theory. This time the people were resolved to brook no more delays or maneuvers. A new attempt by Lafayette to march on Paris with his troops failed. Most of the soldiers refused to obey their commander and fled to Belgium.

August 10 left an indelible mark on the Revolution. Not only did the King and the concept of monarchy emerge the loser from this confrontation; an entire class, the bourgeoisie, was also defeated. The Jacobin Left emerged victorious, against the Girondists and all those who had counseled retreat. But winning a battle is not winning the war. The question was whether the masses could hold their newly won positions. The radical elements who had set the tone on July 14, 1789, had by now grown thoroughly disenchanted with the weak-kneed parliamentarians of Versailles. They now began to ask themselves whether it would not be better to bring both King and Assembly to Paris, where they could keep close watch over them. Thus they could prevent Louis XVI from fleeing and at the same time force the deputies to fulfill their mandates as representatives of the people.

A new voice began to be increasingly heard, that of Jean Paul Marat, who had founded his newspaper *L'Ami du Peuple* in September, 1789. Now it provided the spark (*Iskra*, "the Spark," was the name of Lenin's paper that played so vital a part in advancing the Russian Revolution) needed to fan popular impatience and indignation into a tremendous conflagration. Marat clearly understood that the Revolution would have to be made from below, not from on top.

On October 1, officials of the National Guard had given a dinner in the royal palace in honor of the Flanders regiment. The King and Queen, accompanied by the Dauphin, heir to the throne, appeared to greet the guests. The regimental band played Grétry's air: *O Richard, o mon roi, l'univers t'abandonne!* Pandemonium ensued. Officers tore off the national cockade and trampled it under foot, then put on white and black, the King's colors. When the news appeared in one of the popular papers and was described in Marat's *Ami du Peuple* as a plot to destroy the constitution, crowds took to the streets to demonstrate their resentment. Losing no time, Marat called the Paris districts to arms. The cannon at the Hôtel de Ville were sent off toward Versailles. But in Versailles preparations of a different sort were being made. Things were being readied for the King to move on October 5 to Metz, where he would place himself under the protection of the Marquis de Boulle. At the same time the palace guard was strengthened.

On a motion by Danton, at the Cordeliers Club, the Commune was asked to get Lafayette to intercede with the King and persuade him to withdraw the troops. If this demand went unheeded, then the Assembly should step in and insist on it. The populace went much further than that. On that same October 5, the date of the monarchist escape plot, crowds again took to the streets. A group of women stormed the Hôtel de Ville and won over the soldiers of the guard on duty there.

French women were no mere spectators in the Revolution. They participated directly and vigorously. On October 5–6, 1789, Parisiennes marched on Versailles. On August 10, 1792, they took part in the attack on the Tuileries. They stood guard on the borders of the country and everywhere formed clubs of their own. In *Patriotic Letters of Mère Duchêne*, a book that may be found in the Bibliothèque Nationale in Paris, their feats are recorded with legitimate pride: "I may say in praise of French women that they influenced the winning of freedom by their example, their advice, their speeches, and their acts."

Three women—Olympe de Gouges, Théroigne de Méricourt, and Etta Palm d'Aelders—were in the vanguard of the women's liberation movement of that day. The last-named issued in July, 1791, an "Appeal to Frenchwomen concerning the regeneration of their customs and the need to guarantee the influence of women in a free government." She proposed the creation in each Paris section of a patriotic organization of women citizens, "Friends of Truth." Thus was born the first significant feminist club, the Société des Républicaines Révolutionnaires. These women attended sessions of the Convention and made themselves heard at meetings of the Jacobin and Cordeliers clubs. The reactionaries called them "madwomen of the guillotine" and "Robespierre's devotees." Many women were ready to go to the front and fight against the reactionary troops of the interventionists. Claire Lacombe, a Marseilles actress, presented a petition to the Assembly, asking to be recruited into the army. And she continued: "Lawmakers, you have declared our country to be in danger. That is not enough: you have to strip of their powers those who compromise France's security." Then she bluntly named Lafayette.

Educated in the new spirit in the house of her father, a candy manufacturer and enlightened thinker, Pauline Léon led a delegation of women to the Legislative Assembly on March 6, 1792, demanding that women be given the right to fight against despotism: "Let our weakness," she cried, "be no obstacle. Courage and dauntlessness will make up for it. You cannot keep us from taking our posts unless the Declaration of the Rights of Man does not apply to women. We refuse to resign ourselves to being slaughtered like lambs without having the right to defend ourselves."

At every critical moment in the Revolution, the women in the clubs were aroused and resolute. On May 12, 1793, a women's delegation appeared before the Jacobins, proposing that women from the ages of eighteen to fifty be armed and formed into a special women's unit to fight against the counter-revolutionaries in La Vendée. The women of Paris supported Jacques Roux and the *Enragés*—as the Have-Nots were labeled—in their demands to punish hoarders and profiteers. They lent a special tone to the civic holidays that were so popular during the Revolution: besides serving as meeting centers for the various district federations, these gatherings were a kind of surrogate for the traditional religious holidays that had become empty shells of tradition and routine.

Sharply attacked from many sides during the factional fights, the revolutionary republican women of that day fully demonstrated their loyalty to the Revolution and their passionate zeal to expose the enemies of the Republic. Foes of the Girondists, advocates of a republic of social equality—"We do not want a single person living in misery in the Republic"—adamant in their attitude toward the aristocrats and wealthy classes, these women were the embodiment of devotion to the people. Allied with the *Enragés* by their common hatred of the food profiteers, they inevitably earned the hostility of those in power.

The Girondists accused the Mountain of fomenting popular agitation and leading it into dangerous paths. A series of emergency measures taken at the local and national level to combat high food prices; the sharp drop in value of the currency—the assignats had tumbled 41 per cent in value; shortages and poor provisioning of the markets, the large-scale purchases of wheat for the army having complicated an already bad food situation—all these were denounced as irresponsible and demagogic. But what outraged the Girondists most was *la loi agraire*—the agrarian law.

None of these measures had anything to do with post-Marxian socialism. The men and women who led the great revolutions of the twentieth century would have judged them timid and inadequate. Many of the measures—requisitioning of food supplies, food rationing—imposed on an unprecedented scale in the 1790's were employed by capitalist governments in World War II. Nevertheless, at the end of the eighteenth century they represented a momentous advance: the private property interests were subordinated to the national interest. This was an open breach with the sacrosanct concept of private property. And, in a sense, an anticipation of socialism.

Decisions made in some of the cities highlight this point. In Lyons an official of the municipal government, Lange, established a whole system of nationalized means of subsistence; furthermore, he demanded that prices be determined on the basis of consumers', not landowners', interests. The word *accapareur* (hoarder) became a term of open contempt. Abbé Jacques Roux, in a harsh speech delivered in May, 1792, demanded the death penalty for food hoarders and speculators. His was the voice of the progressive priests who, in contrast to the reactionary, monarchist clergy, spoke on behalf of the people. A parish priest named Petitjean spoke on August 10, favoring direct action against speculation in foodstuffs. He called on the people to break into the hoarders' warehouses and take what was there. For this he was arrested and sentenced to six years in prison; but as a result of popular pressure he was later set free. Marat characteristically threw himself heart and soul into this widening fight for economic equality.

Assassinated by Charlotte Corday on July 13, 1793, Marat passed from the scene. Thus disappeared "the friend of the people," imbued with hatred for the exploiters and fully committed to the cause of the exploited. The people repaid him with deep and genuine affection. The violent manner in which he met his death made his loss felt all the more keenly. Petitions poured in from all sides asking that he be buried in the Panthéon as a martyr of freedom. It was finally decided that he would lie in the Tuileries, with his heart going to the Cordeliers Club. His statue was placed in the Club of the Republicans, together with those of Lepeletier and Chalier, two other patriots who had been victims of Girondist and royalist repression.

Here we cannot pass over the fact—as do so many conservative historians—that it was the terror practiced originally by those on the Right that unleashed the terror of the masses. Counter-revolutionary violence was answered by revolutionary violence preached by the Enragés—Jacques Roux, Leclerc, Varlet, and others—who considered themselves political heirs of Marat. And even further to the Left was Hébert.

All this served to heighten agitation, especially in the long lines waiting in front of bakeries and in marketplaces and among crowds gathered before the warehouses of the rich. The Committee of Public Safety felt it had to intervene. It issued a decree against agitators and put the sale and distribution of food under the control of the authorities.

The demand for more stringent measures against the reactionary plotters extended to the army, where, as we have pointed out, aristocratic officers of high rank and dubious loyalty had been retained. Minister Bouchotte, a sincere republican, tried to eliminate them. This led to an intrigue against Bouchotte; but he was upheld by Robespierre, who openly denounced the maneuver and helped rout the opposition. This in turn gave new impetus to the forward march of the revolutionary government. On the same night that the army question was tackled and clarified, the Committee of Public Safety, on a motion by Couthon, invited Robespierre to take part in its proceedings. Meanwhile the theorist of the revolutionary government, Saint-Just, outlined how and why violence had to be used against the enemy when the alternative was to allow themselves to be crushed by that enemy. He foresaw that the King's party and the entire reactionary camp would utilize the policy of clemency if the government fell into a legalistic trap and put off a decision on Louis XVI's fate month after month, contrary to the interests of the Revolution.

On November 13, 1792, the Mailhe report on the King's trial was placed under discussion. For the first time Saint-Just mounted the speaker's platform. Morisson, a deputy from La Vendée, had raised the question: "Could the King be tried?" answering it in the negative. His argument was that if there was no explicit legislation against it, the principle of inviolability prevailed. Saint-Just evoked the age of Julius Caesar. That tyrant had been cut down in the Roman Senate itself, with no formality except for twenty-three dagger thrusts and with no law save Rome's freedom. In his brilliantly argued speech Saint-Just demolished Morisson's strategy of affording Louis XVI the protective cloak of inviolability and, if that failed, of using every kind of procedural delay as if the man on trial were just any ordinary citizen. Saint-Just demanded that a people's court, not a judicial tribunal, try "this foreign enemy." He transformed an ostensibly juridical question into a political one. Louis XVI had fought against the people and had lost. His writings and his treason were public knowledge. He had behaved not like the king of the French but like the king of a conspiratorial clique. What foreign enemy had caused the people more harm than the murderer of the Bastille, of Nancy, of the Champ-de-Mars, Tournai, and the Tuileries? Saint-Just's speech shook the Convention. Even his opponents were impressed by his logic and clear thinking. In *Le Patriote français*, Brissot the Girondist hailed him as a talent destined to brighten France's luster.

One of the most useful sources of information about the French Revolution is the daily journal *Les Révolutions de Paris*, which appeared from July, 1789, to February, 1794. It was edited by a gifted journalist, de Loustalot, until his death, when he was succeeded by the controversial Fabre d'Eglantine. This publication carried, among other things, the debates of the Assembly sessions. Robespierre's speeches show him less at home in the Assembly than

· at the Jacobin Club, where he felt confident that his listeners were not engaged in intrigues and double-dealing. On October 22, 1792, Robespierre inveighed against "the influence of slander on the Revolution." He asserted vigorously that his charges were not the fruit of his imagination but were leveled "at those who exercise real power under another name" and "at those who hold in their hands all the instruments of their false prestige and control the conduits to public opinion." Even then he accused Minister of the Interior Roland of deploying his agents everywhere to collect the tiniest scraps of gossip that might be used against the Jacobin leaders.

As we have seen, the Girondists stoutly opposed any drastic measures against persons under suspicion—sometimes openly, sometimes surreptitiously. They feared the zeal with which the war for national survival was being led and the enthusiasm of the masses, who instinctively identified with Robespierre and Marat. The Jacobins' revolutionary energy terrified those Girondist deputies who were upset at any appearance, however embryonic, of a feeling for class struggle.

Robespierre was determined to prevent the Republic of Virtue from being undermined by ambition, by money-grabbing and pleasure-seeking. The political theory of the Terror, formulated by Saint-Just, Couthon, Billaud-Varenne, and especially Robespierre, was based on this need to protect the Republic against its enemies. In their eyes the weakness and corruption of those in authority required a temporary stage of a democratic dictatorship. It was a question of choosing between allowing the Republic to be murdered or eliminating its actual or potential murderers. Surrounded by internal and external enemies, from William Pitt and the Duke of Coburg to the vacillating moderates and the agents of counter-revolution, the revolutionary government had to have the courage to abandon certain principles for a while, among them the idea of individual freedom. "No freedom for the enemies of freedom; no freedom to destroy the Revolution."

Robespierre felt that most of his fellow deputies were two-faced and cowardly. And so, on October 28, 1792, he felt impelled to define his own role in the following words: "They accuse us of marching toward dictatorship—yet we have neither army, treasury, general headquarters, nor party. We who are as intransigent as truth, as inflexible, as constant, I would almost say as intolerable as principles themselves." He did not mind feeling alone so long as the people we ·e with him, for the people would not let themselves be corrupted by the corrupters. He provoked his adversaries: those who remained silent when accused themselves. No one who was genuinely on the side of the Revolution, he went on, need fear the Committee of Public Safety, which heeded the people's will. The use of force against the wicked was essential in order to protect the virtuous. Robespierre described the revolutionary government as "the despotism of liberty against tyranny." In his analysis of the theory of the Reign of Terror, the historian Albert Mathiez clearly showed the class-struggle elements involved in the Terror.

Divisions among the various governing committees rendered a crisis inevitable. The Committee of Public Safety had become the strongest organ of rule. By creating its own police force it had incurred the animosity of the Committee of General Security. Personal dissensions complicated the already tangled situation. Robespierre, now the real head of government, was accused of despotism and overweening ambition by Hébert and his friends on the Left—as he had previously been accused by the Girondists from the Right. Lazare Carnot quarreled with Saint-Just. All this was grist to the mill of the falsifiers and schemers, men such as Fouché, Barras, and Tallien, who feared Robespierre's moral probity.

On 8 Thermidor (July 26, 1794), Robespierre launched an all-out attack against his opponents in the Convention. The counter-revolutionary plotters felt that they did not have much time left to act. Saint-Just met with them, but with a sword not with an olive branch in his hand, preferring to die rather than compromise himself with the avowed enemies of the Revolution. On 9 Thermidor of Year II (July 27, 1794), Saint-Just mounted the speaker's platform of the Convention. He had barely begun to talk when Tallien interrupted him and drew loud applause from the gathering when he accused Saint-Just of speaking solely in his personal name since he had dissociated himself and isolated himself from the Committee.

Saint-Just held firm: he felt the need of over-all institutions that would place the Republic once and for all on a solid basis. To him the interests and motives of the various groups were secondary. And he continued: "The divisions within the government have been exaggerated. Not all the days of glory have passed. . . . I warn Europe of the futility of its schemes against the government in power; and I warn the enemies within who claim that the government is too harsh that it will be even harsher if the safety of the Republic demands it."

He condemned the waverers who argued that they were treading on a volcano. The only dangerous volcano was that of revolutionary weakness. He rejected the claim that Robespierre was a tyrant of public opinion. The community was the public conscience. "Was Demosthenes a tyrant?" Saint-Just asked. "In any event his tyranny saved liberty in Greece for a long time." As a man who had emerged from the revolutionary masses, Saint-Just had not squandered his energies in winning over this group or that group. Even among the Jacobins he had played a secondary part. But when the critical moment came and someone had to take command of the sections loyal to the Commune in order to crush the conspiracy, he wasted no time in making contact with men he had scarcely talked with in the past.

The revolutionary journalist Babeuf (called Gracchus Babeuf) was quick to realize that 9 Thermidor meant the end of the Revolution and the beginning of open counter-revolution. His initial reaction was not a sign of his political perspicacity; he did not yet fully grasp the meaning of the victory of the Convention over the Incorruptible, Robespierre. But his eyes were finally opened to the fatal course of events when he was arrested, along with Filippo Michele Buonarroti and other members of the "Conspiracy of the Equals." Their movement, formed to bring about conditions for a thoroughgoing social revolution with communistic overtones, was defeated on 21 Floréal of Year IV (May 10, 1796). Now persecuted indiscriminately by the reactionaries in power, the Jacobins and the *sans-culottes* again drew close to one another. In the working-class districts people looked back nostalgically on "the days of Robespierre" as they demanded bread and the Constitution of 1793.

The best of Babeuf's writings were in his publication *Le Tribun du Peuple*. He knew the revolutionary importance of a newspaper, however limited its circulation, if the political line it defended was clear and represented the true interests of the masses. Babeuf's editorials, as well as his "Manifesto of the Plebeians," which enjoyed great popularity, reveal the nature of his Communist ideas. To Babeuf and the Babouvist conspiracy goes the honor of having been, despite their illegal status, the first organized party in history that put forward the idea of a temporary revolutionary dictatorship. In his view—as later in that of Blanqui and Lenin—such a dictatorship was indispensable for the establishment of a Socialist society. Condemned to death, Babeuf wrote a farewell letter to his family that bespoke his faith in the forward march and ultimate triumph of socialism, despite all the setbacks and disappointments it would encounter on the way. He would not give his enemies the satisfaction of hanging him. An admirer of Greek tragedy, Babeuf imitated one of its heroes and on the scaffold plunged a dagger into his heart. The hangman could execute only a corpse. This was his final gesture of defiance toward the Directory that had dropped its conciliatory mask and was brutally repressing all those who sympathized with Babeuf. As one of Babeuf's biographers correctly notes, his movement marked the emergence of socialism from its prehistory to become the prelude of the great proletarian revolutions of the twentieth century.

On 10 Thermidor, 1794, the guillotine knife fell on the youthful head of the "Archangel of Terror." Elected a deputy from the Aisne district in 1792, Saint-Just had a lightninglike political career. Yet those brief flashes remain as blazing symbols of all young rebels since then who have engaged in action, under whatever revolutionary banner. I have heard Saint-Just's name evoked at a students' gathering in Tientsin, China, as well as behind closed doors at a meeting of guerrilla fighters in Latin America.

André Malraux defined him in a single sentence: "Saint-Just had the calling for the Revolution." "I wanted a Republic that everyone could have loved," sadly wrote Camille Desmoulins. But Saint-Just's formula, in his famous Report in which he demanded that the Convention recognize the Committee of Public Safety as the revolutionary government until peace returned, was "Govern by fire!" And there is also Saint-Just's other statement: "They accuse me of having guillotined many. But I have not guillotined the Revolution."

Saint-Just vowed no compromise with the enemies of the Republic—not with the defeatist republicans or with those who had used the change of regimes to enrich themselves. Even the Jacobins were disturbed when Saint-Just, sent to Strasbourg to stabilize the military situation, set up a revolutionary committee and declared: "Traitors in government offices will be shot." The Jacobins sent an envoy from Paris to soften him. Saint-Just was not impressed: "We are here not to fraternize with the authorities but to judge them." He was an effective political commissar in war, indeed the first in history. He successfully reorganized the army—"politicalizing" it, as we would say today. "I know only one way to resist Europe's attack: by pitting the spirit of liberty against it." The choice of generals, Saint-Just pointed out in his Report, should be entrusted to representatives of the people, that is, to the Convention. The first step was to win over the army by purifying it, if they wanted the army in turn to win victories. Attracting officers by bribes and promises of promotion was a waste of time. Even worse, it would undermine the Republic. Finally, there was one sentence that recurred repeatedly in his arguments: "The Revolution cannot be made with half measures."

His oratory differed from that of the other leaders of the French Revolution in its concreteness and its consistency. "A part of his prestige," Malraux has commented, "comes from his talent which is not, properly speaking, literary. The ensemble of his speeches and statements are not addressed to specialists: his genius was made up of isolated phrases to which his acts gave meaning; and they have spanned the centuries." He was no more eloquent than Vergniaud, no bolder than Danton, no deeper than Robespierre, no sterner than Marat. But his revolutionary appeal took hold. Nobody surpassed him in kindling revolutionary faith. He confronted plotting factions from abroad as well as parliamentary intriguers on the home front. In his analysis to the Convention of the situation brought about by frequent attempts at assassination, he declared: "I don't know if anyone will dare to say it all. I speak to you in utter candor and integrity, resolved to undertake everything and to say everything in order to save our country. Integrity is a force that defies all attempts at assassination. The two factions—the tenderhearted who would spare those who have wronged the nation, and the foreign foe—join to stifle freedom between their two crimes." The "two crimes" were those of open treason and that of "generosity" through concealment.

He was implacable toward Danton, who undoubtedly used part of the secret funds to finance his personal propaganda; toward Hébert, the ultra-left demagogue "who rants against the banks and dines with the bankers"; against young Hérault de Séchelles, ambitious for power and pleasure, corrupt and cynical; as well as toward the agents of the Duc d'Orléans, General Dumouriez, and the Girondists.

On 9 Thermidor, the eve of the fatal day, Saint-Just mounted the podium. The Convention was full to overflowing; most of those in the public galleries had been mobilized by Robespierre's enemies. "His look was stern," wrote Courtois in his report of 9 Thermidor of Year III, "his air was somber." Saint-Just then uttered some of his most memorable words: "I belong to no faction. I have fought them all. And I have fought their efforts to make human vanity win out over public freedom." Tallien, one of the plotters, grew uneasy as he listened. He said to one of his neighbors: "There is Saint-Just on the podium. We've got to finish him off."

When Robespierre, Saint-Just, and Couthon, the souls of revolutionary resistance, were placed under arrest, Saint-Just still had time for an ironic comment: "I am the ruler of France, the new Cromwell." As the hateful Fouquier-Tinville read the decrees that found them guilty, Saint-Just maintained an attitude of great dignity. Disinterested eyewitnesses report that at twenty-six Saint-Just went to the guillotine "quite firm, quite erect." He had written his last words several days before: "I scorn the dust of which I am composed and which speaks to you. You may persecute this dust and kill it. But I defy you to take from me the independent life I have given myself down through the centuries and throughout the heavens."

4

THE REVOLUTIONS
OF 1848

The French Revolution of 1789 reverberated throughout the world.
Its influence reached even into countries that were sunk in a feudal
past. Among these lands was Russia.

Russia has a long history of secret societies. The first important
one, judging from its makeup, was formed by army officers who had
returned triumphant from the Napoleonic Wars. They were disturbed by contradictions in the behavior of Czar Alexander: in
France he passed himself off as a liberal and progressive, whereas in
his own country, Russia, he tolerated the most outrageous abuses
against his own people. The serfs had fought against Napoleon for
the glory of Russia and the Czar; instead of gaining freedom, they
now found themselves more fiercely exploited than before. This
situation seemed intolerable to a group of officers in the Imperial
Guard, who in their campaigns beyond their native land had come in
contact with the ideas of the French Revolution. One group stood
out: that of Colonel Muraviev, scion of an old family, who in 1817
formed a secret society called the Union of Salvation, or the Society
of the True and Faithful Sons of the Fatherland. In a short time the
Union of Salvation attracted some of the boldest and most imaginative members of the wealthy class, who, breaking with their own
class, embraced the cause of reform. One of the best known was
Mikhail Lunin, son of a big landowner and an officer in the Guard.

The secret societies that arose after the Napoleonic Wars laid the groundwork for the Decembrist Revolt of 1825. Later-nineteenth-century historians considered it the first Russian revolution, although long before it occurred there had been the great peasant uprisings we have mentioned above (see Chapter 2), led by the rebel leader Pugachev—"the Russian Spartacus"—who is rarely accorded his due by historians. The outstanding leader of the Decembrist movement was Lieutenant Colonel Pavel Pestel, born in 1793, the son of a governor-general of Siberia. The poet Pushkin, who met him in Bessarabia, described him in these terms: "One of the most original minds I have encountered on my path." Pestel was a member of the executive committee of the Union of Common Welfare, the organization that succeeded the Union of Salvation. In the passionate debates preceding the 1825 revolt, Pestel persuaded his associates to accept the idea of regicide in the event the Czar refused to promulgate a constitution. A confirmed Jacobin, Pestel had been working on an uncompleted treatise, *Russkaya Pravda* (*Russian Truth*), in which he advocated a democratic and indivisible republic, with a single legislative assembly he named the Narodnoye Veche (People's Congress), which would pass laws governing the public welfare. He had a complex personality: generous and at the same time domineering toward some of his Decembrist comrades. Hence many hesitated to follow his lead, fearing to exchange one tyrant for another. Yet his courage in action was exemplary. His *Russian Truth* was more a practical handbook for a revolutionary party than a theoretical analysis of the Russian problem. Pestel advocated a revolutionary party for a "revolution from above," not a "revolution from below." For within himself he had an instinctive fear of the masses—which was one of the weak aspects of the Decembrist movement. The thought of a "chaotic" insurrection, like the peasant uprisings of the past, frightened him and he pinned his hopes on a military coup leading to the violent elimination of the entire imperial family.

By May, 1824, St. Petersburg had become a center for the conspirators, who included Pestel; Nikita Muraviev, the idealistic but ineffective champion of Russian liberalism; Prince Trubetskoy and Prince Obolensky; the poet Kondraty Ryleyev, who recruited many of the participants; and the Poggio brothers, Italian in origin, aroused by the revolutionary movement then sweeping all Europe—in Spain,

Naples, Piedmont, and Greece. During the trial that followed the defeat of the Decembrist Revolt, Alexander Poggio spoke of the impression made on him by the uprising in Spain and the death of the Spanish patriot Riego, whose example he had sworn to follow. (Over a century later Riego's hymn became the national anthem of Spain's Second Republic.)

In November, 1825, Czar Alexander I, grandson of Catherine the Great and, like her, a personable monarch with a far-flung reputation for "enlightenment," died of malaria contracted in the Crimea. For a time the Czar had considered himself a disciple of Jean-Jacques Rousseau, yet he did nothing in a practical way to improve the lot of his people. Now the conspirators could have taken advantage of the confusion that followed upon his death and the struggle for the succession to the throne, had they swung immediately into action. But the "logic of a military revolution" prevailed, and they engaged in protracted discussions. The conspirators found it difficult to agree on a plan for a military coup in the palace culminating in an assault on the new Emperor. Finally, on December 12, the plan was worked out in minute detail. Several regiments of the Imperial Guard, including the Izmailovsky Regiment, the footguards of Moscow and Finland, and the Grenadiers—having all marched to Senate Square in accordance with prior instructions—would refuse to take their oath of allegiance there. After this mass refusal, the Imperial Council and the Senate would immediately convene and name a provisional government. The night before the planned uprising, the poet Ryleyev went from district to district, spurring on the officer-plotters and repeating the detailed instructions. Two of the leaders named to command the rebel forces, Prince Trubetskoy and Colonel Bulatov, were suddenly nowhere to be found and had to be replaced.

December 14 was the day of decision. The conspirators' plan was based on the obviously false premise that Russian soldiers would refuse to fight against one another; and that the forces defending Nicholas I as emperor could not move against those who sought to replace him with his older brother, Constantine. On Senate Square the troops in the conspiracy took their appointed stations. Ryleyev, an ammunition belt slung over his shoulder, made a brief appearance accompanied by Prince Obolensky, who remained there. Pestel had been arrested the previous day. General Miloradovich, military governor of the capital and hero of the Napoleonic Wars, appeared. Marshal Suvorov had called him "the bravest of the brave" and he commanded tremendous respect. Confident that no Russian soldier would dare raise a hand to him, Miloradovich looked on, when one of the conspiring soldiers felled him with a bayonet thrust. Dismayed by the assassination of the redoubtable Miloradovich, the mutineers began to fire their muskets in the air. The conspirators became a prey to indecision and vacillation. Thus Nicholas had time to summon new troop reinforcements.

At one point the rebel troops numbered three thousand. The several regiments involved undoubtedly constituted a revolutionary force. But they lacked decisive leadership. A feeble effort by the insurgent Baron Rosen to win over the Finnish footguards failed. By early afternoon the revolt was crushed. The three thousand insurgents were surrounded by twelve thousand infantrymen and three thousand cavalrymen loyal to Nicholas. A similar attempt at revolt by a southern regiment also failed. Its leader, Sergei Muraviev-Apostol, was killed after a desperate attempt to seize Kiev.

The subsequent public trial distinguished between two groups of defendants: the "top category" of those considered to be the ringleaders, consisting of Pestel, Muraviev-Apostol, Mikhail Bestuzhev-Ryumin, Ryleyev, and Kakhovsky. The lesser group included Prince Trubetskoy, Prince Obolensky, Prince Volkonsky, the Borissov brothers, the Poggio brothers, Alexander Turgenev (condemned in absentia), and several others. The Czar personally questioned the highest-ranking conspirators. Pointing an accusing finger at Trubetskoy, he castigated him: "How was it possible for you, with your name and your family tradition, to get mixed up in this plot? A Prince Trubetskoy! A Colonel of the Guard!"

The five defendants in the "top category" received the death sentence. The Czar exhibited his clemency only by modifying the form of the execution: instead of being hanged and quartered, the five were led to the scaffold and merely hanged. Then they were borne away, still in chains. Before his execution, Ryleyev in his cell wrote a poem on a sheet of metal that was a serene farewell to life. Since Russia had no professional hangmen, they had to bring some in from Sweden. The last words of Muraviev-Apostol were: "They don't even know how to hang well." The day after the execution Czar

Nicholas, accompanied by Archbishop Serafim, attended a solemn service of repentance and thanksgiving.

What was original in the Decembrist movement? It was a clear-cut example of how one section of the nobility identified with the cause of the dispossessed. This group of army officers, descendants of wealthy landowners, fought not to maintain their own privileges but for justice and equal rights for all. They sought to free the great mass of the Russian peasantry from serfdom and poverty and, in so doing, liberate the Russian people as a whole. They formed two groups: the Northern Society led by Pestel and the Southern Society led by Muraviev-Apostol. Their ideas differed in details, but the same spirit of revolt against injustice imbued both groups. The United States Constitution played a decisive part in shaping Pestel's conceptions of what a free society should be; whereas the example of the Spanish fighters for freedom in the Peninsular War against Napoleon inspired him in his struggle against Russian autocracy. Pestel was a centralist but was willing to grant Poland autonomy. His ideas, contrary to what some of his critics assert, were forward-looking and with a distinct socialist tinge. Muraviev was a federalist. Basing himself on the example of the then young United States, he came to conclusions that differed from Pestel's.

The Decembrist movement foundered because of lack of organization and coordination. Both groups, the Northern Society and the Southern Society, were unable to agree on a common program of action and unite their forces. But the fire they kindled remained alive beneath the ashes of defeat. The Decembrist Revolt became an inextinguishable memory. Now at last Russian youth had awakened. In the years and decades to come, Czarist despotism would be unable to lull it to sleep again. At the outset the spirit of revolt flared up among the intellectuals—especially at the universities, where reading circles were formed and Hegel's philosophy was the chief topic of study.

The outstanding teacher was Alexander Herzen, to whom Hegel's ideas together with those of the theorists of French socialism constituted "the algebra of revolution." Like many others of the generation of '48, Herzen felt that an age was drawing to a close and a new era was dawning: "We are on the threshold of a rebirth of the world such as occurred in antiquity. And the present rebirth will have the brain, not the heart, as its vital organ; and socialism will be its arm." Herzen attracted many of those who would soon know the road to Siberian exile. It was a vanguard strongly influenced by the ideas of the Frenchmen Saint-Simon and Fourier, and persecuted for spreading their doctrines. Dostoevsky belonged to one such group, the Petrashevsky circle. Mikhail Bakunin, the anarchist, and Vissarion Belinsky, the outstanding literary critic of that period, belonged to another.

Herzen came to the conclusion that the only way to smash authoritarian rule in his country was from abroad. Accordingly, he emigrated to London, where he founded the first free Russian press. Here were published his periodicals *The Bell* and *The North Star*, which were then sent clandestinely to the new centers of agitation that were sprouting inside Russia. Both periodicals put forward a program with a few limited but immediate aims: the liquidation of serfdom and the establishment of a free press. Beyond that, they sought to prepare the soil for the seed of socialism. For the defeat of the Revolutions of 1848 led Herzen to view pessimistically the immediate prospects for socialism in Western Europe.

In 1848 a wide-ranging series of upheavals shook Europe to the core. In some places and at given moments the participants' ideology, though fluid, undoubtedly contained elements of socialism. Ushered in with tremendous mass enthusiasm, the European Revolutions of 1848 failed one after the other owing to the lack of a clear-cut political line of action. They were preceded by a series of social and financial disturbances: agricultural crises and famine, which in Ireland alone caused more than a million deaths; 750,000 workers unemployed in France; agitation in Hungary led by the poet Sándor Petöfi; nationalist movements among the Serbians, Croatians, Romanians, and Czechs, with the inevitable repercussions in the imperial capital of Vienna; the Milan uprising of March 18–22; a similar revolt in Venice, where a provisional government was formed and a republic proclaimed; and in Germany the victorious political revolution in Baden. Almost everywhere there was a powerful but short-lived revolutionary wave.

The most significant example of this upsurge occurred in France. Prior to the twentieth century France underwent four revolutions:

the Great Revolution of 1789; that of 1830, which toppled from power the older branch of the Bourbons and installed the younger branch, with Louis Philippe—the Citizen King—as monarch; the February Revolution of 1848, which proclaimed the Second Republic; and the Paris Commune of 1871, following upon a lesser revolution, that of September 4, 1870, which ended the Second Empire and established the Third Republic.

After a period of relative social calm, the spirit of revolt reawakened in France. The year 1840 in particular was a year of strikes. The working people sank into impoverishment; their working conditions deteriorated. Wages frequently amounted to only fifteen to twenty sous a day. Workers in factories utilizing copper, arsenic, antimony, and mercury had an average life span of thirty years. Children from six to twelve years of age worked twelve to fourteen hours a day in unsanitary workshops. But even by working all those hours without interruption they could earn no more than fifty centimes. Yet in the Chamber of Peers an aristocrat of that day, Baron Dupin, categorically asserted in 1846: "The working class in France is happy." The Bishop of Chartres struck the same note. Addressing the workers, he exhorted them not to read histories of the Great Revolution and the Jacobins, lest their natural instincts toward kindness be disturbed. He lauded the happiness of the humble. They would enjoy life on earth to the extent that it was "reasonable to expect"; but above all they would find eternal bliss in the next world, if they shut their ears to subversive devils like Proudhon. The Jesuits, quite influential at that time, were also on the side of the counter-revolution.

But the people listened to Pierre Proudhon. At times they did not understand what he was trying to say, but they knew he was trying to improve their miserable lot. Above all, he had uttered the famous phrase "Property is theft," a blunt definition that terrified the bourgeoisie and delighted the common people. Basically, Proudhon was not a man of action. He was a philosopher, a philosopher of poverty, with nostalgic feelings of admiration for Voltaire. He was not enthusiastic about Mirabeau, Robespierre, or Napoleon; but he did admire Voltaire and, in his own way, sought to take his place. But he did not lack a sense of the practical. His proposal to the Assembly to create a people's bank made sense. Fundamentally he shared

Marx's idea that, for the revolution to triumph, the state had to be smashed. But not until Lenin came along did this general concept become a powerful, practical weapon of revolutionary strategy.

Popular ferment in February, 1848, went beyond the plans of the moderate opponents of the regime. The people moved faster than their leaders. They did not take part in the banquets that proved fatal for the monarchy. Instead of making speeches, they built barricades. The wave of popular indignation mounted higher, carrying with it all those who thought they could manipulate the masses, rousing them to action and then holding them back or even making them retreat when they felt they had gone too far. Publications multiplied, most of them selling for one sou. Among them were *Le Peuple constituant* of Abbé Lamennais, a revolutionary priest, Etienne Cabet's *Le Populaire*, Proudhon's *Le Peuple* and *La Voix du Peuple*, and *Le Christ républicain*. Alongside the periodicals there were also the revolutionary clubs: Louis Blanqui's Société Centrale Républicaine, Armand Barbès' Club de la Révolution, and the Club des Amis du Peuple. The working-class periodicals of the period expressed the sorrow and rage of the masses. The poet Charles Baudelaire asserted that he found genuine poetry in them, and now he understood the grandeur of the slogan of the weavers of Lyons: "To live working or die fighting."

Nonetheless, the Republic of '48 did little to change the social structure. Those who rose up against the bourgeoisie were still the inhabitants of the old artisan districts in the Faubourg Saint-Antoine; not yet as in the Commune of 1871, where the working people of Belleville led the fight.

Marx and Proudhon both clearly saw the limitations of the Revolution of 1848. It was undoubtedly an international phenomenon, in which political exiles from many lands took part. It broke out almost simultaneously in France and Germany. But it lacked adequate popular support. "The logic of events has constantly shown," wrote Proudhon, "that by maintaining the monarchical form of society what happened had to happen sooner or later. Because it was unable to define its own principles democracy ended by defecting to monarchy."

The France of King Louis Philippe was the domain of the bankers. A series of scandals exposed the corruption and inequities of the society. They occurred in electoral politics, government administration, and even in "high society." Thus the Duc de Choiseul-Praslin murdered his wife so as to marry another woman; then, in an access of repentance, he committed suicide. Two former cabinet ministers, Teste and Cubières, were tried for misappropriating funds. An army general was brought to trial for the same reason. Civilian and army leaders were thus tarred with the same brush. As against a society and political system that was rapidly losing authority, the working class was constantly growing in numbers and was more and more concentrated in cities. Living conditions for the proletariat were wretched. By contrast, the bourgeoisie's greed for money seemed unlimited. In this they were following the advice of the leading statesman of the regime, the historian Guizot, who had declared: "Take advantage of your hour. Get rich through trade and industry." But at the same time the Industrial Revolution brought ever larger numbers of workers together in workshops and factories, making it easier for them to exchange ideas and strengthening their bonds of solidarity.

On the job, workers discussed the revolutionaries and the reformers of the time: Proudhon, who asserted that property was theft; Louis Blanc, Socialist-oriented, advocate of production cooperatives controlled by the state; and Blanqui, who reflected in his own thinking the polemic already begun between Karl Marx and Mikhail Bakunin. In 1848 appeared the key document of modern socialism, the *Communist Manifesto*, by Karl Marx and Friedrich Engels, written the year before. How like a breath of fresh air it must have appeared to the working people of 1848!

As in many other revolutions, the immediate cause of the 1848 Revolution in France was an unforeseen event. To be sure, 1847 had ended in an atmosphere of crisis. The reasons were diverse. King Louis Philippe had been chosen by 219 deputies representing 100,000 electors. He could claim neither the divine right of kings nor a genuine mandate from the people. The *pays légal* (legal country, in contrast to *le pays réel*, the real country) of 250,000 electors was made up of wealthy bourgeois more noted for avarice than imaginativeness. The democratic opposition opposed the policy of political stagnation at home and military intervention abroad. Taking a leaf out of the English book, the opposition began its nation-wide "banquet campaign." "Reform" became the rallying cry of the day. The oppositionists met, dined, and conspired. Thus, on July 7, 1847, a banquet was held at Château Rouge in Paris. Revolt was in the air. Meanwhile, the secret societies were gaining members by the thousands. One of them, the Society of Egalitarian Workers, became a center of revolutionary agitation. It was one of those moments in history when people suddenly break out of their apathy and, weary of submitting to repressive rule, understand that to make themselves heard they must take to the streets. The end of the July Monarchy of 1830 was in sight.

The authorities grew worried. A banquet scheduled for February 22, 1848, was banned by Guizot. The deputies acquiesced; but not the rank-and-file republicans. The banquet was held in the XII arrondissement of Paris, the Faubourg Saint-Germain. The authorities intervened, and then suddenly the revolt broke out. The masses demonstrated in the streets despite the official ban. In the words of one of the leading participants, "It was an unhoped-for revolt, even for those who made it." Proudhon's comment was: "The February 24 uprising was made without an idea."

On February 24, Louis Philippe summoned to the palace Adolphe Thiers, the man who twenty-three years later drowned the Paris Commune in blood. But things had gone too far for a compromise settlement; the King was forced to abdicate in favor of the Count of Paris and fled to England under the name of Mr. Smith. But this move also failed. The way was now opened for the formation of a Republican Provisional Government that included the poet Alphonse de Lamartine and other moderates as well as the radical "reformers" headed by Louis Blanc. The latter were the only ones who enjoyed the confidence of the people. As often happens in the case of overly "representative" governments, the various groups involved pursued irreconcilable aims. And it was not long before their inner contradictions forced them to mark time futilely. "Reform" became increasingly a formula on paper, devoid of substance. The Palace changed cabinets on February 22, realizing that neither Guizot nor Thiers could stem the tide. A mediocre aristocrat took the helm, but it was no solution. A crowd of street demonstrators tried to reach the Bastille, but were fired on by the guards at the Ministry of Foreign

Affairs; fifty-two people were killed and about a hundred wounded. The following morning, February 23, barricades were built in Paris. There were raids on the arsenals and some members of the National Guard went over to the people's side, to the cry of "Down with Louis Philippe!"

Lamartine headed the Provisional Government in this period, which was known as the "three months of oratorical dictatorship." But one section of the working class preferred action to poetry; so for the first time since 1791 the red flag appeared on the Champ-de-Mars. The Provisional Government that followed upon Louis Philippe's abdication, composed mainly of lawyers and professors, was greeted with demands for genuine political and social change. The weakness of the Provisional Government lay in its inability to take a stand on any of the basic problems of the hour. It vacillated constantly between two tendencies: one group was convinced that it was the government's duty to maintain a kind of people's dictatorship and quickly implement a bold and vigorous program of sweeping economic and political reforms; the other favored a Constituent Assembly that would proceed cautiously so as not to split the forces that supported the Republic.

The result was halfhearted concessions, with no firm revolutionary line. Louis Blanc, the Socialist in the government, succeeded in having "the right to work" recognized, but on the matter of the red flag—which was more than just a minor issue—he had to yield. The radicals attached too much importance to the support of the higher clergy. True, the Archbishop of Paris, Monseigneur Affre, paid tribute to the people, and the Catholic press wrote: "God speaks through the voice of events." But in reality the Church sought only to gain time; basically it viewed what was happening with misgivings and hostility.

Barely a month after the victorious February days the reactionary forces showed signs of their presence. Their initial counterblow was directed at Ledru-Rollin, Minister of the Interior, who, justly resenting the fact that the electoral lists allowed the Right to jockey at will for influential positions, sought to postpone the elections, hoping thereby to give the Provisional Government time to institute electoral reforms without getting bogged down in drawn-out parliamentary debates. On March 16 the "moderates" in the Paris region organized their first protest demonstration. Proudhon, clearly aware of its implications, called it "the first demonstration of the reactionary bourgeoisie." The generals too awaited their moment.

The next day, in response, crowds led by Louis Blanc and Blanqui marched to the Champ-de-Mars. The "Club des Clubs" was in a state of constant alert: "For the Republic the Clubs are a necessity, for the citizens a right." There was a good deal of enthusiasm and oratory, but no continuous and determined effort to make structural changes in the society. So when the Constituent Assembly was finally elected, the reactionary forces, relying on the economic and social crisis and in many ways provoking it, awaited their hour of revenge against the working class and lower middle class, the victors in the February days.

By a decree of June 21 the *ateliers nationaux* (national workshops, the name given by Louis Blanc) were virtually stripped of their usefulness. During the February days these "workshops" brought together industrial workers, white-collar employees, students, and artists. For a time it seemed as if proletarian unity had been achieved. But now, a few months later, the workers had lost some of their outstanding leaders. Blanqui, Barbès, and Raspail were in prison. But the attack on the "workshops" was countered with an outpouring into the streets. On the night of June 22 the watchword for insurrection was given. The next day it broke out.

A huge throng marched toward the Bastille. Barricades appeared on the Rue Saint-Denis. Tempers rose, yet discipline was scrupulously observed. In twelve hours the insurgents had established themselves from one end of Paris to another. Recruiting offices were opened, and ammunition was being made in the back rooms of shops and apartments. The fighting was brief but severe. General Cavaignac, in command of the forces of "law and order," ordered large-scale, ruthless military intervention. The dead and wounded numbered in the thousands. Moreover, once the last barricade was taken and the red flag torn down by soldiers whipped up to a frenzy, many citizens were summarily shot. The bourgeoisie, recovering from its momentary panic, wanted as many workers as possible slaughtered after their surrender. It was one of the bloodiest repressions Paris has known. With its traditional hypocrisy, the bourgeoisie made a distinction between one kind of blood and another: for every bourgeois who fell or every bourgeoise raped, a hundred lives had to be exacted. The masses of workers shot on the spot or after a drumhead trial were not even counted. Twenty-five clubs were closed down. The national workshops and the Socialist newspapers were banned. Over twenty-five thousand were arrested, many sentenced to forced labor, others deported to North Africa. General Cavaignac was hailed as "savior of the country." He was applauded in drawing rooms, feted by the Rothschilds and other bankers.

Was any better proof needed that the event went beyond the limits of a political overturn? However weak and confused in its planning, the 1848 uprising was nevertheless an attempt at social revolution. One idea emerged victorious from the February Revolution: the right to work. But as soon as the workers' uprising was crushed, the wealthy resolved to do away with this concrete achievement. They sought to do this "legally," that is, through parliamentary methods. At the beginning of September, 1848, the Assembly began a full-dress debate on the right to work. A minority led by Ledru-Rollin, reminiscent of Robespierre in the 1790's, sought to incorporate it into the constitution. The discussion was protracted, the parliamentary maneuvers devious. At length the "right to work" proclaimed on February 25 was buried in the Constituent Assembly.

The Jacobins had blazed the trail in the Revolution of 1789. Who were the leaders in 1848? Two men above all, Proudhon and Blanqui. To Proudhon revolution was an irresistible force that, in his view, would lead to a society without ruling authorities. To him, two classes stood face to face: the upper class, which included the aristocracy and the bourgeoisie, and the lower class, consisting of the proletariat or working class. The first class pinned its faith on authority; the second, on freedom. Proudhon believed strongly in loosely federated groups. He had an anarchist's faith in the activities of territorial and local groups, in the democratic management of affairs by citizens grouped in committees, commissions, and councils. By the same token he stoutly opposed a strongly centralized state. (In today's terms, Proudhon was an advocate of political decentralization.)

Blanqui was first and foremost a man of action. Theory played a secondary part in his life. All his energies inside and outside prison—altogether he served twenty-five years in various jails—were devoted to plotting revolution. Long before the idea of "permanent revolution" that caused such sharp differences in the ranks of the Russian Bolsheviks after the 1917 Revolution, Blanqui was a kind of personal embodiment of that idea. To Blanqui and the Blanquists the source of inspiration remained the revolutionary years 1792–1793. They remained deaf to the warnings of Karl Marx, who, especially after September, 1870, warned the French workers of the danger of being misled by the memories of 1792. Tridon, son of a rich businessman from Burgundy, and Raoul Rigault, later Attorney-General of the Commune and head of its political police, were prototypes of the Blanquist movement, which was originally composed of bourgeois youth, bohemian artists and writers, and students who were quickly proletarianized by the march of events.

Proudhon had contempt for those he called the false Jacobins of 1848, such as Louis Blanc and Ledru-Rollin. In his indignation he went so far as to characterize Louis Napoleon as follows: "They say of you that you are just a moron, an adventurer, a madman. However that may be, you are the man we need to destroy the bourgeoisie and wrest the last centime from them." Victor Hugo, on the contrary, despaired when he saw the lethargy into which the defeated masses had fallen. But the truth was they had been betrayed by the liberals of that day who wanted only half a revolution, not the real thing.

For despite all its weaknesses, the revolutionary wave of 1848 reached the farthest shores of Europe. Revolutions broke out almost simultaneously in France, Italy, and over most of the Austro-Hungarian Empire, and there were significant repercussions in Spain, Denmark, Romania, Russia, and the German states.

Of all the German states in 1848, Prussia best symbolized reactionary standpattism. To Kaiser Frederick William III, absolutism alone guaranteed prosperity for the state and its subjects. But when he tried to impose his thinking on the rest of Germany, the national and democratic aspirations of the other German states clashed with this spirit of Prussian dominance and arrogance. The clash in itself provided a revolutionary spark.

In southern Germany a new kind of press, quite different from that of the Junkers—the big landowners of Prussia—made its debut. In

1842 a young liberal-minded banker-industrialist named Mevissen founded the *Rheinische Zeitung*. His interest in social questions led him to make contact with Karl Marx. So it was in the columns of the *Rheinische Zeitung* that the founder of scientific socialism wrote numerous articles analyzing all sorts of world problems. In fact, these pieces provide invaluable source material for knowledge of an era in which the class struggle had begun in earnest. (Those who find it difficult to read Marx's monumental *Capital* will find his newspaper articles far more accessible.)

In its origins German radicalism was strongly influenced by the Hegelian school of philosophy. But these young or "Left" Hegelians soon sought a rapprochement with the workers, realizing that without their help no struggle against the authoritarian state could get very far. Once again we encounter a revolutionary priest. A Catholic priest from Saxony, Johannes Ronge, became a champion of social reform. "Rongeanism" was the political expression of the insurgent Church, and Ronge's movement grew until it embraced some eighty thousand followers. Metternich pointedly warned German governing authorities of the danger of not taking it seriously. Metternich's Holy Alliance was not just a doctrine; it was a gendarme ever on the watch for subversive activity.

Now, as schools of Socialist thought began to develop in Germany, the whole country began to be aroused. The Grand Duchy of Baden was quite near France; so it was not accidental that revolt began there. When news arrived of the 1848 uprising in Paris, the streets of Karlsruhe were quickly filled with a throng demanding a republic. The disturbance spilled over into the states adjoining Baden. In Bavaria the advocates of a new order seized on a trivial local incident. In mid-March rumors spread through Munich that the dancer Lola Montez, mistress of Bavarian King Louis I and notorious for her support of extreme counter-revolutionary groups, was going to appear. Noisy demonstrations ensued. Homes belonging to the ballerina were burned. Louis I was forced to abdicate.

Soon the German Revolution of 1848, violent at times but more often tepid and virtually without bloodshed, reached the Hanseatic cities in the north. In Prussia, where the government viewed with disinterest and Olympian disdain what was transpiring in the other German states, the Revolution burst forth on March 18 with greater fury than elsewhere. Barricades rose before the horrified eyes of self-important Prussian bureaucrats who could not comprehend what was going on. The rebels had few arms: only several of the thirty-six cannon of the King and small arms mostly from hunting clubs. The makeup of the insurrection was quite broad and heterogeneous, including students, intellectuals, petty bourgeois, artisans, and workers. Although poorly armed, the rebels made things difficult for the government, which, feeling the very principle of authority had been violated and assailed, soon made itself somewhat ridiculous in the eyes of the average Prussian, who had long been used to the harshest sort of rule. This challenge to authority was something unheard of, unprecedented. For a moment the new king, Frederick William IV, even thought of quitting Berlin and taking up residence in Potsdam for reasons of safety. In any event, the immediate result of the March days was that Prussia's position as the paramount state in Germany was shaken.

As a consequence of the March uprising, a cabinet of liberals was formed in Prussia. But divisions soon appeared in its ranks. Moreover, the liberals became panicky when the barricades were built and a majority of the radicals, not content with a mere change of façade, demanded basic changes in the police state. Most important, the absence of firm leadership in the Revolution brought a return of the reactionaries. This is the ever-recurring tragedy of the liberal or pseudo-Socialist Left: its vacillation, its timorousness, its fear of the mobilized masses.

The Prussian nobility, on the other hand, had learned its lesson well. Once the momentary panic was over, it hastily took steps to organize a more solid political base by creating the Conservative Party and founding its press organ *Die Kreuzzeitung*, the newspaper of the Junkers. Meanwhile, the King, sensing a threat to the authority of the Crown and frightened by the Frankfurt parliament, dissolved the Berlin Assembly.

As in France, so in Germany the 1848 Revolution lacked revolutionary boldness and over-all socialist thinking. In *The Campaign for a Constitution for the Reich*, Engels notes that peasant support of the uprising was vital—but in order to win that support all the feudal taxes had to be abolished and paper money had to be printed forthwith. So the German Revolution of 1848 ended in defeat. None of the concrete aims had been achieved: the creation of a single unified nation; the destruction of the repressive administrative and police apparatus of the state; and the liberation of the German masses from capitalist domination.

Alexander Herzen, living in France during the Revolution of 1848, wrote from Paris in his *Letters from Italy and France, 1848–1849*: "Europe is too old, it does not have enough strength to adapt its behavior to the level of its thinking. After so many long and glorious struggles, Europe has earned the right to repose. In its aspirations for a profound regeneration of the nations, Europe may be replaced by the United States of America and by Russia."

As for America, the usually discerning Herzen was wrong, as he acknowledged years later. True, the United States benefited from many German exiles, '48ers who emigrated there when their revolution failed and imparted new life to the working-class movement in the United States. But gradually their influence in their newly adopted land faded. In his forecast concerning Russia, however, Herzen hit the mark.

Herzen felt that the archaic Russian *mir*, a type of village community with joint ownership of land, would provide fertile soil for the growth of socialism—but it would be a socialism free from the corrupting capitalist influences of the West. It was a question, therefore, of working on the enormous human potential of the Russian peasantry and directing it toward revolutionary action. Herzen's ideas strongly influenced the Russian revolutionary movement in the 1860's. The first revolutionaries to appear on the scene, after the serfs were freed in 1861 under Alexander II, were disciples of Herzen. Attention now focused on the struggle within Russia. Herzen himself had critically revised his original ideas about other nations and peoples. In his youth he had manifested enthusiasm for William Penn, even writing a play about the Quaker leader who had sought to open the doors of America to all free men. After 1848, however, he changed his mind about the United States and expressed doubts about the firmness of its principles. "Basically a calculating nation," Herzen wrote. "Apparently it is losing the evangelical fervor that imbued its founders." Herzen continued to admire Hegel's philosophy and phenomenology to the very end, but had increasing doubts about the practical application of Hegel's doctrines: Hegel "is incapable of action and full of prejudices. At bottom he remains a German."

Meanwhile Karl Marx's *Capital* appeared, with a new and scientific theory of socialism. Outlining new tactics of struggle for all peoples, the book made a deep impression on revolutionary circles in Russia. Georgi Plekhanov, an outstanding Russian Marxist, has described the profound impact of Marx's writings in a country in which theories of direct action had taken hold. Plekhanov himself was one of the first to go abroad, to Switzerland, to make contact with the young Marxist movement. It marked the first step toward the founding of the Russian Social Democratic Labor Party, with Plekhanov at its head. The new party took a position against the two older Socialist movements, the Narodniki (Populists) and the Narodnaya Volnya (Will of the People). Plekhanov, who corresponded with Marx and his party, agreed with Marx's position concerning the leading role of the industrial proletariat. Thenceforth the Russian Marxists did not share the enthusiasm of other Russian groups for the peasant-based *mir*; nor did they believe the peasantry could serve as a springboard for the development of socialism.

Moreover, Plekhanov's Social Democrats did not countenance terrorist actions. Their main concern was to organize the working class, even though that class was still scanty in numbers in a Russia where industrial capitalism was still in its early stages. By contrast, the Populists—and Herzen agreed with them in this—did not think it necessary to postpone action until the development of capitalism and, with it, the rise of an industrial proletariat. They believed in the historical power and the creative capacity of the individual.

If Herzen was the theoretician of populism, Nikolai Chernyshevsky was its most powerful leader. An unusually attractive and original figure, Chernyshevsky is the symbol par excellence of the policy of direct action in mid-nineteenth-century Russia. He was born in 1829 in Saratov, on the Volga, the son of a high dignitary of the Russian Orthodox Church. At that time Saratov was a kind of frontier city, dividing European and Asian Russia. Chernyshevsky has left us a vivid picture of Saratov in pages written in the prison-fortress of Peter and Paul, where he also translated Rousseau's *Confessions* into Russian. He tells us, for example, that not until the early years of the nineteenth century did his family know the luxury of having sugar with its tea. On the other hand, the shelves in the library of his family house were filled with books on Russia's medieval past. Hence by early adolescence he displayed an interest in classical languages and culture and subsequently became an outstanding linguist, with a thorough knowledge of Latin and Greek, as well as French, English, and German. Knowledge of German made him familiar with the German philosophers and, like Herzen, he studied Hegel closely. He also had an intimate knowledge of the French Revolution and admired Robespierre; but it was an event closer to hand, the 1848 Revolution in France and other European countries, that "politicized" him completely.

From the age of eighteen he had been in rebellion against the state of affairs in his native land. The Revolutions of 1848 impelled him to take the decisive step from political thinking to political activism. In the summer of 1848 he wrote of his "admiration for the West" and his conviction that "in comparison with Westerners, Russians are of little account. They are men; we are children. We have not had class wars and at best have made only the barest beginnings." Significantly, he spoke already of "revolutionary socialism."

Chernyshevsky was opposed to the ideas of Saint-Simon as well as those of Blanqui. He was put off by the "idealization of old feudal relations" on the part of the Saint-Simonians, which he considered pure and simple romanticism. Blanqui, in his opinion, was attempting to make a revolution before objective conditions for it were ripe. To him, the basic attitude of a true revolutionary was to keep a firm grasp on reality without being lured by opportunistic "realism" that only looks for alibis to avoid risks. In his opinion of Blanqui, Chernyshevsky was, I feel, mistaken. Lenin was closer to the truth when he called Blanqui "unquestionably a revolutionary and a fervent partisan of socialism" and distinguished between Blanqui and the Blanquists, who, in the Paris Commune of 1871, adopted an incorrect political line and through sectarianism isolated themselves from the masses.

A study of the Revolution of 1848 written by Chernyshevsky in 1859 created a stir. It was an attack on the liberals "and it doesn't matter how the reactionaries exploit this essay." Chernyshevsky predicted the political downfall of Count Cavour, the outstanding figure of Italian liberalism. The basic weakness of liberals every-where, he asserted, was that they were obsessed with the "proper middle way." They repudiated violence and sought to "safeguard principles" even though the reactionaries trampled them under foot; and all the liberals could do then was to complain. But genuine radicals were not afraid to act even if they were taxed with "lack of judgment and intellectual balance." They did not fear "getting burned," if by acting they served the people's cause.

Reviewing previous efforts toward socialism, Chernyshevsky drew special attention to the Chartists' movement in England and the June, 1848, days in France. He acknowledged that they had been weak, halfhearted attempts that had failed. Yet despite their failure they had helped to kindle hope in a Socialist future. And his own faith in that future was unshakable. It was in 1859, when he wrote his famous essay, that he broke with the liberals once and for all. He preferred to go it alone, along his own road. But he was far from alone. By his side were men such as Dobrolyubov, gifted writer and publicist, and a large segment of the student body. Chernyshevsky was certain that he could not long avoid imprisonment. Even had there been no intercepted letter from Herzen, which the latter in his *Memoirs* described as "a fatal lack of prudence," the Czarists would have found some other pretext for sending him to jail. He spent over twenty years in various Russian jails and prison camps. In one of them he was with his close friend the poet Mikhailov. And much of his revolutionary work was done while he was behind bars.

The Revolution of 1848 caused profound reverberations through-out Russia—as had the earlier French Revolution of 1789. In 1848 Russia seemed somnolent, inert, in the tyrannical reign of Nicholas I (1825–1855). Then came the shock of revolutionary ideas. Western books, smuggled into the country, made the rounds of universities and literary societies—translations of Fourier, Louis Blanc, Proud-hon, and many others. Two opposing groups emerged: one sought to renew the past, gazing fondly at the Decembrists of 1825, and dreaming only of freeing the serfs and obtaining a liberal constitu-tion. The other, the Nihilists, were convinced that the only way out was the destruction, root and branch, of the society that was stifling them.

One of those affected by this latter group was Fyodor Dostoevsky. Emerging from the St. Petersburg School of Military Engineers in 1843 with the rank of second lieutenant, Dostoevsky soon resigned from military service to devote himself entirely to writing. Strongly influenced by Vissarion Belinsky, a giant of Russian literary criticism, he was briefly attracted by socialism. Sentenced to death for his revolutionary activities, he was reprieved at the last moment and returned to literature. Thereafter his views became increasingly religious and Slavophile, but he never lost his deep compassion for the common people. When he died, in 1881, the funeral procession that followed his mortal remains to the monastery of St. Alexander Nevsky numbered some twenty thousand. The government was very uneasy because in that throng were hundreds if not thousands of Nihilists indistinguishable from the rest of the crowd. This was a people's way of showing its sorrow at the loss of the great writer. And it was one among many portents of things to come.

Until Lenin created the Bolshevik Party in 1903 and gave it a Marxist content in which theory was inextricably combined with action, the revolutionary movement in Russia proceeded by fits and starts. Periods of great militancy and initiative were followed by intervals of passivity and despair. One example of this alternating pattern is offered by the secret societies. In 1876 one of the most interesting of these societies, Zemlya y Volya (Land and Liberty) appeared. A heterogeneous group, it brought together intellectuals and workers. Among the former were some young women from the highest social circles, educated at the Smolny Institute in St. Petersburg, which virtually every noblewoman in the empire had attended. In courage and idealism these young women revolutionaries vied with, and often surpassed, the men. Many of them had studied medicine at Swiss universities, mainly so that on their return to Russia they could register as practicing physicians or midwives in the villages and carry on revolutionary work there. Rereading the Russian writers of that period, one is struck by the social dedication of the members of Land and Liberty. Constantly operating under conditions of political illegality, they were everywhere hounded and persecuted by the Czarist police.

The work of organizing demanded a great deal of their time. The most pressing need was to set up an underground press. Not only must it be safe from spying eyes; it also required skilled linotypists, many of them self-taught. Since the open purchase of supplies would immediately put the buyers under suspicion, members had to resort to a stratagem later frequently used with success. Trustworthy comrades who had learned the compositor's craft went to work in large printing establishments of the capital. Every night they left the plants with their pockets full of old, virtually worn-out characters of type. With these they were able to set up a small printing press and bring out an illegal leaflet or newspaper.

Within the Land and Liberty organization, two main tendencies soon appeared. The more impatient members recommended direct action forthwith; and when the following summer Vera Zasulich, on her own, shot to death Trepov, the notoriously repressive police chief of St. Petersburg, she was acclaimed as a heroine by the youth. This trend was strengthened with the return of Alexander Soloviev from the Volga area, where he had been in charge of revolutionary agitation. Two years of political work in Samara had taught Soloviev much about the way one had to approach the peasants and win them over to the revolution. Contrary to some of the intellectuals in the group who were skeptical about the revolutionary potential of the peasantry, Soloviev did not feel that the peasants were closed to Socialist doctrine. But he knew that it would take a very long time to organize and train them in the secrets and techniques of illegal work. Meanwhile the important thing was to arouse the masses by a few bold strokes. If Vera Zasulich's pistol had had a bigger propaganda effect than all the underground literature combined, one could imagine the consequences of an attempt to assassinate the Czar.

Soloviev's mind was made up. Reaction had to be smashed in the person of Alexander II. He confided in a few of his most trusted comrades. An incident of the previous year was still fresh in their memory: a careless slip-up had revealed to the police the plan to blow up the Czar's yacht in the Black Sea by means of mines laid by some sailors who sympathized with the movement. The revolutionary movement also had its sympathizers in the armed forces, especially in the artillery and the navy. Soloviev waited one day for Czar Alexander II to leave the St. Petersburg Winter Palace and shot at him. But he missed. When the police pounced on Soloviev they saw him bring his hand to his mouth. They rushed him to a pharmacy and forcibly applied antidotes that prevented the swallowed poison from taking effect. For six weeks Soloviev was tortured; but he did not reveal the name of a single comrade involved in the shooting attempt. Finally, weary of their futile questioning, the authorities hanged him.

This loss did not demoralize the radical wing of Land and Liberty. Nevertheless, a compromise was reached: the organization as such would refrain from all terrorist acts, but individual members were free to proceed as they chose. This solution preserved at least a semblance of unity between Plekhanov and his Marxist adherents and the direct-action group deeply committed to new assassination attempts.

The Czar's movements were closely studied, particularly the route which he was to travel during the coming months on his return from the Crimea. The police were on full alert. Despite the conspirators' precautions, one of the men assigned to making bombs, Kavatkovsky, was discovered and executed. The hardest problem of all was to transport the dynamite to the railroad line by night. Yet the group managed somehow to set land mines in seven different spots, and one of their number posed as a switchman. He took up his position in a little hut and was ready, if the explosions failed, to derail the train. At a signal from Sofia Perovskaya, daughter of a governor-general of St. Petersburg, the fake switchman pulled a switch and the train on which the Czar was thought to be traveling flew off the rails. But Alexander II had changed trains midway en route.

Large-scale arrests and executions followed. Sofia Perovskaya, also involved in the previous attempt, again escaped. The calmness of the woman was as great as her courage. In her peasant dress, and with her naïve and childlike manner, she fooled the authorities time and again. Her friends called her, in memory of Saint-Just, "the avenging angel."

Efforts to assassinate Alexander II resumed. Since it was virtually impossible to get at him in the streets, a revolutionary named Chalturin, a carpenter by trade, devised a plan to kill the Czar in his own palace. He entered the Winter Palace as a workman and, during one of the court functions, placed small sticks of dynamite in the cellar. In the ensuing explosion the imperial family emerged unscathed: Chalturin was buried in the debris. Nevertheless, the death sentence still hung over Alexander II. Eventually, in 1881, he was felled by a bomb tossed at him by a revolutionary named Grinevitsky as he was returning to the palace after reviewing a parade. This time too the police had changed the procession's route at the last moment. But Sofia Perovskaya, who was following it, had time to notify two comrades stationed elsewhere and then guided them to a spot where they could most easily slip through the double row of soldiers.

Shortly thereafter Sofia Perovskaya was executed. She was the first Russian woman to mount the scaffold for the revolution. Vera Zasulich, who had killed a governor, not an emperor, had been freed as a result of popular pressure. Perhaps the Czarist government had thought that, by showing leniency in the case of the Trepov shooting, it would induce the conspirators to give up their plan to finish off the Czar.

To unite peasants and workers in the same revolutionary movement required extraordinarily hard work in Russia, as indeed almost everywhere else. For this has always been one of the basic problems in the march of socialism, if we take the word "socialism" in its broadest sense.

Thus in Russia when Alexander III outlawed the Narodnaya Volnya group, in the early 1880's, most of the peasant masses remained indifferent. Their inertness was deeply disappointing to the revolutionary intellectuals of Narodnaya Volnya. For it was these Narodniki, or Populists, who, having attracted a group of militant workers to their ranks, pinned all their hopes on arousing the mass of the peasantry against Czarist tyranny and landlord exploitation. But to the disillusioned Populists the peasants of that day seemed to have surrendered themselves completely to mysticism and vodka. Yet this was a temporary eclipse, which in their despair a good many intellectuals of the period exaggerated. The over-all course of Russian history abounded in peasant uprisings. To turn one's back on the peasants, to stop believing in them in a predominantly agricultural country, meant in fact renouncing the revolution.

From one revolutionary stage to another, the appearance of a new great writer—novelist, poet, playwright, or critic—seems to epitomize or mirror the moods and attitudes of a people. Such was peculiarly the case with Leo Tolstoy. The Tolstoys were originally a German family which had settled in Russia at the time of Peter the Great. Many of them became well-known figures in their adopted country and they enjoyed high standing in its economic and social life. This was further consolidated when Count Nicholas Tolstoy married Princess Maria Volkonsky, and they became parents of the future author of *War and Peace*.

Leo Tolstoy entered the University of Kazan in 1843. His student years were frivolous and turbulent; he was near the bottom of his class in studies. He was a notorious woman-chaser and a gambler, though not with quite the same passion as his fellow writer Dostoevsky. But in the Russia of that day no one with any sensitivity could remain totally indifferent to the poverty of the masses. If at first Tolstoy rejected the most divergent philosophical systems, as he grew older he came closer to socialism—a socialism interpreted in his own special way.

He distinguished himself as a young officer in the Crimean War by his total disregard of death. Then when he retired from military service he lived in St. Petersburg, where he devoted himself to study and writing. One of his earliest works, the trilogy *Childhood, Boyhood, and Youth* (1852–1857), was strongly influenced by Rousseau. The aristocratic society of the Russian capital both attracted and repelled him, this ambivalence marking virtually every period in his adult life. But gradually his contact with the highborn began to make a rebel of him. He thought of founding a new religion. This was the period of his: *A Confession* (1879), *What I Believe In* (1882), and *What Then Must We Do?* (1886), all socio-religious in nature. Meanwhile he wrote literary masterpieces: *War and Peace* (1865–1869), *Anna Karenina* (1875–1877), and *Resurrection* (1899–1900), novels that are astonishing in their creative force and descriptive power. His portraits of women, especially Natasha Rostov in *War and Peace* and Anna Karenina in the novel of that name, are among the finest in world literature. Yet in 1898 he could publish a violent diatribe against what he called pure art: *What Is Art?*

On his large estate at Yasnaya Polyana, where from the 1860's on Tolstoy spent the bulk of his time, his inner doubts and self-questioning drove him to individual rebellion. (In the year of the centenary of

Tolstoy's birth, celebrated throughout the Soviet Union, I was able to visit Yasnaya Polyana personally and see many mementos of his inner torment.) Moreover, the spectacle of the wretched conditions of those who worked the land made him a decided partisan of the peasants' cause. His feeling for social injustice intensified as his personal relations with his family grew strained. Then came his total renunciation of all personal property and possessions, including the income from his numerous writings. He refused the Nobel Prize for Literature, and finally, in October, 1910, accompanied by his intimate friend and follower, Dr. Chertkov, he left his family home for good. In a farewell letter to his wife he spoke of "the impossibility of any longer leading a life of luxury" that clashed with his convictions. He tarried briefly in the monastery of Chamardino; then he traveled on to the little town of Astapovo, where on November 10 he died of a lung infection in the tiny railway station. He was still a rebel when he died; the Holy Synod adamantly opposed any religious ceremony for the deceased.

Tolstoy was probably the greatest Russian writer of all time. He was on the side of the people, confusedly, contradictorily, but on their side nonetheless. In the beginning the Russian working class showed no great sympathy for him because of his belief in nonviolence and his condemnation of violence in political struggle. But at his death they felt the loss as one of their own.

Tolstoy's novels deal much more profoundly with the social struggles of his time than do the works of other great Russian novelists. With incomparable genius they reveal the mainsprings of a Russian society divided into two worlds that barely know each other: on the one hand, the men and women on whom Peter the Great stamped the outer forms of Western civilization; on the other, the rest of the population—merchants, artisans, soldiers, peasants. Above all, Tolstoy was the interpreter—without a peer in the Russian language—of the state of mind known as nihilism. "I have lived fifty-five years in this world," he wrote. "With the exception of fourteen or fifteen years of my childhood, I have lived thirty-five years as a nihilist, in the real meaning of the term. Not a Socialist and a revolutionary, with the distorted meaning that frequent use has given those words, but a nihilist—that is, devoid of any faith."

War and Peace—which many consider the greatest novel ever

written—gives a picture of Russian society during the Napoleonic Wars of 1805–1815. As we read about the fields and farms, the Court, the soldiers, and the battlegrounds, we realize with what compelling powers of observation Tolstoy has noted the variable influence of environment on human beings. In this respect, despite Tolstoy's passionate denial, we may detect a certain socialist element. The French entry into the Kremlin, the mysterious flames rising over Moscow in the night, Count Pierre dreaming of killing Napoleon and thus achieving martyrdom, as the sacrificial victim of his people—all these incidents in the overpowering novel reveal a Tolstoy sensitive to social injustice, whom his disciples looked upon as the first apostle of social goodness. In Tolstoy's books one feels the presence of the Russian people readying themselves for impending struggles, and one remembers their countless peasant revolts of the past.

Giuseppe Garibaldi, born in Nice in 1807 and dead in 1882, although not directly identified with the Revolutions of 1848, mirrored in his person the violent atmosphere of the period. The Italian rebel-patriot was ready to espouse any cause he found just. As early as 1834 he was involved in a political conspiracy with followers of Giuseppe Mazzini. An early fondness for the sea took him as a cabin boy to Odessa, and from there to Brazil, where he fought on the side of opponents of the government. Taken prisoner, he escaped and led a sailors' mutiny in Rio Grande do Sul province, where he routed those who had previously pursued and tortured him. After this victory over reaction Garibaldi sought other fields of activity. In Uruguay he headed a legion of eight hundred Italians fighting against Uruguayans who supported the odious Argentine dictator Juan Rosas. With three small boats he defeated a fleet three times bigger than his own. His courage infected all of his followers. He proceeded on the theory that not numbers but the spirit of the activist fighting group was decisive.

Echoes of his feats in South America resounded in Italy. There he fought against the Austrian overlords and achieved tremendous popularity, and was elected to the Roman Constituent Assembly. His first legislative act was to declare in favor of an Italian republic. Persecuted for his "subversive" activity, he returned to America, this time to New York and California. Then he went to China as a captain in the merchant marine. But his real aspiration was to free his native land of reactionary influences and unite it. His Sicilian expedition in 1860 brought him to the summit of his glory. He became a hero of the masses in the Risorgimento movement to unify Italy, and a bright political career opened up before him. But he scorned it, for he detested the trappings of officialdom. He felt happiest in the red shirt of his volunteer army. It was not that he lacked parliamentary talents, as he had shown in his sharp debates with Count Cavour. But it was in the street, not in the assembly hall, that he lived to the full. His famous cry of "Rome or death!" sums up his dual personality of patriot and revolutionary.

Garibaldi hated the Austrian and Prussian rulers. In the Franco-Prussian War of 1870 he led a group of Italian volunteers to fight against the Prussians; in 1871 they occupied the city of Dijon. His French campaign crowned a heroic life. Yet, though still young in heart and spirit, he was full of bullet wounds and saddled with debts. The French parliament voted him a generous pension to aid him in retirement. But he hated the very idea of retirement and refused to accept anything from "a government responsible for France's woes." Nevertheless, when he died in 1882, the French Chamber of Deputies adjourned its session as a sign of mourning.

With him disappeared an individual unrivaled in militancy. Some years earlier, the French diplomat Alexandre Walewski, sent by Guizot to Argentina and Uruguay, returned to report that Garibaldi "was a genius, capable of any exploit and equal in the art of warfare to our best generals in France."

Garibaldi's name is writ large on every new revolutionary outburst in Italy. (It was the Garibaldi Battalion, together with the Abraham Lincoln Brigade and volunteers from many other lands, that provided the greatness of the International Brigades in the Spanish Civil War of 1936–1939.) Garibaldi was a genuine example of revolutionary internationalism in action.

5

THE PARIS COMMUNE

Most French workers on the eve of the Paris Commune lived near the poverty level. In Marx's famous phrase, they really had nothing to lose but their chains. By 1870 the French working-class movement had finally emerged from the years of intimidation, police repression, and naïve faith in promises of social justice made during the Second Empire—deceitful promises advanced by the opportunist politicians of the time. A series of strikes in the Lyons region and in other industrial centers preceded the Commune and heightened social tensions. Important members of the First International, such as Eugène Varlin, led the workers in these protests, and the International was gaining increasing support among the working class.

Two great lessons emerge from the events of the Commune. First, although the economic and social crisis was profound, it had not yet reached the point at which, in Lenin's terms, the very foundations of society are shaken and irreconcilable class antagonisms rise to the surface. Napoleon "the Little" counted particularly on war to check the advance of the liberal bourgeoisie and the working class—but this war aroused the patriotic people of Paris against the French accomplices of Bismarck. The rebellious movement was, however, limited to the capital; the rest of France was virtually unaffected. Inevitably this weakened the Commune.

The second lesson is that the division between the virtuous poor and the wicked rich is much too simplistic a concept. Marx had clearly pointed out that a bourgeois is not necessarily evil as an individual, nor is a proletarian necessarily a superior type of human being. The respective classes of both are what count; it is this that indelibly stamps their social relations.

The date of March 18, 1871, faithfully commemorated every year in France, symbolizes one of the decisive revolutionary acts of the working class—in which courage and resoluteness mingled with blundering. Individual moments in the Paris Commune justify Marx's designation of France's style as "dramatic." Over-all, the Commune was a celebration of revolution—in which human beings died amid passionate speeches and songs. At the end it was absolute tragedy; but its seventy days were full of joy, hope, and light.

It was preceded by treason on the part of the ruling class. Adolphe Thiers, the representative of the French bourgeoisie, came to terms with the Prussian leader Bismarck against the nation. At the end of February, 1871, an armistice was signed in the Franco-Prussian War. Thiers had accepted as a condition that thirty thousand Prussian troops occupy Paris. The French National Guard rejected the armistice as a surrender and resolved to defend Paris on its own. The pledge to defend the city against Bismarck and Thiers rallied the people around the National Guard. The 1871 uprising involved all the people of Paris, except, of course, the reactionary minority: the Parisian workers, delegations from the political clubs, members of the First International, and a host of others, with their determined and fearless wives. They fought to the music of guitars in an atmosphere of springtime joyousness in the midst of death. Theirs was a mélange of greatness and illusion which many subsequent historians, including the most sympathetic, fail to understand. Too many of the scholars are dismayed when they recall the innumerable obstacles that from the outset blocked a victorious denouement, despite this outpouring of courage. But it was a mark of Marx's genius that he was able to separate fundamentals from anecdotic details and include in his theory the premise of a dictatorship of the proletariat when the counter-revolution threatened. One thing is clear: without the Commune everything progressive and revolutionary in republican France in the twentieth century would not have existed. From March 28, 1871, when the Commune was proclaimed on the square in front of the Hôtel de Ville, until May 28 of the same year, when the last pockets of resistance were wiped out in the streets of Belleville, this popular revolution developed with extraordinary élan as one crisis succeeded another.

On March 29 the Commune held its first session, under the chairmanship of its oldest member, Beslay. Various decrees were issued, including one that called for a government takeover of public services. Another provided that the executive committee should be newly elected each week. The first "bureau" consisted of Proudhonians and Blanquists, proportionately represented. Ten committees were appointed: military affairs, finances, general security, food, foreign affairs, and education being the most important. The following day Beslay set up his office as commissar in the Bank of France. On April 1 the first skirmishes occurred with the Versailles troops who tried to enter the city by way of the Neuilly bridge. The following day the troops seized Courbevoie, thus endangering the defenders' main line of communications. The people of Paris reacted vigorously: fifty thousand men gathered quickly in Montmartre, with a single cry: "To Versailles!" Meanwhile the Commune continued to pass laws. "In view of the fact that freedom of conscience is the first of the freedoms," a decree was adopted providing for separation of Church and state. An appeal was addressed to the population: "Despite the moderation of our attitude, the royalists have attacked. Elected by the people of Paris, we have a duty to defend our great city against guilty aggressors. With your help, we will defend it."

Now the Commune made its first mistake. In the orders for attack issued April 3, the generals of the Commune placed enthusiasm above effectiveness. The attack, although well planned, was carried out without taking the enemy's strength into account. The royalists counterattacked, producing a disorderly retreat of the "federated" troops, who lost two brave generals, Flourens and Duval. Cluseret, at least, was saved: he had been a Union officer in the United States Civil War, had later become an art critic, and was now promptly named commander-in-chief. He surrounded himself with the best persons available, among them the Polish-born Dombrowski. The Commune lost no time in protecting itself against its enemies within Paris. A decree of April 5 established swift procedures for eliminating agents of Versailles, defeatists, and speculators. Newspapers hostile to the Commune were suppressed.

On April 9 the *Fédérés* under Dombrowski's command fought magnificently. The people's morale rose. Women led by Louise Michel and Elizabeth Dimitrieff took a prominent part in the struggle. The slogan was quite clear: "We must conquer or die." The resistance organization was broadened to attract members of the professions. On April 13 the Federation of Artists of Paris was formed—their aim "a government of the arts by the artists." They were ready to fight when necessary and at the same time to raise the cultural level of the people. Everything was to be for the people and by the people. The general tone of the manifesto foreshadowed the "Declaration to the French People" drawn up on April 19 by the Proudhonian journalist Denis and the old Jacobin Delescluze: "In the painful and the terrible conflict in which Paris is once again subjected to the horrors of siege and bombardment, Paris and the whole nation must know what the revolution is, its reason for being and its goal. What is it striving for? The recognition and consolidation of the Republic." And further on: "The communal revolution, begun by popular initiative on March 18, inaugurates a new era of experimental, positive, scientific politics."

The Paris Commune was a key event in the long march toward socialism. It confirmed the Marxist theory regarding the role of the working class in the fight for liberation. Thanks to the struggle waged in Paris, wrote Marx on April 17, 1871, the fight of the working class against the capitalist class and its state had entered a new phase; and whatever the outcome, a new point of departure of universal importance had been achieved. As for Lenin, in discussing the Soviets he pointed out that their power had the same characteristics as those of the Paris Commune. The Commune combined spontaneity with the creative capacity of the revolutionary people as a whole. To be sure, the Commune had no single leader of the stature of Lenin. Yet at certain moments the masses rise to the necessary heights and, even in the midst of defeat, leave their imprint on the history of their own time and thereafter.

In the Commune, arming the people was the work of the masses. They did not wait for the support of the section of the army that patriotically resisted Versailles and the Prussians. True, the lack of military experience limited the effectiveness of some operations, and some were badly coordinated. Nevertheless, the principle of arming the people was established as an inherent element of all true revolutions. Many years later this principle was broadened: military training was essential for cadres called upon to lead the revolutionary action of the masses and the guerrillas.

The Commune demonstrated the capacity of the working class for initiative and imagination. The measures it recommended for the people's welfare could easily have been adopted by a liberal government, but they were not; and so the masses undertook to fill the vacuum. Analyzing this situation, Lenin commented: "When the bourgeoisie refuses to confront these problems, the proletariat solves them violently by means of a revolution. For example, the Paris Commune."

The partisans of "law and order" believed, of course, that once the Commune was defeated, socialism would cease to be a menace for a long time to come. Marx, in his *Civil War in France*, demolished this theory of a bourgeois victory. Vividly describing the events of 1871, Marx links them with the February days of the 1848 Revolution, in which, as we have seen, the Social Republic made itself heard, although still in a minor key and without the profound reverberations of the Commune. In the Commune that term "Social Republic" acquired "positive form." It was the first attempt in history to set up a workers' government. The working class showed complete confidence in its destiny, capable of competing with, and surpassing, the bourgeoisie in the art of government.

The machinery of government was set up democratically by elections in the various city districts. Delegates from these districts constituted for all practical purposes a government capable of acting in the legislative and executive spheres. It was a government responsible to the working class: its members could be, and were, replaced by a majority vote of the representatives elected from the various districts. Marx acknowledged that this was still only a primary type of government organization. But inasmuch as it was based on the workers' recognition of the need to provide an effective substitute for the old apparatus of oppression and not simply to leave things to the mercy of revolutionary improvisation, it represented progress toward the final liberation of the working class.

In his prologue to Marx's *Civil War in France*, Engels summed up the achievements of the Commune in the following terms: on March

26 the Commune was elected and on March 28 officially proclaimed. On March 30 it proceeded to recruit a standing army, recognizing the National Guard, to which all citizens capable of bearing arms had to belong, as the genuine representative of the armed forces.

Toward the end of April some signs of disorganization in the armed forces and in the distribution of food at the main combat centers appeared. These gave rise to acrimonious discussions, and for the first time unity was broken. Now a minority confronted a majority—and it was not always on basic points. Still, the people continued to fight with enthusiasm in the streets of Issy-les-Moulineaux, Billancourt, and elsewhere. Some incidents, though slight, were significant. For example, the artists' battalion of the Commune opposed a scheme by a group of ultras to destroy the cathedral of Notre-Dame. They took the first steps toward revolutionary city planning, asserting that it was possible to save Notre-Dame as a meaningful historical landmark yet cleanse Paris of everything designed exclusively for the comfort and ostentation of the rich.

On May 1 the building of barricades gathered momentum. It mirrored the people's determination to fight to the bitter end. The idea of forming a Committee of Public Safety came to the fore again. The *Journal Officiel* of May 2 published a brief decree without any preamble: "The Commune of Paris decrees: Article 1. A Committee of Public Safety will be immediately organized. Article 2. It will consist of five members appointed by the Commune on the basis of individual balloting. Article 3. The most extensive powers over the delegations and committees will be given this committee and it will be responsible solely to the Commune." The newly elected members of the Committee of Public Safety were: Antoine Arnaud, Léo Meillet, Ranvier, Félix Pyat, and Charles Gérardin.

In the middle of May, as the situation worsened, the defeatists and traitors began to stir. Within the very leadership of the Commune dissension increased. The minority group—that is, the Proudhonians and members of the First International, who counseled a more moderate policy—withdrew to their respective districts and accused the majority of setting up a dictatorship in the name of the Committee of Public Safety. The reaction of the clubs and trade-union groups was: continue the fight, but on condition that unity be re-established and maintained. Where men fell in battle women took their place. The Central Committee of the Union of Women for the Defense of Paris on May 6 issued its manifesto against conciliation and capitulation. It concluded: "The present struggle can only end in victory for the people."

In the second half of May the military situation became critical. Five Paris districts were under enemy fire. The foe shot every prisoner that fell into their hands. In view of the worsened situation, the minority group returned to their posts in the Commune. War measures alternated with plans for making education secular and giving the theater a more social role.

As far as war measures were concerned, attention was focused on building barricades. This is apparent from Delescluze's proclamation of May 21: "We have had enough of militarism! No more general staffs with their gold braid. Make way for the people, for the fighters with their arms bare." It was the final phase of desperate heroism. The members of the Commune prepared to die, each one in front of his section.

On May 24, in a battle in which there was no longer any pretense of unified military command, the resistance was ferocious in some spots, such as the Left Bank and around the Hôtel de Ville. The Versailles forces, who had retaken the Bank of France, the Stock Exchange, and the Louvre, were temporarily halted. On May 25 and 26 the *Fédérés* continued to fight among dead bodies and ruins. Women and children brought them as much ammunition as they could. On Sunday, May 28, the last resistance points were taken by storm. Even the wounded dragging themselves along the ground continued to shoot. But it was the last act.

Then commenced the brutal repression. Officially 50,000, in reality probably 100,000 arrested; more than 30,000 were shot. Yet, despite their tragic sacrifices, the people of Paris bequeathed a never-to-be-forgotten message to the working class of all countries. An old French Socialist whose forebears had fought in the Commune told me in the 1920's: "My party is not for the Russian Revolution, but I am. And do you know why? Because the Russian Revolution vindicated the Commune." The phrase is fraught with meaning. The French proletariat failed, for reasons we have indicated; the Russian proletariat triumphed. The victory in October, 1917, vindicated not only the Paris Commune but also all the previous actions of the working class that had been smothered in blood and repression.

The repression in 1871 was atrocious. History shows that the "white terror" always exceeds the "red terror" when political passions put opposing class interests against one another. The hatred of the wealthy in society for those who challenge their self-proclaimed right to rule and to unrestrictedly enjoy their wealth knows no limit. Hence the anger and desire for revenge of the victorious reactionaries in the period following the collapse of the Commune. To find a historical parallel to the merciless repression of 1871, one must go back centuries to the campaigns of extermination waged by a Genghis Khan or a Tamerlane. Jean Gaucon in his book *The Paris Commune* estimates that more Parisians were killed in eight days of the repression than the Prussians killed during the entire war of 1870–1871.

When the struggle was over, the fate of the leaders of the Commune was as follows: of the seventy-nine members on May 21, one, Delescluze, had fallen at the barricades; two, Durand and Rigault, had been shot; two others, Brunel and Vermorel, seriously wounded; three wounded slightly, among them Frankel. To these one must add three thousand dead and wounded Communards.

No attempt by the leaders of the Commune to spare lives once they realized the hopelessness of prolonging the struggle was heeded by the foe. The fortress of Vincennes was surrendered to the enemy by its commander, Faltot, a veteran Polish and Garibaldian revolutionary. He gave up the fort without a shot, requesting that its officers be spared. A futile gesture: the Communards were put up against the wall and executed. They fell on the very spot where the Duc d'Enghien had fallen to Napoleon's firing squad. Then Marshal MacMahon issued his order of the day: "Paris has been liberated. Order, work, and security are restored." What really was restored was the frenzied rage of the reactionaries. In 1848 workers whose pardon had been publicly announced were executed. The same thing happened twenty-three years later. In the selfsame manner of the triumphant counter-revolution, Thiers promised pardons and amnesty. In fact he gave a free hand to the soldiery to settle accounts while he declared: "Socialism is finished for a long time."

Prisoner status was not respected. Many prisoners were shot out of hand by the Versailles policemen, after being handed over by German soldiers. In La Roquette prison 1,900 persons were shot forty-eight hours after the fighting was over. Similar shootings occurred at Mazas, at the Ecole Militaire, and in the Parc Monceau. In the Châtelet district the authorities preferred for appearance' sake "to proceed by legal means." Military courts were set up and the prisoners filed past them. On an average the trial of an accused lasted one minute. Eight out of ten received death sentences from these tribunals. In the Lobau district collective verdicts were pronounced against groups of prisoners so as not to waste time. In many places wives accompanied their husbands and asked to be shot with them. Eugène Varlin, an outstanding revolutionary, who remained on the barricades to the last, was found in a crowd of people. Although he merited prisoner-of-war status, he was seized and sentenced to death on the spot. Exhausted from having been on his feet all day, he was executed sitting on a chair. From afar, absorbed by the responsibilities of government, Thiers decided not to intervene. His only comment was: "Perhaps this terrible spectacle will serve as a lesson."

Thiers' newspapers vied with one another in fomenting hatred and demanding new victims. The liberals did not dare open their mouths. Léon Gambetta himself could only say, "The heroic days are over." There were too few prisons—both regular jails and improvised ones—to house the political detainees. The victors settled the problem by mobilizing cattle carts in which the prisoners were transported to forts that had long since been abandoned as army barracks because of their state of decay. There the prisoners waited for the "judicial" process to unfold. At one point the authorities even feared that the soldiers under their orders might refuse to continue to shoot down defenseless Frenchmen.

Apart from those executed summarily, there remained some 40,000 as evidence that the law was being respected. But, just as in 1848, or even more harshly, the guiding motive was the complete extermination of the revolutionary parties so as to guarantee a long period of calm. This attitude was shared by the Bonapartist officers, who were in a majority in the army when the Commune collapsed. When Thiers proclaimed a state of siege in the *département* of Seine-et-Oise, he helped create an atmosphere of repression in which no effort was spared to leave the working class in disarray for years to come.

Beginning in August, 1871, about fifty military courts were established. This was a conscious effort to impress the general public and convince them, by means of this façade, that justice was being meted out. The accused had to defend themselves without access to lawyers of their choice. When they spoke they were constantly interrupted, and their court-appointed attorneys—named by military judges—strove not to defend them but to hasten their conviction. None of this, however, prevented Ferré, a convinced fighter for socialism, from addressing the court in these words: "If you let me live, I will not stop denouncing the assassination of my brothers by the committee on pardons. If you are not cowards, kill me!"

Lesser crimes were punished with the same harshness as more serious ones. Even men who had risked their lives to save Generals Lecomte and Thomas were condemned to death. On November 28 a series of "legal" executions began—all carried out "with due regard for the penalty exacted by law." The first on the list were Ferré, whom we have just mentioned, and Rossel; and the executions continued well into 1873. A majority fell under the bullets shouting: "Long live the Commune!" Others died a slow death, at forced labor or in prison camps in exile. A few managed to escape from France, but Cabinet Minister Jules Favre pursued them with demands for their extradition—and reactionary governments granted the demand in violation of human rights. The International of Reaction opposed the Workingmen's International. The panic caused by the Commune knew no national boundaries. The "financier of the Commune," Jourde, who with other exiled Communards was working near Strasbourg, was handed over to French authorities in exchange for a promise from Thiers to Bismarck to collaborate on a large-scale building project on the border. The lives of Communards were like easy money, bartered away without a qualm.

Thus ended a terrible war that reached record heights of cruelty and barbarism. If we add to the 20,000 Communards murdered on the spot the 13,000 executed "according to law" or who died in decaying fortresses or on filthy cattle carts, we see why Talès was justified in commenting: "In one month the repression of the Commune movement caused more victims than did the French

Revolution in two years." Indeed, even pro-monarchist historians have estimated a maximum of 2,600 victims in fifteen months in the Terror of 1793. What took place after May, 1871, was a punitive expedition against the entire population of Paris. But here let us quote Ferré again: "No matter how many you kill, the working class will regain its militancy in the not-too-distant future; and in the battles of this century and the next for human emancipation and dignity the memory of the Commune will serve as a stimulus and a lesson."

Up to the beginning of June the mass assassinations reached the figure of 17,000. This figure came from the Ministry of Justice itself. In reality, however, 20,000 would be closer to the truth. Sympathizers were rounded up along with participants. The hunt was on for the alleged "arsonists" and *"pétroleuses"* (women incendiaries). Any woman surprised in the act of lifting a bottle of alcohol or a box of matches to do her cooking risked being arrested and in some cases shot. The wounded were in an especially exposed situation. Some of those transported by the International Red Cross were forcibly removed from the cattle carts in which they had been dumped. The mere fact of having a wound, even an on-the-job accident, invited summary trial and execution. Bourgeois republicans were mistaken for Socialists. Deputy Millière, a liberal, who had taken part in the barricade battles but who was not a member of the Commune, was arrested and shot in front of the marble columns of the Panthéon. Dr. Moilin, suspected of Socialist sympathies, suffered the same fate. Foreigners were targets of hatred and fear. Dombrowski's Polish origin cost the lives of Poles who had nothing to do with politics, much less with the Commune.

This outbreak of vengeance cannot be attributed to an irrational outburst of fearful people during the days of the Commune. Nor was it the sanguinary reflex of a group that panicked and lost control of itself. It was the calculated work of the counter-revolutionary government determined to teach the working class a lesson, so that it would never again be tempted to challenge the social order. Directives came from on high; there was no trace of generosity in them. It was a policy of harshness, coldly conceived and deliberately put into practice, oblivious of the fact that French citizens, not invading Prussian soldiers, were being slaughtered en masse. When the decisive moment came—the hour of truth—many of the liberal sympathizers with the Commune abandoned the heroic fighters to their fate.

The defeat of the Commune gave the conservative forces in France only a brief breathing spell. Inspired by the revolutionary Louise Michel and others, a powerful anarchist trend emerged from the people's uprising in Paris. For the first time in history anarchism on a world scale made itself felt. It spread to other countries, gained strength in Italy, and became a political factor in Spain. (At this time of writing, it is still a force to be reckoned with in the struggle to eliminate the Franco dictatorship.)

Possessing its own theory, tactics, and methods of struggle, anarchism attracted to its ranks persons as diverse as the Russian aristocrats Bakunin and Kropotkin, the French poet Laurent Tailhade, the fiery Italian agitator Malatesta, guerrilla fighters of great courage such as the Spaniard Durruti and the popular Catalonian leader Salvador Seguí, called the *Noy del Sucre.* Anarchism was not a monolithic movement, either in substance or in style. As a matter of fact, in its origins it revealed three distinct trends: One that may be termed moderate and evolutionary, led by Proudhon, the French "philosopher of poverty." Its chief interest was to raise the standard of living of the working class by creating cooperatives and organizations for mutual aid. The second, anarcho-Communism, was distinctly violent and militant, as was its outstanding leader, Bakunin. The third, influenced to some extent by the teachings of Karl Marx, was for years a strong influence in the trade-union movement, under the name of revolutionary syndicalism, or anarcho-syndicalism.

Louise Michel, born in 1830, was a revolutionary so totally committed that no temporary defeats, no disappointments in her fellow human beings, could dampen her indomitable spirit. Her exile to far-off New Caledonia, far from dismaying her, prompted her to undertake new tasks: teaching the native New Caledonians how to read. To that end this former schoolteacher-turned-revolutionary learned the native dialect. She won the affection of the most savage tribes living isolated in the jungle, whom white men scarcely dared approach. The Kanaka rebellion that broke out in 1878 had Louise Michel as a precursor and a guide to action. She had an unforgettable beauty of spirit and person. Aging survivors of the Commune whom the present writer encountered as a youthful student in Paris still spoke glowingly of her beautiful eyes. The ideological disputes within the anarchists' ranks did not interest her. "Action above all" was her slogan. In her youth she had written poetry dedicated to Saint-Just. She was one of the first to adopt a new method of struggle—"direct action." Almost a century later this remains the core of anarchist tactics.

The anarchists' preference for direct action, for lightning blows that would make bourgeois governments totter, and their differences with the advocates of scientific socialism created a deep division in the international labor movement. Curiously enough, it was in quiet, untroubled Switzerland that the various trends in the working-class movement of the period came together and then split violently apart. The initial congress of the First International took place in Geneva in September, 1866. Louise Michel had already gained a reputation in the French political clubs and societies of France, where Napoleon "the Little" was denounced and ridiculed. Everywhere she became known simply as Louise, president of the Club of the Revolution. In Switzerland too, anarchism reorganized after the 1872 Congress of the First International at The Hague, when the followers of Marx and Bakunin split with one another. Anarchism became an independent, libertarian movement, freed of what it considered the restrictive and moderating influence of Marxism. In Berne, a city of lovely fountains, romantic towers, and elaborately sculptured clocks, the libertarian paper *Le Révolté* first appeared as a mouthpiece for the partisans of direct action, members of the anarchist Fédération Jurassienne (the Jura Federation).

From anarchist theorizing and cries of "Long live anarchism!" and "Down with the bourgeois!" that burst forth at meetings and street demonstrations, the anarchists moved quickly to put their new theories into practice. Direct action was aimed in the first place against autocracy and authoritarianism in all its forms. Assassinations and attempts at insurrection erupted from one end of Europe to the other. Revolvers and bombs supplanted discussions concerning a political program. At every meeting she attended Louise Michel would say: "First, let's make the revolution and then we'll see." As we have seen, a beautiful Russian student, Vera Zasulich, assassinated the hated chief of police Trepov in St. Petersburg in 1878. With Louise Michel, Vera became the idol of young people in the universities and factories who found the Marxist theoreticians too ponderous and slow-moving. A wave of violence swept European society. Caught up in it were rebels who had broken with their own bourgeois class as well as precursors of the new society; it embraced princes and workingmen, men and women who worked in laboratories and in factories, veritable "sweatshops" that employed children as well as grownups, against which Victor Hugo fulminated and which provided a backdrop for many of Emile Zola's novels.

The bomb that exploded in the Winter Palace in St. Petersburg failed to kill Alexander II; but in 1881 he was assassinated by Russian nihilists. In September, 1883, a German printer named Rheinsdorff made an attempt on the life of Kaiser William I. His trial touched off a massive campaign against "the present state of affairs" that engulfed all Germany, despite its highly disciplined and tightly controlled society. A spectacular assassination attempt in the French Chamber of Deputies on December 9, 1893, marked the beginning of a series of violent acts that continued until 1894. An object was hurled from the spectators' gallery while the Chamber was in full session. It exploded and felled numerous deputies, who lay in pools of blood. The police arrested a man named Auguste Vaillant and questioned him briefly. Vaillant declared he was an anarchist: to bring about the social order he deemed necessary, he had decided to strike at the source in order to "warn" the deputies. "Let the deputies feel the people's anger upon them! Then perhaps they will decide to vote juster laws."

Auguste Vaillant had had a wretched childhood. One day, when he was seventeen, he was so famished that he entered a little restaurant and ate his fill. When the time came for him to pay his ninety-centime check, he revealed his penniless plight to the restaurant owner, who had him arrested and sent to prison. When he emerged from prison Vaillant frequented anarchist groups, where he heard praise of names like Louise Michel and Ravachol. Ravachol, on being sentenced to death, had shouted "Long live anarchism!" and in prison had tried to win the prison guards over to his ideas. Vaillant too became an anarchist and began to read widely—history, astronomy, mathematics, philosophy. One of his major accusations against the existing social order was that it kept the people in ignorance "so that they do not notice the social hell in which they live."

He emigrated to Argentina and wrote enthusiastic letters to his anarchist comrades in France, describing the savage and terrible beauty of the Chaco region. He lived among the Indians and became one of them, viewing them as human beings not yet corrupted by the bourgeoisie. In that forbidding Chaco wasteland, beset by malaria and tropical heat, where panthers came out on the railway tracks and hurled themselves at the engines, Vaillant managed to assemble a few dozen persons and founded a philosophical club of which he was the guiding light. Then he returned to France and tossed his bomb in the Parliament. His trial was a sensation, especially after experts testified that had the mechanism exploded at the base of the speaker's platform instead of in mid-air, a hundred deputies might have been killed or seriously wounded. Witnesses called by the defense all described Vaillant as a cultured, kindly man, always ready to help his fellow human beings. Despite a broad movement on his behalf to have his sentence commuted, Vaillant was executed. His burial place became a kind of shrine in which flowers were left, sometimes accompanied by notes threatening vengeance. The latter soon materialized. A few days after Vaillant's execution a bomb exploded at the Café Terminus in the Saint-Lazare railway station. The man who planted the bomb, Emile Henry, was also executed. His last words to the court were defiant: "In this war without quarter which we have declared on the bourgeoisie, we, the anarchists, request no pity. Others will fall after me. But what you will never be able to destroy is anarchism, which has been born in the womb of a decaying society."

Attacks occurred in restaurants, churches, and the most fashionable spots in Paris. Direct action was attempted in the provinces as well. The President of the French Republic, Sadi Carnot, was visiting the World's Fair in Lyons on June 24, 1894. As he was going toward the Grand-Théâtre, where a gala performance was being held in his honor, a man approached his carriage, flung a pamphlet enclosing a bomb, and shouted: *"Vive la Révolution!"* Carnot fell mortally wounded. This time it was not a Frenchman but a young Italian, Caserio, aged twenty-one, who said he wanted to punish the President for having denied a pardon to Vaillant.

Louise Michel epitomized the women of the Commune. Once when she was arrested and informed each morning that on the following day she would be shot, her reply was: "As you please." But she was far from alone. There were many other sister revolutionaries, from the elegant Elizabeth Dimitrieff to Jeanne Moussu the laundress. Born in Russia in the province of Pskov, an extraordinary linguist, awakened to politics by the books in the library of her father, a former hussars officer who received publications from abroad, Elizabeth Dimitrieff emigrated to London, where she became a close friend of Karl Marx and his family. For Marx she was an invaluable source of information about events in Russia. She helped send underground literature to her native country and made available to Marx books by Chernyshevsky and others. Marx showed his high esteem for her by giving her an important mission to Paris in 1871. She took part in the Union des Femmes, the women's organization for the defense of Paris and care of the wounded, and became one of its leading spirits. This organization brought together women of various classes: schoolteachers, dressmakers, housewives, and sweatshop workers. Historians of the Commune, including some who are obviously hostile to it, all speak of Elizabeth Dimitrieff's air of distinction. One of them, describing her as wearing a large feather-decorated hat and a red scarf, says that she was a striking model for a painting of the Revolution. Shortly thereafter her red scarf was replaced by a cartridge belt.

She was a woman of ideas and action. She made her comrades rethink their views on the role of women in politics; and in circles that had hitherto resisted, she won acceptance of the principle of equal rights for women, specifically of equal pay for equal work. For that day and age it was a revolutionary concept that ranks among the outstanding achievements of the Paris Commune. When the Versailles troops entered Paris on May 21, the reformer in her gave way to the fighter. Building the future was temporarily sidetracked. The problem now was to build barricades.

Another Russian woman, Anna Vassilievna Krukovskaya, daughter of General Krukovsky, joined the Communards. Her father had threatened to cut her off financially if she meddled in politics. Her response was to go to work in a printing shop where she identified with the workers and joined one of the revolutionary clubs.

In general, however, there were few foreign-born women in the movement. Just as the First International was not the sole driving force of the Commune, so the Union des Femmes was not its only fighting organization. Above all, there were the clubs: for example, the Club of Proletarian Women, which assigned specific tasks to its members. On May 20, Citizen Valentin bade the other women in her club "guard the gates of Paris while the men go out to fight." The response was most impressive. Louise Michel frequently presided over sessions of the Club of the Revolution, with headquarters in the Church of Saint-Bernard de la Chapelle. In the Club of the Social Revolution, a seamstress, Blanche Lefebvre, mobilized the women needleworkers. There were days of study as well as political agitation. Until the moment came for taking up guns, the clubs discussed the elimination of capitalist exploitation and the participation of the workers in the profits of the enterprises where they worked. It was by no means Marxian scientific socialism. But it did indicate Socialist sentiments, a feeling for socialism.

In the bloody final week of the Commune women were in the vanguard of the resistance. With bare hands they erected barricades, cleaned rifles, supplied the Communards with food, kept alive their fighting spirit. The women were the last to surrender. When, all around her, men were falling from bullet wounds, Eugénie Rousseau, a hairdresser, made a flag out of her shawl and shouted to a group of survivors: "Here comes Dombrowski! We are saved! Long live Dombrowski! Long live the Commune!"

All sorts of weapons were used against the reactionary onslaught. Although anticlerical, the Communards had refrained from harming a single church. Now, as the Versaillais advanced on Paris, fires broke out. Marx justified the Commune's "using fire strictly as a defensive measure." Women fought in the midst of the flames. An English eyewitness depicts a women's battalion, armed with Snider carbines, shooting accurately and fighting like demons. Others described them as "lionesses."

Enemies of the Commune later reveled in drawing a portrait of *pétroleuses* seized with a fury of wanton destruction, a can of kerosene in their hand, and giving themselves to men between setting fires. But in an article written in August, 1871, after denying that the leaders of the Commune acted on orders from the Central Committee of the First International, Marx branded stories about the *pétroleuses* as "one of the most hateful slanders devised in a civilized country." Indeed, the courts-martial could not identify a single *pétroleuse* caught in the act of setting a fire. This did not prevent them from shooting hundreds of women and deporting thousands more to the prison fortresses of French Guiana. Marx stated categorically: "Everything that was set on fire was done so by men."

Reputable authors who later wrote about the Commune drew a distinction between fire as a weapon of war, a defense measure of the *Fédérés,* a violent response of the people to the violence of the Versaillais, and fire for the sheer pleasure of destruction. Clearly, a kind of collective hysteria took possession of the "law and order" minions who saw *pétroleuses* in every nook and cranny of Paris. This was like the notorious *grande peur* of 1789. Today, too, it inspires absurdities such as the "red menace" and the "yellow peril," particularly when the Soviet Union and China are concerned.

In his penetrating analysis of the Commune, Marx, whom we have so frequently quoted, indulged in no romantic outbursts. This would have been contrary to his critical temperament and scientific attitude. Both he and Engels foresaw the advent of revolution in France; so in 1870 they posed the problem of who in Paris would be in a position to assume leadership of the revolutionary movement. Leading members of the Commune later came to Marx for advice. "Your opinion concerning the social reforms to be achieved," wrote Léo Frankel to Marx, "will be extremely valuable to our committee." Despite illness, Marx was unremitting in his efforts on behalf of the people of Paris who had taken up arms. He sought to convince the Commune leaders that the working class could not simply lay hands on the state apparatus ready-made, "but must smash the military and bureaucratic machinery of the bourgeois state and establish the dictatorship of the proletariat." From March 18 on, Marx and Engels recognized the class character of the Commune: workers or their elected representatives predominated in it. Thus the Commune's decisions bore an unmistakable proletarian stamp. Nevertheless, in the economic field many important things were neglected. Engels noted the Communards' respectful attitude toward the Bank of France. "Yet," he wrote, "the Bank in the hands of the Commune would have been worth more than ten thousand hostages."

In his report to the General Council of the International Association of Workingmen, "to all the members of the Association in Europe and the United States," Marx excoriated "the monstrous Thiers," who for more than half a century had held the French bourgeoisie under his spell and who was "the intellectual expression of his own class corruption." He ridiculed Thiers' alleged patriotism: "Certainly no government would have dared direct the guns of its own forts against Paris except the very government that had previously surrendered those forts to the Prussians." The working class, said Marx, did not expect miracles from the Commune. They did not propose a ready-made utopia that could be introduced by a decree of the people. In his *Civil War in France*, Marx wrote: "They know that in order to work out their own emancipation and, along with it, that higher form to which present society is irresistibly tending, by its own economical agencies, they will have to pass through long struggles, through a series of historic processes transforming circumstances and men."

So, despite all its shortcomings, the Commune still stands out as a historic achievement of the masses. It was a people's uprising—an example and guide to other peoples. As Marx said: "The great social measure of the Commune was its own existence and action."

"The corpse is in the earth and the idea is on its feet"—these words of Victor Hugo were often heard in the midst of the campaign for amnesty that marked the last days of the "Assembly of Misfortune," the name given to the parliament that adjourned on December 31, 1875, after shamefully remaining deaf to popular demands for clemency. In the voting on May 18, 372 deputies were against amnesty, and only 50 in favor, while Léon Gambetta, like so many other confused and vacillating liberals at all crucial junctures in history, abstained. In the Senate, Victor Hugo pleaded passionately for amnesty.

The press of the genuine Left renewed its vigorous campaign. A Paris newspaper, *La Révolution Française*, defying fines and imprisonment, published the opinions of exiled members of the Commune. Despite the continuing harsh repression, the Socialist Party was not "pulverized," as Thiers had announced to the agrarian-minded Assembly. Finally amnesty came, and the amnestied exiles returned to Paris, where special welcoming committees of republicans and radicals greeted them everywhere.

This was the balance sheet of casualties in the Commune: 30,000 men, women, and children killed in battle or in the resistance that ensued; at least 3,000 dead in exile; over 30,000 condemned to jail terms averaging nine years in duration; 70,000 women, children, and old people deprived of their usual support, driven into penury—that was the balance sheet in blood and vengeance of a bourgeoisie that called itself virtuous and Christian.

But the Commune became a landmark in history. No amount of sophistic and pseudo-intellectual analyses by dry-as-dust pedants seeking to pile criticism on criticism and error on error can dislodge it from the place of honor it holds in the march of socialism. It was a magnificent effort to give power to the working class.

In the *Revue des Deux Mondes* (Vol. 4, 1871) a certain Emile Beausire, one of the most vicious detractors of the March 18 uprising of that year, emitted the opinion that those who thought the Commune was finished once and for all were greatly in error: "The Commune has died? Oh, no! The Commune has not died! It lives on in the ruins it has left. It continues in the false ideas that gave rise to it. In the passions it represented and which have survived its fall." Confirmation once again—from an unlikely source—that every great mass movement leaves its indelible mark.

6

THE
RUSSIAN REVOLUTION

During his years of exile Lenin's strength lay in the fact that he was the least exiled of all. Outside Russia, Lenin maintained constant contact with the genuinely revolutionary elements on the inside and closely followed what was happening in his native land. His clear political line always paralleled the evolution of events. He showed unusual foresight, yet never tried to speculate on the future, as did other Russian revolutionaries; nor did he indulge in heady or romantic improvisations. Lenin was the realistic revolutionary par excellence, solidly rooted in the Russian earth, although separated from it geographically by thousands of miles.

From the outset of World War I, Lenin had accurate data on the military and political situation in Russia. He knew that the Czar had sent his armies to the front, in a hastily organized offensive against the German army, in order to aid his French allies, despite warnings from the most qualified Russian generals. Thus General Shilinsky, who in August, 1914, commanded the northeastern Russian front, declared that the Russian offensive designed to aid France was doomed to early failure. The chief of the general staff, General Yanushkevich, shared that opinion. On August 30, 1914, the Russian Foreign Minister, Sasonov, told French Ambassador Paléologue: "Samsonov's army is routed. We had to make this sacrifice out of consideration for France."

On the tenth anniversary of World War I, Paul Milyukov, head of the Constitutional Democrats ("Cadets") in 1914 who went into exile when the Revolution triumphed, confirmed this viewpoint when he wrote: "Never should we have expected Russia, without time to mobilize and effectively train its forces, to send millions of its sons into the trenches for a foreign cause." Yet, though not in Russia, Lenin discerned more clearly than all the political leaders within the country how the war would develop. Hardly had hostilities begun when he wrote that Czarism "would not be able to mobilize its forces" effectively. For Russia was a giant with feet of clay. Its bourgeoisie and big landowners made a pretense of fervent patriotism but were chiefly concerned with getting rich from the war. Frequently in his writings of that period Lenin refers to them as "merchants of war" to whom sacrifices were unthinkable. Sacrifices were only for the common people.

Monopoly capitalism was beginning to dominate the Russian economy. The war gave it new impetus. In the textile industry alone—after all, soldiers did have to wear uniforms—profits of a hundred firms rose from 60,000,000 rubles in 1913 to 174,000,000 in 1915. Over-all industrial production went from 5,620,000,000 rubles in 1913 to 6,831,000,000 in 1916. But along with war profits and wide-open speculation and corruption, the people's poverty intensified. In the autumn of 1915 ration quotas for the cities dropped almost to a hunger level. The army received only about half the amount of foodstuffs assigned to it.

This was the Russian reality in the very first year of the war. Lenin understood its revolutionary potential. The two words "bread" and "peace" were uppermost in his mind—and became watchwords in October, 1917. From 1914 to 1917 he kept his eye on his goal, without a moment's vacillation. At the same time, he knew that to exploit the revolutionary possibilities there had to be within Russia a group of trustworthy men and women, loyal to the Bolshevik idea and free from the confused thinking of the other groups in opposition.

The Russian parliament—the Duma—reflected the weakness of the allegedly liberal trend. In the Duma the rightists predominated, the numerically strongest faction being the "Octobrists," headed by powerful landowners such as Mikhail Rodzianko, who possessed vast holdings at Ekaterinoslav. (Years later, on one of my many visits to the Soviet Union, I saw his lands transformed into collective farms.) The second-largest bloc of deputies was the "Cadets," led by Paul Milyukov, whom we have mentioned above. The working class was represented by five deputies: Petrovsky, Muranov, Badaiev, Samoilov, Shchagov, all Bolsheviks. In November, 1914, they were arrested and sent to Siberia. With the arrest of these Bolshevik deputies the vacuum created in the left-wing opposition in the Duma was filled by Alexander Kerensky, of the Social Revolutionaries. He was not of the same stripe. An eloquent orator, with the word "people" frequently on his lips, he proved weak indeed when, with the fall of Czarism, he became head of government during the first stage of revolutionary upheaval.

To Lenin one of the most important revolutionary tasks as the war continued was to set up a party organization within the army itself. A secret report of the Czarist police, discovered and published after the 1917 Revolution, stated: "The followers of Lenin, who are gaining ground in the Russian Social Democratic organizations, have made large-scale distributions of leaflets in the most important cities—Petrograd, Moscow, Kharkov, Kiev, Tula, Samara—demanding an end to the war, the fall of the present government, and the establishment of a republic. They are trying to infiltrate their propaganda in army circles."

In the midst of the war Lenin wrote his *Imperialism: The Highest Stage of Capitalism*, a work that profoundly influenced the controversy about the nature of the war and gave left-wing Socialists who disagreed with the official attitude of the Second International a solid weapon with which to fight against the abandonment of true Socialist aims. Here was an answer to those who maintained that one had to support one's own country, right or wrong. In it Lenin argued against Karl Kautsky and Rudolf Hilferding and their concept of super-imperialism, as well as against Nikolai Bukharin and his theory of the automatic collapse of capitalism. He reaffirmed his belief, voiced as early as 1915, in the possibility of the victory of socialism in a single country. On this point he differed with Leon Trotsky, who considered such a victory impossible. Moreover, Lenin opposed any policy that sought artificially to rebuild the Second International.

Nevertheless, attempts to rebuild it continued: first at Lugano, Switzerland, where the Socialists of the Allied nations met in

February, 1915; then in April of the same year, when the German and Austrian Socialists met. In London, at a similar conference, the English Socialists insisted that the war be looked upon as a war of liberation. There Trotsky clashed with Maxim Litvinov, who, realizing that he could not present the Bolshevik point of view because of the attitude of the majority of those present, issued a protest and left the hall. The resolution adopted by the London conference called for an Allied victory and the rebuilding of the Second International after the war.

Lenin replied to every maneuver that sought to give the appearance—in words alone—of a rebirth of militant socialism. He denounced such efforts: "The Second International is dead, conquered by opportunism. Down with opportunism! Long live the Third International, cleansed of deserters!" He was not diverted by the fears of some of his friends that by insisting on his own viewpoint he would remain alone. "Alone? No. I shall be left with a position, a clear political line, something the others do not have." By his criticism of the behavior of the Second International when World War I broke out, Lenin laid the basis for the Third International. At a conference of Bolsheviks held in Berne, Switzerland, on September 6–7, 1914, Lenin characterized the war as a capitalist, dynastic, and imperialist war, denouncing as a betrayal of socialism the attitude taken by the principal leaders of the Second International.

On November 1, 1914, a document of the Russian Social Democratic Labor Party (Bolsheviks) presented Lenin's "Theses" on the war. Thus began a ceaseless effort to reunite all dissident Socialists and form a solid and cohesive Socialist left wing, united across national boundaries in their opposition to the war. Here, clearly, was the first step to an alternative to the Second International. On the following March 27 the foreign sections of the Bolshevik Party met at Berne and decided: to vote against any new war credits; to ask Socialists to leave the bourgeois governments they were participating in; to set up illegal organizations everywhere; to begin propaganda for troop fraternization at the front and for revolutionary actions by the working class. They further asserted that a policy not accompanied by revolutionary actions only fostered illusions, misled the masses, and turned into an instrument of secret diplomacy. The Berne gathering also took a stand against Trotsky and his newspaper *Nashe Slovo*, whose slogan was "Neither victory nor defeat," and against the idea of re-establishing the Second International following a proclamation of general amnesty.

In an article that appeared at that time, Lenin restated with new arguments the Marxist position toward war: "The workers cannot fulfill their historic mission if they do not undertake a struggle against those renegades who are slavish and lacking in character."

At the Zimmerwald Conference (1915) he fought to obtain a strong resolution condemning all forms of Socialist support for the war. When one of the German delegates, Georg Ledebour, attacked him by saying it was easy to issue revolutionary appeals to the masses after having taken refuge abroad, Lenin replied that the prosecuting attorney of the Czarist government had accused him in similar terms—but he, Lenin, expected a different kind of language from a Socialist. Finally Lenin decided to sign the manifesto that emerged from the Zimmerwald Conference. He was ready to march hand in hand with unstable elements inasmuch as the Zimmerwald statement, despite its limitations, was, in his own words, "a step forward toward an ideological and practical break with opportunism and social-chauvinism."

This did not prevent Lenin from being inflexible in the realm of ideas toward those Socialists who distorted Marxist teachings and indulged in intellectual and philosophical dilettantism. His letters to Maxim Gorki, then in Capri, insisted on the obligation of a party member to fight against any propaganda he was convinced was mistaken and harmful. He criticized the "leftist" opportunists, reserving harsh language for Trotsky, whom he called "a careerist and factionalist." He waxed ironical over "Bogdanov and Co.," and at one moment said he agreed with Plekhanov against Bogdanov.

I arrived in Switzerland in 1916 from Berlin, where I had taken part in the first anti-war demonstrations, by the side of Rosa Luxemburg. As soon as I came to Switzerland, I was able to follow closely Lenin's campaigns in Zurich, Berne, and elsewhere. At the Zimmerwald Conference, near Berne, held in September, 1915, Lenin already assumed leadership of the left-wing group that held: "This war is not our war." They were not numerous, only eight delegates in all; yet Lenin insisted that a small group with a clear political line is more effective than a group twenty times larger that lacks a guiding revolutionary principle.

In writing *Imperialism: The Highest Stage of Capitalism*, Lenin used the Central Library of Zurich. From time to time he had to report as an émigré to the Swiss police. In one of his statements to the police he defined his status: "I am neither a deserter nor an insubordinate person but a political émigré from the 1905 Revolution." A confidential police report at the beginning of 1917 indicates that Lenin and his wife had a joint monthly income of 200–250 Swiss francs.

March 15, 1917, was a decisive date in his period of exile. After eating, he was getting ready to go to the library when a Polish Socialist comrade arrived and told him: "Haven't you heard? The Revolution has broken out in Russia." Lenin ran to the building of the *Neue Züriche Zeitung*, where important last-minute bulletins were posted on the outside wall. Yes, a general strike had begun in Petrograd. Soldiers were fraternizing with workers. From that moment Lenin thought only of returning to Russia. Now every day he had to spend in Switzerland became unendurable. He sought to lessen his tension by giving lectures. On March 27 he spoke in Zurich on "The Tasks of the Bolshevik Party in the Russian Revolution." Already he foresaw the triumph of the October Revolution.

The historical process of revolution knows periods of slowdown, but these are simply preparatory stages for new eruptions. When a people digests its revolution, to use one of Victor Hugo's images, like an immense boa constrictor that has just swallowed a tiger, it feels tired and sleepy; then other peoples carry forward the constant struggle against exploitation and shame. Hegel has described history as a constant forward march of the world spirit, in which peoples and nations succeed one another, from one era to another, in pursuing a goal that can never be given up because humanity's fate is indissolubly linked with it. Where one least suspects it, inert masses rise up, and they in turn stimulate the energies of other peoples worn out in the course of a century-old struggle. Over the vast European land mass and extending far into the Asian continent a new and numerous amalgam of peoples was about to make an impressive entrance on the stage of revolution. Russians, Poles, South Slavs, and many others—they were now displaying powerful signs of life and making themselves felt in every direction.

From his early years in exile in Switzerland, Lenin had been writing books and pamphlets that laid the basis for the subsequent success of the October Revolution in 1917. In the summer of 1905 his brochure "Two Tactics of Social Democracy in the Democratic Revolution" appeared. In contrast to what he considered dangerous confusionism on the part of the Mensheviks, Lenin stressed the Bolshevik position: the working class was the only genuinely revolutionary class, the driving force of the democratic revolution. The Mensheviks, on the other hand, argued that the political leadership of the democratic revolution should be left to the liberal bourgeoisie, while the workers within the general movement should limit themselves to demanding higher wages and more humane labor legislation. His polemic with the Mensheviks did not prevent Lenin from trying to promote in every way possible the unity of the working-class movement. This, he asserted, was indispensable if they were successfully to confront Czarist power, which, though weakened after the defeat inflicted on Russia by Japan in the Russo-Japanese War (1904–1905), still possessed an oppressive apparatus capable of crushing a disunited opposition. Lenin corresponded diligently with the Central Office of the Second International, with a view to eventual negotiations for party unity with the Mensheviks.

For this was one of Lenin's strong points: he combined firmness in defense of principles and freedom from any trace of opportunism with flexibility in relations with other political organizations fighting against Czarism. He was not a leader who insisted: "Join me, or I won't have anything to do with you." He was always ready to come to an understanding with the other Socialists, while maintaining a clear-cut line of doctrinal separation between him and the others. (This same conception of revolutionary tactics was applied many years later when the Chinese Communists rose to power in their country.)

In retrospect, no one can overestimate the importance of Lenin's stay in Switzerland in forming the Bolshevik Party and preparing the Russian Revolution. From May, 1895, to April, 1917, he spent large stretches of time in that land, studying, writing, and speaking at public and private meetings in Geneva, Berne, Lausanne, and Zurich. Although he admired the Swiss landscape, he was less enthusiastic about his Swiss comrades, with the exception of a few who adopted his revolutionary line. He had come to Switzerland as a young man, as a delegate from the Social Democratic group of St. Petersburg, to make contact with the "Emancipation of Labor" group of Russian exiles led by Georgi Plekhanov. Returning in 1895, after his first visit to Switzerland, by way of Berlin, Lenin, to his great regret, was unable to visit Friedrich Engels there. Engels, seriously ill, died on August 15, 1895, in London.

In 1900 Lenin returned to Geneva and proposed to Plekhanov that he collaborate on the newspaper *Iskra* (*The Spark*), which owed its title to the reply of the Decembrist revolutionaries to the poet Pushkin: "From the spark the flame will burst forth." *Iskra* was born at the dawn of the new century. It was a small paper, as befitted an illegal publication that had to be introduced into enemy territory. Printed at various places—Leipzig, London—it was later reproduced in Baku, where it utilized mats smuggled in from abroad. Lenin has described the beginnings of *Iskra*: "We were a small, solid group, traveling along a steep and difficult path, firmly holding one another's hands. We were surrounded on all sides by enemies. But stoutheartedly we always refused to compromise." To those who claimed that one had to "adapt oneself to reality," Lenin replied: "No! We must change reality!"

Lenin lived with his wife, Nadezhda Krupskaya, and her mother in Sécheron, the working-class suburb of Geneva. A good portion of his meager income went for letter-writing: sometimes as many as three hundred letters a month when the paper had to suspend publication. He was not dismayed by the diminishing number of his collaborators. At one point when the creation of a "collective of propagandists" was being considered, a comrade visited Lenin from St. Petersburg and asked him how many were in the "collective": "At the moment one—myself." Krupskaya wrote in a letter to Maxim Litvinov: "We must admit we are in a precarious position. It's terrible not to have money. The Mensheviks are much better off in that respect. We have had to begin the paper on credit. But we do not despair." When the paper could not be issued, letters and pamphlets substituted for it. In this regard Lenin set an example for all revolutionary movements that came after him. No lack of money, no reduction of personnel to a bare minimum, could justify the lack of political activity. He worked as much as he could with what he had. And in due course this work was richly rewarded.

From Geneva, Lenin gave direction to the movement within Russia. His replies to questions addressed to him from inside his country were clear: thus, workers in the Baku oil fields who had gone out on strike, or comrades who asked him how to behave in court as political defendants, felt implicit confidence in his advice. In the second-named instance Lenin advised his followers always to name the party, to call it "our party," but never to reveal a thing about it. He cautioned them not to be impressed by attorneys who urged their clients to say they were nonpolitical in order to gain their freedom. Lenin stressed that a courtroom attitude combining firmness with reserve would gain new adherents for their cause.

Deeply versed in French social history, Lenin reserved his greatest admiration for the Jacobins. In conversations with Russian comrades in Geneva, he ridiculed Martov, who, at a meeting of Mensheviks, had declared that there was nothing in common between Social Democracy and Jacobinism. Earlier he had criticized Vera Zasulich for viewing the forward march of the working class through the eyes of the liberals. "Real revolutionary Social Democrats know perfectly well what Jacobinism is," he repeated on several occasions. When he argued he was vehement but controlled—and always dialectical. As an orator he was neither wordy nor flamboyant, but he had a driving force like that of a locomotive engine. He smiled when opponents called him "Robespierre-Jacobin." He would reply: "The Jacobin position in struggle was put to the test by history at the end of the eighteenth century. It was not a struggle in kid gloves, not a sentimental struggle; it accepted violence when necessary, and was not a prey to dejection caused by so-called questions of conscience. Naturally, those who place above all the sacred respect for what they have defined as democratic principles cannot understand what it means to be a Jacobin. Nor can it be understood by those to whom revolution is mainly an intellectual game, and who think that one can attain the heights of audacity in thought and language without going out in the streets. Nevertheless, one has to go out in the streets, even though the guillotine is being built there. The responsibility for blood falls on those who resist the inexorable march of history. Without a Jacobin position it is impossible to make a good bourgeois revolution —let alone a Socialist revolution."

Lenin waited impatiently for news from Russia about the workers' demonstration in Kiev and the spreading strike wave there. That was in 1903, two years before the 1905 Revolution. To a comrade who had just arrived in Geneva and told him that a Bolshevik had addressed a thousand persons in Rostov, Lenin answered, not without a touch of envy: "That's a real meeting! When I was in St. Petersburg I was satisfied if I could talk in front of fifteen workers." But to Lenin, talking before fifteen workers was not a waste of time. Surely one of the reasons for his eventual success was his belief that at the outset one did not have to have a large number of adherents to engage in political activism. The essential thing was the homogeneous character of the core of activists, however few and insignificant they might appear to others. This meant that in the years 1902–1903, prior to the mass upheaval in 1905, he relied on a Jacobin-style group which, though small, was utterly determined to fight. During these conversations in Geneva, with Krupskaya at his side, his interest quickened whenever someone who had just come from Russia narrated in detail clashes between strikers and the police. "It is not a question," Lenin said, "of being able to fight in a figurative sense. It is not enough to be able to fight brilliantly with the pen or the spoken word. It is good that the students march onto the streets with the red flag unfurled, shouting: 'Down with autocracy!' But autocracy will not be demolished with the trumpets of Jericho. We must begin to destroy it physically, with massive blows."

One day the conversational theme was the nineteenth-century Russian novelist Goncharov. Lenin saw in the hero of one of his novels a caricature of a revolutionary. But he found this useful as a warning to vacillating comrades. "I would like very much to take not one but many of our comrades and shut them in a room to read *Oblomov*. And when they beg for mercy, saying they can't stand it any longer, I would ask them: 'Now, do you understand what Oblomovism is? Do you realize that it is planted inside of you? Have you decided once and for all to free yourself of that sickness?' "

In praising Jacobinism, Lenin also sought to establish what he considered their correct theory of the dictatorship of the proletariat as an instrument for keeping the Socialist revolution alive after the seizure of power. At times, even when he was under severe attack, he took a stand against those who in the name of alleged political realism preached compromise among the various political groupings. "They, the Girondists, are the opportunists," he would assert, always thinking in terms of the French Revolution. With due regard for the changed circumstances in his own time, Lenin felt that Jacobinism meant three things: acceptance of dictatorship of the proletariat; second, centralism in the organization of the party; third, discipline in the party. "Let us not be fooled by those who in the name of freedom of ideas speak of 'blind submission' and 'barracks discipline.' Many of them reflect anarchist phraseology and the customary petulance of intellectuals."

Curiously, when it was not a question of politics and the problems of socialism, Lenin in these Geneva conversations showed himself to be much broader and more understanding than some of the other comrades touched with Oblomovism. Take, for example, the subject of the poet Pushkin, whom Lenin loved. Later, after the victory of the Russian Revolution, during a visit to the Moscow School of Fine Arts in the early 1920's, he shrugged his shoulders disdainfully when several students claimed that Pushkin was a bourgeois. To Lenin, he was the greatest poet Russia had had.

The Revolution of 1905, although a defeat, was a kind of dress rehearsal, rich in lessons, for the October Revolution in 1917. Stalin (then called Koba) supported Lenin from his modest post as a local leader in Georgia and continued to support him in the bitter Bolshevik-Menshevik controversy that followed the defeat. To the Mensheviks, in the situation then prevailing in Russia, it was the middle class that had to lead the Revolution. The Bolsheviks did not yield on this point. In their view, the working class had to assume leadership of the Revolution. On the other hand, they conceded that the Revolution had to be "democratic and bourgeois" and nothing more. This realistic approach to the possibilities in any given period was characteristic. Revolutionary realism led Lenin and, later, Stalin to the formulation of the principle of "timely retreat" which Mao Tse-tung later developed in his theory of revolutionary war. Indeed, Lenin wrote after the failure of 1905: "The revolutionary parties must complete their education. They have learned now to attack. Now they must learn that victory is impossible so long as they do not know both how to attack and how to retreat correctly." Of all the revolutionary and opposition groups that were beaten in 1905, the Bolsheviks staged the most orderly retreat.

Both Lenin and Stalin, from quite different levels at that time, were convinced that the eclipse of the revolutionary movement after the Revolution of 1905 was temporary. The street demonstrations on the occasion of Leo Tolstoy's funeral justified that hope. In 1912 the workers struck in protest against the shooting down of "agitators" in the Lena gold fields in Siberia. World War I, despite the introduction of "military rule," did not succeed in stifling the revolutionary unrest. The agitation continued in various forms, extending to the battle front and fortifying the home front for the decisive days ahead. In St. Petersburg strikes and demonstrations at the end of 1916 in commemoration of "Bloody Sunday" in the 1905 Revolution, signaled a new and turbulent entry of the Russian people on the stage of history.

One month before the October Revolution of 1917, Stalin, who acted as a liaison between Lenin, in hiding, and the Bolsheviks' Central Committee, presented a memorandum by Lenin entitled "Marxism and Insurrection." "To treat insurrection in a Marxist manner," wrote Lenin, "means to treat it as an art. We must proceed, without a moment more of delay, to organize the general staff of the forces of insurrection. We must distribute our forces; place the regiments in which we have the greatest confidence in the most important places; surround the Alexandreisky Theater, where the so-called Democratic Assembly is assembled; seize the Peter and Paul Fortress; capture the communications buildings and establish telephone contact with all the factories." Feeling that he was too far away from the capital to outline in detail the political orientation the impending uprising should have, Lenin submitted his memorandum as a suggestion. Within the Central Committee a lively discussion of the memorandum broke out. Years later, after Lenin's death, Trotsky accused Stalin of having played a double game on that occasion. Yet the evidence indicates that here too Stalin supported Lenin.

Stalin also supported him during the controversy over the Treaty of Brest-Litovsk. Lenin proceeded from the viewpoint that the

Soviets were incapable of pursuing a revolutionary war. Consequently they had to make peace. The leftist Communists did not agree with Lenin. They insisted that despite all the sacrifices they had suffered on behalf of Russia, the Russian Revolution had to remain faithful to the cause of European revolution. Stalin voted with Lenin and his party faction for peace. To him the European revolutionary movement was only a possibility: the Russian Revolution was a reality; its fate could not be risked for such a possibility.

Rereading *Imperialism* afresh today, one is impressed by an aspect to which insufficient attention has been paid. I refer to Lenin's ever-present sense of the practical. He wanted the work to be published legally inside Russia. Hence he worked hard to use a language that, on the one hand, would leave no doubt whatever as to his position and intentions, and, on the other hand, would have a certain moderation in style that would enable it to appear within Russia and gain widespread distribution among the workers. We cannot stress this too often: Lenin always envisaged a political question from a strictly realistic point of view. Thus his wish to see his own government defeated in the war did not derive from his hatred of the Czarist regime, which was profound indeed, but from his realization that its defeat was indispensable for the Revolution to triumph. That is why he assailed the "Social Patriots" so sharply. It was not so much that his Socialist conscience was outraged by their attitude; but they constituted a serious obstacle to revolutionary action.

During those war years the main aim of his writings was to prevent the reactionaries from escaping defeat by exploiting the sense of confusion prevailing in the pacifist movement. His "Theses" written in October, 1915, dealt extensively with this point. In summary he wrote:

First thesis. Regarding the summoning of a Constituent National Assembly. It is not enough to demand it. It must be made clear who should summon it. If this task is left to the Czar, one can say goodbye to the Revolution. It must be summoned by the popular forces, through their political organizations and with a very concrete program: a democratic republic, confiscation of large landed estates, and an eight-hour day for the workers.

Second thesis. Convince the workers to slow down their work in the armaments factories then operating in Russia.

Third thesis. Socialist propaganda should be extended to the farms and urban neighborhoods. This Socialist propaganda should be in the form of a program containing specific demands: freeing the deputies of the Duma arrested for having voted against war credits; immediate cessation of hostilities as soon as a worsening in the military situation creates a situation favorable to such a demand. Concrete demands. No eloquent pronouncements.

Fourth thesis. Support councils (Soviets) of worker-delegates and similar institutions. Give them a very specific plan of work and avoid too many empty discussions. They must be considered organs of revolutionary power, and those who lead them must have a high sense of responsibility.

Fifth thesis. An analysis of the outlines of the future Russian Revolution, which at the beginning will be a bourgeois-democratic revolution.

Sixth thesis. Despite all demagogy, do not promise revolutionary measures that cannot be attained.

Seventh and eighth theses. With regard to alliances with other revolutionary forces: this is possible with the Social Democrats if they really move into action. Impossible with revolutionary chauvinists.

Ninth thesis. Connected with the previous thesis. With unusual foresight it warns that, after the victory of the Kerensky revolution, an attempt will be made to continue the war at all costs. "We are against chauvinists, whether they are republicans or revolutionaries. We are against them and in favor of the unity of the international working class in the name of the Socialist Revolution."

Tenth thesis. Reply to the question: Can the working class assume the leadership of the bourgeois revolution in Russia? It answers this question in the affirmative.

Eleventh thesis. Contains the whole program of international action of a revolutionary Russia in which the Bolsheviks have taken control. "We shall propose peace to all the nations at war, on condition that they free the colonies and all nations that are oppressed and deprived of their rights. Neither Germany, nor England, nor France will accept this. Then what do we do? We shall have to undertake revolutionary wars." That is, wars of national liberation—the thesis that fifty years later engaged the Moscow-Peking Communist world. In October, 1915, Lenin left nothing to chance. His "Theses" is essential reading for an understanding of the course taken by the Russian Revolution.

From the day in March, 1917, when Czarist power was dislodged from its centuries-old position until the day eight months later when workers' power was established, Lenin kept his bearings in the midst of a highly fluid, dramatic, and contradictory situation.

In 1967, on the occasion of the fiftieth anniversary of the October Revolution, a host of memoirs, books, and special issues of periodicals were published. These publications, containing vast amounts of documentation, exposed the slanders and absurdities of Lenin's detractors in the years following the Bolsheviks' assumption of power. Incapable of infusing new life into the Socialist movement, the Socialist leaders of the Second International between the two world wars as well as after World War II, most of them mediocre and wrongheaded, tried to distort Lenin's great work—in theory as well as in practice. But by his contribution to the march of socialism, by basing the Russian Revolution on firm foundations, Lenin changed the future of the world. He made the twentieth century the century of the great revolutions—the century of socialism. His towering figure stands out as one who continued and successfully carried forward the ideas of Marx and Engels.

In the fourth thesis above, the one concerning workers' councils (Soviets), there is a point that most of Lenin's biographers seem to have glossed over. In a speech given in January, 1917, in Zurich, on the occasion of the twelfth anniversary of "Bloody Sunday" in the 1905 Revolution, Lenin discussed this problem at some length. Significantly, at that moment he did not yet attribute unusual importance to the workers' councils; indeed, he assigned them a rather subsidiary role. In 1905, the Workers' Soviet of St. Petersburg, headed by a lawyer with no party affiliations, Khrustalev-Nosar, played an important part. Precisely because Khrustalev was a non-party man, he was able to unite all the others and avoid the punishing in-fighting of various factions. In the light of the 1905 experience, Lenin sought to avoid giving the Workers' Soviets a distinctively Bolshevik stamp; and in fact he gave them a secondary role. Events after February, 1917, and the weakness of the Kerensky government, however, caused him to change his mind: now he saw in the Soviets a powerful instrument by which to seize power.

Once he returned to Russia, Lenin lost interest in the Constituent Assembly because he believed that the Soviets were superior to parliamentary democracy. He allowed the Social Democratic and Social Revolutionary parties, temporary winners in the parliamentary jousting, to waste their energies in the scramble for jobs and the votes on minor questions. There was one exception: continuation of the war. To Lenin this was *the* major question. Kerensky listened readily to the Czarist generals who, supported by French and British diplomats and agents, thought they could still salvage the military situation. Lenin did not think this was possible; moreover, he felt a choice had to be made between war and revolution.

When the right moment arrived, Lenin threw all the weight of his influence on the side of the Workers' Soviets. He was aided in this by a comrade with outstanding organizing ability, Vyacheslav Molotov. In the inter-party fight between Kerensky and Molotov for their respective groups in the St. Petersburg Soviet, Kerensky shone as an orator, whereas Molotov was more adept at the patient job of proceeding step by step, until a solid organization was built.

Lenin's political will to power—his vision and determination—contrasted with Kerensky's lack of political will: when the issue was joined, he was bound to win. He was undaunted by the fact that he was in a minority; he was used to leading a minority to victory. In February, 1917, the Bolshevik Party had barely 24,000 members. In the vital centers of St. Petersburg and Moscow its membership numbered 2,000 and 600, respectively. In numbers it seemed overwhelmed in the midst of the Social Democrats and the Social Revolutionaries, the latter enjoying greater mass support at that time. But whereas the other leaders allowed themselves to be swayed by the ever-changing situation, Lenin knew at all times what he wanted. His revolutionary logic was compelling. In every one of his actions during those decisive days, he concentrated on preparing the Revolution. At the first All-Russian Congress of the Soviets, in June, 1917, Lenin answered the Socialists: "The Citizen Minister of Communications [Tseretelli] has stated that in Russia no party is ready to assume total power. I reply that there is one party. All the parties are struggling for power, as they should. And our party does not deny that. We are ready at any moment to assume total power."

Among Kerensky's many mistakes was his failure to pay prompt attention to the agrarian question. Thus he lost the support of the soldiers, a majority of whom were peasants in uniform. Lenin, on the other hand, adopted the slogan: "Peace and Freedom" and added to it: "Bread and Land." With his consummate sense of the practical, he dealt with the agrarian question and at the same time won over the peasants and soldiers. He made a distinction between the active members of the Social Revolutionary Party and the masses of soldiers and peasants who supported it. The same was true of the Mensheviks. He would willingly have collaborated with Martov, who led a small group of internationalist-minded Mensheviks and for whom Lenin had great personal esteem. But apart from the fact that Martov had very little influence on the masses, he insisted on following a policy equidistant from the various opposing factions.

Lenin fought against Kerensky's government but without allowing the reactionaries to exploit the existing differences in the opposition. His aim was to replace the government with workers' power. Yet when General Kornilov tried to stage a *coup d'état* in the summer of 1917, Lenin forgot the persecutions his supporters had suffered at the hands of the Kerensky government and ordered the Bolsheviks to support that government. This order by Lenin brought the Kronstadt sailors, vital shock troops of the Revolution, to St. Petersburg to defend the Kerensky government against the uprising of the Czarist generals.

Despite his back-breaking organizational work, Lenin found time to write one of his most important works, *The State and Revolution*, two months before the decisive attack. In it Lenin proposed five revolutionary democratic measures: (1) fusion of all banks into a single bank, with its operations controlled by the state; (2) nationalization of monopoly capital groups, including the sugar, oil, and metallurgy combines; (3) abolition of secret commercial agreements; (4) forced cartelization: that is, all industrialists, merchants, and employers in every category must join cartels or syndicates; (5) compulsory formation of consumers' societies.

At one point, around September, 1917, Lenin was virtually

isolated in his own party. He was convinced that they must proceed directly toward an uprising. Trotsky supported him in this, but a majority of the Bolshevik leaders were opposed. Discussions went on until October 10, when at a secret session of the Central Committee the differences were resolved. Lenin won the day. By a resounding majority, with only two votes opposed, a motion in favor of an immediate uprising was passed.

As military disasters occurred, the atmosphere in and around the Imperial Court lent itself increasingly to all sorts of intrigues and plots. Nicholas and Alexandra had a weakness for seers and charlatans. Years before the war a Frenchman notorious for his spiritualist experiments had resided in the palace. In a séance around the "magic" table the spirit of the previous Czar had appeared and counseled his son to rule with a firm hand. Such "spirits" were useful to the reactionaries, who consistently opposed all types of reforms. Later the ghosts of the imperial chamber became a flesh-and-blood reality: a peasant from Pokrovskoya in Siberia, Grigori Rasputin, entered upon the scene. His exploits have since become an inexhaustible theme for cheap, sensationalist books and films.

Supported by Anna Virubova, confidante of the Czarina, and claiming to be the only one able to cure the heir to the throne of his hereditary hemophilia, Rasputin became a veritable maker and breaker of cabinet ministries. In him the Germans had a powerful source of influence at the Court. The British ambassador to Russia during World War I, George Buchanan, has given specific details of pro-German machinations at St. Petersburg. By April, 1915, the Czarina—she was called "the German woman" in some circles of the national-minded nobility—told Czar Nicholas II about a letter from "Ermin," in which the Germans made concrete suggestions for a separate peace. "Ermin" was the nickname of the Czarina's brother, the Grand Duke of Hesse. Stockholm was suggested as a likely place for a meeting between Russian and German envoys. Rumors of the letter spread, and those who were hostile to Empress Alexandra made the most of the report. Buchanan writes that possibilities of a palace revolt were hinted at. During a dinner at the embassy, a Russian friend who held a high government post told him that the only question to be decided was who had to be eliminated: the Czar, the Czarina, or both.

This was a defeatist, not a win-the-war, outlook. Toward the end of the autumn of 1916, Lenin—whom I saw in Zurich—knew that his political analysis of the situation and his proposals for an activist policy were gaining ever wider support within Russia. The strike wave in October, 1916, had lessened in intensity; but the severe winter that followed and the steeply rising prices of foodstuffs convinced him that the workers and peasants would be forced to take to the streets. Lenin's prophecy was accurate. On January 9, 1917, the anniversary date of a brutal police assault on a workers' demonstration during the Revolution of 1905, factory meetings organized by the Bolsheviks were held in many areas. From the factories the workers marched into the streets: in Moscow, in front of the Bolshoi Theater, cries of "Down with the war!" could be heard. A fine sketch by the artist Savisky shows the violence of the encounter with the mounted police. A report from the chief of police to the government stated: "The idea of a general strike is gaining ground daily, and is becoming as popular as it was in 1905."

Note how preoccupied the Czarist authorities were with what had happened twelve years before—another confirmation of the theory that no serious revolutionary effort is lost. What may seem at the moment a defeat for socialism proves to be—if the struggle has been rightly fought—the germ of new victories.

Throughout January, 1917, one strike followed another. It was a mounting spiral that could not be checked. Now the villages joined the cities—St. Petersburg, Moscow, Nizhni Novgorod, Baku—in the insurrectionary movement. Constant requisitioning of grain and livestock had ruined the countryside. Hatred for the rich peasants, the kulaks, was intensified when it was seen that they even exploited hunger by first hoarding, then selling their cereals at exorbitant prices.

On February 5 the government resorted to the traditional measure employed when faced with an incipient revolution: mass arrests. Its sole effect was to broaden the base of the opposition. On February 14 the Mensheviks called on the workers to demonstrate in defense of the Duma. But the Russian working class was not overly enthusiastic about the future of the parliament; they already had experience with the workings of formal democracy. The workers of the Putilov factory paraded that day with red flags on which were inscribed:

"Down with absolutism! Down with the war!" As the afternoon of February 28 drew to a close, there was a feeling of combat in the air. The first skirmishes of the preceding twenty-four hours had ended with a victory for the forces of "law and order." But the victory was short-lived. The Russian proletariat had learned its lesson from the Revolution twelve years before. If they meant to win, this time they had to make contact with the soldiers. This was a much more realistic policy than that of those left-wing parliamentarians who claimed to be close to the masses and able to anticipate their reactions. As soon as these contacts between workers and soldiers commenced, the government realized what a serious turn in events had occurred. Rodzianko, presiding officer of the Duma, sent an urgent message to the Czar's headquarters, urging the immediate formation of a government that would enjoy public confidence. Documents published later revealed the Czar's reaction. "That fat Rodzianko," said Nicholas II to Fredericks, his Minister of the Interior, "getting excited as usual. He has written me a lot of nonsense. I wouldn't even dream of answering him."

The soldiers, on the other hand, answered the workers' appeals. Lieutenant Kirpichnikov, of the Volinsk regiment of the Imperial Guard, persuaded some three hundred soldiers to join him in the workers' demonstrations. The revolutionary fever spread rapidly from one district to another. Armed workers aided soldiers who were defying their officers, flouting military discipline, and declaring common cause with the people. Among the regiments that followed the Volinsk were the Preobrazhensky and the Lithuanian. In a few hours St. Petersburg was alive with trucks and private cars loaded with armed soldiers and sailors, filling the air with rifle salvos and shouts for the Revolution. The Czar's headquarters issued an order to repress the movement regardless of the number of victims. But this time the Revolution had the Bolshevik Party, which, despite its small membership, was undoubtedly the strongest, clearest thinking, and most determined of the existing political parties in Russia. Moreover, in Lenin it had a leader of genius.

Ten months before the actual seizure of power, in fact from the very first day the revolutionary forces took to the streets, leadership had passed into the hands of the Bolsheviks. And Czarist repression came up against a man with a will of steel who all his life had concentrated on one theme: revolution.

The Czar chose General Ivanov, notorious for the harshness with which he had stifled the Kronstadt uprising in 1905, to lead the troops against the disorders in St. Petersburg. But as they approached the outskirts of the city, many of them went over to the Revolution. The High Command, realizing that further efforts in that direction would only increase the number of rebellious units, renounced the attempt to capture the capital. They turned back; and Nicholas II had to beat a hasty retreat.

On this occasion, no time was lost in setting up an effective mechanism for the people's resistance. The very night the workers and armed soldiers poured out onto the streets of St. Petersburg en masse, a Soviet of the city's deputies, delegates, and workers was formed. The first phase of the Revolution was now safeguarded. As for the role played by the Soviets in 1917, it is instructive to note Lenin's reaction to the duality of public power in March of that year: on the one hand, the provisional government of the liberals; on the other, a new and second form of power, the Soviets. Here in embryo was a form of workers' government, with its precedent in history, the Paris Commune. Writing at this time, Lenin quoted from Marx's opinion of the Paris Commune, applying Marx's comments to the Soviets in 1917.

In Lenin's view, we repeat, Soviet democracy was superior to parliamentary democracy. But the essential point was that, once the Revolution began, it had to remain in the hands of those capable of defending it and of thwarting any reactionary counter-coup. Hence Lenin saw nothing wrong in allowing the existing National Assembly to function as a kind of Upper Chamber, so long as real power was increasingly concentrated in the Soviets. For in 1917 the liberal bourgeoisie in Russia represented a bourgeoisie without power and without a program.

Once the October Revolution had triumphed, Lenin displayed his many-sided abilities as a revolutionary leader and statesman in the difficult first two years of the infant Soviet Republic. The first serious crisis arose in the spring of 1918; should the Soviets sign a separate peace with the Germans, a harsh, Prussian-style peace, or should they continue in the war and jeopardize the whole future of the Revolution? Lenin's closest friends and collaborators agreed with the Left Social Revolutionaries that it was better to go down fighting, red flag held high, than to accept the humiliating Treaty of Brest-Litovsk. Lenin, however, saw things differently. With unusual clarity and a distaste for empty theatrical gestures, he hammered home his viewpoint. Since they could no longer make war, they must make peace and arouse the masses to protect and consolidate their Revolution.

Arguing against the utopian extremists and the syndicalists, Lenin wrote in 1920 his *Left-Wing Communism: An Infantile Disorder*. For decades since, his ideas in this booklet have been tendentiously interpreted and exploited, whenever bureaucratic "derevolutionized" leaders have sought to hold back the masses marching ahead of them in the fight for true socialism.

Again Lenin showed his realism in the spring of 1921, with the introduction of the NEP—the "New Economic Policy." His first step was to suspend the forced requisition of grain. He had never felt that by a single move one could convince millions of small peasant proprietors of the need for socialized agriculture in Russia. The NEP allowed the Russian peasant, once he had delivered a portion of his crop to the government, to dispose of the rest as he saw fit; at the same time, it re-established small businesses and small-scale industry. The state retained the key elements of the economy: banks, foreign trade, heavy industry, and the railroads. Many foreign Communists, notably the well-known Dutch Communist Hermann Gorter, sharply criticized the NEP. But it enabled the Soviets to overcome one of the major crises in the newborn revolutionary state.

In 1917, when the order was given for a revolutionary seizure of power, the Kamenev-Zinoviev group in the Bolshevik Party did not believe in the possibility of a victorious uprising. Desirous of maintaining party unity at such a crucial moment, Lenin sought to win them over. He did not succeed. Their stubborn opposition continued throughout the Revolution. In fact, even after victory the Kamenev-Zinoviev group doubted that the Bolsheviks could retain power. Despite this, Lenin did not remove them from party leadership. Quite the contrary: just as he considered his previous differences with Trotsky at an end, so it was with Kamenev and Zinoviev, who had sided with Trotsky at every critical juncture. Never reproaching them for their vacillations, Lenin entrusted them with tasks of the utmost importance.

In the first months after the October Revolution, Lenin sought to associate with the Bolshevik Party other genuinely popular forces uncompromised by a "win the war at all costs" policy. He succeeded briefly in this until the Brest-Litovsk Treaty; thereafter, however, the Left Social Revolutionaries ruptured the temporary coalition and stubbornly opposed the Bolsheviks. Between March and November, 1917, the Social Revolutionaries had split. The right wing went along with Kerensky, the left wing with Lenin. In the elections for the National Assembly the peasants had voted overwhelmingly for the Social Revolutionaries; but at the same time they had voted for land expropriation, which put them closer to Lenin than to Kerensky. Therefore it was logical for the Left Social Revolutionaries to align themselves with Lenin and the Bolsheviks. So until the split caused by the Brest-Litovsk Treaty, Bolsheviks and Left Social Revolutionaries worked together, some of the leaders of the latter group entering the Council of People's Commissars, the new revolutionary government. With the signing of the Brest-Litovsk Treaty, Lenin realized that he would face an almost impossible situation. Yet neither this prospect nor the ensuing split with the Left Social Revolutionaries, nor the skepticism of his closest collaborators, made him yield. He was convinced that he was right; and within a few months events confirmed the correctness of his position.

After signing a separate peace with Germany, the Bolshevik government had to give up all thought of economic aid from the Allied powers. This was not all. The Entente decided to blockade Russia. Its ports closed, Russia was isolated from the rest of the world in the midst of a desperate economic situation. Meanwhile the Germans had occupied the wheat-rich Ukraine and deprived Russia of the coal of the Donets Basin as well as the oil of the Caucasus, thus forcing a great many factories to shut down. Russia's former allies now became her implacable enemies. Nor was Germany any kinder after Brest-Litovsk, though Lenin had never counted on her "generosity." Now the blockade was complete: it was revolutionary Russia against all the others, a Russia cut off from its grain-growing centers, its most productive regions, and its seaports.

But it had a leader with unique qualities. Many of his closest associates were dismayed, first by the Brest-Litovsk Treaty, then when the Soviets were purged of a number of officials who had played an honorable part in the seizure of power but who now proved to be an obstacle in establishing a genuinely revolutionary state. Lenin, however, remained undaunted. He did not abolish the Soviets, although he might easily have done so in the first flush of victory after the October Revolution. He retained them as the symbol of the Revolution. But, encircled by a totally hostile world, he needed an unusually strong and clear-eyed government capable of extricating itself from one crisis after another. For there was no lack of crises—domestic and foreign. From 1918 to 1920 food rations for the workers were extremely meager. But at least there was no inequality in a time of scarcity. There was no bourgeoisie that could speculate and buy on the black market while workers' wives had to line up for hours and hours at the stores. Two years later there was famine. In the summer of 1922 I visited Russia for the first time. I was a member of the Nansen Mission, headed by the great Norwegian explorer who was a friend of Lenin's. Nansen had undertaken relief work in the Ukraine while the Americans, headed by Herbert Hoover, were mixing humanitarianism with politics in the Volga region. At that time few foreign diplomats stationed in Moscow gave the Bolshevik regime more than two more years of life. Some of them told me confidentially that economic difficulties would accomplish what military intervention had failed to achieve: put an end to the Bolsheviks.

In the midst of these critical problems Lenin felt himself sustained by the Russian workers, conscious of the fact that theirs was the first victorious working-class state in history. Their pride increased when at the Genoa Conference in April, 1922, Westerners met Russians for the first time since the October Revolution and accorded diplomatic recognition to the young Soviet state. I was in Genoa as a journalist, before leaving for Russia with the Nansen Mission. There I had interviews with Chicherin, the Soviet Foreign Commissar, as well as conversations with British Prime Minister Lloyd George and Walther Rathenau, German Foreign Minister. Both these men predicted an early demise for the Bolshevik regime; both were wrong.

Inevitably, in studying the Russian Revolution, one must deal with the Stalin-Trotsky struggle. At bottom, this fight centered on the question of "socialism in one country." At the Fifteenth Party Congress of the Soviet Communist Party, Stalin raised the question: Who would defeat whom? Lenin, in 1921, raised the same question when he introduced the New Economic Policy (NEP). Would the Soviet Union be able to coordinate its socialized industry with its rural economy, eliminate tradesmen and private capitalists, and do business on a Socialist basis; or, on the contrary, would private capitalism prevail and split the working class from the peasantry? From 1924 on, Stalin increasingly stressed the theory that it was possible to build socialism in one country. This idea appears in Lenin's last writings, in 1923, but it was Stalin who made it the basic doctrine of the Bolshevik Party. As such, it was the guide to Soviet domestic and foreign policy in the years ahead. In contrast to Stalin's assertion that a wholly Socialist society could be built in a single country, Trotsky maintained his concept of international and permanent revolution.

To translate the theory of "socialism in one country" into reality, Soviet industry had to be developed no matter what the cost. This was the signal for the introduction of the Five-Year Plans, a move which even many of Stalin's opponents grudgingly praise. The first Five-Year Plan ran from October, 1928, to October, 1933. The country was forced to increase its imports sharply in order to procure the needed machinery; money was not spared to attract foreign technical specialists. The effort was tremendous; and the results were plainly visible during World War II, when the U.S.S.R. faced a highly industrialized Germany on the battlefield. In the midst of the world economic crisis that followed the American Depression in 1929, the Soviet Union, thanks to Stalin's policy of all-out industrialization, was the only country without unemployment. The theory of "socialism in one country" resisted all anti-Stalin critiques and emerged strengthened. Its supreme test came in World War II, from which the U.S.S.R. emerged a winning power. Undoubtedly, without the Soviet Union the Allies would have found it extremely difficult to defeat the Axis powers.

To carry through his policy, Stalin played party politics to the hilt, setting one faction against another until he could assert his undisputed leadership. But no one with any sense of objectivity can deny him a key role in the fundamental problems of the Revolution. Here, therefore, we should like to trace the line he followed, at crucial junctures of his much-debated activity, from the outset to the end of his life.

Born Iosif Dzhugashvili in Gori, Georgia, near Tiflis, in 1879, Stalin attended school in that region. He early showed himself to be a diligent student endowed with an impressive memory. But he was not yet a Marxist, despite the claims of later commentators. He did, however, possess a deep feeling for social injustice. His stay in a theological seminary, from October, 1894, to May, 1899, furthered his cultural development and at the same time aroused his interest in the exploited classes. His family heritage contributed to this awakening: his father was the son of Georgian peasants, who only a few decades previously had been serfs. To carry on political work—even of a rudimentary nature—Stalin joined with a few other rebellious seminarians. To deceive the monks in charge, they had to pretend to feel a sense of their religious vocation. On leaving the seminary, Stalin knew what direction he had to take. The Russian Social Democratic Labor Party had just been founded in Minsk by a handful of Socialists. Stalin instinctively felt that no group, however small, should be disdained if it followed a firm, clear, and logical political line. As we have seen, this was a basic revolutionary attitude of his mentor, Lenin.

Stalin's revolutionary beginnings show him to have been a cautious, reserved, and wary activist in the underground movement. Around the turn of the century he was an organizer and wrote for a publication called *The Struggle*. His articles were simple and clear. The paper was, of course, an underground publication, because "since it defended the interests of the workers, the authorities could not possibly tolerate it. We did not have to fear censorship since we did not submit to it." *The Struggle* echoed the line of Lenin's *Iskra*. Many chroniclers have told how exciting an occasion it was when each new issue of *Iskra* arrived in Russia. But Stalin was not content to be merely an echo of the great voice from abroad. In his own style he repeated Lenin's arguments, and identified himself completely with the Bolshevik ideology. Lenin's influence on the twenty-year-old revolutionary was decisive. As far as action was concerned, Stalin favored street demonstrations, because in the streets the workers could get a better training in struggle than behind the closed doors of a meeting. Organizing street demonstrations became a specialty of this young would-be revolutionary: the success of the first May Day demonstration in the Caucasus, in 1901, gave proof of his skill.

Taking the *nom de guerre*, first of Koba, then of Stalin, the young revolutionary was well known within two years. In 1903, while serving sentences in the jails of Kutais and Batum, he was elected to the executive committee of the Transcaucasian Federation. There, as elsewhere, he defended Lenin's ideas in the inner-party controversies that foreshadowed the Bolshevik-Menshevik split. At the Russian Social Democratic Congress of Brussels (1903), the Mensheviks accused Lenin of seeking to impose a barracklike discipline on socialism. To Stalin the discipline never seemed excessive. He defined the Party as a militant group which, less numerous than the working class, was superior to the latter in consciousness and experience, and more cohesive than any other workers' organization. Many years later cohesiveness was the basic reason for his impatience with many of the original leaders of the Party who, brilliant though they were, sought to introduce into the Party a diversity of views about the same problem. Stalin never believed that one could be a member of the Party, accept its program, and continue to engage in factional activity. Bolshevism had to be a monolithic party in victory and thereafter.

In the struggle launched against the Workers' Opposition in 1921, the group led by Shliapnikov, former Commissar of Labor, and Alexandra Kollontai, which asserted that the trade unions as direct representatives of the working class should plan and direct the national economy, Stalin was on the side of the Party. A few dissident leaders were expelled from the Party, but no severe punishments were meted out. Those who sympathized with the Workers' Opposition were replaced by elements more loyal to the Party line, among them Vyacheslav Molotov. Many years later,

during the attacks on Stalin that followed the publication of the
Khrushchev report in 1956, Molotov was the only one of the old-time
Bolshevik leaders who refused to take an anti-Stalin stand, even
though it led to his being stripped of all his posts.

Throughout the civil-war period, the highest organ of the Party—
the Political Bureau (Politburo)—consisted of five members: Lenin,
Trotsky, Stalin, Kamenev, and Bukharin. When Stalin was later
named general secretary of the Party, his power was publicly
confirmed. But in fact this power had been increasing even before
Lenin's death, even though many, including Party members, were
not aware of it. This increasing power of the general secretary
disturbed Lenin, as did the sharp antagonism between Stalin and
Trotsky, both of whom Lenin described as "the most capable leaders
of the present Central Committee." A whole volume would be
required to describe the main incidents in the intense factional fight
that followed Lenin's death in 1924. In a famous "postscript" of
January 3, 1923, to his political will of December 25, 1922, Lenin
foresaw the dangers of excessive personal power and anticipated the
impassioned and terrible controversies of the ensuing years.

Until Stalin emerged as the head of the Party, the combinations at
the top varied: at the outset a triumvirate of Stalin, Zinoviev, and
Kamenev within the Politburo was aligned against Trotsky while
Lenin was still alive. Lenin died in Gorki on January 21, 1924. All the
evidence from the funeral speeches presents Stalin as having served
under Lenin without any disagreement on crucial questions. He
appeared humble and saddened, publicly asserting that no one could
fill the immense vacuum left by the disappearance of the creator of
the first working-class state in the world. But a few months after
Lenin's death, at the end of 1924, the opposing viewpoints clashed.
In opposition to Stalin's belief in socialism in one country, Trotsky
advanced his theory of the permanence of the revolution, as well as
its universality. This was the heart of the confrontation. Then came
some of the other problems that beset the Soviet Union until the
outbreak of World War II: differences over agricultural policy, the
development of industry, and military policy. These clashes reached
a dramatic and sanguinary climax in the trials of the 1930's and the
subsequent repression and executions. But in the midst of so many
personal tragedies, Stalin held firmly to a position that subordinated

everything to the survival of a revolution which he felt was constantly being threatened from within and without. To judge Stalin from the time of Lenin's death to his own death merely as a crude, bloodthirsty despot obsessed with a hunger for power, as do many Western writers and historians, is to go counter to historical truth.

Once Trotsky left the War Commissariat, the triumvirate in the Politburo set up to "contain" him lost its *raison d'être*. Thus, for example, Stalin and Bukharin agreed in the mid-1920's that the revolutionary period in Europe was over; whereas Zinoviev and Kamenev soon emerged as "Left" Communists, protesting against the "opportunism" of the other two leaders. There was one moment when Zinoviev and Kamenev came close to Trotsky's position: another moment when Bukharin drew away from Stalin. The alignments shifted, until by 1929 Stalin had definitely asserted his control. In my view, a comprehensive study of this whole period demonstrates that Stalin's opponents were unable to judge correctly or appreciate his qualities as a political leader and a statesman.

The survivors of a war that cost the U.S.S.R. twenty million lives—a fact too easily forgotten only a few years later when alliances shifted and to many Soviet Russia suddenly became the main enemy, whereas Germany, the wartime aggressor, became the friend—remembered Stalin's great speech less than twelve days after Hitler's troops invaded the Soviet Union. It is one of the great speeches of World War II, worthy of a place alongside the famous speeches of Winston Churchill. On that day Stalin declared: "There is no place in our ranks for cowards, deserters, and sowers of panic. The Red Army, the Navy, and the Soviet people must all fight for the smallest parcel of Soviet earth, fight to the last drop of blood for our cities and villages. All places of work must intensify their labor and produce more and more. Wherever Soviet units are forced to retreat, they must take with them all railroad stock. The enemy must not find a single locomotive, a single coach, not a pound of bread or a can of gasoline. All utilizable material that cannot be transported must be destroyed. In occupied territories guerrilla units shall be formed, designed to demolish roads, bridges, telephone lines; and they shall set fire to forests as well as enemy arsenals. Comrades, our forces are vast. The insolent enemy will very quickly learn this. All the might of our people must be set in motion to crush the enemy. Forward, to victory!"

In 1946, on my first visit to Moscow after World War II, I still heard praise of that speech. At that moment Stalin's popularity was at its peak. After a dinner at the French Embassy, the ambassador, General Georges Catroux, took me into his office and spoke to me at length about Stalin. He said that if at that time Western-style elections had been held, with a genuinely secret ballot, Stalin would have been elected with an overwhelming majority.

In the years that followed the publication of the Khrushchev report in 1956, Stalin's achievements were assailed in every respect. Those who had praised and glorified him while he was alive were the most outspoken in their condemnation. The same hands that had applauded Stalin frenziedly during his lifetime now hailed every new attack on his memory. Yet for all the hatred he has inspired and will inspire, Stalin was far superior in many ways to the majority of his detractors, once his most devoted adherents. In this he was like Robespierre, who inspired such frenetic hatred in his time yet has since been justly praised for his invaluable contribution to the French Revolution.

Apart from attributing to Stalin every conceivable mistake in the conduct of World War II, many have accused him of ineffectively utilizing the possibilities offered by the peace. This latter point is less known to the general public; hence it is worthwhile examining, however briefly, Stalin's work as a peace negotiator—on the basis of published documents, most of them from Western sources.

Stalin's approach to diplomacy was a combination of Clausewitz's and Lenin's. Clausewitz, the outstanding theoretician of warfare in Imperial Germany, held that war was a continuation of politics by other means. Lenin subscribed to that view—but added his deep insights as a revolutionary. To Lenin (Eighth Congress of the Soviets, December, 1920), "the very existence of the capitalists is in itself a war against the Socialist world." But it was also Lenin who wrote in that same period: "Even the person most firmly dedicated to the ideas of Communism must master the art of agreeing to indispensable practical compromises, zigzags, maneuvers of conciliation and retreat, in order to hasten the event [the realization of Communism]." In World War II, Stalin held strictly to Leninist doctrine both during the period of pre-negotiations (1942–1943) and during the three great conferences of Teheran, Yalta, and Potsdam. On the strategic level, alliances with the opposing ideology were inconceivable. But on the tactical level, provisional alliances could be made when necessary, provided they were subordinated to the greater interest of socialism. Even with this proviso, a wide area was left for diplomatic maneuvering. Stalin used this to good effect; and official documents show him on many occasions superior to his allies—including such statesmen of stature as Roosevelt and Churchill.

The signing of the German-Soviet non-aggression pact in August, 1939, met with shock and deep disapproval in the West and in progressive circles throughout the world. When Hitler violated the pact in June, 1941, Stalin in his first speech to the Soviet people on July 3, 1941, as German troops were advancing on Soviet territory, explained why he had signed it: "What have we gained with the signing of the non-aggression pact with Germany? We have obtained for our country eighteen months of security, during which we have had an opportunity to prepare ourselves to rebuff the assault of Fascist Germany, in the event that they risked attacking our country despite the pact. What has Fascist Germany gained and what has it lost by treacherously violating the pact and attacking the U.S.S.R.? It has gained a temporarily favorable position for its troops; but it has lost politically, revealing itself to the eyes of the entire world as a bloody aggressor. There is no doubt that this momentary military advantage is nothing but an episode, whereas the advantage won by the U.S.S.R. on the political level is a factor of considerable scope and long-term in nature, on which future military successes of the Red Army will be based." Later, when the war was over, Stalin explained how he had been influenced by the vacillations of the British and French governments, following the Munich Pact, and by the existence of a powerful current, especially in England, that wanted the Nazis to turn east and attack Soviet Russia. On this point the then Soviet ambassador to Great Britain, Ivan Maisky, in his *Memoirs* has furnished impressive evidence. In his March, 1939, report to the Eighteenth Party Congress in Moscow, Stalin made a distinction between the "aggressive" capitalist powers—Germany, Italy, and Japan—and the "non-aggressive" capitalist powers—

chiefly France and England—even though, as he stressed, the latter were also capitalist powers. Subsequently, of course, the U.S.S.R. became the ally of the Western powers in the fight against the Nazi-Fascist Axis.

Regarding Stalin's technical competence, we have the testimony of the U.S. general John Deane, who was profoundly impressed by his knowledge of armaments and military matters. Other Western generals who participated in inter-Allied conferences, with rare exceptions, found Stalin extremely well informed, down-to-earth, and opposed to long-winded speeches and vague formulas. This was also Winston Churchill's impression. Referring to his first visit to Moscow, Churchill reported to the House of Commons on September 8, 1942, that for him it was a most interesting experience to meet Prime Minister Stalin. The Soviet Union, he declared, could feel satisfied to have a leader of such stature in its hours of anguish. He was an unusual personality, a man of unflagging courage and will power, sober and even brusque in his language. Prime Minister Stalin gave Churchill the feeling of cold and clear-eyed objectivity, totally free from illusions. This was also the opinion of General Charles de Gaulle, judging from his *Memoirs*: Stalin could disorient his adversary, but was incapable of fooling himself.

In negotiations he bargained hard, seeking to obtain a maximum of advantages for his country, whether it was a question of opening a second front, territorial problems in eastern Europe, or representation in the projected new international organization, the United Nations. But at the proper moment he also knew how to retreat, without "losing face." In the lengthy negotiations preceding the Teheran Conference, the first encounter of the three great leaders of the anti-Axis alliance, Stalin bided his time. The military situation did not yet permit him to participate in a meeting of that kind on an equal level with his allies. The battle of Stalingrad, then in progress—the outcome of which, a major defeat for Hitler, changed the whole course of the war on the Eastern Front—justified Stalin's rejection of the date first proposed by Roosevelt—January 15, 1943—for a "summit" conference. Undoubtedly Stalin preferred to wait, so that he could come to the conference table with a military victory that would earn admiration for the Russians. So it was with the hope that the balance of power among the three major allies would be modified as a result of Soviet military successes that Stalin postponed the meeting date several times. During this period of preliminary negotiations Stalin proved to be an astute diplomat, very sure of himself. All the documents published by the U.S. Department of State as well as marginal comments by various non-Russian participants in the three great inter-Allied conferences portray Stalin as both hard and adroit, knowing always what he wanted, but not forgetting either what he had once said about Hitler, that the latter's basic mistake was that he did not know when to stop.

At Teheran, the first of these conferences, Stalin was content to obtain a single immediate advantage: Operation Overlord, the opening of a second front in Europe, which he insistently demanded. As a result, a date was set for Operation Overlord: May, 1944; a disembarkation in France would be undertaken as a subsidiary to the main operation, and the command would be named without delay. Those who attended Teheran agree that Stalin at various moments showed unexpected flexibility in his tactics. Comments he made during the conference reveal that after every storm he was eager to restore cordiality, especially after he got what he wanted. To General Alan Brooke he said, with a hearty handshake, "The best friendships are those based on misunderstandings." To Churchill, constantly worried by the spread of Communism, as if already preparing for his famous "Iron Curtain" speech at Fulton, Missouri, five years later, which ushered in the Cold War, Stalin "confided" in passing: "It isn't that easy to install Communist regimes." Stalin successfully negotiated the Polish-Soviet border problem; he succeeded in getting the question of the Baltic States eliminated from the agenda, and obtained other, lesser concessions. Over-all, he managed to obtain the maximum from a diplomatic situation which, at the outset of the conference, could not have made him feel very optimistic.

At Yalta, during seven days of conference, February 4–11, 1945, Stalin formulated four important demands for which he vigorously fought during the arduous discussions with Roosevelt and Churchill: (1) German reparations, (2) partition of Germany, (3) territories in the Far East, and (4) multiple representation in the United Nations. The Western powers had more numerous demands, over a wide range of problems.

On the question of the United Nations, Stalin was conciliatory. He yielded with regard to the voting procedure in the Security Council and the question of multiple representation in the General Assembly. Obviously, he attached only relative importance to the United Nations. He looked upon it more as a forum embodying the parliamentary traditions and preferences of the Western powers than as an organ of execution. When the twentieth anniversary of the United Nations was celebrated in 1965, Stalin's initial skepticism concerning that international body was widely shared in the East as well as in the West.

On the German question Stalin held fast to the position that all necessary steps must be taken to prevent a repetition of what happened after World War I, when, barely twenty years after losing the war, Germany was again able to defy the world and attack it. Although the concrete terms of a division of Germany were not fully discussed at Yalta, Stalin managed to have the principle of dismemberment formulated in such a way that it would later offer no escape clause for any of the other members of the Allied coalition. In the matter of German reparations, Stalin had the advantage of dealing with the problem on the basis of a thoroughgoing study of its various aspects. Maisky's presentation of the Soviet position at Yalta is a model of how to engage in a conference of this type—with all the dossiers, all the detailed documentation at hand to support one's arguments.

Various comments made by Stalin at Yalta in the course of the discussion reflect his lack of confidence in Churchill, his suspicion that the great British leader—whose fighting qualities Stalin had genuinely lauded at Teheran—sought to prevent Germany from being too weakened in the postwar years. Alert and mistrustful, Stalin seemed to anticipate the shift in alliances in the near future, in which the enemies of yesterday would become friends, and vice versa. Stalin got from Yalta everything the favorable turn of military operations on the Eastern Front permitted him to get. Now he was negotiating from a position of strength, yet he was careful not to make exaggerated demands, and above all not to antagonize President Roosevelt.

At Potsdam, the last of the three great conferences, his co-participants were different. Roosevelt was dead, succeeded by Harry

Truman. And during the second part of the conference, instead of Churchill and Eden, defeated in the British national elections, Stalin faced Clement Attlee and Ernest Bevin. During the first part of the Potsdam Conference, on July 19, 1945, Stalin condemned the Spanish regime of General Franco and asked his allies to break diplomatic relations with Madrid and support any new non-Fascist regime. The English were opposed to this. Franco had promised not to quarrel with them over Gibraltar. Stalin insisted that Franco's regime ought to be condemned in a general statement about Europe. But here Stalin did not carry his anti-Franco offensive to its logical conclusion. He was satisfied with Franco Spain's exclusion from the United Nations. Had he demanded instead that, in view of the dispatch of the Spanish Blue Division to Russia to fight on Hitler's side against the Soviet Union, Franco be included among the war criminals to be judged at Nuremberg along with Goering and the other Nazi leaders, Franco would have fallen in 1945 and Spain would then have been liberated.

Potsdam was the broadest of the three conferences. This time each of the principals was surrounded by a veritable team of experts. On the Soviet side Molotov stood out: hard, capable, and a man of character, as he subsequently proved during the dangerous period of "de-Stalinization" in the U.S.S.R., the only one among Stalin's old associates who did not renounce his leader. Germany was again the main subject at Potsdam. But now viewpoints were sharper than heretofore. To the English the problem was primarily one of reorganization. Truman also insisted on the need for administrative machinery to fill the big vacuum caused by the collapse of the Third Reich. As for Stalin, he wanted Germany to pay to the limit of its capacity, thus deferring its recovery and any temptation to indulge in new military adventures. It was during the Potsdam Conference that the following comment was attributed to Stalin: "The Germans are the Germans. I don't trust them, not even those who belonged to the Communist Party. The only correct policy toward Germany is that of extreme vigilance." At Potsdam, Stalin proved to be adept in the technique of "correlation"—that is, whenever his allies advanced a subject that did not please him, he opposed it with another demand related to the first one, in order to prepare the ground for turning the last demand into a concession. Whether it was a question of Poland, the Mediterranean, or the Far East, Stalin never lost his temper, whereas his opposite numbers frequently displayed irritation. But he always found an opportune moment to soothe them. His reaction to the Allies' initiative in giving Japan an ultimatum, without consulting him, was surprisingly mild. The one thing that concerned him was how he could make the Western powers formally invite the Soviet Union to enter the war against Japan. This was a diplomatic maneuver that demanded delicate handling, and it proved successful.

In the course of the three conferences Stalin was interested solely in concrete and limited objectives. He allowed his co-participants to formulate the grandiose concepts and concentrated instead on a few essential points. For these he fought stubbornly, in line with the Leninist conception of always keeping one's adversary in check and thus forcing him on the defensive, but without being intransigent in principle. At times Soviet concessions seemed quite generous, as in the organization of the United Nations. But almost always these concessions concerned abstract principles, not basic questions that directly concerned the Soviets.

It has often been said—and rightly—that victory in World War II would have been impossible without the Soviet Union's contribution, without the twenty million Russian dead. This made it difficult for the Western powers to oppose some of the Soviet demands and put them in a position of inferiority, so to speak, in the negotiations. Especially was this true at Potsdam. To convince oneself of this, one has only to look at a map of Europe in 1945 and view the military positions of the various Allied powers. But such had not been the case at Teheran, when Operation Overlord was discussed. There Stalin had on his side only his dialectical skill and fighting spirit. In résumé, only the lack of sober judgment that characterized the period of "de-Stalinization" can explain why Stalin was not given his due as an outstanding negotiator, as one who fought for a peace favorable to his country with the same energy he displayed in guiding its war effort.

Stalin was attacked by veteran Stalinists from every point of view. In the broad de-Stalinization campaign launched after the Twentieth Congress of the Soviet Communist Party and renewed at the Twenty-second Congress, which I attended as a journalist representing several newspapers, one of the reproaches most frequently leveled at Stalin was that he had ignored all signs of Hitler's impending attack on the U.S.S.R. When in 1965 Moscow issued a stamp commemorating Richard Sorge, a key figure in the Soviet intelligence apparatus, new life was given to the theory that Stalin had disregarded the most serious warnings sent him in the late spring of 1941—a season that proved decisive for the fate of the world.

Richard Sorge was a colorful personality. In Tokyo, where he operated, he had a reputation as a Nazi charmer, irresistible to Europeans and Japanese alike. Malicious tongues later gave as one of the chief sources of their information the wife of the German ambassador to Tokyo, noted for her beauty. As a cover Sorge worked as correspondent for the *Frankfurter Zeitung*, where his "inside" stories created a sensation.

The Soviet intelligence service early realized what unique qualities Sorge possessed. Born of a Russian mother and a German father, who as an engineer had worked for a German oil company in Baku, Sorge was handsome, built like an athlete, and unusually cultured, equally at home in German and Russian and proficient in English, Chinese, Japanese, and French as well. His linguistic talents proved highly useful. A youthful admiration for Lenin led him, one year after the death of the Communist leader, to join the Soviet Communist Party. When eight years later Hitler rose to power in Germany, the Soviet intelligence service felt that a German-Japanese alliance was inevitable. What better man to choose for Tokyo than Sorge? So in May, 1933, posing as a fanatic Nazi, Sorge persuaded the German press that he would be useful in the Japanese capital. An incident that occurred during the Spanish Civil War helped open all doors to him. During a public argument with a Soviet journalist, Sorge and the journalist came to blows when Sorge lauded the victories of Hitler's air force over the Spanish Republicans. This was one of his many dodges. He became an intimate friend of the German ambassador in Tokyo and helped that envoy when work piled up in the Embassy, among other things deciphering coded dispatches from Berlin. Thus the German secret military code came into his hands, and soon thereafter into the hands of the Fourth Bureau of the Soviet Red Army. As he constantly refined his role as an agent, Sorge gathered a group around him, headed by two Japanese anti-Nazis, Hosumi Ozaki, with whom he had become friendly in China, and the painter Miyagi.

The confidential reports Sorge sent to his superiors in the Soviet Union were so authentic that they left no room for doubt. In May, 1939, he sent word that Hitler was planning to crush Poland, then France and England, and finally the U.S.S.R. He even included an exact date for the offensive against Poland: September 1, 1939. In 1941 he revealed the famous "Barbarossa plan" aimed at the Soviet Union. Increasingly sure of himself, Sorge indicated that at the end of May, 1941, preparations for mobilization against the U.S.S.R. were under way, employing 150 divisions of the German army. But his most sensational revelation was the news that the Japanese were not going to attack the Russians in Siberia—thus enabling the Red Army High Command to withdraw forces from the Far Eastern front so as to withstand the German onslaught. Sorge played a vital part in the defeat of the German army at the gates of Moscow.

Stalin did not believe the Germans would attack the U.S.S.R. As we have said, this was one of the most serious criticisms leveled against him after his death. When he received a telegram from the Red Army's Fourth Bureau casting doubt on the veracity of his information, Sorge was in despair. In June, 1941, Hitler attacked the Soviet Union. Thereafter, Sorge was believed unreservedly. He did not enjoy his triumph for long. Japanese counter-espionage authorities began to suspect him, and Sorge was taken to Sugamo prison. He was not executed immediately; the Japanese sought to wrest from him all the information they could. But he did not weaken, and one day the prison guards saw him dance a few steps. It was the day of Stalingrad. But with this memory there was the torment of November 7, 1944, the date chosen for his execution because it was the anniversary of the Russian Revolution.

The anti-Stalin campaign eventually produced a counter-movement. Twelve years after Stalin's death, and nine years after the sensational revelations made by Nikita Khrushchev that shook the world Communist movement and seriously hurt the Left everywhere, Stalin's name was applauded in Moscow—first on the occasion of the speech commemorating the victory over Hitler, and then in the movie houses where films of World War II were shown. Foreign observers who, on May 8, 1965, witnessed these demonstrations in the Soviet capital agreed that Leonid Brezhnev, then general secretary of the Soviet Communist Party, was surprised by the favorable reaction to the mention of Stalin's name. And in the motion-picture theaters, when the well-known figure of the wartime leader was flashed on the screen, the initial response was one of astonishment, then loud applause at subsequent appearances during the film. All at once Stalin seemed more alive than ever. The victory the Soviet people celebrated in the spring of 1965, as they glanced back twenty years, was to many Russians Stalin's victory, whereas Khrushchev had been relegated to the position of an anonymous Soviet citizen. Stalin's name was again applauded in the U.S.S.R. when U.S. aerial assaults on North Vietnam, ordered by President Lyndon Johnson, made even influential Western newspapers carry headlines such as "AMERICA IN ALL-OUT WAR." The international situation had taken a dangerous turn for the worse. In Paris and London, as well as Moscow and Latin America, people asked themselves: Who can restrain Johnson? Inevitably the comment was made: "If Stalin were alive, Johnson would not have dared." And suddenly one grew aware of the precariousness of the policy of peaceful coexistence. Remembrance of that disturbing period was a subject of deep concern in left-wing circles. The most powerful nation on earth, the United States, had gone over to the offensive in the name of a capitalist system that fought against yielding world domination.

Freed of the pressures exerted on those who unconditionally followed Moscow's political line—which for a long time avoided any objective evaluation of Stalin's personality—an outstanding figure in world socialism, György Lukács, paid homage to him in his writings. Lukács, probably the most noted Marxist literary critic of the Stalin and post-Stalin era, who at eighty-two was still working twelve hours a day in Budapest to finish his *Aesthetics*, publicly dissented from those on the Left, Communists as well as non-Communists, who vied with one another in tearing down Stalin's work. The great Hungarian philosopher-critic had no special reason to feel affection for the late Soviet leader. During the "purges" of the 1930's, Lukács was living in Moscow and spent many a night waiting for the police to come and arrest him. He had probably grown used to the idea that one day he would be shot. Nevertheless, he wrote: "To us, the determining factor is the over-all perspective of the movement; and from that viewpoint it is impossible to deny that under Stalin socialism strengthened and consolidated itself."

Stalin represented a second revolution within the Russian Revolution. To be sure, in the world Communist movement Lenin remains first—the founder and creator of the first working-class state. But the problem posed by Lukács—without Stalin would the first working-class state have survived?—is historically valid. This question provokes violent responses and protests. Many on the Left see in Stalin only the man who had his leading associates murdered, the man of the purges and the Siberian concentration camps. Others hesitate to rise to his defense for fear of incurring the same hatred that surrounded Stalin when Khrushchev's "secret report" was made public. I once heard a veteran Stalinist, in a moment of deep sincerity, say: "To defend Stalin requires more courage than making the Revolution," and he added that he would not dare to do so publicly. But it is not a question of defending Stalin; it is a question of analyzing his contribution to history. Now, within the Soviet Union itself, since the fiftieth anniversary of the October Revolution, we are beginning to read comments by marshals of the Red Army and articles by noted Soviet historians which would not have been published only a few years ago.

From the time he became undisputed head of the country until the years of World War II, Stalin, displaying an energy unequaled since the time of Lenin, used his power to lay the bases of Socialist construction in the U.S.S.R. Isaac Deutscher, a well-known anti-Stalinist, points out that the outstanding reformers in Russian history—Ivan the Terrible and Peter the Great—as well as great reformers of other countries, seem of lesser stature than the giant figure of General Secretary Stalin. The Stalin era, or second Russian Revolution, if we may term it thus, enabled the country within ten years to beat back the tremendous assault of the Axis armies. This is a fundamental fact, in the face of which accusations by repentant Stalinists of the 1950's that Stalin lacked ability fall flat. Other observers, non-Communist historians as well as Western military leaders and diplomats, agree that, had it not been for Stalin's planned economy, the Soviet Union would have succumbed to the Hitler invasion. German military experts are of the same opinion, even though it does not make them happy to admit it.

Forced industrialization under Stalin, by means of successive Five-Year Plans, proceeded during twelve years of peace, regardless of the sacrifices. But it was not attempted under wartime pressures or improvised to meet an emergency; it was carefully planned. Hence it enabled the U.S.S.R. to resist successfully the Nazi aggressors; and it accounts for the present-day strength of the Soviet Union as the second most powerful nation in the world, competing with—and in some areas outstripping—the United States. Soviet planning set an example for the other Socialist countries even after Stalin had died and was discredited. It meant the transformation of a whole society. Again, we may cite Isaac Deutscher, who asserts that Stalinist Russia in twenty years did the work of twenty generations.

How shall we judge the effects of de-Stalinization? In the first ten years between the Twentieth and the Twenty-third Party Congress of the Soviet Communist Party—the decade 1956–1966—de-Staliniza-tion went hand in hand with a process of disintegration hitherto unknown in the Communist world. This is of serious, indeed of historic importance for the world Socialist movement. I use the word "Socialist" in its broadest sense to include the Communist parties in various countries and all other genuine left-wing parties and trends in the national liberation movements. Unquestionably the de-Staliniza-tion set in motion by the report read by Khrushchev on February 25, 1956, to the delegates of the Twentieth Congress of the Soviet Communist Party, assembled in secret session to hear him denounce "Stalin's crimes," to use the official expression, weakened the Left. On this point even the staunchest supporter of Moscow's position during the ten years of turmoil in the world Communist movement would find it hard to argue the contrary.

In 1956, in a letter addressed to the Twentieth Congress, Mao Tse-tung wrote: "The Communist Party of the Soviet Union has been and will continue to be an outstanding example for the Communist parties in every country in the world. It is the first 'shock brigade' of the world revolutionary movement." Compare this statement of Mao's with what has since been said and written in China concerning the Soviet Communist Party; or compare it with the declaration of the Chinese delegation on the occasion of the Twenty-third Congress of the Soviet Communist Party in the spring of 1966 and one sees what a change in attitude has occurred. Not just in China and Albania. In all the countries in Eastern Europe, with regimes similar to that of the U.S.S.R., in all the Communist parties throughout the world, in all left-wing and national liberation movements, the political, psychological, and ideological shock of de-Stalinization has been tremendous.

In the late 1960's the world Communist movement, once solidly united under Stalin, was unable to check the process of polycentrism (to use Palmiro Togliatti's word) that had set in with the revelations of the Khrushchev report. Stubborn efforts by the Kremlin were unavailing. At the Budapest meeting in March, 1968, Mikhail Suslov, a leading ideologist of the Soviet Communist Party, enjoyed a tactical success when all the Communist parties gathered there—with the exception of the Romanians, who had left the meeting—voted unanimously to prepare a new "big Communist conference" to be held in Moscow. For four years the Russian leaders had sought to convoke such a conference. In itself this objective seemed at first sight difficult of attainment. To bring the world Communist movement together in a new common front, without seven of the fourteen parties in countries where the Communists were in power—notably, in China, Vietnam, North Korea, Cuba, Albania, Romania, and Yugoslavia—might gain approval of the leadership of the other parties favorable to the Soviet position, but would hardly win the enthusiasm of the masses in those countries. Approval by the Communist leaders who did attend the Consultative Conference seemed less significant after the Romanians quit the gathering. None of the others followed suit, not daring to risk Soviet displeasure; but Suslov, in turn, had to make certain concessions in order to achieve unanimity, which was embodied in the final communiqué. Contrary to his original plan, Suslov had to agree that ideological questions would not be included in the agenda for the forthcoming Moscow Conference as agreed upon by the sixty-six Communist parties in Budapest.

The Romanians had announced beforehand that they would come to Budapest provided that no "labels" were attached to any Communist party and that no absent party was attacked. When they were accused of being nationalists and the Chinese accused of nationalism and many other things, the Romanians left the conference. Moreover, other Communist parties were plainly dissatisfied that their request to extend an invitation to "other anti-imperialist forces" to attend the planned Moscow gathering was turned down.

Of the influential Western Communist parties at Budapest, the Italian Communist Party appeared to show little enthusiasm for a world Communist conference to be held in Moscow without China's participation. The head of the Italian delegation, Berlinguer, said in this connection: "We have criticized the positions of the Chinese Party from the very first. Nevertheless, we do not forget that the People's Republic of China is a target of Western policy and a threat to American imperialism. We are well aware that China, by virtue of the position it occupies and deserves to occupy in Asia and in the international community, may be able to make an important contribution to the cause of world peace and the struggle against imperialism."

No, the Communist world did not reveal close-knit unity at Budapest and thereafter. Most of the parties continued to be aligned with Moscow, though they affirmed "unity in diversity." But some of their supporters wondered whether the Communist movement was losing its revolutionary élan.

7

THE FIGHT FOR
TRUE SOCIALISM

The First International—the International Working Men's Association—lasted from 1864 to 1876; it was the first organization which vigorously fostered the idea of class solidarity beyond national frontiers. To be sure, there had been other noteworthy attempts to unite the progressive forces of Europe: Mazzini's "Young Europe"; the "Democratic Association" founded in Brussels, of which Karl Marx was vice-president; the "International Committee"; and others. But whereas all these movements attracted only a minority of revolutionaries, the First International genuinely represented the European working class.

Its creation coincided with strikes that aroused widespread attention: the brass workers in Paris, the Belgian workers in Liège, Antwerp, and the mining districts. At international gatherings in Brussels and Basle, the First International proclaimed the necessity and legitimacy of the strike weapon. Within the First International two main trends fought for control: that of Marx and that of the Russian anarchist leader Bakunin. Escaping from a Siberian prison and settling in Italy, Mikhail Bakunin won to his point of view workers in the more recently industrialized countries, especially Italy and Spain. In Spain one of Bakunin's disciples, Fanelli, headed the Madrid and Barcelona sections of the First International. This accounts, at least in part, for the strong roots anarchism has had in Spain—maintained, despite numerous crises, down to the present day. Between the time of the First and Second Internationals the two main trends confronted each other constantly. Thanks in large measure to the skill of Friedrich Engels, these dissensions were overcome—at least enough to permit organizing on an international scale. At the Brussels Congress, August 18–23, 1891, the Marxists definitely won the day—in the domain of principles as well as tactics.

All the congresses of the last part of the nineteenth century that were convoked with a view to re-establishing the First International, were involved in constant debates between the two main tendencies. A retrospective study of these debates is extremely valuable, for they represent important stages in the march of socialism. At the London Congress of 1886, the main theme was the urgent need to rebuild the International, but there it was more of an emotional matter than a strong ideological position. The leading proponents were those who had in the past opposed the move: the anarchists and the opportunists, or "possibilists." In the first phase of the rebuilding process the Marxists fought with the anarchists; in the second phase, the Marxists were in sharp disagreement with the opportunists or revisionists. At the Congress of Ghent "politicism" got the upper hand over "anti-politicism," and the idea of renouncing political action was rejected. At this Congress the anarchists found themselves isolated.

Engels followed all these efforts to rebuild the International with passionate interest, but he never allowed his zeal for unity to dull his critical acumen. He was not enthusiastic about an International rebuilt on the basis of confusion and led by opponents of Marxism. During this period he wrote and spoke much on this general theme. Then in 1889, when the proposal by the possibilists to convoke a world congress seemed to gain ground, Engels took the matter firmly in hand. The French Congress of Troyes and the trade-union congress of Bordeaux declared themselves in favor of calling an international congress in Paris that same year. Both gatherings leaned toward a Marxist-oriented congress. But, basing themselves on the decisions of the London Congress, the possibilists tried to broaden the congress as much as they could. Engels quickly intervened. He persuaded the German Socialist Party to insist on a preliminary conference at The Hague to decide on this crucial question. Under Engels' guidance the French followers of Jules Guesde and the Germans then called the Paris Congress with two aims: on the one hand, against the extreme Left as represented by the anarchists; on the other, against the opportunists of the Right. In London, Eleanore Marx-Aveling, Marx's daughter, carried on intense propaganda on behalf of the Paris Congress, which met on July 14, 1889, a historic date—the hundredth anniversary of the fall of the Bastille.

"All Europe," wrote Engels, "was represented there." In numbers it surpassed the preceding International. There were 395 delegates from the leading European countries: Germany, England, Belgium, Austria-Hungary, Holland, and France. There were also Russians, Swedes, Norwegians, Danes, Spaniards, Italians, Czechs, Portuguese, Bulgars—and even delegates from the United States. Among the Russians, Georgi Plekhanov was pre-eminent: he had been the first to raise the banner of Marxism in his country. Emphatically he told the Congress: "Only as a working-class movement can the revolution triumph in Russia." Hitherto the revolutionary groups in Russia had pinned their hopes on the peasantry, but Plekhanov, the Marxist, did not share that opinion.

This was a genuinely Marxist congress. It opposed the possibilists and trade-union syndicalists who vainly sought to steer it along a different course. Indeed, the syndicalists held a separate meeting that attracted little attention, in contrast to the impressive congress opened by Paul Lafargue, a son-in-law of Karl Marx. Three resolutions summed up the different positions: one recommended collaboration with the possibilists; another called for drawing a definite dividing line between Marxists and revisionists; and the third called for negotiations between the two trends. The third resolution, advanced by the German Wilhelm Liebknecht, was finally adopted. Nevertheless, the general directives left no doubt as to which trend had won: "The working class must fight for the seizure of power and the expropriation of the bourgeoisie." Struggle! That was the word that breathed through the text the Congress adopted. Meanwhile the following immediate demands were formulated: an eight-hour day; regulation of women's work; other reforms in social policy. Following the example set in the United States, the delegates unanimously proclaimed May 1 as labor's holiday and decided to celebrate it for the first time on May 1, 1890. There was but one resolution on war and peace: war will disappear when labor is free and socialism has triumphed.

Engels' spirit was reflected in all these decisions; and the anarchists, disdaining political action, were boxed out. A new International—the Second International—had come into being. The working class now had a powerful weapon of struggle and a sure path to tread; but it was not an easy path.

The bourgeoisie whipped up a frenzy around the Second International, seeing its hand in every violent event everywhere: bombs in Florence and Pisa; assassination attempts in Berlin, Naples, Madrid, and St. Petersburg. But neither then nor thereafter was the Second International a secret society dedicated to acts of terrorism. Its headquarters were well known; its origins and activities were a matter of public record. The working class would have been much stronger, however, had not revisionist tendencies reappeared with the founding of the Second International. As the class struggle gained in intensity, not all Socialists felt the same urgent need for militancy.

The history of the Second International, as reflected in its many congresses, may be summed up as the fight against the "worms"—as the conservative-minded Socialists were called by one of the founders of the organization. The worms, entering the body of the organization, threatened its very existence. The struggle over doctrine was a dramatic one, involving clashes between partisans of revolutionary socialism and defenders of reform and accommodation. Those who now, in the final decades of the twentieth century, feel pessimistic when they witness the splits in the world Socialist camp, would do well to turn back and study the stubborn polemics that marked international Socialist gatherings after the initial Paris meeting of 1889 and learn a valuable lesson from them.

As we have seen, the Brussels Congress (1891), with 380 delegates representing the international working class, had opened with the slogan of unifying the forces of the proletariat. Among the old questions discussed were electoral tactics and relations with the bourgeoisie. Then in 1890 the anti-Socialist laws passed by Bismarck in 1878 were repealed. It was a victory for German Social Democracy, which now became a legal party. In its Erfurt Program it abandoned its last illusions of utopian socialism, rid itself of

Lassallean influences, and adopted a purely Marxist platform. Nevertheless, certain incidents showed that the revisionists were still trying to regain their lost influence—as in their Volmar agrarian program and in insistent attempts to create an independent trade-union international. The polemics heightened in intensity when the problem of war was debated. Two trends clashed with increasing sharpness. The German Wilhelm Liebknecht and the Frenchman Edouard Vaillant favored an educational campaign to expose the motives and intrigues of the war party, supported by industrial and financial circles. The Dutchman Domela Nieuwenhuis, an anarchist who was allowed to present his point of view and participate in the discussions, demanded deeds, not words: strikes and a refusal by anti-war advocates to be sent to the front.

The possibilists—the revisionists of that day—used the rhetoric of revolutionaries. Yet even in the Erfurt Program, destined to influence the International for many years to come, and despite its radical-sounding Marxist language, opportunism managed to infiltrate. The Erfurt Program evaded the issue of the dictatorship of the proletariat. Its opportunist escape clauses, energetically fought by Engels, were all the more dangerous in the program, yet it became a model for all the other parties in the Second International.

The first Congress of the new Second International met in Zurich, Switzerland, in 1893, in an atmosphere of heightened international tension. On the one hand, there was the conflict between Germany and Russia because the Germans had raised customs levies on grain, a matter serious enough to threaten armed conflict. On the other hand, there was social unrest in many countries: 200,000 miners on strike in England; a political strike in Belgium, calling for extension of voting rights; and diverse social movements in other lands—all indicative of the rising class-consciousness of the working class. Georgi Plekhanov demanded a clear stand against Germany's aggressive policies toward Russia. The two chief spokesmen of German Social Democracy, Wilhelm Liebknecht and August Bebel, wavered when a strong anti-militarist resolution was adopted, fearing a loss of popularity in their own country if they adopted such a position. This accounted for attempts by the German delegation to justify their refusal of a revolutionary general strike in the event of war. They were opposed, they said, not on principle but because of the practical difficulties of carrying out such a strike in a capitalist regime.

At Zurich, Engels appeared before the international working class for the last time in his life. He exhorted them to stand firmly on their principles and reject opportunist ideas. He pointed to the continuity between the First and Second Internationals, stressing, however, that the latter was much stronger than the former. "If Marx were alive," declared Engels, "he could be proud of his work." Nevertheless, until the final months of his life, Engels warned unremittingly of the danger of sacrificing principles and theory to numbers and respectability in the movement. Winning over votes or members from the petty bourgeoisie by making concessions to the bourgeoisie was not, he reiterated, the road to socialism.

Nor, according to Marx and Engels, was the road to socialism to be found in the theories of Ferdinand Lassalle, which, in the mid-nineteenth century, had many adherents, among them the first Socialists in the United States.

Ferdinand Lassalle, founder of the Social Democratic movement in Germany, came from a family of wealthy German Jews in Breslau. In Paris he met Louis Blanc, who, like himself, believed that capitalism could be changed into socialism by universal suffrage and progressive reforms. At the outset Lassalle and Marx worked together on the *Neue Rheinische Zeitung*, Lassalle devoting himself mainly to questions of philosophy and philology. Soon, however, he drew away from Marx, whose theory of class struggle shocked him. Lassalle believed more in evolutionary development and was inclined to accept the state as an instrument of gradual change that would lead to the establishment of socialism. In other matters his approach to political questions of a general nature was a discerning one. He realized the true meaning of the 1848 Revolutions as uprisings of the people against outmoded political forms and the efforts of the Holy Alliance, set up by the Congress of Vienna, to protect the ruling dynasties of Europe. He was an effective organizer of the working class, founder of the Allgemeine Deutscher Arbeiterverein (General Confederation of German Workers). He was also a brilliant polemicist and pamphleteer. In one of his brochures, "The Italian War and Prussia's Mission," he argued tellingly that no force could prevent the unification of Italy. In another pamphlet that was widely hailed in its day—"Power and Law"—Lassalle maintained that in the state of Prussia no one could talk of law. As an agitator he was often superb, but too often state-oriented in his theories. Bismarck himself one day told the German parliament how much he had been impressed by Lassalle after meeting with him. And the workers in the Rhineland flocked to his meetings and lectures.

He was also a romantic who paid for his romanticism with his life. He had fallen in love with a Fräulein Helene von Dönniges, who was also courted by the Romanian Count von Racovitza. As a result of this rivalry, the two men fought a duel at Carouge, a suburb of Geneva, on August 28, 1864. On August 31, Lassalle died of wounds received in the duel.

In the history of socialism, Lassalle holds a place of honor. Despite profound differences with Marx, he agreed with him in considering the working class the creator and representative of a new era in history. Although it was founded by Lassalle, German Social Democracy soon came under Marx's influence. Brilliant, with a great power of appeal for the masses, a spokesman of the working class who retained the refined habits of a dandy, Ferdinand Lassalle was a fighter in his own way. Yet he never attained Marx's level of power as a historian, a philosopher, and the founder of scientific socialism.

Despite internal differences, the Second International soon proved that it was a significant factor in world politics, taken seriously by friends and foes alike. It was a people's parliament that included some of the outstanding public figures of the time. Their names are well known: the Germans August Bebel, Wilhelm Liebknecht, and Karl Kautsky, the Belgian Emile Vandervelde, the Briton Keir Hardie, the Italians Turati and Bissolati, the Russian Plekhanov, and the Spaniard Pablo Iglesias. The French, with a number of talented orators and leaders, were divided into a left wing headed by Marx's disciple Jules Guesde, Vaillant, and the aging Blanqui; and a right wing led by René Viviani and Alexandre Millerand, joined later by Aristide Briand. And above all there was Jean Jaurès, capable on his own of rousing an entire congress.

The Dresden Congress of the German Social Democrats (1905) revealed, as no preceding congress had, the dividing line between the reformists and the left-wing Socialists. Several local groups opposed to the reformists demanded that they be expelled from the party. August Bebel, a highly respected leader, made a violent verbal attack on the revisionism of his German colleague Eduard Bernstein. But in the final analysis his speech was more brilliant than effective. The reformists parried the blow and retained the key posts in the party. The clinching argument of the opportunists was that party unity had to be safeguarded above all.

During those very days, in another land, revolution became a reality. After the Russo-Japanese War, the Russian revolutionaries exploited the crisis in the discredited Czarist regime and moved into action. In the course of this action a new Socialist party was born: the Bolshevik Party. Bolshevism took shape under the guidance of that extraordinary leader, Lenin, and went on—as we have seen—to victory in the October Revolution of 1917. A party that made the dictatorship of the proletariat the very heart of its conception of struggle was bound to jolt those other Socialist parties that preferred parliamentary reform to revolution. Within Russia the Bolsheviks from the outset took a stand against the Mensheviks, who in their eyes represented right-wing opportunism, despite their brilliant speeches and radical-sounding phrases. In the center were Leon Trotsky, the Jewish Bund, and the Social Revolutionaries. Now a new party, hewing strictly to the Marxist line of class struggle and maintaining iron discipline, challenged the socialism as expounded by German Social Democracy. Since it was the Germans who from the 1900's on had achieved the greatest success among the Socialist parties of the West, in terms of both the size of their membership and the quality of their leaders, the Bolsheviks, right down to the outbreak of World War I, waged their strongest polemics against the German Social Democrats. The Bolsheviks were concerned not only with specifically Russian problems or with the usual international issues; they also appealed to the peoples under the colonial yoke, considering them allies and urging them to revolt against the imperialist homelands.

To the Bolsheviks the general strike was not a topic of discussion merely indulged in by parties to give their congresses a certain air of Jacobinism; it meant instead a genuine desire for action, a concrete weapon of struggle, a means of mobilizing the masses and preparing them for armed revolt. Their concept of masses did not exclude any section of the population that could be enlisted in the fight: land-hungry poor peasants belonged, as did workers, but leadership had to be in the hands of the working class. The Bolsheviks insisted on the Socialist nature of the next revolution; and their most authoritative spokesman, Lenin, was convinced that it would begin in Russia.

The appearance of the Bolsheviks as an independent force was greeted with reservations—even by such an outstanding left-wing Socialist as Rosa Luxemburg. In 1904, Lenin and she exchanged polemics concerning the timeliness of the new party. At the meeting of the "Bureau" of the Amsterdam Congress, Plekhanov sought to eliminate the Bolsheviks on the pretext that they did not represent a special trend of their own. But the two delegates sent to Amsterdam by the new party, Liadov and Krassikov, held firm and were finally permitted to give a report, which dealt with the dictatorship of the proletariat. After these initial confrontations in the "Bureau," the Amsterdam Congress opened in an atmosphere of considerable tension and expectation.

Owing to the high level of its debates, the Amsterdam Congress of the Second International was one of the most impressive ever held. Jean Jaurès fought like a lion against the Germans. There was one moment in which the great French Socialist leader clashed sharply with the two most prestigious German Socialists of that day, Bebel and Kautsky. Nor did he waver even when his criticisms aroused the hostility of a majority of the Congress delegates. Anticipating in uncanny fashion what would happen at the outbreak of World War I, Jaurès waxed ironical about "the rules of action, or rather inaction, which today govern German Social Democracy." The Germans, Jaurès concluded, have no revolutionary tradition. The achievements won by the German working class were handed down from above. They were not earned on the barricades. "No," Jaurès thundered at the German Social Democrats, "power is not yet yours, since you cannot even offer the international working class the hospitality of your capital in which to hold a meeting. You hide your inability to act behind the clarion calls of theoretical formulas which your eminent Comrade Kautsky will continue to furnish us." Next he turned to Bebel, who had characterized the republic as a bourgeois institution. "Careful! True, a republic at this moment is not everywhere the necessary expression of economic and social progress; but in France, by its origin, by a series of events: in 1791 the petition of the Champ-de-Mars, in 1792 the entrance of the people into the Palace of the Tuileries, in January, 1793, on the Place de la Concorde, where the head of Louis XVI fell, in 1830, in 1848, and in 1871 the Commune—the Republic has been the result of a revolutionary movement that has created modern France. That is why the French proletariat, in the name of its class, and faithful to its traditions—from Babeuf and Buonarrotti to Blanqui—defends the republican regime and republican freedom."

Eduard Bernstein spoke in rebuttal. Once a courageous fighter against Bismarck's anti-Socialist laws and a capable editor of the party organ *Der Sozialdemokrat*, Bernstein was now the chief revisionist in the party. Along with large enterprises, he said, there was also a place for medium and small ones. The petty bourgeois and the peasant are here and will not soon disappear. Hence there is a chance to improve the condition of the working class, even in a capitalist state. Proceeding from these premises, Bernstein went on to revise Marx's theses. He had a heated discussion with Kautsky and an even more violent one with Rosa Luxemburg, who stressed that possibilism and the opportunist tactics that accompanied it could only lead to the defeat of the working class. In the question of the mass strike, Jaurès was on the side of Rosa Luxemburg, with Lenin also supporting her, favoring it as a weapon of action that would increase the fighting capacity of the working class. But it is interesting to note that, by contrast with today's revisionists and right-wing Socialists, even the leading theoretician of revisionism seventy years ago, Eduard Bernstein, voted at Amsterdam in favor of the resolution for a general strike. At the beginning of the century the most conservative Socialists were Marxists by comparison with the bureaucrats and careerists who lead many of the Socialist parties today.

A humanist in every fiber of his being, Jean Jaurès believed it possible to win over the most enlightened section of the bourgeoisie to the revolutionary cause. But he realized that, for practical purposes, his influence was limited to the working class. His integrity and the manner in which he understood the role of the intellectual in politics prevented him from substituting his desires for reality, or from improvising a new intellectual theory of revisionism that the opportunists could exploit. In his many writings he demonstrated robust thinking and a deep feeling for literary style. Among these was his monumental *Socialist History of the French Revolution,* which sheds light on aspects of that world-shaking event hitherto neglected by advocates and adversaries alike.

Jaurès was sensitive to every teaching of history. Although strongly attracted by parliamentary life—and no one in the halls of parliament has rivaled him as an orator in France—he never forgot that the field of genuine struggle lay elsewhere. Nor was it a contradiction that the great fighter for peace spent so much time on the problem of national defense. His thoughts on this score were summed up in a book of considerable significance: *L'Armée nouvelle (The New Army),* bearing the subtitle: *The National Defense and International Peace.* But even that volume was a contribution to peace in that it proceeded from the premise that in a world of rapid social change the antagonisms between the various forces of aggression had to be settled peaceably. He asked: "How can we raise the possibilities of peace to their highest level, for France as well as the insecure world surrounding France?" Only an army free of caste and class differences, argued Jaurès, would guarantee the fatherland and peace. Only such an army would have the means and incentive to defend the France of the Revolution against an aggressive militarism inspired by diametrically opposed aims. His recommendations were for the creation of a people's army in which each and every citizen was a potential defender of the nation. He wanted the barracks' spirit abolished, as well as the professionalism and arrogance of officers' cliques who felt above their troops and behaved like a self-contained caste. He sought an army capable of attracting millions of free men. "There is no real defense possible unless the nation participates in it with its mind and heart. An armed nation must also be a 'thinking nation.' " Jaurès favored an army similar to the Swiss militia but adapted to French conditions—a genuine army of defense fully devoted to maintaining peace and freedom. When all peoples built their armies in that spirit and assigned them similar tasks, a new era would begin in Europe.

Socialism in Western Europe faced a new problem when the Russians passed from theory to full-scale revolutionary action. The Russian Revolution of 1905 confirmed Rosa Luxemburg's viewpoint. With her superb dialectical skill she fastened on what was happening in the most revolutionary country on the continent to combat the wavering theoreticians and to laud the power of the masses. She was eager to take personal part in the Russian Revolution, but illness prevented her from undertaking such a long journey. As soon as she was well again she boarded a train for Warsaw and threw herself completely into the struggle, where she met, among other comrades, Leo Jogisches.

Those were days of great tension in Warsaw. Armed encounters with the soldiers had already occurred. A state of war had been proclaimed, and new mass demonstrations were being prepared, in open defiance of the police ban. On March 4, 1905, Rosa Luxemburg and Jogisches, using false names, were arrested, held at the Warsaw Town Hall, and were soon revealed to the police under their true identity. Rosa Luxemburg was taken to the Warsaw fortress and so badly manhandled that she fell ill again, this time gravely. The doctors insisted that her life was in peril if she were kept there; and since she had German citizenship she was finally set free at the end of July. Leo Jogisches, on the other hand, was sentenced to eight years' forced labor. However, a bold escape enabled him to continue the fight. Rosa Luxemburg managed to get to St. Petersburg; and after a brief stay in Finland she returned to Germany, where her presence was urgently needed. The Russian Revolution of 1905 had jolted German Social Democracy out of its smugness and its hankering for a comfortable, prosperous life. It was shaken in its assumptions and values, and now began to ask if it too, in the not-too-distant future, would not have to assume a much more militant stance, particularly in view of the increasing aggressiveness shown by the reactionaries.

The Russian Revolution of 1905 had repercussions even in the most faraway places, including countries that hitherto had been considered totally sealed off from any social demands. It echoed in Persia, Turkey, China, and India. But of course it was in the Socialist parties of the West and in circles of the Second International that the uprising of the St. Petersburg workers made the deepest impression.

The Socialist movement soon took a leftward turn. In some parties, opportunists were expelled—thus Millerand, Briand, and Viviani were excluded from the French Socialist Party. The question of a mass strike again became a live issue. Even the threat of one forced the Austrian government to introduce an electoral law along the lines demanded by the Socialists; in the ranks of the German party too, the left wing was strengthened. Rosa Luxemburg and Parvus introduced the thesis of permanent revolution, which Trotsky later developed and broadened. This state of mind was reflected at the Stuttgart Congress of the Second International, whose 881 assembled delegates included most of the best Socialist minds of the day. For the first time a delegation of Bolsheviks led by Lenin was seated: thanks largely to their efforts, the Congress agreed that any war resolution to be presented and voted upon, if it was to be effective and win over the masses, had to be conceived and expressed in the spirit of revolutionary Marxism. But in the course of the impressive debate that ensued, the German Socialists tried to hedge. Bebel insisted on a distinction between offensive and defensive war; he had indicated once before that if it was a question of marching against absolutist Russia, he would march; this, despite the fact that, as a Marxist, he had always presented capitalism as the true cause of war. The *enfant terrible* of the Congress was the French anarcho-syndicalist Gustave Hervé, who, years later, turned into chauvinistic superpatriot and ended up as a Nazi collaborator in France. At Stuttgart the young Hervé called for a general strike and an armed uprising should armed conflict break out.

Of the French Socialists who spoke, Jules Guesde and Jean Jaurès were the two with the greatest authority. Guesde considered the general strike utopian; Jaurès, on the contrary, considered it a potentially effective weapon against war if preceded by a broad-based anti-militarist campaign that would expose those who instigated and promoted a warlike foreign policy. It is not enough, Jaurès insisted, to denounce the warmongers in parliament, the press, and elsewhere. To get the masses to march they must be informed of the truth.

The final resolution at Stuttgart led to heated encounters between French and German Socialists. Lenin, in his writings, ably analyzing

the proceedings of the Congress, declared that the Socialist movement had to focus on one goal: not to replace war with peace, but to
replace capitalism with socialism. As always, Lenin sought a clear
political line as the first and essential condition of victory. He put the
higher interest of socialism above the polemics regarding offensive or
defensive war, asserting that socialism was the only sure guarantee of
peace. Thus he laid the bases for his "war theses," which, once
World War I erupted, inspired the controversial slogan: "Turn the
imperialist war into civil war."

In the course of the Congress discussions, Lenin succeeded in
getting passed his amendment to Bebel's resolution, which strengthened it considerably. Lenin's amendment stated that if despite all
efforts to stop the war it should nevertheless break out, every
measure should be taken to demand that hostilities come to a halt,
that the true causes of the conflict be ascertained, and that the
masses be informed of them in order to hasten the overthrow of
capitalism. At the same time the resolution stipulated that Socialist
members of parliaments in all the Socialist parties of the Second
International were obliged to vote against war credits. Over-all, the
Stuttgart resolution represented a considerable advance over the
previous resolutions voted at Amsterdam and Paris. Peering well into
the future, Lenin sought to create a united Socialist left wing on
which the new policies could be firmly based. Unity in the Socialist
left wing, however, ran into a number of difficulties. To begin with, it
was weak in numbers. Then, too, there was factional sniping by a
number of opposition groups and individuals, among them Leon
Trotsky, with whom Lenin had many differences until the victory of
the October Revolution. Between congresses Lenin engaged in
polemics with Karl Kautsky, whom he criticized for his "surface
radicalism"; with Georges Sorel, the French syndicalist theoretician;
and especially with the German right-wing revisionists who in 1912
proposed an alliance between Socialists and middle-class liberals and
whose opportunism reached such a point that they no longer
opposed the taxes on which war budgets were based. Answering
Kautsky, who had favored the admission of the British Labour Party
into the Second International, Lenin maintained that that party,
lacking a genuine Marxist ideology, would only serve to strengthen

the right wing. On the other hand, he was no more indulgent toward the left-wing sectarianism of a Hyndman in England or an Avramov in Bulgaria.

When the Copenhagen Congress met on August 28, 1910, it presented a kind of world parliament of the working class. There were thirty-three countries represented: all the European countries and the most important nations in North and South America, as well as Japan, South Africa, and Australia—all in all, 8,000,000 dues-paying members. In his opening speech Emile Vandervelde rightly stressed the world power of the Second International. Struggles in various lands were reflected in the atmosphere of the Congress: in Spain there was police terror against the masses who were hostile to military adventures in Morocco; a strike involving 300,000 workers in Sweden; the beginnings of a nationalist revolution in Turkey; agitation in Persia and India; political awakening in China. Hence it is not surprising that colonialism was once again a central issue. Here unity was difficult to achieve because of the obvious nationalist tendencies in various parties of the International. On the Czech question, for example, the Austrian Socialists led by Renner were unyielding. The German trade-union leader Legien treated the Czechs as "foreigners." Thus the Congress resolution was not applicable to "Czechia" (a pejorative term for the Czech nation).

The resolution on peace and disarmament was also strongly influenced by the revisionists, who wanted to obtain disarmament through parliamentary means. Another hotly debated question was whether cooperatives should be considered instruments of struggle or organizations useful for coming to an understanding with the bourgeoisie. Jules Guesde, supported by Lenin, was for the first proposition, whereas the Russian Social Revolutionary Chernov and the German Elm wanted to make the cooperatives a key factor in social reform.

From one congress to the next, the world situation worsened. The imperialist powers sharpened their weapons, and between England and Germany there was a bitter rivalry for control of the seas. Militarist Germany, with the restless, unpredictable William II on the throne, sought world hegemony. In Africa the clash was almost at hand: the conflict between Germany and the Western powers over Morocco brought them to the brink of war. The "Bureau" of the

French Socialist Party sent a round-robin letter to its sister parties calling for an emergency meeting of the International, but the Germans and the English held back, and so the initiative failed. The German Socialists were moving steadily to the right. Even in Kautsky's writings there were disturbing comments—as, for example, a tendency to discern anti-war as well as frankly pro-war trends in capitalism. This attitude on the part of the German Social Democratic Party was reflected at the 1912 Chemnitz Congress. Meanwhile the Socialist movement continued to make headway. In Germany there was the great election victory of 1912, in which the number of Social Democratic deputies rose to 110. In France there were 1,400,000 votes for the Socialists, enough to elect 103 deputies. But in more than one instance these gains were made at the expense of principles. This slide into opportunism was at times slowed down by the revolutionary behavior of the masses. Thus, under their pressure the Congress of the Italian Socialist Party expelled the ultra-revisionist Bissolati, who had gone so far as to approve Italy's war against Turkey.

On the eve of the Congress of Basle, which took the form of an extraordinary session before the outbreak of hostilities in the Balkan Wars, an article by Kautsky appeared in which he dealt with the relative ineffectiveness of extreme anti-war measures such as a general strike or an armed uprising, and emphasized propaganda instead. Lenin, unable to attend the Congress, asked Plekhanov to present his viewpoint, which was opposed to Kautsky's. But the Congress leadership, fearing that any discussion might compromise the unity of the various groups, shut off the debate on the Lenin-Kautsky disagreement. The Basle Congress itself lasted only two days. It ended somewhat dramatically with a solemn session in the cathedral, during which the bells of Basle tolled an appeal for peace. All the delegates, including the right-wing groups, took an oath to fight resolutely against the threat of war that hung over them like a cloud. Keir Hardie evoked the might of 45,000,000 Socialist voters in Europe alone. Viktor Adler foretold the doom of the warmongers in Austria if the Hapsburg dual monarchy continued its policies of provocation. Not all who participated in the Basle Congress, however, remained true to the oath they had sworn; but one delegate, at least, did: Jean Jaurès. He became a tireless champion of peace. His voice was heard for the last time on the international scene at the last Congress of the Second International before the outbreak of war, in July, 1914.

World War I broke out on July 28, 1914; one of its first casualties was the international Socialist movement. In Germany only Karl Liebknecht—Wilhelm Leibknecht's son—voted in the Reichstag against war credits. I was a living witness to the moral and political cave-in of the German Social Democratic Party. At Leipzig, where I was studying, I worked closely with the Socialist Youth. When war was declared I saw how many of my young Socialist comrades succumbed to patriotic propaganda that thundered: "All Germans are one." Similarly in France, where the French Socialist Party adopted the slogan of Union sacrée—sacred unity—and voted for the war credits after having criticized their German comrades for the same action. The French Socialist Sembat entered the cabinet. In Russia, Plekhanov spoke out for war against Germany, the violator of treaties, as it had shown itself to be when it invaded Belgium. As may be seen, this was a pell-mell abandonment of all the pledges made to the international working class. Who was mainly responsible for this ideological collapse? Even now it is impossible to single out any one group as exclusively responsible; but the German-Austrian aggressors bear a heavy responsibility since they had taken the first step toward a general conflict. In any event, the Basle oath was shattered. The headquarters of the Second International was moved to London.

There was one notable exception. One group kept the Basle oath: the Russian Bolshevik Party, unanimous in its "no" vote on the war credits. A firmer and more principled attitude in 1914, like that of the Bolsheviks, would have prevented most of the Socialist parties, during the next few decades, from slipping into one compromise after another. The Bolsheviks, for their part, were not content merely to vote against the war credits; like Karl Leibknecht and Rosa Luxemburg later in Germany, they began strong agitation among the masses under the slogans: "Overthrow the Imperial Government" and "Turn the imperialist war into a civil war." Another of their slogans was "Fraternize with the soldiers at the front," an appeal which as time went on proved unusually effective.

Following an entirely different course, the Second International, which, despite everything, had for twenty-five years rendered important service to the cause of socialism, now began to lose the confidence and support of the masses. Inevitably, new and younger Socialists arose who sought inspiration in the teachings of the Socialist leaders of the past and in those contemporary Socialist groups and individuals who refused to adopt the position of the reactionary bourgeoisie in either camp of the warring powers and who reasserted the need to resume the fight for socialism.

The opportunist trends were many, bearing various labels: in France, there was "Millerandism," named after the French Socialist who had moved into the bourgeois camp at a time when nothing justified his defection; in Germany, there was "Bernsteinism," which sought to give right-wing socialism a theoretical underpinning; in Britain, the more conservative leaders of the labor movement, invoking patriotism, exploited the war to wage their fight against the more radical Socialists. The latter, stoutly opposed to Prussian imperialism, sought nevertheless to maintain intact the solidarity of the international working class.

Whereas some of those who previously had been considered members of the Socialist Left, such as Kautsky and others, now argued that defense of one's country was a fact, that the working class had a stake in that defense, and that the collapse of the Second International was merely a transitory event, Lenin ridiculed what he called Socialist patriotism. He wanted medals awarded to those who had become "social patriots" and "social chauvinists": one side of the medal to bear likenesses of Kaiser William II and Czar Nicholas II and the other side the heads of Plekhanov and Kautsky. If at the outset of the war there had been more Socialists like the German deputy Frank, who volunteered for the front and was killed in action shortly thereafter, it would not have taken a year after the initial battles for many of the Socialist leaders, who had forgotten everything they had said or written before hostilities erupted, to realize that their change of attitude was not shared by an important section of the working class in their respective countries. The masses soon began to get fed up with the frightful slaughter. By 1915 some of the Socialist leaders who had hitherto unconditionally supported their government suddenly began discussing the need of preparing for a return to peace.

A manifesto issued by Kautsky, Haase, and Bernstein drew

attention to the increasing inclination of the ruling class to proclaim war aims that differed from their first official proclamations and that revealed an annexationist spirit. Similarly in France, Jean Longuet, Marx's grandson, and some of his associates kept their distance from the *Union sacrée* government and from Socialists like Renaudel, who supported it completely. These were somewhat tardy but significant shifts. Much in these initial pacifist attitudes, however, was timid, confused, or contradictory. By contrast, Lenin raised uncompromisingly the banner of revolutionary internationalism.

Once World War I was over, efforts to revive the corpse of the Second International quickened. The "social patriots"—who had collaborated with their bourgeois governments—and the "centrists" met in 1919 in the Swiss capital and launched the so-called Berne International. Nevertheless, there were Socialists, such as the Belgian Vandervelde, who refused to sit at the same table with the Germans; and most of the delegates attributed primary guilt and responsibility to Germany. The Germans too were absolved, however, despite the bloody repression by the postwar Social Democratic government in Germany, in which workers who at war's end fought for a Socialist Germany were shot down on the streets.

In that same year, 1919, a new meeting of the revived Second International was held in Amsterdam, followed by an attempted World Congress in Lucerne—a rather ambitious name for the venture inasmuch as barely fifty delegates attended it. Enough, however, to reveal the differences between the right-wing Socialists and the centrists who called the treaties of Versailles and Saint-Germain imposed treaties (*Diktats*). In the end, however, they accepted a compromise resolution on the question of the treaties in exchange for a resolution condemning the policy of blockade and intervention against revolutionary Russia. In Leipzig, also in 1919, the independent German Socialists convened a congress. Under the leadership of Kautsky, Bernstein, and Haase, they had broken away from the party in the midst of the war and constituted a separate faction. Here for a passing moment the majority of the delegates went on record in favor of the Soviet system, a theme which provoked heated discussions at future gatherings. A new conference was held in 1920, from which the German, Austrian, and French centrists stayed away. The main resolution dealt with two very controversial subjects: war guilt and the dictatorship of the proletariat. With the centrists absent, the conference revealed a frankly anti-Russian tone.

In the midst of the struggle between the moderate and revolutionary Socialists in the first decades of the twentieth century, a powerful figure emerges: Rosa Luxemburg. Personally and politically, she was an extraordinary leader, endowed with genius, a Marxist thinker of the highest order. Unjustly neglected after her tragic assassination in 1919, she was the subject of two books that appeared in 1966. In them she comes to life again, at the very heart of the controversy caused by the Sino-Soviet rupture and the crisis in the world Socialist movement. Of the two books, the later one—*Rosa Luxemburg* by J. P. Nettl—is the best-documented biography in English of the revolutionary heroine. I was fortunate enough to have been closely associated with her, so I am excerpting from my personal notes a few salient comments on her life and activity in the German Socialist movement and the Second International, where her voice—like that of Jaurès—rang out prophetically on the very eve of World War I.

When Rosa Luxemburg returned to Poland, after her studies in Zurich, Switzerland, she undertook with Leo Jogisches to reorganize the Polish working class into a party well grounded in theory and revolutionary in spirit. That spirit was a distinctive trait of Rosa Luxemburg's—a woman who combined unusual sensitivity with a profound and original mind. Jogisches, also a Pole, was a friend from her Zurich days and the person closest to her. In Zurich the future author of *Capital Accumulation* also met such Russian Socialist leaders as Plekhanov, Axelrod, and Vera Zasulich. On her return to Poland, Rosa Luxemburg felt that her main task was to convince the Polish working class that the road to follow was not that of Narodnaya Volya (Will of the People), that is, of the populist Socialists attracted by individual terror and "Blanquism," but the road of Marxism. In her activities she soon moved to Germany, where the Socialist movement was already a force to be reckoned with. At first there was a tendency to see in Rosa only a talented polemicist, a fiery agitator who impressed the more stolid Germans.

They had not yet discovered in her the theoretician, infinitely more subtle and discerning than the prestigious German Socialist leaders whose reputation dominated the Second International.

Rosa Luxemburg did not go along with the general sense of complacency as the German party grew in numbers and strengthened its positions in parliament; she sought instead a party nourished by a revolutionary substance, not relying on files and briefcases but forged in struggle. Only struggle, she asserted, makes the party a live and effective thing; only struggle deepens and strengthens class sentiments. Intelligent leadership of a party means knowing when to choose the proper moment to intervene; yet it must also maintain a long-range and over-all view of events. Hence, it must not fear a possible momentary defeat if the general interest of the cause demands it. The specter of "defeat," a frequent excuse for doing nothing, did not faze Rosa Luxemburg. "Only step by step, stride by stride, retracing the Calvary of its own bitter experiences, can the proletarian revolution attain complete clarity and maturity"—in those words she summed up her concept of the march of socialism.

Her concept of the general strike, the subject of one of her most important pamphlets—and virtually every pamphlet she wrote was as valuable as a full-length book—illustrates the way in which she merged theory and practice in analyzing problems. She thought it absurd to look upon the general strike as an isolated act that could be carried out by decree. The general strike had to occur at a specific moment in the class struggle, as a result of years of revolutionary propaganda and action.

After a brief stay in France following the Russian Revolution of 1905, where she made contact with Jules Guesde and Edouard Vaillant, two of the militant leaders of French socialism, Rosa Luxemburg went to Germany. There, to avoid harassment by the Prussian police authorities, she made herself "respectable" by a *pro forma* marriage with the son of an old friend, Gustav Lübeck. He helped her thereby acquire German citizenship and, once that goal was attained, disappeared from her life. In a short time her strong personality attracted attention in a party that numbered many leaders of renown. She was soon completely involved in an extensive controversy over the proper theory and tactics of socialism, in which she immediately took a stand against the revisionist-opportunist trend that was beginning to make headway. The party's success in gaining new members and the favorable outcome of several strikes led by the trade unions under Social Democratic guidance did not lull her critical spirit. To Rosa Luxemburg these victories tended to exaggerate the importance of parliamentary and trade-union gains, achieved as they were at the expense of revolutionary content. Prosperity accompanying or following a period of relative social calm had deceived a number of Socialist leaders who found it more comfortable to conceive of a peaceful advance of socialism to power than to lead the masses in struggle by spurning facile solutions and compromises. Rosa Luxemburg was not deceived. With penetrating insight, she foresaw the sharpening of the workers' struggles in Germany as militarism became more aggressive and imperialist. She demanded of the Social Democratic Party tighter discipline and intellectual firmness to enable it to face up to the big battles that were approaching.

Rosa Luxemburg's dialectical talents were outstanding. The Socialist historian Franz Mehring called her *Capital Accumulation* "the finest and deepest work since Marx's *Capital*." Her brilliance and irony were shown to best advantage in the polemic with Eduard Bernstein—a polemic that began with his earliest writings and continued for years in the Socialist press and at party congresses. Now, more than a half century later, Rosa Luxemburg's writings seem unusually relevant to our time.

Influenced by the French Socialist historian Louis Héritier, who wrote critically on the revolutionary movements in France in 1848, Eduard Bernstein in the years prior to World War I began to assail revolutionary radicalism as the main obstacle to the achievement of socialism. He was supported by a group of intellectuals and professors, including Werner Sombart, who was then very much in vogue. Mingling economics with history and adept at improvisation and the play of ideas, Sombart had created a theory of the working class that was accepted by a section of the enlightened bourgeoisie.

But Rosa Luxemburg did not treat all adversaries alike. She fenced with Sombart without taking him too seriously. She played with him as Karl Marx had toyed with the economists of his day. One of her replies to Sombart drew the professor out of his attitude of self-assumed superiority and forced him to recognize in Rosa "a fanatical theoretician, but with a respectable intelligence." With Bernstein, however, things were different. He was a more important opponent, for around him was a group of Socialists who always invoked Marx's authority but insisted that his theories be brought up to date. Revisionism advanced in Marxist dress, until Rosa Luxemburg laid down the challenge in a pair of articles that drew widespread attention and served as the basis for the theoretical debate at forthcoming Socialist congresses. Bernstein himself was forced to acknowledge that she was a profound thinker, richly endowed with talent and fighting spirit.

When general mobilization was decreed in 1914, Rosa Luxemburg, always physically frail, was sick from a recurring heart condition. Yet she got up out of bed and went to see her closest comrades, who were supposed to constitute the left wing of the Social Democratic Party. Among the leaders, Haase and Ledebour had, at the outset, declared they would not vote the war credits. Ledebour was a former actor, a fiery orator, impressive in his cape and long unruly hair, more passionate than Haase. But later, after lengthy discussions within the Socialist parliamentary faction, the leftists yielded on the pretext of maintaining party discipline. The history of socialism is full of such instances in which party discipline has won out over principles. But discipline could not stop Karl Liebknecht inside the German Parliament, or Rosa Luxemburg on the outside. Rosa by herself was worth virtually an entire party, especially when it had practically ceased being Socialist from one day to the next. On her own she traveled throughout Germany to arouse the people. The party press refused to print her articles, except for a small newspaper in Gotha, which thereby risked suspension by the government. Within a short time, Franz Mehring, Clara Zetkin, and Karl Liebknecht had joined her in signing a declaration of principles.

I shall never forget Rosa Luxemburg during those first days of World War I. She was a living example of what a single individual can do in a concrete situation, provided that person sticks to a revolutionary position and scorns the attacks of former comrades who have deserted the struggle. Around Rosa Luxemburg a group formed, very tiny in the beginning, but confident of ultimate success because of their clear and consistent political line.

From Rosa Luxemburg's lips, in the days preceding her arrest in 1916 after one of the mass anti-war demonstrations she organized, we can hear her harsh opinion of the causes of the collapse of the Second International on the outbreak of World War I: "It was inevitable. The International was the first to surrender its belief in its own power. When during the last days of July, 1914, we met at Brussels to see what could be done, apart from Jaurès, who was determined to try everything to prevent the war, and Keir Hardie, who was ready to call for a general strike in England if general mobilization was decreed in his land, the others had given up the game as lost before anything was even discussed. And anyone who had followed the Socialist movement in the preceding years could not plead surprise. It was infested with revisionism. And the worst were the top leaders of Marxism, the so-called infallible theoreticians who had set themselves up as 'untouchables' in Germany. Kautsky, to name just one. In *Die Neue Zeit* he gives us proof of his 'flexibility.' Most ingenious! There are two materialist conceptions of history: one for peacetime and one for wartime. The appeal in the *Communist Manifesto* has been broadened to read: 'Workers of the world, unite in peace and slaughter one another in war!' "

Rosa Luxemburg answered vigorously in *Die Internationale,* in the only issue of that publication that saw the light of day. It was a controversy of long standing, not only against Kautsky, for whom Rosa Luxemburg had hitherto always shown respect, but against the majority of the German party. Just as she had fought against nationalist trends in the Polish Socialist Party, when she was a member of that body, so in the German Social Democratic Party and in the Second International she worked tirelessly to inject a more militant concept of struggle into the movement. In the revisionist tendencies of her day, Rosa Luxemburg sensed the appearance of a factor whose consequences completely escaped the others, including those who thought themselves very radical.

Loyal in principle to the Russian Revolution, inspired by the militancy shown by Lenin and his co-workers at a moment when any vacillation on their part would have jeopardized the Revolution, in view of the weakness of the Kerensky government and the threats of a Bonapartist putsch, Rosa Luxemburg nevertheless felt obliged to express her reservations constructively, to help the revolutionary

German working class formulate its program and orient its policies after the war. Her position was, as usual, straightforward and clear. To her there was no contradiction in her defending the Russian Revolution and at the same time pointing out its errors and seeking to avoid them. She was not able to finish her critique of the October Revolution, written during the last months she spent in prison. But in the scant fifty pages she wrote, she expressed her viewpoint with clarity. What was happening in Russia seemed perfectly understandable to Rosa Luxemburg, an inevitable chain of causes and effects, including among the former the policy of aggression of German imperialism and the defection of the international working class, which could not or would not fight unequivocally on the side of the first working-class state whatever may have been its initial mistakes.

It would be absurd, said Rosa Luxemburg, and worthy only of "parlor Bolsheviks" to demand of Lenin and his collaborators that in the circumstances in which they found themselves they establish a beautiful democracy and a flourishing Socialist economy. Lenin had shown genius in discerning what tactics had to be followed in the first revolutionary period. Every revolution puts to the test the political wisdom of its main leaders; and only that party achieves victory that chooses the correct aims and directives and goes forward with sureness of will, not heeding the siren voices that seek to divert it from the path, whether they be calls for the re-establishment of inner unity or threats to its existence. So wrote Rosa Luxemburg.

It was the lesson of the English Revolution of 1642, as of the French Revolution of 1789. Descendants of Lilburne's Levelers and the French Jacobins, the Bolsheviks took power in their own right. They were the only ones who saw clearly in the midst of a chaotic situation, further complicated by outside events. On this point Rosa Luxemburg identified herself completely with Lenin. Her reservations came later, particularly on the agrarian question. Acknowledging that while in prison she did not possess adequate study material, but judging that this did not substantially affect her general viewpoint, she asserted that Lenin's slogan "Go and take your lands" might, at the moment it was launched, have been the only way of gaining the support of the peasants in the face of the counter-revolution. But in itself such a measure foreclosed, or greatly complicated, prospects for ultimate land socialization. What was being created was not social property but another form of private ownership. Antagonisms between country and city were thus intensified—private property in the rural areas, collectivization in the cities. She feared that this antagonism would slow down the movement of the Russian Revolution by engendering all sorts of friction with the peasantry.

Her second objection was of a lesser nature. She referred to the dissolution of the Constituent Assembly. Rosa Luxemburg agreed with Lenin's decision not to place the future of the Revolution in the hands of an Assembly elected in the Kerensky period and one that mirrored the confusion and vacillations of the Mensheviks and the liberal Cadets. She felt, however, that another Assembly should have been convoked in its stead. Without worshipping parliamentarism, she felt the masses needed ways and means of expressing their desires. A new Constituent Assembly might have contributed to this end. Here again one encounters the influence of the English Puritan Revolution of the seventeenth century. For seven years the Long Parliament accomplished its mission, reflecting all the changes in the people's attitude—from the first polite skirmishes with the Crown to the abolition of the House of Lords, the execution of Charles I, and the proclamation of the Republic.

One other German Socialist stood out in bold relief—proof again that under certain concrete conditions a single individual can effectively compensate for an entire group. Lacking revolutionary élan, the German Social Democratic parliamentary faction had become demoralized and impotent, but one person did emerge from their docile and submissive ranks: Karl Liebknecht. Whenever he began to speak in parliament the conservative deputies scowled and sneered, the scars on their cheeks received during their traditional student duels reddening and deepening. The hall became charged with passion and seething hatred. Liebknecht began one such speech on the eve of war by attacking a decree of the Governor of Frankfurt regarding teaching methods in the schools. The decree sought to ridicule "the illusions of brotherhood among peoples and international pacifist sentimentality." "If the duty of teaching the truth"—rejoined Liebknecht—"had any meaning in our country, what we would have to teach is the truth behind the state of siege. Show them what lies behind this aggressive and warlike authoritarianism. We would have to enlighten the youth as to what interests this war is serving. Then the assassination at Sarajevo would appear in its true light. We would see that certain circles in Germany and Austria looked upon it as a godsend, because that assassination gave them the pretext they longed for to go to war."

Liebknecht's words created an uproar. The bell of the presiding officer, Count von Schwerin-Löwitz, could not quiet the storm of protests from the right-wing benches. From the benches of the so-called Left, Liebknecht's presumed party comrades, no one rose to support him. He did not need such support. His voice was heard above the tumult: "That is the truth! [New protests, ringing of the chairman's bell.] That is the truth! It was only a pretext. The necessary mask. . . ."

The chairman finally succeeded in making himself heard: "I must ask Deputy Liebknecht to apologize forthwith." Liebknecht went on: "That is the truth! The trouble is you don't want to hear it." Voices arose: "Out with him! Throw him out on the street!" "Yes, go ahead, avoid the truth! *You* should get out! *You* won't listen to the truth!" The setting, the era, the temperament were all different; but at that moment it was like listening to Saint-Just at the French National Convention in 1792.

Count von Schwerin-Löwitz was anxious to get rid of Liebknecht, but, like a good Prussian, he wanted to do it according to the rules, so he had to wait until the third call to order before proceeding against the defiant deputy. Liebknecht now attacked the professors and scholars who spouted chauvinist propaganda: "Worthy representatives of the arts and sciences! But we still have the working class. [The deputies stirred uneasily. Then there was deep silence in the hall, followed by a second call to order.] The working class is our hope. From here I cry out to them, to those in the trenches as well as those on the home front! Lay down your arms and turn against the common enemy . . . !" Several rightist deputies started to rush toward Liebknecht. The chairman ordered everyone back to their seats. *Ordnung muss sein!* (Order must prevail!)

Then came the vote. The results were as expected: by a whopping majority the Chamber voted sanctions against Karl Liebknecht. He was ordered to leave his seat, so with firm stride he quit his place and left the hall. The Sacred Union was shattered. The working class, betrayed by its leadership, now had new leaders in Karl Liebknecht and Rosa Luxemburg. The two names remained linked until death—that is, until their assassination.

Between the two there is a third figure, inevitably a participant in the forthcoming tragedy. This was Sonia Liebknecht, Karl's wife, Russian-born, a bright, sensitive woman torn between political solidarity with her husband and the fear of losing him. Rosa Luxemburg cheered her up by writing to her from prison. Rosa's letters to Sonia have since become a part of German literature. Her talents as a writer—hitherto largely overlooked because she had written articles in simple language addressed to workers in the Left Socialist newspaper, the *Leipziger Volkszeitung*, or basic Marxist texts—now blossomed. Here is one example from a letter by Rosa to Sonia Liebknecht: "In your letter you ask: Why all this? Soniushka, life has always been this way: sorrow, separation, yearning. One must look for beauty, for a better side, in every situation. At least I have always done so. And not because of any elaborate wisdom, just simply because it came out of me. I wish I could be by your side to distract you, to talk with you, and make you feel the truth of this unique way of defending oneself!"

Again: "My new imprisonment fills me with bitterness. Why is it given to some human beings to decide the fate of others? Forgive me: without wanting to, I have to joke about it for a moment. In Dostoevsky's *Brothers Karamazov* there is a Madame Hohlakova who, constantly beset with worries, goes from one person to another asking the same questions, without even waiting for them to answer. Soniushka, the whole history of humanity—is based 'on the power of some human beings over the others.' It's a fact that has its roots deep in the material conditions of existence. Only a long and painful future process will be able to change it. We now find ourselves at the beginning of that process and you ask: 'Why, why all this?' Why? Because there are no concepts that can be applied to all of life and its forms. Why? Why are there butterflies in the world? I don't know; but each time a butterfly flutters into my cell I get an inner feeling of release. . . .

"Thank you for the Galsworthy novel. I finished reading it last night. I liked it less than *The Man of Property*, and of course that has nothing to do with its social content. When I read a novel I'm only interested in its artistic merit. In Galsworthy I find a certain obsession with being clever; one sees that Shaw and Oscar Wilde disturb him. His irony is subtle, but forced. I think that an artist can give his characters all the ironical thrust he wishes, but not laugh cynically at them. Gerhart Hauptmann's *Emanuel Quint*, for instance, is a bloody satire of modern society, as good as any that has been written for a great many years now. Nevertheless Hauptmann refrains from wounding for the mere pleasure of convincing us of his wit. So in the end we confront the world of petty miseries with wide-open eyes, in which there appear to be even the faint traces of a tear. Galsworthy, on the other hand, with his casual witty remarks, makes me think of a dinner companion sitting next to me—every time a guest enters he feels obliged to whisper some malicious gossip about the newcomer in my ear.

"Personally I feel quite well. In a tiny garden, here, or in the country I feel better than in the midst of . . . a Party congress. To you I can say this without your suspecting that I am about to betray socialism. You know that, despite everything, I shall die at my post, in a street brawl or in a prison fortress. But my most intimate 'I' belongs more to the ants than to the 'comrades.'"

German Social Democracy turned its back on the Kaiser; it also turned its back on socialism. Basically, it had not changed. Some had had illusions when, at the end of World War I and the defeat of the imperial armies, the first republican government was formed. Made up of three Majority Socialists—that is, right-wingers—and three Independent Socialists, from a group that vacillated between fits of weakness and shows of strength, the government despite everything seemed somehow leftist. But Cabinet solidarity lasted only briefly. The antagonisms that had divided the Majority and the Independent Socialists during the war were now sharpened in the postwar period, causing constant clashes within the government. Meanwhile the counter-revolution advanced. As so often in history, the reactionaries set themselves up as defenders of the vested interests, of social privileges and wealth. The speed with which they acted and their lack of scruples in choosing their methods of attack gave them an advantage over the leftist forces. Feigning humiliation at Germany's defeat and eager to make up for the harm inflicted on the country, the army—conquered by the Allied powers—thought only and continually of revenge. Revenge abroad and revenge at home, saddling the civilians with the loss of the war.

From one end of Germany to another, reactionary elements engaged in conspiratorial activity: "Leagues to fight Bolshevism," patriotic militias, *Freikorps* (volunteer corps), multiplied. They bore various labels but all had a single aim: liquidate the Revolution. One of the preferred methods was to infiltrate the new people's organizations. Army officers and Junkers—big landowners—had succeeded, absurd as it may appear, in taking control of the "Soldiers' Councils." The generals gave guidance, as in the heyday of the Kaiser's reign. Without any orders from the government, General von Winterfeld marched on Aachen and Cologne "to re-establish order." The high command of the army in the Baltic region hastily organized a "division of iron," with a view to stopping the onrush of the Bolshevik wave, to use the language of the right-wing press. The Republic was only six weeks old—no one could accuse the reactionaries of having lost time.

Faced with the threat of a rebirth of militarism and aware of the government's lack of vigor, only one revolutionary force, the Spartacists, moved into action. (The situation foreshadowed what happened in France in the 1930's, when the slogan became: "Rather Hitler than the People's Front!") The Spartacists organized open-air meetings, usually on the Alexanderplatz in Berlin, a working-class neighborhood. They remained out of doors because no one would rent them a hall.

Once again Rosa Luxemburg and Karl Liebknecht were looked to and idolized by the masses. Liebknecht was not a good speaker, but he was an extraordinary agitator. His language was direct: "After four years of slaughter humanity has been thrust into the forge. With hammer in hand the working class is here, ready to forge a new world. They told us: the National Assembly, it's through them you'll get your freedom. But the National Assembly doesn't mean anything but political democracy. We see other countries in Europe and America where political democracy has ruled for some time and where capitalism also rules. The political power the working class won on November 9 has already been partly snatched out of its hands. On the pretext that they were indispensable for demobilization, the government has kept the former generals and officers, who now are doing nothing but plotting against the Republic. The generals who led Germany into ruin are now manipulating the guardians of order. Instead of appearing before a revolutionary tribunal, they set themselves up as judges. . . ." "Revolutionary tribunal! That's what we need!" Such shouts were heard from various places in the crowd. A soldier got up on the speakers' platform and shouted: "If we had shot a few dozen officers and bourgeois, they wouldn't be plotting now against the people." "Long live the Red Army!"

Liebknecht's speech on Alexanderplatz was a desperate appeal. On the one hand, it sought to arouse the conscience of the Socialist government and alert it to the seriousness of the intrigues by the reactionaries and the army officers. On the other hand, it was an exhortation to the masses to launch a counter-offensive. Liebknecht further declared: "They accuse us of wanting terror. The very same ones who had no compassion when they saw German youth dying in the trenches for a false ideal tremble at the prospect of violating the so-called basic principles of society. What basic principles? The basis of exploitation and shame, the crime of years upon years against the people. We only want the Revolution to follow its course. The order they claim to defend is a springboard for the reactionaries to regain their former positions. That is why we say: 'Arm ourselves to defend the Revolution!' If the government of Socialist leaders is derelict in doing its duty, we shall see to it that the working class fulfills it. Workers, soldiers! Your road is clearly marked. Join the revolutionary ranks. Form the Red militia. Demand the disarming of the reactionaries!"

As on other occasions in history before and after 1919, the reactionaries chose a Socialist, Gustav Noske, to keep the working class in check. Taking the notorious General Hoffmann as his chief of staff, Noske defined his policies in a single brief order: "Anyone caught on the streets with weapons in his hand fighting against the government will be shot." Along with the repression, the campaign of lies and slanders against Liebknecht and Luxemburg intensified. Government circles spread the rumor that the two had fled. Their friends no longer knew where to hide them safely. They had to be moved from the friendly house of a Dr. Bernstein in the Hallische

Tor section to a worker's apartment. The right-wing press pulled out all stops in reviling them. But it was the Social Democratic paper *Vorwärts* that took the lead in inciting its readers to assassination with doggerel verse! "Go to the cemetery; you will bury hundreds of your brothers. [Victims of Noske, of course! *Author's note.*] Proletarians! Karl and Rosa? Don't look for them. They are not there!"

But Karl and Rosa were at their combat posts. Rosa replied to Noske in *Die Rote Fahne (The Red Flag)*: "In 1831 Cabinet Minister Sebastiani announced complacently to the French Chamber: 'Order rules in Warsaw,' while Pankievich's soldiers bloodily entered the outskirts of the city and then, after a terrible onslaught, completed their shameful slaughter. 'Order rules in Berlin,' Ebert and Noske proclaim. They hail the warriors they meet on the streets of the capital, fighting against their own people, and crown their bayonets with withered laurels. Receive the praises of the bourgeoisie! Parade beneath their terraces! They will cheer you with fluttering handkerchiefs, joyous in their delirium because at the last moment you have saved not only their social status but also the honor of the German army. Parade, army of victory!"

The army of victory crowned its repression with the dual assassination of the two great leaders of the German working class. Seized in their final hiding place, the house of a comrade in Berlin-West, Rosa Luxemburg and Karl Liebknecht were taken to the Eden Hotel, headquarters of the Cavalry Guards division. As Liebknecht left the hotel to enter a car that was to take him to jail, a cavalryman named Otto Runge rushed forward and struck his head three or four times with a rifle butt. His bleeding head was bandaged with a makeshift handkerchief and the car took off. Soon, however, a flat tire was detected, or allegedly detected. Liebknecht had to get out of the car and was ordered to proceed on foot. Behind him followed his escort, four officers and several soldiers—more than enough for a single wounded prisoner. A volley of shots rang out. Liebknecht fell dead.

Warned that "something serious has happened," hearing rumors of her husband's death, Sonia Liebknecht crisscrossed Berlin in a desperate, futile search. The setting sun blinded her eyes at times, but she kept on looking. Liebknecht's corpse, like that of any unknown, had been hauled to the emergency room at the Botanical

Gardens by the officer in charge of the escort, Captain Pflugk-Hartung.

Twenty minutes after Liebknecht had left the Eden Hotel, Rosa Luxemburg, weak and wasting away, came out. The very same soldier, Otto Runge, who had of course remained scot-free after his assault on Liebknecht, was still on guard duty. Brutally he struck the woman prisoner with his rifle butt, and she almost fainted as she entered the waiting car. Her head, uncovered, was bowed. Lieutenant Colonel Kurt Vogel had only to stretch out his arm to kill her. One shot was enough. Soldiers grabbed the corpse and dumped it into the canal near the Cornelius Bridge. I had to write Rosa Luxemburg's obituary for *El Sol*, the Madrid newspaper. Never have I written an article with a heavier heart.

In the period after World War I, the right-wing Socialists came to the rescue of the threatened bourgeoisie, assenting to anything rather than to seize the favorable situation to build socialism. The Social Democrats, in the person of Noske, already notorious for his suppression of the sailors' mutiny in Kiel, took on the task which members of the liberal bourgeoisie shunned: persecution of the Spartacists and the vanguard of the working class. Not having troops of his own, Noske turned to the old imperial officers and, whether by accident or by design, surrounded himself with the most reactionary ones, who took a special delight in squaring their personal accounts with the Revolution. It was in this framework that General von Luttwitz's expeditionary corps operated, everywhere taking the offensive against the Spartacists. For days there was fighting around the building of the Socialist newspaper *Vorwärts*, until the Spartacists were driven into illegality. Such was the situation at the beginning of January, 1920, when I reached Berlin.

The Russian Revolution was the great dividing line that led to significant changes in the world Socialist movement. The year 1920 saw an extraordinary swing of Socialists into the Communist camp, beginning with the German Independent Socialists. The shift spread quickly to other parties. In France it led to an open split in the Socialist Party, a great many members leaving to form the Communist Party. The same thing happened, to a lesser degree, in Great Britain and elsewhere. To check this pro-Communist swing of the workers, the centrists created a halfway organization which with deliberate irony they called the Second and a Half International, that is, midway between the Second and the Third. It was an ingenious attempt to bridge a gap in the workers' ranks that was increasingly widening, but in the end, the grounds for compromise proved to be illusory.

From the end of the war to the rise of the Nazi movement, many chances to advance the German revolution were lost. Had the Left been only half as aggressive as Hitler's followers, it could have strengthened its position. It might not have been able to set up a Socialist regime forthwith, but at least it could have laid the basis for one. As in retrospect we analyze the problem objectively, we must acknowledge that the leadership of the workers' parties shares responsibility for the failure. The masses below, though they did not always respond to revolutionary appeals, gave proof on various occasions of their potential for struggle—provided they were properly led and had a clear political line to follow.

Without a vigorous response from the workers, the first attempt at a right-wing *coup d'état* would have succeeded more than ten years before Hitler came to power. Taking advantage of Noske's tolerance of revenge-seeking officers of every stripe, the military plotters came together and merged their various gangs of adventurers and murderers. One of them, a Captain Erhardt, who had fought in Africa and during World War I had commanded a torpedo-boat flotilla, distinguishing himself in the naval battle of Skagerrak and the fight for the Baltic islands, exploited his war record to the full. In 1919 he organized the first important *Freikorps*, "the anti-Communist volunteers," who were specialists in assassinating left-wing leaders. Other anti-republican officers, such as Colonel Bauer and Commander Pabst, vied with Erhardt in forming shock brigades. With their joined forces, on March 13, 1920, the Erhardt brigade advanced on Berlin and occupied the city. They needed a civilian figurehead to lend an air of respectability to their putsch, and they found such a one: Wolfgang Kapp, son of an 1848 revolutionary who had emigrated to the United States. Kapp now became the nominal head of the uprising; and the Kapp Putsch became a precedent and example for later Hitlerite activities. Kapp "decreed" the end of the country's legal government, the dissolution of parliament, and proclaimed himself Chancellor of the Reich and Prime Minister of Prussia. He appointed von Jagow, a notorious police chief, Minister of the Interior, and named von Luttwitz Army Minister. The right-wing Socialist Winnig, who held a high post in East Prussia, joined Kapp; on the other hand, the most intelligent and farsighted general in the Reichswehr, Hans von Seeckt, remained loyal to the republican government. His position enabled him later, within the framework of the Weimar Republic, to reorganize a German army which, in size and significance, quickly went beyond the restrictive clauses of the Versailles Treaty.

At first it looked as though the Kapp Putsch might succeed. Newspapers controlled by the insurgents printed a series of victory communiqués. The Social Democrats called a general strike, but the Communist Party, on the other hand, initially decided not to lift a finger in defense of the bourgeois order. Nonetheless, the general strike call and appeals for sabotage were widely heeded. Whatever grievances they may have had against the Social Democrats' policies of compromise and surrender, the workers decided to fight in defense of the legitimate republican government. When the government returned to Berlin from Stuttgart, where it had taken refuge, there was widespread jubilation.

That would have been the moment to press for Socialist policies, inasmuch as the working class was aroused and indignant at the audacity of the anti-republican putschists. When the general strike ended on March 20, the trade-union movement, led by Legien, presented a series of concrete demands to the government: sweeping changes in the government of the Reich and the state of Prussia, with the appointment of reliable progressives to key posts; dismissal of all reactionary civil servants; immediate socialization of those branches of the economy ready for it, beginning with the construction industry; and the ouster of Noske from the government. The last point was granted. Two Socialists with a reputation for political courage and energy, Otto Braun and Carl Severing, entered the Prussian government as Prime Minister and Minister of the Interior, respectively. (But years later, in 1932, at a decisive moment in German history, when the anti-Fascist opposition should have joined ranks and fought Hitler, Braun and Severing proved as weak as the

Social Democrats they had criticized in 1920, ending their careers as defeated, discredited men.)

The chance to revitalize the influence of the working class was lost. With the defeat of the Kapp Putsch, a series of more or less Socialist measures could have been introduced, but the *Betriebsräte-gesetz* (Law for Factory Councils) passed by parliament fell far short of the workers' minimal demands. Its only immediate effect was to annoy those who had fought to defend republican institutions. When under the leadership of the Independent Socialists and the Communists a march on the Reichstag was held, the police broke up the demonstration, leaving dead and wounded among the demonstrators. As a result of their more militant policies, the Independent Socialists now gained in popularity. In the elections of June 6, 1920, they increased their seats in parliament from 22 to 81, whereas the right-wing Majority Socialists lost 55 seats. Nevertheless, there was no real unity of action among the parties of the Left; local rebellions and uprisings broke out sporadically, without, however, yielding results. One of the most violent occurred in 1921 in central Germany, under the leadership of Max Hölz, a working-class leader who was a war veteran and who, after forming a federation of young Protestants, joined the Communist Party. Many died in the Max Hölz uprising, and Hölz himself, accused of having murdered a big landowner, was sentenced to life imprisonment but later, after seven years in various prisons, was pardoned in 1928.

In the struggle between the abortive revolution and the reactionaries bent on regaining their lost power as quickly as possible, some of the best minds of the German Left were lost. The reactionaries *always* acted with unbridled fury, whereas on many occasions the Left vacillated. Even so, despite the reactionaries' greed for wealth and power, they would not have won so easily without the help of the pseudo-Left, which hated the true Left more than it did the class enemy. Thus in Munich, Kurt Eisner, one of the finest Socialists in Germany, fell. He had been forced to share power with the right-wing Socialists, who impelled him, against his will, to summon the Bavarian parliament at a bad time, simply as a gesture to those who believed strongly in parliamentarianism; but then and later, in Germany and elsewhere, it was one of the reasons for the

Socialist retreat. The Bavarian Diet met on February 21, 1919. As Eisner was walking toward the parliament building, shots rang out and Prime Minister Eisner fell dead. His assailant was a fanatic, anti-Semitic aristocrat, Count Arco-Valley.

The workers reacted vigorously to the assassination, and a few weeks later, on April 7, they proclaimed the Soviet Republic of Bavaria. The left-wing Socialists, the Independents, participated in the movement under the leadership of the brilliant poet-dramatist Ernst Toller, whereas the Communist Party led by Eugen Leviné sought to delay the proclamation of the Bavarian Soviet, feeling that it was premature. Leviné, of Russian origin, was a brilliant, experienced Socialist who had become a Communist. But once the first Soviet Republic in Germany was proclaimed, Leviné and his followers supported it with all their energy. The Bavarian revolutionaries thought they could join with Austria, where a revolutionary movement was under way, and thus serve as a bridge to Hungary, where the Hungarian Soviet Republic had just been declared.

In the Munich Soviet was an anarchist writer of great talent, Erich Mühsam, a powerful agitator with a biting pen, who was very popular in German literary circles. But the outstanding political figure in the Soviet was another anarchist, Gustav Landauer. Sharply at odds with the increasingly bourgeoisified and bureaucratic Social Democrats, Landauer reflected the ideas of Kropotkin and Bakunin, and had succeeded in forming an active group that worked in the underground. Yet Landauer was also ready to work with Socialists and, later, Communists. He and his friends were grouped around the magazine *Der Sozialist*, which, in contrast to many similar publications written in a dull and heavy-footed style, was extremely well written; even persons outside the movement were among its gifted contributors.

The Bavarian Soviet Republic was short-lived. Local reactionaries, supported by the right-wing Socialist Hoffmann, fought back, and Munich soon became the scene of violent struggles. The workers, however, held firm, and a more radical Soviet Republic replaced the earlier one. Hoffmann's reply was predictable. His government, set up parallel to that of the Soviets, brought sufficient troops into Munich—100,000 in all—to deal a decisive blow. They entered the Bavarian capital under orders to crush the Communist movement.

The workers resisted for a week, but then the radical experiment collapsed, and the white terror began. Gustav Landauer, who for so long had practiced Tolstoyan nonviolence, who had never forsworn his humanitarian idealism, deliberately choosing the cabinet post of Minister of Education and Popular Enlightenment in the Bavarian Soviet, was assassinated by a band of soldiers. The victorious reactionaries lost no time in meting out death sentences to Leviné and others. Mühsam and Toller were sentenced to long prison terms.

I was well acquainted with the German Socialist movement and its leaders from the years preceding World War I to the advent of Hitler to power in the 1930's. In 1928 I returned to Germany. The turbulent years were over—years of pre-Fascist coups such as the Kapp Putsch, the assassination of Foreign Minister Walther Rathenau (hated as a progressive and a Jew), the Munich trial of Adolf Hitler and General von Ludendorff, and street fights all over the country which pitted armed reactionaries against working-class groups. Now the German people were quiet and eager to have a good time, enthusiastic about sports, hiking, and dancing. At the Café Wien, gathering place for foreign journalists, anyone who dared suggest, after the fiasco of Hitler's 1923 Beer Hall Putsch in Munich, that the Nazi menace was not entirely over, was derided as a spoil-sport. The Social Democrats had just won an impressive electoral victory, gaining 153 deputies, and seemed to be in control of the situation for some time to come.

The aging Marshal Hindenburg dutifully played the parliamentary game: a broad coalition cabinet was set up, its Chancellor Hermann Müller, a Social Democrat who had signed the Treaty of Versailles, reason enough to earn the hatred of the Right; Gustav Stresemann was Minister of Foreign Affairs; and the indispensable Severing was Minister of the Interior. The new face in the Cabinet was that of Rudolf Hilferding, a Socialist, as Finance Minister, of whom great things were expected. Hitler's followers, on the other hand, had suffered a sharp setback in the 1928 elections. There were barely twenty extreme-right-wing deputies in the new Chamber.

Among the Social Democrats of that day were several personalities of interest. One of them, Rudolf Breitscheid, looked like a British lord and was so proficient an orator that the parliament was packed every time he spoke in debate. During World War I he had a clear record of pacifism. In 1917 he had joined the Independent Socialists and thenceforth I was in constant contact with him. The last time I saw him was in 1934, at the time of Captain Röhm's revolt against Hitler. I met him in Paris on the Place de la Concorde; he was very excited and brimming with a confidence I could not share. In exile in Paris, he continued to fight against Hitler. But just before he was about to leave for the United States, the Nazis caught up with him and sent him to the Buchenwald concentration camp, where he died. In his own way Breitscheid had been a good Socialist, but he was too fond of his talents as an orator and more at home in the parliament than in street fighting.

Another German Socialist of the 1920's, much more militant and with greater political insight, was Paul Levi. I met Levi in Switzerland while Rosa Luxemburg was in jail. Our common admiration and affection for Rosa made us friends, and this friendship lasted until his death. Closely associated with Rosa Luxemburg and Karl Liebknecht, Paul Levi became a Communist when they did. When they were assassinated, he became the outstanding representative of the newly formed German Communist Party, and in 1920 was elected to the Reichstag on the Communist slate. Those were days of abortive Communist coups, such as the above-mentioned 1921 uprising in central Germany led by Max Hölz, and others that ended in failure. Levi had serious reservations about these attempts to seize power, and wrote a series of closely reasoned pamphlets entitled *Unser Weg*, in which he sought to analyze why the coups had failed. The official leadership of the Communist Party deeply resented these writings and expelled him from their ranks, so shortly thereafter he joined the Independent Socialists. Soon he became the spokesman of the left wing of that party, where he exerted considerable influence on the young people in the movement. Active as a journalist and writer, he also carried on an extensive law practice devoted mainly to the defense of political prisoners. His last great case was his defense of a man named Bornstein in a slander suit against the lawyer Jorns. The case itself was an outgrowth of the double murder of Rosa Luxemburg and Karl Liebknecht, and involved efforts to keep the murderers out of jail. During the trial Levi's indictment of Jorns was one of the great legal speeches of our century. But Paul Levi was not fated to see the end of this noteworthy trial. Victim of a terrible attack of fever, he jumped from a fourth-floor balcony to his death. It was not suicide: Paul Levi was too much a revolutionary and too deeply involved in struggle to take his own life. Nor was it assassination. It was a fatal moment of delirium that deprived German socialism of one of its outstanding leaders, who never tired of warning his comrades that the weaknesses of the Social Democrats and the mistakes of the Communists would lead the German working-class movement to disaster.

The activity of a handful of Socialists in Austria and Germany during World War I saved socialism from total decline and disrepute. A few Socialists at least took the path of struggle. In Austria the Socialist Fritz Adler, sitting at a table near the Prime Minister, Count Stürgkh, shot and killed the head of government, thus defying official Socialist theory concerning the futility of individual acts of terror. Those who knew Friedrich Adler found it hard to imagine him with a gun in his hand, shooting the wartime Prime Minister. Yet he had done it, and as a result the Austrian workers were roused to action. The shot was the signal for the strike of the Vienna munitions workers.

The strikes spread to Germany, where at the outset they had no significant social content. Thus the strikes in Berlin and Saxony, involving some 200,000 workers, put forward typical trade-union demands; but these were accompanied by a demand to end the state of siege and a declaration in favor of a "clean peace." It was still not much; but at least it marked a beginning of Socialist consciousness in contrast to the line of blind, patriotic obedience that the Party had been following. The negative factor was the lack of dynamic leaders, for with Rosa Luxemburg and Karl Liebknecht in jail, there was no one even remotely capable of taking their place. As has often been reiterated in this book, personality does count, no matter what the dangers and excesses of the "cult of personality." A few youthful leaders, scarcely known to the masses, tried during this period to give more political content to the strikes. I knew some of them personally, and their concept of "politicalizing" strikes derived chiefly from Rosa Luxemburg; but their efforts foundered.

Between the two world wars the European Socialist movement had several centers of Socialist thought, one of which was Vienna. The group of Austro-Marxists around the publication *Marx-Studien* included noted theoreticians such as Max Adler, primarily an educator; Otto Bauer, a keen polemicist who stoutly defended the Russian Revolution; Rudolf Hilferding, author of *Finance Capital*; and others. During World War I, Max Adler and Otto Bauer had fought, together with Friedrich Adler, against "social patriotism" in the Karl Marx Club. The club was shut down by the Austrian authorities after Adler's assassination of the Prime Minister intensified Viennese opposition to the war. The anti-war campaign was not limited to theoretical debates; it took the form of mass action. The first big strike before hostilities ended broke out in Wiener Neustadt, an industrial city about twenty-five miles south of Vienna, in protest against a 50 per cent reduction in the bread rations. Again resounded the cry of "Bread, bread, bread!" heard by Rosa Luxemburg a year and a half earlier in Berlin. The masses were in a militant mood and the government was uneasy. Two days later the Social Democratic newspaper *Arbeiter Zeitung* wrote that the people did not want to "continue the war against Russia just so the Austrian Emperor could add King of Poland to his string of titles."

"The war," wrote Otto Bauer, "has taken the workers out of the factories and workshops and brought them into the trenches, where they suffer unspeakably. In the trenches their hearts fill with hatred of the hoarders and war profiteers who get rich on the masses' misery, and against the generals and officials who live a life of luxury and pleasure. Years in the trenches have given them faith in violence." (This same theme of violence preoccupied the Spanish Left, thirty-five years after the advent of the Franco dictatorship.) The Austro-Marxists did not reject violence when it was the people's reply to the violence of the counter-revolution, which sought in every way to halt the advance of socialism. In this regard it is instructive to follow the course of the debate in the ranks of the right-wing Social Democrats. Max Adler, for example, contended that the fundamental shortcoming of formal bourgeois "democracy" was the absence of genuine democracy. In this pseudo-democracy, Adler observed, the power of the ruling class was masked, not suppressed; the parliamentary system, even overlooking the different "loopholes" of the various electoral systems, did not guarantee self-determination for the people. On the one hand, the deputies, once elected, constituted a relatively independent body not subject to controls by the voters; on the other hand, the prevailing ideas in every era are those of the ruling class and little by little "the [elected] representatives of the people" adjust to those ideas.

The Austro-Marxists were not Communists, although Austrian Chancellor Dollfuss branded Otto Bauer in open parliament: "You are a Bolshevik!" He was not; but in contrast to other Socialists, Bauer had understood the great importance of the Russian Revolution for the future of socialism. And his group had been profoundly impressed by Lenin's *State and Revolution*, which had appeared shortly before the decisive days of the October Revolution. They had admired the way in which Lenin, basing himself on texts by Marx and Engels regarding the relations between the working class and the state, had for the first time traced the path leading from theory to action, thus plugging one of the gaps in Marxist thought. As Marx and Engels had drawn lessons from the Paris Commune in a preface to a later edition of the *Communist Manifesto*, so Lenin insisted on the point that the working class could not simply take possession of the state apparatus and make it function for its purposes; it had to smash the old state machinery immediately after the victory of the revolution. The left-wing Austrian Socialists digested these theories of Marx and Engels, as updated and completed by Lenin, on the nature of the bourgeois and the proletarian state and the need for a dictatorship of the proletariat. Did all this clash with the idea of democracy, bourgeois style? But what was this democracy, in most cases, if not the juridical form of the dictatorship of the rich? This was the question the Austro-Marxists posed in their polemics with the right-wing Socialists regarding *State and Revolution*. When Ferdinand de los Ríos journeyed to Moscow on behalf of the Spanish Socialist Party and, in the course of a discussion with Lenin, passionately uttered the word "freedom," Lenin replied: "Freedom? For whom? Is that freedom going to help ease the plight of the Andalusian peasants in Spain?"

The distinguishing feature of the Austro-Marxists—Otto Bauer, Max Adler, and the others—was that without ever indulging in the anti-Communism of the right-wing Socialists, and realizing the enormous historic significance of the Russian Revolution, they did not unconditionally accept all its results. To the Austro-Marxists the first Soviet constitution corresponded to the economic and political conditions of a backward nation. They themselves preferred workers' councils, which they considered to be a more authentic way of representing the revolutionary working class. The workers' council, Max Adler noted, represented all the workers in a factory, without distinction as to their political affiliation as such, or their specific brand of socialism, whether Socialists or Communists; hence in his view it constituted a form of direct democracy, going much beyond bourgeois democracy. With the workers' councils the working class as a whole would develop a sharper consciousness of its role. There were undoubted risks in this form of rule as in anything tried for the first time; but there was also much promise.

Otto Bauer analyzed with discernment the differences that split the Socialist movement into two camps—the one revolutionary, the other reformist. The results of bourgeois revolutions had disappointed the working class. In the Revolution of July, 1830, in Paris, the workers fought for freedom, but the only practical consequence of that revolution was that the state passed into the hands of the landowning nobility and financial aristocracy, while the workers were deprived, as before, of their rights as citizens. Thenceforth the most enlightened sections of the working class realized that they must fight against the bourgeoisie as well as against feudalism and absolutism. Germany began its bourgeois revolution much later than did England and France. The German radical intellectuals, learning from history, set their goals far beyond those of preceding revolutions, such as that of July, 1830. But only with Marx and Engels did the class struggle appear as the decisive factor, the point of departure for revolutionary socialism. For the first time the young revolutionary Socialist movement clearly defined its strategy in the bourgeois revolution. At the outset the workers would fight with all their might against the established authorities; then, exploiting the breakthroughs in the old order made by the bourgeois revolution, they could lay the foundations for a complete social transformation along Socialist lines. Thus the Paris workers in 1848 fought altogether differently from their predecessors in 1830. Having fought in February for the bourgeois republic, in June they built barricades to overturn that republic. It was a prelude to the Paris Commune of 1871.

Reformism, or revisionism as it was called in Germany, where the most extensive debates developed, stood in sharp contrast to revolutionary socialism, mainly because of the emphasis it placed on the "real" difficulties in the path of a Socialist revolution. It insisted that the prosperous state of capitalism made it virtually impossible for the working class to bring about socialism by force and violence. Under the influence of reformism the Socialist parties were gradually adopting "realistic" political policies: that is, abandoning basic principles and thus leading inevitably to the collapse of the Second International when World War I broke out. "In that year," wrote Otto Bauer, "in only one country in Europe did socialism retain its revolutionary character. That country was Russia." For all their differences with the Bolsheviks, the Austro-Marxists such as Bauer and Max Adler were quite different from the majority of the leaders of the Socialist parties who hated the Russian Revolution far more than their own respective bourgeois governments. In the wide-ranging polemic concerning the dictatorship of the proletariat, Otto Bauer reminded his readers: "At a given moment the Great French Revolution had to resort to the terrorist dictatorship of the proletarians in the suburbs of Paris, to jettison the remains of feudalism, to defeat the domestic and foreign intrigues of the counter-revolution, and to guarantee the victory of the bourgeois revolution."

As French socialism developed in the twentieth century, one great figure projected the power of his thinking and life style across a movement that had split into two, into Communists and Socialists. Both groups subsequently honored his memory and claimed allegiance to his teachings; and today, almost sixty years after his death, one can see the name of Jean Jaurès on the masthead of the official organ of the French Communist Party, L'Humanité.

I have never forgotten Jaurès; he was probably the greatest orator I have ever heard, even though I come from a country—Spain— where oratorical talent has sufficed to turn a mediocre politician into a party leader or prime minister. Spain has known really great orators too: in the nineteenth century, Castelar; during the Second Spanish Republic, Manuel Azaña and Indalecio Prieto. But Jaurès' vibrations were universal: in 1914, and until the day of his assassination, all of humanity who hated war spoke through his voice. For Jaurès, a man of ideals and total integrity, was spurred by a conscience that would not be quiet; this enabled him to pass safely across the narrow boundary separating day-to-day politics, with its ups and downs, from revolutionary politics focused on the future, without ever losing sight of the supreme goal: socialism. Compared with the Guy Mollets of our time, Jaurès looms like a giant; it is even painful to mention the two names together. His own culture was vast, but without pedantry or improvisation; he was born in France, a land in which the life of the mind and the classical disciplines are still held in high esteem. A powerful apostle of peace, Jaurès campaigned against war on a level commensurate with his magnificent spiritual qualities. He had pinned his hopes on arousing his contemporaries to the worst enemy of modern society, war. His scorn for the patrioteers who constantly slandered him as "an internationalist without a fatherland" was boundless. Throughout his life he carried on this never-ending campaign against war. Many of his friends as well as his foes called him "the dreamer"; yet it was he who saw how relentlessly and inevitably international events were driving toward war, displaying far more insight than the political leaders dubbed "realists." He lost no opportunity to warn of the peril of war and to arouse the people to the plots of the militarist cliques. In parliament, in the press, at international Socialist congresses and gatherings, at mass meetings, the voice and pen of the great French Socialist named, defined, and analyzed the threat, assailing the cynicism of some and the defeatism of others—who refused to believe that the masses could be effectively mobilized against the governments and privileged classes who looked upon war as a political or financial transaction.

Jaurès did not hesitate to carry his anti-war campaign to the main headquarters of militarism, the Germany of Kaiser William II, which was continuing a bellicose tradition that went back to the era of the Prussian Frederick the Great. The German government, fearing Jaurès' influence over those who listened to him, instructed its envoy, Radolin, to suggest discreetly that a lecture Jaurès was preparing to give in Berlin be postponed. The emissary's mission failed. The *Vorwärts* of Berlin printed Jaurès' text in full, and at a packed

Socialist meeting specially called for the purpose, the German deputy Robert Fischer read the speech. If we make allowances for some of the pacifist phraseology of that day and substitute appropriate current phrases for the Prussian militarism of 1914, the speech holds up surprisingly well. In it Jaurès warned that peace was jeopardized if one allowed the forces of aggression to keep the initiative and dominate the situation, while the peace forces were ashamed to develop their full potentiality as an opposition. He appealed to the working class to lead the fight for peace. "The working class," Jaurès asserted, "fears war not out of weakness or sentimentality, but because it realizes that if it breaks out it will be difficult to emancipate the working class and free the people." Later he declared: "In peace the growth of democracy and socialism is certain. The revolution may emerge from a European war, and the ruling classes would do well to bear this in mind; but there can likewise emerge a series of counter-revolutions, the furious reaction of exacerbated nationalism, stifling dictatorship, monstrous militarism, a chain reaction of reactionary violence, petty hates, reprisals, and enslavement. We do not want to play that barbarous game of chance. We do not want to sacrifice thereby the inevitable advance of European socialism."

He exhorted France to follow a policy of friendship with the other nations of Europe, seeking issues and areas of common interest to set against fallacious national chauvinism. The provocative policies of the chancelleries, which could easily lead to war, had to be opposed by the policies of socialism, of international solidarity. "On this basis we pool our common efforts and pin our hopes. That is how we can establish working-class and Socialist internationalism, capable of rising above the disorder and national antagonisms." Thus ended Jaurès' speech, which succeeded, albeit briefly, in winning the applause and support of the German working class.

Jaurès considered nations to be genuine cultural units, each of them possessing innate value and promise. They did not deserve to be attacked by a foreign land thirsting for power and domination. Each one of them had a personality of its own; and all of them should form a federation held together by their common desire for peace and international cooperation—an anticipation of the idea of the League of Nations and the United Nations. He saw the evolution of socialism as a series of victories and defeats, advances and retreats, demanding constant vigilance, readiness for sacrifice, and utilization of every available opportunity to strike a blow against the counter-revolution. It was a dialectical approach as formulated by Hegel and then given revolutionary content by Marx. Jaurès insisted on this process of advances and retreats: he warned that if this were not understood, the sure road to socialism would not easily be found. An idealist by temperament, Jaurès had learned from history that when the reactionaries really felt threatened in their material interests, they tossed overboard all their fine phrases about freedom, fatherland, religion, and love of humanity. The masks came down. (Thus when fascism came to Europe in the early 1920's, it was defended as a system of law and order by those who had been gripped with fear when the October Revolution triumphed in Russia and ushered in the first working-class state. Some of Jaurès' writings prefigure the rise of Fascist tendencies in Western Europe in the 1930's—when there were war cries such as "Rather Hitler than the People's Front!" in France and "Rather Franco than the victory of the Spanish people!" in Spain; and when embattled Madrid, fighting alone against international fascism, embodied Jaurès' dream.)

In 1914 the French Marxist Jules Guesde engaged in a polemic with Jaurès as to the effectiveness of international mass strikes in preventing a war. This served as a pretext for Charles Maurras, monarchist and anti-Semite of the extreme Right (in World War II he collaborated blatantly with the Nazi occupiers of France), to distort the meaning of the controversy. In *L'Action française* for July 18, 1914, Maurras wrote: "Mr. Jules Guesde has accused Mr. Jaurès of high treason. Well said. But is he going to dissociate himself from that traitor?" *Le Temps*, the prestigious newspaper of the enlightened bourgeoisie, joined its voice to that of the monarchist paper and spoke of Jaurès as "public enemy number one." Maurras returned to the attack; day after day he intensified his campaign of hate against the great Socialist leader and fighter for peace. He began to suggest his physical elimination—hinting that "our policy is not merely one of words. Realism in one's ideas must correspond with the seriousness of one's acts. By seriousness of one's acts we mean someone who expresses his patriotic indignation by a blow that silences anyone who persists in his treason."

Jaurès considered it beneath his dignity to debate with Maurras, despite the latter's redoubtable reputation as a writer and journalist. Without deigning to reply, and heedless of the stream of insults and threats, he continued his anti-war activity. On July 28 he went with Vaillant, Marcel Sembat, Jean Longuet, and Jules Guesde to Brussels, where the Second International was to convene the following day. In Brussels, at the "Cirque Royal" before an audience of many thousands, Jaurès issued a final appeal to the people of the world, across all national boundaries.

His last speech before the outbreak of hostilities was at Vaise, near Lyons. Reading it today, one feels it as a cry of desperation, a kind of final testament. Jaurès saw catastrophe at the door. He vigorously denounced colonialism, upbraided Austria for her attempts to dismember Serbia, attacked Czarist Russia for its weakness and indecisiveness that caused the German militarists to treat it with contempt and hastened their decision to deal from "positions of strength." (The same expression again gained widespread currency during the Cold War of the 1950's and 1960's.) As against the so-called sacred obligations of the secret treaties, Jaurès set the morally superior obligations of "the public treaty with Humanity." And the last words in the last speech he ever made before an international gathering accurately foresaw what would come to pass: "If against all the laws of reason war breaks out, in the beginning it will carry along with it many blinded by militarist and nationalist propaganda. But when the disasters follow one another, the people will say to those responsible for them: 'Get out, and may God forgive you!' " Jaurès hoped against hope for a last-minute change of heart on the part of the various governments that would avert war. But he knew this would happen only on one condition: if the working class everywhere moved into action and set up a united front against the war. Here was Marx's "Workers of the world, unite!" passionately uttered in a last-minute effort to stave off war.

Jaurès was a tragic figure. His magnificent brain refused to allow him to accept illusions as realities. He realized by now that no one could stop the war, but he did not let the thinker in him prevail over the fighter, at a moment when all that mattered was action. He knew that because of his unyielding fight against the war he was isolated even among his French Socialist comrades, and hated beyond description by the French reactionaries. He must have sensed his killers stalking him. After the Brussels Socialist Congress of July 14–18, 1914, a torrent of slander and denunciation swept over him.

On his return from Brussels, Jaurès did all he could—in parliament, in government circles, and in the press—to save what could be saved. His admirable article of July 31, 1914, in *L'Humanité* was a kind of swan song, in the midst of frenzied, fast-moving events that rendered clearheaded analysis virtually impossible. "When one thinks," wrote Jaurès, "of all the harm this war is going to cause, one asks if the most insane or the most depraved of men are capable of ushering in a similar crisis. All Europe, with its most powerful nations, is going to be involved in it. At this last decisive hour men in responsible positions who can still make the people hear them must raise their voices in an appeal to reason. The danger is immense, but not insuperable." And Jaurès called upon the Socialists to demonstrate everywhere. He summoned all Socialist Party members of the Seine Federation to meet at the Salle Wagram, "to show that we are capable of measuring up to the hopes that the International places in us."

Meanwhile Jaurès had led a group of Socialist deputies, including Renaudel and Longuet, to meet with Prime Minister Viviani. Then he went with a group of friends to eat a hasty dinner at the Croissant Restaurant, next to the office of his newspaper, *L'Humanité*. They sat down at a table near the entrance. He was still giving last-minute instructions for the makeup of the next issue of his paper and admiring a photograph of a little girl shown him by a friend at a nearby table when a shot rang out through the open window. A woman's voice screamed: "They've shot Jaurès!" The restaurant was in an uproar. Friends gathered around the wounded man, now stretched out on a couch. He was still alive. A doctor rushed in, then he turned toward the horror-stricken crowd and said: "Messieurs, Monsieur Jaurès is dead." The news hit Paris like a bombshell. The government pasted up wall bulletins condemning the assassination and calling the death a loss to the nation. The press was unanimous: with disgusting hypocrisy even Maurras' paper, *L'Action française*, which had whipped up such frenzied hatred against Jaurès, carried a eulogy of the departed Socialist leader. In *L'Humanité*, Marcel Sembat wrote: "They have taken him from us in this terrible hour when France needs him more than ever. Oh, madmen who reviled him, now you may have an idea of his greatness and his worth." "His death is a European catastrophe," the British press wrote.

The news of the assassination came to me in Leipzig, where I was meeting with students of many different nationalities, Russians among them, to intensify our anti-war campaign. That same afternoon several hundred students came out on the streets of Leipzig to demonstrate for Jaurès, until the police charged our ranks. We all realized that now that his voice was stilled the militarists were in the saddle; the war machine was in full motion.

Jaurès had warned of the holocaust to come; he was impotent to stop it. His voice was joined by others: Tolstoy, Romain Rolland. Among the masses anti-war sentiments and appeals to revolt against the imperialist war developed unsuspected strength. Today Jaurès appears to us as a great figure in a transitional period when there were still illusions that the conflict between the privileged bourgeoisie and the working class could be settled in an orderly and conciliatory manner. Under Jaurès' leadership the French Socialists had fought against every reactionary attempt to exploit the basest instincts of the people, among them anti-Semitism. In the 1890's anti-Semitism had exploded in France, during the famous Dreyfus Case, in which a Jewish army officer was wrongfully accused and convicted of espionage by corrupt militarists who used him as an innocent "front." As soon as Emile Zola issued his powerful "J'accuse" letter, Jaurès supported him wholeheartedly in the columns of La Petite République. Jaurès used the Dreyfus Case to attack class justice. "Today there is a complex of laws designed to protect the basic inequity of our society: laws that sanction the privileges of capitalist property, the exploitation of workers by the employers. We want to smash those laws, if need be by revolution. But alongside those unjust laws there are others that sum up humanity's meager progress, modest guarantees of what humanity has wrested, bit by bit, down through the centuries and as a result of revolutions. Those are the laws Zola invokes. We Socialists will defend them against the decorated officials, against the generals who dream of coups d'état."

In France the Congress of Tours (December, 1920) saw a split in the

Socialist Party and the creation of the French Communist Party. Nevertheless, the French working class always retained a desire for eventual unity over and above party differences. From time to time this feeling was heightened when the reactionaries stepped up their efforts to halt the march of socialism. This was signally demonstrated in the 1930's, in response to the fascist provocations culminating in the attempted coup of February 6, 1934. Faced with a rightist attempt to change the parliamentary majority by force, compel the government to abdicate, and eventually proceed to a complete overhaul of the regime along the lines of Mussolini's Italy and Hitler's Germany, the French democratic forces all came together in defense of democratic institutions. Radicals, Socialists, and Communists joined forces. Once again the working class was fighting for freedom, even though that kind of freedom would not solve their own problems.

The first to take to the streets, in answer to the Fascists who had staged their riots in front of the Chamber of Deputies, were the Communists. They organized the counter-demonstration of February 9. Unlike trade-union movements elsewhere that were interested solely in the fight for wages, pensions, and immediate demands, the French C.G.T. (General Confederation of Labor) was highly political. So on February 12 it issued a call for a general strike. The intervention of the trade-union movement proved decisive. Organized, disciplined masses gave a show of strength, demonstrating that in France Fascist dictatorship was not an inevitable stage, that fascism could be effectively fought if the masses were properly mobilized.

Intellectuals joined in this effort, responding to the appeal of the anthropologist Paul Rivet, the scientist Paul Langevin, the writer Alain (Emile Chartier), and many others to band together to prevent "France from being subjected to a regime of oppression and warlike poverty." These were the same intellectuals who two years later, in 1936, headed the movement of international solidarity for the Spanish people, popularizing the anti-Fascist slogan *"No pasaran!"* ("They shall not pass!"). The Organizing Committee of the People's Mobilization, forerunner of the Popular Front government that came to power in 1936 with the Socialist Léon Blum as Premier, was composed of some ten national organizations, among them the

Radical-Socialist Party, the Socialist Party, the Communist Party, the two national trade-union federations (the C.G.T. and the C.G.T.U.), the League of the Rights of Man, and the World Committee against War and Fascism. It was not easy to find a basis of agreement among such diverse elements. Thus the Communist Party favored the broadest possible program of immediate demands in order to attract as many people as possible but without attempting structural reforms that might frighten off the middle classes; whereas the Socialists and the C.G.T. emphasized structural reforms and nationalization of industries, which were not to the liking of the Radicals. These differences were overcome when agreement was reached that during the election campaign each party would present its own program and would vote for it on the first ballot; on the second ballot a week later, however, all members of the Popular Front would support the common program of the Front. And in 1936, when Léon Blum was given the task of forming the first Popular Front government, he made that program the program of his government.

What was undeniably most striking in France was the Popular Front of the masses rather than the Popular Front of the political leaders. Political developments there were bound to have repercussions on the anti-Fascist movements in other countries. In Vienna in 1934 the workers replied to the Nazi onslaught by arming themselves and taking to the streets. This was also the response of the Spanish people in July, 1936, who, after the electoral victory of the Frente Popular in February, 1936, defended the Spanish Republic against the insurgent generals and Fascists in the bloody civil war that lasted until 1939. All these people's movements struck a similar note: they replied to counter-revolutionary violence with revolutionary violence.

In the general movement toward socialism, British laborism has always held a very special place, differing from the rest of European socialism in the secondary role it has accorded Socialist theory. One simply cannot compare German, French, Italian, or Russian Socialist literature prior to the October Revolution of 1917 with books on socialism appearing in England during the same period. The average British Labourite, as well as his leaders, looked with misgivings and even some contempt at his comrades on the Continent: in his view they were wasting their time studying Marx and trying to adapt Marxist teachings to the new realities of the political, economic, and social scene. Yet one cannot deny that the British working class was the first to resist its exploiters in an organized way and that, on occasion, it moved forward in exemplary struggle. But in the course of the years the British Socialist movement, numerically strong and supported by powerful trade unions, has encountered a series of disappointments and defeats. Why? Because it lacked a Socialist position based on genuinely Socialist thinking; because it failed to analyze problems in a scientific and revolutionary spirit. The Labourites have been able to win elections, but a few months after they assume power, the question arises as to whether all those efforts were worthwhile when one sees the Labour government behaving on essential matters in more or less the same way as their opposition, the Conservatives. In fifty years of activity the Labour Party has not enriched its stock of Socialist ideas. Will it ever justify Marx's high hopes? Well over a century ago he assigned to the British working class the glorious task of showing the workers of the world the road to emancipation.

Historically the English working class was one of the first to challenge the power of the ruling capitalist class. Its record is full of high points and low moments, heroic episodes and humiliating compromises. Socialism was born in England with a decidedly idealistic and romantic tint, altogether different from what was later known as scientific socialism. In its origins British socialism was the generous dream-child of a philanthropic manufacturer, Robert Owen, who believed that the working class could solve its problems without having to form a political party. He failed to realize that the power of the bourgeoisie, solidly anchored in English politics, required the creation of an opposing political power capable of ending an exploitative social system which Owen himself morally condemned with the utmost vehemence. Yet despite his limitations, there was undoubtedly an element of the social revolutionary in Owen: he advocated the appropriation and control by the workers of all the means of production.

From 1900 on, "evolutionism" held sway in the British Socialist movement. The prestige of the centuries-old Parliament attracted even those who considered themselves in rebellion against it. It was the mother of all parliaments, with impressive rituals and a membership that included offspring of the oldest families in the country; hence the British Socialists felt both attracted and intimidated by Parliament. On the other hand, the classical parties—the Conservatives and the Liberals—graciously consented to democratize it. Of course, their "kindness" was motivated by their desire to win support among the masses. So all the major parties vied for the votes of succeeding generations; and the Fabian Socialists soon became the most devoted practitioners of infiltration tactics and reformist techniques.

When I was a young student at the London School of Economics, the Fabian Society included in its fold distinguished intellectuals and social planners of the stature of Beatrice and Sidney Webb. A few Socialists of the Independent Labour Party sounded more militant in their Sunday speeches in Hyde Park; but their anti-capitalist militancy was more emotional than solidly analyzed. The Fabians, more conservative, at least knew what they wanted; they offered administrative measures which, in their opinion, would open the road to socialism, and they were able to persuade large sections of the British people who demanded a clear, concrete analysis of their daily problems. The Socialists in the Labour Party, on the other hand, gave the impression of uncertainty and lacked qualified leaders—hence they found themselves in an inferior position vis-à-vis the Fabians. Had they been better grounded in Socialist theory, however, their working-class base and the sincerity of their anti-capitalist sentiments might have won them a larger number of followers.

As it was, they relied more and more on "trade-unionism." The trade unions, with their growing membership and financial resources, increasingly dominated the British labor movement for a long period of time; they were the backbone of the emerging Labour Party that had begun to challenge the Tory-Liberal monopoly of British politics. The trade unions took part in the creation of the new party and significantly shaped its course of action. In the newly formed Labour Party the Fabians were the moderate wing; elements from the Independent Labour Party constituted its radical wing. From the outset this left wing was weak and has basically remained so throughout the years. It has been a non-Marxist Left, generally unreceptive to Marxist theory.

At his best moments a Liberal like Lloyd George could give the Labourites lessons in courage. Receiving a Labour delegation toward the end of World War I, Lloyd George, then Prime Minister, told them that at that moment society was like molten metal. They could stamp it with any mark they wished, provided they did so with firmness and determination. Unfortunately the Labour leadership lacked both qualities. From time to time the masses themselves, however, showed signs of courageous initiative. At the Leeds Convention in 1917, under the impact of the Russian Revolution, a resolution was voted demanding "the establishment in every city, in every urban and rural district, of councils of workers' and soldiers' delegates (soviets), in order to stimulate and coordinate the activity of the working class." The resolution proved to be nothing more than a noble gesture—the Labour Party leaders and their real bosses, the trade-union leaders, stymied it. At least the Fabian reformers did not pretend to be revolutionaries. They did not try to deceive anyone; they maintained that if all the reforms they advocated were put into effect and constantly updated in line with the constantly evolving economic realities of the country, socialism would one day be attained. They proposed the nationalization of those industries considered "ripe to become public property": coal mining, gas and electricity, transportation, iron and steel, and the Bank of England.

After World War I the British Labour Party appeared to be much more revolutionary. Beginning with the 1918 Party Congress, much more stress was laid on its Socialist label, as demanded by a great many of the members. The new party constitution claimed "to guarantee the workers, manual workers as well as brain workers, the entire product of their labor and the fairest possible distribution of that product, thanks to the collective ownership of the means of production and the best possible system of administration and control for the people in all industries and all services." Behind this program there was no real militancy, no genuine determination to fight for its realization. In the final analysis everything was left to the good will of Parliament and the good sense of an enlightened bourgeoisie. Thus socialism was turned into a vast bureaucratic and parliamentary operation, with the Labour Party constantly subjected to the will of the trade unions, who held the real power. Now and then the feeble, vaguely Socialist trend represented by the Party "rebels" challenged that power, but easily yielded.

Following World War I the Labour Party was elated when its parliamentary representation rose sharply until it replaced the Liberal Party as His Majesty's official Opposition. At bottom the English bourgeoisie was delighted. Socialism was going to be tamed under the double influence of the trade unions and the parliamentary game, both of them conservative influences. When the Labour Party first came to power, in 1924, it was for a short time and little was accomplished. But that brief tenure was much less damaging to Labour's prestige than the second Labour government, of 1929–1931, in which Ramsay MacDonald turned his back on the interests of the working class and fought to "save the pound" with such zeal that not even a Conservative government could have done more. From the Left there were cries of betrayal when MacDonald sacrificed the Labour Party in order to join a coalition with the Conservatives and Liberals to form a so-called National Government. But actually this desertion of socialism was not an abrupt one; for years MacDonald had ceased to believe in the working class. The memory of the General Strike of 1926 called in defense of the striking miners was fast receding.

World War II accomplished what middle-of-the-road British socialism had failed to achieve—it shook up English society and discredited compromise solutions. The weakening Empire fell apart when the colonial peoples stirred and resolved to gain their independence by their own efforts. Labour was given an unexpected opportunity to come to power again in the July, 1945, elections, with tremendous popular support and a powerful majority in Parliament. One factor among several that played a part in the elections was the Spanish War. The Labourites had pledged themselves to repair the harmful consequences of the Baldwin-Chamberlain non-intervention policy by now helping the Spanish people regain their freedom. But once in office the Labour Minister of Foreign Affairs, Ernest Bevin, did just the opposite; indeed, his policy toward Spain did much to strengthen the Franco dictatorship. In the jails of Spain the Labour government was cursed, much as the Spanish people had cursed the Non-Intervention Committee during the 1936–1939 war. The alliances had changed: the enemies of yesterday were the friends of today. Bevin's anti-Communism led inevitably to his benevolence toward Franco. But one concession to the reactionaries never stands alone; it calls forth others. So British socialism continued in the grip of this basic contradiction: promising socialism in words, receding from it in deeds.

Again, the 1966 election campaign gave new proof of the feebleness of Socialist thinking in the British Labour Party. Harold Wilson, the party leader, was praised by friendly news organs because in his political judgments he was a "realist," not a Socialist. The Manchester *Guardian* hailed him as "the best conservative Prime Minister the country has known in a long time." Note the word "conservative." The 1966 elections ended with a sweeping Labour victory: a majority of over one hundred seats in the House of Commons and five years in which to carry out its program. Yet few either in England or abroad felt that Harold Wilson would move "left," even though in earlier years he had belonged to the left wing of the Labour Party. Only in the City of London, in financial circles, was there any uneasiness as to whether Wilson, or a substantial section of his party, would interpret the decisive electoral victory as an endorsement of socialism. It would be ironic, wrote the London *Financial Times*, inasmuch as the Prime Minister has shown himself to be an essentially pragmatic leader, free of all the fetters of dogma. Now he would have an opportunity to prove that he was not an old-style Socialist, that in domestic as well as foreign policy he could overcome the viewpoints and prejudices that prevailed in the Labour Party in the 1930's. To the wealthy classes a Socialist could earn respectability without ceasing to be a Socialist. "What is Harold Wilson today, a Socialist or a Labourite?" many asked. One thing no one could deny: he was one of the most intelligent persons in British political life in many years, although he seemed to work so hard to disprove that fact. Some of his skill now had to be displayed in smoothing out the differences in the Labour movement, even within the parliamentary group. This was rendered easier since Labour had a comfortable working majority in Parliament, compared with the thin edge it possessed after the 1964 elections.

But many who had been shocked when a British Labour Prime Minister supported—not once but repeatedly—the U.S. bombing attacks on North Vietnam nevertheless pinned their hopes on

Wilson. With such an ample majority in Parliament, he could now begin to dissociate himself from the policies followed by President Lyndon Johnson in Vietnam—policies that outraged even many of the British Conservatives. Still, on the day after the electoral triumph of 1966, nothing could be taken for granted. When a person gets used to governing without being too much disturbed by principles, he always puts off his return to a principled position to another—and better—time. Which means, in essence, when he again sits on the Opposition bench.

In foreign policy, Wilson surely received some reward for changing from a left-wing Labourite to a British Prime Minister: the Americans acclaimed him. He had a chance to appear as the great statesman of the Atlantic coalition, capable of lifting NATO out of the crisis into which it had fallen as a result of General de Gaulle's refusal to allow France to become a dependent of the United States, as Britain was. He could decide Europe's fate for the 1970's; in a word, lend new vitality to Western policy, while at the same time working to improve East-West relations, glancing more toward Moscow than Peking. Right after the election victory of 1966, many U.S. publicists stressed that one of Wilson's missions would be that of holding de Gaulle in check. Political strategists in Washington were trying to play the Socialist Wilson against the reactionary French President, who refused to align his country with the Americans in their Cold War policy of containment of socialism.

In domestic policy, not too much was expected of Wilson. It was hoped that with his comfortable governing majority he would give more of a Socialist tinge to his government than in the preceding year and a half, when he had a bare working majority of three or four M.P.'s to impose his so-called "unpopular measures." Actually they were not so unpopular among the upper classes, who were compensated by a revival of the economy, as they were among the workers, who were called upon to collaborate in this "cleansing" operation—a "floating pound," export subsidies, and an agreement not to put forward "unreasonable" wage demands. With such policies it was not surprising that the Labour Party increasingly lost voter support and, in the general election of 1970, suffered a resounding defeat at the hands of the Conservative Party led by Edward Heath.

In its long history the British working class has often given proof of its mettle, and some of its leaders have risen to the occasion. One of those moments was the General Strike of 1926; and one of those leaders, the mineworkers' general secretary, Arthur Cook. Interviewed forty years later, in 1966, one of the survivors of "the nine days that shook Britain," Lord Davidson, in 1926 a high official in Prime Minister Stanley Baldwin's government, told how he had been responsible for the Cabinet's information services. His most difficult task was to censor some of the comments by Winston Churchill, who edited the *British Gazette*, the government's own publication. Churchill was among those who wanted to take over the BBC (which seemed to him biased in its commentaries). Baldwin (the Prime Minister) had decided not to negotiate with the trade unions until they gave the order to call off the strike. "They must surrender completely," he said; for to him it was essential not to allow an outside organization, the T.U.C. (the central trade-union body), to dictate to an elected government. The two hard-liners in the Cabinet were Churchill and Lord Birkenhead, both of whom demanded drastic measures against the strikers.

In the workers' camp, Arthur J. Cook was a Marxist and a strong believer in direct action. He was not intimidated by the deployment of military forces ordered by Baldwin. Warships appeared in the Thames; soldiers with fixed bayonets protected the cars commandeered to replace the autobuses. Submarines were used as power sources in place of the power plants shut down by the strike. The workers replied by stoning the strikebreaking cars and fighting with their fists against "scabs"—members of aristocratic clubs, middle-class junior executives, and university students who took over workers' jobs. (In 1926 the students were not with the strikers; today it would probably be a different story.) Photographs in the pro-government press showed beautiful Lady Mountbatten, surrounded by duchesses, doing housework, or Lord Weymouth driving a strikebreaking car. When the strike was over, social columns of the newspapers were filled with descriptions of how the upper-class women flocked to beauty parlors for manicures to repair the ravages of the strike. The workers' wives who had stoutly supported their husbands went virtually unmentioned.

Cook was not the only workers' leader who remained steadfast throughout the strike. The president of the Miners' Federation, Herbert Smith, a much older man, was summoned by Prime Minister Baldwin and his ministers a few days before the outbreak of the strike to listen to "a final offer." He turned down the offer with a gesture the Conservatives were not used to seeing. Even Ernest Bevin (the same Bevin whom I heard as Minister of Foreign Affairs after World War II propose to the General Assembly of the United Nations that the diplomatic blockade of Franco Spain be lifted) fought on the side of the strikers from his command post at the London headquarters of the Transport and General Workers Union. One member of Parliament, Shapurji Saklatvala, related to the wealthy Tata family in India and a Communist M.P. from Battersea, strongly supported the strikers and was sentenced to prison because he appealed to the soldiers not to fire on the workers.

Among the Northumberland miners, three of the survivors who had been imprisoned in 1926, interviewed forty years later, showed no "remorse." On the contrary, they were proud of having participated in one of the finest shows of strength the British working class has ever manifested. The workers lost the battle, but they forced the wealthy classes to alter their position and finally take into consideration the demands of the genuine class of producers. One of the three miners' leaders, Arthur Wilson, said some years later: "In jail I read Lenin. I entered prison very close to the Communists. I haven't changed." Nevertheless, the heads of the T.U.C. refused an offer of 2,000,000 rubles from the All-Russian Council of Trade Unions that might have enabled the strike to continue.

Yet despite outstanding struggles such as the General Strike of 1926, many British workers have traditionally remained in respectful awe of the upper classes. That is why even now, in the second half of the twentieth century, a substantial portion of the working-class vote goes to the Tories. Some observers see England as the only nation in Europe immune from the great ideological appeal of the French Revolution. The upheaval of 1789 left Britain intact. Hostile to what was happening in France, the English bourgeoisie scornfully rejected Jacobinism and for a long spell exploited the workers' inclination to compromise and accommodation. British conservatism demonstrated its shrewdness in its untiring efforts to keep the working class within bounds of moderation and self-control—virtues that were praised as distinctive traits of the national character. A British worker is "un-English" if he is swayed by political passions and becomes an "extremist," like the unruly masses abroad. Good manners, above all, must prevail, in imitation of the behavior of the upper classes.

In the light of the Socialist revolutions of the twentieth century, there is something melancholy about the waste of social energy of a working class as potentially powerful as the English working class has so long been. Since 1848 the revolutionary spirit of the Chartists has all but disappeared from the English proletariat, leaving behind a general feeling of disappointment and inability to pit its strength against that of the bourgeoisie, which in turn has done its utmost to remove the class struggle from the British scene. Without an opponent resolved to engage it in a real life-and-death struggle, the English bourgeoisie has been able to enjoy the luxury of appearing as the most progressive of its time—meanwhile ushering in the industrial revolution without the risks of the accompanying political revolution.

"Class-consciousness," as far as the workers were concerned, developed very slowly in England from the time of Robert Owen and the Chartists until the formation of the Labour Party. When the party was eventually formed, it was more Socialist by inclination than Socialist in thought. Unlike the situation in other European countries, the English workers have rarely had the aid of intellectuals, to give a philosophical underpinning to their occasional revolts against the established order. Indeed, one of the chief obstacles to the development of socialism in England is the attitude on the part of many British intellectuals that Marxism may be good for the other countries but not for their own. When they considered it a moral duty, a spiritual imperative, or a matter of intellectual curiosity to interest themselves in questions of social justice or the welfare of the poor, it was the Fabian Society they found most to their liking. The Fabian Society was undoubtedly useful; it was also highly respectable. It sought practical solutions; it did not have outsized ambitions; it focused empirically on problems with a view to introducing legislation limiting the abuses of the rich and tidying up the administration of public affairs. The Fabians thought that by thus reforming the state and the municipalities a kind of automatic socialism would take effect, without unduly alarming the bourgeoisie and so jeopardizing the chances for bettering the living conditions of the masses. Socialism was looked upon as a crusade. Even when the protest movement against the unequal distribution of wealth attracted such brilliant publicists as Robert Blatchford, spokesman of the Independent Labour Party, no new ideas were contributed to Socialist theory.

Laborism was born too late to stamp its innovative ambitions on British politics. But it was also born without real faith in the strength of the working class; hence it was more interested in winning a few more seats in Parliament than in the revolutionary education of the masses. By entering full swing into the parliamentary game, laborism created its own checks and restraints. The English bourgeoisie felt completely reassured when it encountered a labor leader like Hugh Gaitskell, with his reputation as an intellectual which enabled him to face down the uneasy intellectuals grouped around Aneurin Bevan who formed the left wing of the Party.

In the years after World War II, anti-Communism played an important part in the development of the Labour Party, while it was in power as well as in the Opposition. Foreign Minister Ernest Bevin, for example, shocked even the conservative U.S. Secretary of State James Byrnes by his aggressive hostility toward the Russians. Bevin's speeches at the United Nations differed in no way from the language a Conservative foreign minister would have delivered in his place. This former strong man of the British trade unions turned diplomat did not hide his aversion to the fight against colonialism; and he frequently stressed that he did not have the slightest intention of contributing to the breakup of the British Empire. I often saw him talking in the corridors of the United Nations, emphasizing that the collapse of the British Empire would only lead to a worsening of the living standards of the voters who had pinned their hopes on a Labour government and voted it into power. Similarly, when Harold Wilson became Prime Minister, the defense of the pound sterling and, above all, continuing support for close cooperation with the United States crippled the Labour government's freedom of action.

What British laborism did not see was that a social revolution had to begin with a political revolution. The British working class suffered for a long time from the lack of clear, strong Socialist thinking. Chartism, which began as a promising movement in the first half of the nineteenth century, partially filled the political vacuum for a while. But its program remained essentially reformist: it sought universal suffrage, free elections, remuneration of M.P.'s, the secret ballot; it retained confidence in the free play of the parliamentary mechanism.

Historically, therefore, Owen and the Chartists were valuable as precursors of socialism; but they lacked a firm political line such as that which emerged from the teachings of Marx and Engels. Unlike France, England was not the site of a thoroughgoing bourgeois revolution. The idea of revolution—which is essentially a political act—was far from the thoughts of the leaders of the British labor movement. They were content to wrest a few concessions, some of them more apparent than real, from the dominant capitalist class. But the basic structure of England's aristocratic and highly stratified society remained intact. Lacking a political party free of the traditional prejudices of a nation extraordinarily conscious of its superiority, the English working class, even though it has shown its courage in many individual actions, does not seem to be aware of its potential power. It has been satisfied with "gradualism"—with gradually improving its wages, reducing its hours of work, and thus participating albeit quite modestly in the profits of an Empire which, even in sharp decline, still possesses substantial world markets and sea power.

After World War II, the American Left began to decline until, by the 1970's, it was a small, weak political force. The American Left has never had the full-bodied support of a working class imbued with the kind of militancy that suffuses every revolutionary movement. During World War II, discerning European political leaders of the Left who came to the United States in flight from Hitler's occupation armies were surprised by the conservatism of the American workers and their leaders, by their lack of interest in Socialist ideas. It was interesting to compare the ways in which an American trade-union leader differed from his European counterpart. The latter was struck by the life style of the American trade-union official—his salary, so much higher than anywhere else in the world, the house he owned, and his social relationships. But even more shocking was the absence of any sense of class struggle as international socialism understood the term. In those years one of the few leaders in the American trade-union movement who impressed his European colleagues as having this sense of class struggle was John L. Lewis, head of the United Mine Workers' Union.

Inevitably, this inability of American workers to understand the more "politicized" workers in the rest of the world—we have touched on this theme several times above—helped to weaken the American Left. Hence, when a determined effort was made in the 1940's to set up a more powerful Left in the United States, McCarthyism, in the next decade, found fertile ground in which to operate. Senator Joseph McCarthy's "talent" consisted in fastening upon some of the outstanding figures of the American Left and picking them off, one by one. Under various pretexts, chiefly that they were "Reds," they were dismissed from their jobs in newspaper offices, radio networks, the motion-picture industry, and other private enterprises. Two years of McCarthy's wild denunciations poisoned the air in the United States. For too long his witch hunt proceeded relentlessly and without sufficient challenge, mainly because those threatened by McCarthyism failed to unite and fight back.

I was eyewitness to this lack of determination. One day in New York City, I was invited to a gathering in the home of a well-known radio commentator. Present were about thirty writers, journalists, artists, and Hollywood movie people, all of them targets of Senator Joe McCarthy. I was the only non-American present; perhaps the reason I enjoyed this distinction was my record in the Spanish Civil War. At this meeting the participants discussed at length how best to counterattack McCarthyism. Called upon for my view, I insisted that the only way McCarthyism could be stopped was by united action. I suggested that a dozen or so well-known American intellectuals write a letter to *The New York Times*, couched somewhat along these lines: "We are all Americans. If *any* foreign country—the Soviet Union or any other—attacked our country we would fight to the end to defend the United States. Meanwhile, however, we cannot stand by and allow Americans to be exposed to the wild charges of a reckless senator. We call upon all those who share our feeling that Senator McCarthy is discrediting our country in the eyes of the world and creating a situation unworthy of American democratic traditions and intolerable for free men and women, to unite in a movement 'Against McCarthyism, for the defense of freedom of thought in the United States.' " Could this have aroused the conscience of the American people? At any rate, I felt it was worth trying.

Actually, the United States has been the weakest section in the march to socialism. When students in Europe and Latin America assailed the "Establishment," they could count on sympathy and support from the workers; in the United States, however, they could not involve the workers in their struggles. Hence at Berkeley, Columbia, and every other campus in the nation, they fought largely alone. When they finally appealed for a student-worker coalition against the war in Vietnam and for "free universities," the labor leaders disdained them, preferring instead to concentrate on making the workers' life more nearly like that of the capitalists. The trade unions in the United States simply did not want to hear about socialism. By and large, their attitude on the Vietnam War was outrageous. Not only did they not protest against the war; they backed it eagerly. They were pillars of support for succeeding Presidents: Kennedy, Johnson, and Nixon, chiefly because the war provided better pay for the workers. It is not only George Meany and the other top officials who are to be blamed. Many a steelworker or building-trades "hardhat" was delighted to make more money from "overtime" while giant B-52 bombers and napalm brought death to the Vietnamese people. Politics was not their business; that was left to the politicians. Consequently, the many praiseworthy efforts of the American peace movement, the Socialist-oriented activities of the intellectuals, students, and women's groups, were limited in their effectiveness because of the almost complete lack of support of the American working class.

Outside the United States the American labor movement is considered an appendix of American capitalism, and viewed with mistrust if not contempt. Even those Socialist sections of the European labor movement that get help from some American trade unions have little respect for their benefactors. But it has not always been thus. For example, the workers' movement in St. Louis, Missouri, in the 1850's, deserves mention in any history of nineteenth-century socialism. It was led by the '48ers, most of them German revolutionaries who, forced to leave Germany after the 1848

Revolutions, emigrated to the United States in search of political asylum. The German-American labor movement was led by Herman Kriege, associated with Marx and Engels in Europe and well versed in scientific socialism. Another outstanding early Marxist leader was Joseph Weydemeyer. Wilhelm Weitling brought out a publication, *Die Republik der Arbeiter* (*The Workers' Republic*); and in New York City a Socialist gymnastic society was founded. The *Communist Manifesto*, published at the end of 1847, soon crossed the Atlantic, and in various industrial centers of the United States branches of the First International—the International Working Men's Association— began to spring up, supporting the ideas of Karl Marx.

In the years preceding the Civil War, American workers fought not only for higher wages and fewer hours of work but also for an end to the institution of slavery. This was their answer to the barbarous concept of the slaveholders, expressed editorially in one of their representative organs, the Charleston *Mercury*: "Slavery is the natural and normal condition of the laboring man." So it was not surprising that when war came in 1860, many volunteers, white as well as black, came from the workers' ranks and fought on the side of the North. In 1873 the German section of one of the most important branches of the International Working Men's Association in the United States issued the first number of the *Arbeiterzeitung*, which preached working-class solidarity and cogently analyzed the problem of poverty in each recurring industrial crisis in America. In those days Lassalle, as well as Marx, had his adherents in the United States. The Lassalleans founded the Social Democratic Party of North America in 1874, which competed with the Marxians for the workers' support. In that era workers and their leaders were highly political in their thinking. But when, at the beginning of World War II, I suggested one day in New York to Sidney Hillman, a labor leader of stature, that he ought to publish a Socialist paper for the American workers, Hillman replied to me: "A Socialist paper here? Our workers read the *Daily News*." When I commented that the leaders were responsible because they had not taken the trouble to educate their members politically, Hillman said to me: "You are a hundred per cent right."

The meetings of the early Social Democratic Party were often broken up by the police or by paid gangs hired by the more reactionary capitalists who did not even want to hear the word "socialism." The Party gradually declined in membership and eventually disappeared. But it was not long before another, the Socialist Labor Party, founded in Newark in 1877, took its place. It drew members as a result of the big railroad strikes of the day; soon it boasted of a group of capable speakers and lecturers who brought home to the United States the lessons of the recent Paris Commune. The Party led labor struggles; it also taught Socialist theory. It won considerable support. (This was the period of the "robber barons," of James Russell Lowell's valedictory address on democracy, as well as Edward Bellamy's *Looking Backward*, a utopian novel that was socialistic in content.)

In the 1880's Chicago became the center of the leftist, militant trends in the American labor movement. From Chicago came the first call to declare May 1—May Day—labor's national holiday. May 1, now widely celebrated throughout the world, originated in the United States; and on that first occasion 3,500,000 American workers marched. Their main slogan was for an eight-hour day, but there was an unmistakably revolutionary atmosphere at the demonstration, which the authorities were quick to grasp: in the ensuing days police assaults brought death and injuries to many workers.

A new militancy was abroad in the land. It was noticeable in many directions, one of them the labor-backed campaign of Henry George for mayor of New York City (1886). George ran a close race against the candidate of Wall Street and the business interests. Engels commented from England on the phenomenon: "The Henry George Boom has of course brought to light a colossal mass of fraud, and I am glad I was not there. But in spite of it all it was an epoch-making day." The same militancy permeated the Industrial Workers of the World (I.W.W.), whose activities rose to a peak in the years preceding World War I. The main difference between the I.W.W. and the Socialists concerned the merits of direct action as contrasted with electoral and parliamentary action, but this was not the only divergence. One group in the I.W.W. led by William Z. Foster, later a leader of the U.S. Communist Party, argued the question of "dual unionism." Foster, well acquainted with the French trade-union movement, had close relations with the Vie Ouvrière group, which in the early 1900's enjoyed considerable prestige and influence among the French working class. Subsequently this policy of "boring from within," first used in the British trade unions, became popular in many trade-union circles in Europe.

Other left-wing European Socialists who influenced the radical wing of the American labor movement included Lenin and Rosa Luxemburg. The latter's writings on mass strikes were closely studied. Thus, when the periodical *The New Review* was founded in January, 1913, its editorial board was dominated by right-wing Socialists and moderate trade-unionists. Soon, however, the left wing, following the tactics of "boring from within," moved the publication closer to advocacy of more revolutionary methods. (In those years intellectuals of various shades of opinion sat on the editorial board, including W. E. B. Du Bois and Walter Lippmann.) In those years too, American workers were at least curious about revolutionary struggles led by workers in other countries. Thus Tom Mann, leader of several big strikes of miners, dockworkers, and railwaymen in Great Britain, became famous for his "Don't shoot!" open letter to the soldiers; and he was invited to speak in the most important cities in the United States. The membership of the I.W.W. was never large; and its financial resources were always precarious. Nevertheless, it made up in militancy for its meager finances and was a far more important revolutionary force than the American Federation of Labor, despite the latter's millions of members and large treasury.

The outstanding leader of the American Socialist Party in the first decades of the twentieth century was Eugene V. Debs, a former railwayman and trade-union leader. He was a commanding figure among the masses, esteemed both for his personal integrity and for his lifelong devotion to Socialist principles. His stand against American participation in World War I, which he called an imperialist war, brought him a ten-year prison sentence—after a speech in Canton, Ohio, in 1918. From jail he ran as candidate of the Socialist Party for the presidency in 1920 and polled close to a million votes. Among the Socialist-minded journalists, two were outstanding: Lincoln Steffens, the noted "muckraker," and his young follower John Reed, both well known for their reporting in the U.S. campaign against the Mexican revolutionary leader Francisco (Pancho) Villa from 1914 to 1916, and both of them contributors to the radical magazine *The Masses*. Later Reed became a Communist and was in Russia in 1917, where he won Lenin's confidence and was an eyewitness to the October Revolution. His vivid description of this event in *Ten Days That Shook the World* quickly made the book one of the classics of twentieth-century revolutionary literature. Among the Marxist theoreticians one may mention Louis B. Boudin, who in 1907 wrote *The Theoretical System of Karl Marx*, subsequently translated into German, Russian, and several other languages.

With such a past one is entitled to hope that one day the American labor movement will cease being an exception in the world and will again become "politicized." But for that to happen a fundamental change in its leadership and direction is required. The labor movement in the United States will have to show solidarity with causes outside its own narrow purview, its own strictly trade-union business: it will have to consider sympathy strikes, twenty-four-hour political strikes, and concern for causes that are Socialist in content. How can it expect solidarity from others if it does not show the slightest trace of solidarity toward them? Moreover, one can hardly expect original Socialist ideas or theory to emerge from a labor movement that does not feel the need to support any Socialist publications of national importance. This in a nation now well over 200,000,000 inhabitants, whereas little Switzerland, with a population of roughly 5,250,000 and a reputation as the most bourgeois country in Europe, has three Socialist daily papers.

This "depoliticization" of the American labor movement weighs heavily on the whole future of the United States. I am not referring to low-level political consciousness—such as participation in national, state, and local elections on the basis of the Samuel Gompers "reward your friends, punish your enemies" theory or the in-fighting for power and control in the local unions. I refer to the fact that the workers have largely become a heterogeneous mass without class-consciousness or the most elementary ideas about socialism. Mainly responsible for this "depoliticization" have been the labor leaders, who have made no effort to educate the workers politically and in many instances have not even tried to educate themselves. But without the millions of men and women in the trade unions, no movement with goals higher than that of mere creature comforts or individual well-being can win power in the United States. To achieve socialism, the support of the labor movement is indispensable.

The Socialist parties of the West have fallen into low estate. To measure this decline, let me quote a well-known French historian, Bernard Lavergne. Analyzing the problem of the dangers inherent in a presidential regime as favored by a section of French public opinion, Lavergne recently wrote: "Under de Gaulle the presidential regime, however much I detest the system, has nonetheless given results beneficial to France and world peace. But suppose the Socialist Guy Mollet had been President of the Republic elected for seven years and not subject to recall, instead of having been Prime Minister in a parliamentary regime that could unseat him—what disasters would have overtaken France?" The argument is not lacking in substance. As head of government in 1956, Guy Mollet involved France in the Suez adventure against Egypt, which had such a dismal denouement. And he did so without authorization from the French parliament or the unanimous agreement of his Cabinet. So it is fair to ask what Guy Mollet would have done had he been granted the same powers as de Gaulle. On the other hand, the Fourth Republic, in which Guy Mollet was one of the leading figures, found itself politically and morally—though not constitutionally—impotent to put an end to the Algerian War and recognize Algeria's complete independence. Mollet's socialism was weak and faint-hearted. With de Gaulle in power the war in Algeria ended, a whole new African policy for France was initiated, China was recognized, better relations with the countries in the Socialist camp—countries Mollet hated and feared—were established. And France's dependence on the United States, the trait common to all the preceding French governments, was sharply altered.

In his *Critique of Hegel's Philosophy of Law*, the young Karl Marx gave an example of how Socialists must confront even the most difficult situations. Marx, agreeing with his friend Ruge, acknowledged that there was no people more divided than the Germans or less prepared for a revolution of the classic French type. On the other hand, it was possible to move the German people toward a different type of revolution, one that was basically more far-reaching in that it would bring about structural changes in the economy and prepare the ground for socialism. This could be accomplished if they could win over to revolutionary action a new class that had appeared in history: the working class.

To abolish the German feudal and police state, the manicured hands of the bourgeoisie were not enough. What was needed was a fighting force capable of attracting to its side all the oppressed strata of the population, relying on more than just windy, empty phrases. In 1830 the French bourgeoisie toppled Charles X from power solely thanks to the workers who fought on the barricades. To young Marx the only German policy worth supporting was one that led to a complete democratic revolution. Marx's insights remain valid, far beyond the confines of Germany, more than a century and a quarter later in the era of Socialist revolutions.

8

THE
SPANISH REVOLUTION

In October, 1934, the Spanish Socialist movement was in a revolutionary posture without parallel in any other Socialist Party in the world at that time. What other group in the Second International could measure up to the Asturian miners, predominantly Socialist in orientation? Their leaders—Amador Fernández, Graciano Antuña, Inocencia Burgos, and Juan Antonio Suárez—were as a matter of fact centrists rather than left-wing Socialists. Except for the Austrian Socialists under Julius Deutsch who fought against fascism in Vienna and in the Spanish Civil War, no other Socialist group matched the Asturian miners in revolutionary ardor and conviction. It was they who had halted the first attempt to install fascism in Spain, two years before the Franco uprising of July, 1936. That is why it is legitimate to call October, 1934, a major event in the history of socialism.

In the years before 1934 the Asturian masses had followed their centrist leaders in every attempt at gradual reforms—attempts that had instilled a feeling of pride in the creative capacity of the working class. Asturian socialism had its "statesmen," such as Manuel Llaneza, who enjoyed a national reputation as an organizer and was respectfully listened to in official Madrid circles in matters involving labor disputes. Asturias was the experimental center of the cooperative movement, of study centers for workers, of progressively run enterprises such as the San Vicente mines. In the course of this constructive activity, many Asturian workers were trained; so when

October, 1934, came, they proved as apt for revolution as for progressive work in the trade unions.

At the outbreak of the 1934 Revolution, the local and provincial labor leaders, mainly Socialists, were in a position to take over leadership in the Asturian region. They defied the established government that sought to turn the clock back and abolish the modest reforms instituted by the Republic since its proclamation three years before, in 1931. Unfortunately, the Republic did not have the courage to go to the root of the problem and make basic structural changes in Spanish society. The dead weight of decades of alternating do-nothing governments of Conservatives and Liberals still remained—and both parties served the interests of the privileged classes.

In Asturias the order to demonstrate on the streets came on the night of October 4–5. Some reformist Socialist leaders—or revisionists, if you prefer—alarmed by the revolutionary élan of the October, 1934, revolt, assert in retrospect that it was basically a republican, not a Socialist, movement. They may say what they want; the evidence proves that the order issued that night implied a fight to seize power. The order was given with that idea unmistakably in mind: the miners poured out on the streets to give Spain a Socialist state; otherwise they would not have demonstrated. If the Socialist leaders in Madrid had a more limited goal in mind, they kept it well concealed.

The facts speak for themselves. From the very outset, once the first municipality in the mining area was seized, the Asturians set up a revolutionary Socialist, people's regime. The apparatus of the bourgeois state was swept away, and a new Socialist administration was organized. In Mieres, La Felguera, Gijón, and elsewhere, the *Casas del Pueblo* (Houses of the People—i.e., workers' centers) became for all practical purposes the town halls. Militias, mobilized in the name of the working class, were organized; they were the beginnings of a People's Army. The Socialist paper *Avance* set the tone when it spoke of "the insurrectional proletarian state." Apart from thousands of dead and wounded, 30,000 Asturians were imprisoned. In those days, when reaction was furiously unleashed, no one in the Asturian jail cells would have dared to assert that he had fought solely to defend a bourgeois republic that had deceived the masses. So if we analyze the October, 1934, Revolution in Asturias in its many-sided aspects, we see that it contained all the elements of an attempt to install a dictatorship of the proletariat. Dictatorship of the proletariat—not of any one specific party or organization. Although it was led by the Socialists, Communists, anarchists, and other working-class groups participated with equal enthusiasm and equal rights in the movement.

Thirty-four years later, in 1968, revolt again flared up among the Asturian miners, and once again a lively polemic arose: Are the Spanish people potentially revolutionary or not? The defeatists kept harping on the apathy of the masses, but the truth is that all their efforts to prevent violent actions and their condemnation of violence proved a failure as anti-Franco agitation increased. And as in 1934, the most militant and dynamic elements in the opposition, coming from the most widely divergent parties, began to unite in a single movement. The heads of the traditional opposition parties, even though they controlled the apparatus of propaganda and organization, were not heeded—rejected above all by the youth—when they counseled moderation. And some of them, under pressure from below, were forced to change their stance and adopt a more revolutionary attitude, at least in appearance. This was a significant fact, foreshadowing the course Spain will follow once Franco has disappeared. Neither a monarchist restoration as sought by a bourgeoisie that has for decades loyally supported General Franco, nor a republic unable to transform the country socially—like the one that marched under republican colors against the Asturian miners— has any chance of enduring, even though it may be set up in the initial period of uncertainty. The precedent of October, 1934, and shortly thereafter the magnificent behavior of the Spanish people in their 1936–1939 war against domestic and international fascism, mark the road of Spain's future.

No chronicle of the workers' struggles in Spain can omit mention of the peasants' movement. As this book is being written, the peasants' movement has again won the attention of the most imaginative and determined elements of the anti-Franco opposition. In this connection the major work to consult is by Juan Díaz del Moral, *Historia de las Agitaciones Campesinas Andaluzas* (*History of Peasant Disturbances in Andalusia*). Díaz del Moral, a notary from

Bujalance, has painstakingly noted and analyzed events in the province of Córdoba, adding a large amount of data excerpted from publications of the two main leftist movements in the Andalusia of his day, the anarchists and the Socialists. Peasant disturbances have a long history in Andalusia, and it is worth noting that prior to the nineteenth century popular uprisings in Andalusia never focused on the question of land. They were violent explosions against tyranny. As early as the end of the fourteenth century we find a rebellious priest, Fernán Martínez, archdeacon of Ecija, defying the warnings of his Church superiors, arousing the masses of Seville, and spreading his movement throughout Andalusia. Some of the agitation was directed against Jewish merchants, accused of exploiting the peasantry, and many Jews were forced to "convert" to Christianity—these were the "converted Jews" (Marranos) of the last period of the Middle Ages. Then there was the memorable uprising of Fuente Ovejuna in 1476, commemorated to this day on the world stage in the play of that name by Lope de Vega. It deals with the assault on the palace of the local tyrant, Commander Hernán Gómez de Guzmán, and contains a chorus as fresh today as it was five hundred years ago. When the judge asks: "Who killed the Commander?" the collective shouted answer is "Fuente Ovejuna!" "And who is Fuente Ovejuna?" "All the neighbors in this village. Fuente Ovejuna, all for one!"

In 1652 a peasant revolt broke out in Córdoba during which handwritten and printed leaflets circulated clandestinely. They bore harsh accusations against the King and incited the people "to end the tyranny of governments." The uprising was later called "the hunger riot"—but hunger was a permanent, not a transitory, phenomenon in Andalusia. This was a distinctly political revolt against the highhandedness of the Crown, in which the insurgents seized the cannon from the fortifications of the Calahorra and hauled them to spots chosen for their defense. In a short time some eight thousand rebels had seized the city of Córdoba.

In the nineteenth century Socialist ideas from abroad, especially the teachings of Charles Fourier in France, took root in Andalusia. The Loja insurrection in 1861 was of a markedly Socialist hue—in reality a mixture of republican and Socialist sentiments, with such slogans as "Long live the Republic!" and "Death to the Queen!"

Anarchism too penetrated the Andalusian countryside, particularly the teachings of the Russian Bakunin and the Frenchman Proudhon. R. Mella, one of the most learned and intelligent Spanish anarchists, maintains that the teachings of Proudhon were "the credo of the majority of the people" in Spain. Federico Urales attributes the popularity of anarchism in Spain to the spirit of individualism and revolt that flourished among the Arab philosophers of Córdoba, giving rise to mystics, artists, great captains, and explorers. A number of books and publications kept the agitation alive and prepared the ground for mass strikes. These included Malatesta's writings; Kropotkin's *The Conquest of Bread*, for a time the most popular book among the Andalusian peasantry; the articles of Anselmo Lorenzo; and a host of publications that appeared and faded away, from the *Indicador anarquista*, a manual with simple directions for making bombs cheaply and planting them without great risk, to *Tierra y Libertad* and *La Anarquía*. In all this there was more enthusiasm than organizing ability, and scant concern for coordinated action to enhance the prospects of success. Nevertheless, the general strike of April, 1903, reached sizable proportions and was accompanied by unusually militant manifestos. "If they don't grant our demands, tomorrow Córdoba will burn." "If tomorrow you see the guns flash, don't be afraid; if the bourgeoisie has guns, we have dynamite." During the grain harvest the struggle intensified, recalling the militancy of the Jerez peasants during the 1892 revolt. The repression was harsh. But neither the closing down of the workers' centers nor the mass jailings ended the agitation, which lasted until 1905. Only then, with hopes of victory gone and hunger ever-present, did the revolt die away.

The basic fact that emerges from a study of the disturbances in Andalusia throughout the nineteenth century and in the first third of the twentieth is the existence of a high degree of revolutionary potential. Periods of calm alternated with periods of struggle, but the feelings of revolt could never be completely smothered. The Spanish peasants who in the 1970's walk bowed and seemingly resigned to their fate will stand up straight as soon as they have a clear and correct political line to guide their deep-seated, inextinguishable spirit of revolt. The farmworkers' organization of Espejo, which survived the collapse of the general strike and remained a strong center of propaganda until 1918, is proof of the efficacy of such a political line.

Paralleling the anarchists' activities in Andalusia was the Socialist movement. The Fourier-type Socialists were led by Fernando Garrido and the official Socialist Party by Pablo Iglesias. The latter had visited the province of Córdoba in 1886 in the company of the typesetter Francisco Alarcón Vega, who had been forced to leave Madrid as a result of a printers' strike and had settled in the provincial capital of Córdoba, where he founded the Córdoba Socialist group which began to organize the farmworkers.

The Bolsheviks' seizure of power in 1917 stirred Andalusia, where the protest movement was for the moment at a low ebb. One forgets that in those days anarchists and Socialists alike felt the victory of the Russian working class as their own: let me cite as evidence enthusiastic articles hailing the Revolution in such diverse publications as *Tierra y Libertad*, *Solidaridad Obrera* in Barcelona, and *La Voz del Campesino* in Jerez. By 1918 the masses in Spain were again in a mood to present their demands. The Socialist Gabriel Morón made a vigorous effort to activize Socialist groups in his region despite barrages of right-wing propaganda. Castro del Río was among the towns in the forefront of anarchist agitation. "As always," writes Díaz del Moral, "the most important factor was the newspapers and pamphlets. Those of Sánchez Rosa and of *Tierra y Libertad* were sold in the thousands. Editions of *Abogado del Obrero* (*The Worker's Advocate*) came out in rapid succession. In this period, more than in the previous one, anarcho-syndicalist literature flooded the entire Córdoba region."

Panic set in among the big landowners and government officials identified with their interests. The conservatives fostered the Catholic trade unions in an attempt to counter the influence of the syndicalists and Socialists. The Catholic Church, especially the top hierarchy, played its traditional part in Spain as the upholder of law and order. Although the tensions abated after 1919, there were sporadic outbreaks of rebellion, and the peasants were still imbued with a feeling of hatred for social injustice. Those who believed in the electoral process voted for the Socialists; others revived their anarchist workers' centers at the first possible opportunity. So in 1936, when the Franco rebellion broke out, despite the fact that the agrarian reforms introduced by the Spanish Republic in 1931 had been woefully weak, the peasants were the first to join the people's militia.

During most of the nineteenth and twentieth centuries, the working class in Catalonia has been in the forefront of the fight against the various forms of reactionary rule. As early as 1831 the Society of Weavers was organized in Barcelona, and for a long time the textile industry was the most important sector of the Catalonian economy. The Society's immediate aims were to guarantee the right to organize and strike and to obtain unemployment relief for the many weavers who were being increasingly thrown out of work owing to the introduction of machinery. The first factory run by steam power, the Bonaplata plant, was burned down by the workers, who continued organized resistance against the employers and local authorities, who were acting in collusion. Thus was born the *Batallón de la Blusa*, mentioned by Stendhal during his trip to Catalonia in 1837. The scattered resistance groups organized into a federation. Then in July, 1855, the Catalonian weavers called the first general strike recorded in Spanish history, putting forth these demands: a ten-hour day, a reasonable wage scale, a ban on work by children under twelve, and the right of association. Barcelona, which then had a population of 180,000, saw 40,000 strikers join in the action. This general strike was an event for all Europe, not for Spain alone, and it increased in violence as the authorities increased their repression: monasteries were burned in protest against the support given the employers by the Catholic hierarchy. The strike was imbued with a decidedly republican spirit: the monarchy, the employers, and the high clergy constituted the threefold enemy.

The First International came to Spain in 1870. In 1866, when the Geneva meeting of the International discussed Marx's proposals, there were no Spanish representatives present, but in October, 1868, Fanelli, an Italian deputy and long-time radical, who had fought for the Roman Republic in 1848 and for the freedom of Poland in 1863, came to Spain. At the first Congress of the International held in Barcelona, the apolitical tendency gained the upper hand, and the newspaper *La Federación*, which had begun by advocating a federal republic, gave up its republican campaigns. Differences between

Marxists and Bakuninists quickly came to light, reflecting deep differences within the International.

At the outset the Catalonian workers were receptive to Marxist ideas. The U.G.T. (*Unión General de Trabajadores*), destined to play an important part in future Spanish labor struggles, was formed in Barcelona in 1888. Gracia Quejido, one of the most intelligent leaders of the early Spanish Socialists, saw clearly that the transfer of the U.G.T. headquarters to Madrid was a mistake; but his opinion did not prevail. The fact is that the anarchist movement grew strong in Barcelona and throughout Catalonia, stimulated as well by a parallel growth in neighboring France, where such well-known intellectuals as Laurent Tailhade, Paul Adam, and Octave Mirbeau were anarchist sympathizers and where the movement itself had outstanding leaders such as Jean Grave and Sébastien Faure.

The May Day celebration in 1890 came as a shock to the Spanish bourgeoisie, for all resistance groups, the apolitical ones as well as the U.G.T. supporters, went out on strike. A state of war was decreed and troops patrolled the streets, now thronged with workers. The anarchist publication *El Productor* added to the tensions by printing statements by Kropotkin and Malatesta. A series of assassination attempts took place: a bomb exploded at the Ministry of National Production; another in the Plaza Real; and on September 24, 1893, a worker, Paulino Pallas, tossed two bombs at General Martínez de Campos during a military parade. Pallas, shot by a firing squad at Montjuich, died courageously, forcefully reasserting his belief in anarchism and crying out: "The revenge will be terrible!"

His warning was fulfilled, for less than two months later, on November 7, at the opening of the opera season at the Teatro Liceo, two bombs were hurled from the top gallery, killing twenty-one people and wounding many others. The toll would have been higher, but only one of the bombs had exploded; the other, undetonated, was found in the skirt of a woman killed by the first bomb. The repression against the anarchists was extremely severe. The perpetrator of the bombing could not be found, but "to serve as a lesson" four anarchists—José Codina, Mariano Cerezuela, Manuel Archs, and J. Sabat—were shot at Montjuich, even though there was no evidence connecting them with the bombing. The Montjuich castle became the symbol of police terror. On June 7, 1896, during the

Corpus Christi procession, another bomb was thrown, resulting in ten dead and forty-four injured. This bombing led to the famous Montjuich trial. But first there was a general roundup of anarchists throughout Spain. In Catalonia as well as Valencia and Aragón, the Guardia Civil arrested all those remotely suspected of sympathy for the anarchists and led them in chains through the streets under a blazing summer sun. When they fainted from exhaustion, they were revived by blows from clubs. At Montjuich itself torture was the order of the day. At a series of protest meetings in Madrid and elsewhere, concrete evidence of the tortures was presented and demands were made for a new trial for the Montjuich prisoners. One of the phrases used by the presiding judge at the trial, Lieutenant Colonel Marco, "Shutting our eyes to reason . . ." became notorious throughout Spain.

The protest campaign spread abroad to Paris and then to London, where it was led by an unusually interesting man, Fernando Tarrida del Marmol, a chemical engineer from Sitges and son of a Catalonian manufacturer. (I later became personally acquainted with him when I studied in England.) Among the literature on the Montjuich trial, the best book is by Ciges Aparicio, a capable writer and the governor of Palencia, shot by the Franco forces at the beginning of the Spanish Civil War in 1936. In the summer of 1897 an Italian anarchist named Angiolillo killed the Prime Minister, Cánovas del Castillo, at the bathing resort of Santa Agüeda, in an attempt to avenge the Montjuich trial. Then there was the *attentat* by Mateo Morral, who, on the day of Alfonso XIII's wedding in 1906, tossed a bomb from a Madrid balcony at the King, but did not hit him.

The Moroccan campaign of 1909 was highly unpopular in Spain, and incidents occurred every time troops left for the African battlefield. In July of that year the protest movement in Barcelona assumed greater proportions than anywhere else. The anarchist federation Solidaridad Obrera was in favor of a general strike, but in reality it was the workers who walked off their jobs on their own and completely halted the life of the city. Here in the very center of apolitical anarchism was an eminently political strike! The political consciousness of the masses, especially the women of Barcelona, was very high. What ensued was "the tragic week of Barcelona"—with more than a hundred dead and many more hurt. The authorities, anxious to crush this movement, looked for its leaders; and the police, taking their cue from the Madrid government, fastened on Francisco Ferrer. Ferrer, a teacher by profession, was the founder of La Escuela Moderna (The Modern School). Himself wealthy, he nevertheless felt close to the people; and his innovative ideas on education had aroused the hostility of the Catalonian bourgeoisie and clergy. His arrest made sensational news inside Spain and abroad, and many feared for his life. Shot on October 13, 1909, he died shouting: "Long live The Modern School!" His execution aroused the fury of millions of Europeans, and violent demonstrations took place—in Paris, Brussels, Milan—just as, twenty years later, when Sacco and Vanzetti were executed in Massachusetts. More than sixty years after his death, Ferrer is still remembered in many countries, above all in Brussels, where there is a statue in his memory.

In the years immediately preceding World War I, strikes increased in Catalonia. The war enriched the employers and led to workers' demands for higher wages. One of the most important strikes, in 1913, occurred in the textile industry and spread throughout Catalonia, involving some 200,000 workers. The syndicalists soon had their own organization, the powerful C.N.T. (Confederación Nacional del Trabajo). The first moderate demands for wage increases were met, for war profits were high. One textile manufacturer told his friends he felt like commissioning a golden statue of Kaiser William II, out of gratitude for his war orders. Thus, part of the swollen profits went to keep the workers satisfied, and as a result strikes virtually ceased for a time.

But the war brought other problems—political problems that went beyond wages and working conditions. Spain was fertile ground for the activities of German espionage and thus also for Allied counter-activities in that field. Moreover, the working class realized that once the wartime boom was over, they would have to pay the costs of an inevitable depression. Defensive measures were therefore in order, and one of these was a movement for trade-union unity. At the end of 1916 representatives of the U.G.T. and the Catalonian syndicalists, including their leader Salvador Seguí, met in Zaragoza, for their first real contact after a lengthy period of mutual distrust. The general strike of 1917 sealed the pact signed at Zaragoza, with members of both groups participating fraternally in the movement. In its way it anticipated the U.H.P. (Unidad de Hermanos Proletarios—Unity of Proletarian Brothers) in Asturias in 1934. In 1917 too, at a famous gathering in Sans, a unified trade-union movement was formed, and the various unions covering a single industry—for example, the carpenters, cabinetmakers, upholsterers, etc., in the wood industry— merged. Following the formation of "El Unico" (One Union), labor strife intensified, culminating in the epoch-making strike of La Canadiense, the popular name for the vast enterprise Fuerza y Riegos del Ebro, created by a Canadian businessman named Pearson, which produced all the electric power for Catalonia. Consequently, shutting down La Canadiense meant virtually paralyzing all industrial activity in that region.

The strike was led in a way that was a credit to the Catalonian working class and refuted the theory that anarcho-syndicalism was nothing but chaos and confusion. To every repressive step taken by the government, the strike leaders replied with actions that undermined the government's authority. Having suspended constitutional guarantees, the government introduced press censorship. In turn, the C.N.T.'s organ, *Unico*, applied labor censorship. The richest and most influential paper in Barcelona, *La Vanguardia*, rejected labor censorship until a group of workers appeared in the editorial offices, revolvers in their hands, and ordered everyone out on the street. When the employers sent out armed strikebreakers, the workers responded in kind. In this interplay of violence, Layret, a labor lawyer and genuine democrat, was killed; crippled in both legs, he was an easy victim of "the law-and-order assassins."

The Canadiense strike attested to the popularity of one of the most remarkable figures in the entire Spanish labor movement, Salvador Seguí, an anarchist of outstanding intelligence and compassion. Mario Aguilar, a noted journalist who died in exile without finishing his *Memoirs*, has left us a warm and penetrating portrait of this working-class leader. Close to the masses, Seguí, while in Madrid, also made a profound impression on such renowned intellectuals as Miguel de Unamuno and José Ortega y Gasset.

In France the once flourishing anarchist movement emerged considerably weakened after World War I. The war itself had been condemned in a manifesto that appeared a few months before August, 1914, bearing the title "The Anarchist International and the

War" and signed by thirty-five of the best-known anarchists in the world, including Enrico Malatesta and Emma Goldman. The manifesto asserted that wars will exist so long as there are states rather than a society free of all coercion. But the war, and the subsequent Russian Revolution, split the movement. The International Anarchist Group in London denounced the anti-German stand taken by Kropotkin and Jean Grave, declaring in 1916 that they rejected "all clichés in foreign policy with which governments seek to lull their peoples." A similar split developed with respect to the October Revolution. While Malatesta cried: "Anarchy, yes; Bolshevism, no!" at the convention of the C.G.T. (Confédération Générale du Travail) in Clermont-Ferrand at the end of 1917, Merrheim, one of the most powerful anarcho-syndicalist leaders, appearing on behalf of the metalworkers' union, spoke vehemently against the majority attitude toward the Russian Revolution. "Our indignation knows no limits when we see how the men of the October Revolution are slandered." Merrheim's speech created a sensation. The then head of the French government, Georges Clemenceau, interested solely in winning the war, asked Merrheim to go to Russia and see Lenin and Trotsky, but Merrheim, now the head of the trade-union opposition, declined Clemenceau's request on the ground that it came too late. Anarchist activity then lessened perceptibly in France.

Another outstanding figure in the period of direct action was a soldier named Lecoin, who in 1910 refused to fire on the workers during a railwaymen's strike against which the government had mobilized the army. He was court-martialed, and his courageous attitude before the military court gave the anarchist movement a new hero whom the anarchist papers hailed. For in that period the anarchist press was widely read: *La Guerre sociale*, brilliantly edited by Gustave Hervé, was the most widely read of all. In Paris the workers pored over it by candlelight during meetings in narrow rooms on back streets or in concealed cellars to avoid police surveillance. In London the few copies that arrived were quickly snapped up by the handful who knew which newsstands sold them. One of Hervé's articles, "Tolstoy and the Soldier Lecoin," was an imaginary dialogue with the author of *War and Peace*. In a sense the prosecution of Lecoin for having refused to fire on striking railwaymen connected anarchism with pacifism and dramatically posed the problem of "conscientious objectors"—a problem that bothered French governments in both world wars and reappeared during the Algerian War. Lecoin emerged from his court-martial a much larger figure. Even the bourgeois press accepted the high-mindedness of his motives, although deploring the fact that he had fallen under the influence of anarchist propaganda. To many anarchists, on the other hand, Lecoin's deed was that of a totally pure and dedicated person, offsetting some of the ill repute anarchism had earned through the notorious Bonnot gang in Paris, which, claiming to act in the interests of anarchism, staged holdups, bank robberies, and assassinations that terrorized the country for a time.

In his prison cell at La Santé, Lecoin wrote anti-war pamphlets. When he got out of jail, during one of his intervals of freedom in 1917, he assailed those responsible for the war. Two individuals stood out in his mind as the main culprits: French President Raymond Poincaré (*"Poincaré la guerre"*) and Gustave Hervé. Hervé, who had defended Lecoin years before, had subsequently gone over to "the camp of the super-patriots," and by so doing had, in Lecoin's words, "betrayed the cause of anti-militarism."

The fight against the war brought together persons of diverse views. In the Librairie du Travail, Leon Trotsky developed his theory that the war was only the first act in a gigantic world upheaval that would everywhere end in the triumph of the Revolution. Such an outlook did not wholly satisfy Lecoin. To him the immediate task was to fight against war on all levels and to denounce the war-makers: in the first place the government, in the second place those who lived and profited from the arms industry—and both were inextricably intertwined. But when peace came, Lecoin did not feel that his tasks were over. Although broken in health as a result of long years in prison, he plunged headlong into the protest campaign for Sacco and Vanzetti in the 1920's. As secretary of the French Committee for Sacco and Vanzetti, he organized a huge mass meeting in Paris in which he succeeded in getting the Socialist Léon Blum to speak on the same platform as the anarchist Sébastien Faure.

When the Algerian War began, Lecoin was old and exhausted. But the question of "conscientious objectors" revitalized him. Again his name appeared in the newspapers: in January, 1962, he served notice on General de Gaulle that he was commencing a hunger strike and would not end it until the French parliament dealt with that problem or the executive intervened to see that "true justice" was done. When President de Gaulle heard that Lecoin had entered into a coma, he said to a meeting of his Council of Ministers: "Lecoin must not be allowed to die." The French government proceeded to take more humane measures to change the status of conscientious objectors, similar to those in force in England. It was Lecoin's final contribution to revolutionary pacifism.

The Spanish Civil War of 1936–1939 involved many aspects of revolutionary socialism. The first militia forces, the Spanish guerrillas in the summer of 1936, were made up chiefly of peasants and workers. Later, elements of the most diverse social groups—General Escobar of the ultra-reactionary Guardia Civil; Air Force General Emilio Herrera, former gentleman-in-waiting of King Alfonso XIII; General Vicente Rojo, Chief of the General Staff and a conservative; Admiral Valentín Fuentes, and others—were integrated into the newly reorganized armed forces of the Spanish Republic. Within two years this army was transformed into an effective and impressive military force—as acknowledged by German officers who fought on the side of General Franco. Nevertheless, what gave the Spanish Civil War its historic dimension was the original nature and content of the people's armed response to Franco's uprising backed by Hitler and Mussolini. And it was this that brought to Spain the magnificent volunteers of the International Brigades.

But within the war itself perhaps the most revolutionary act was the effort to continue the resistance in the central region after the fall of Catalonia in 1939. With Juan Negrín, I was the chief proponent and most stubborn advocate of this policy, which emerged from the meeting held by the Republican government in the French city of Toulouse shortly after the last Republican soldier had left Catalonian soil. The reasons for the success of the rebel offensive in Catalonia are closely bound up with the "Non-Intervention" policy adopted a few weeks after the outbreak of the war in 1936 when a Socialist, Léon Blum, headed the French government. Our ability to fight effectively on the Catalonian front was fatally weakened by the failure of much-needed arms shipments to arrive. I heard General Rojo tell the small committee in charge of coordinating our war effort how crucial it was for us to receive a large convoy of arms acquired by the legal government of Spain before the Fascists mounted their offensive in Catalonia. Yet at that very moment the arms were being detained in France. General Rojo, a professional soldier of unusual competence and unswerving loyalty to the Republic, insisted that without those arms we would be unable to withstand the impending enemy attack. Hitler's agents within the French government were well aware of the importance of that convoy and intensified their efforts to retain the arms in France. Ironically, they were released after the fall of Catalonia and added to Franco's military arsenal.

With Catalonia lost, there remained the central region. By utilizing the geographical features of that part of Spain, the Republican government could have continued the war for a time, even if Madrid fell. The decision to continue the war in the central zone was taken by the Council of Ministers at a meeting in Toulouse, France, on February 9, 1939. I am committing no indiscretion if I now recall that President Manuel Azaña considered the war completely lost when Catalonia fell. In his view, any attempt to continue fighting in the central zone was sheer madness. President Azaña's attitude strongly influenced several ministers at the Toulouse session. It is also worth noting that by then Azaña had decided to step down as Spanish President on the same day the French government recognized General Franco. The Cabinet discussion was a long and stormy one. The sole Communist minister in the government, Vicente Uribe, immediately supported our proposal to return to the central zone and continue the war.

In my comments, I concentrated on one point: the outbreak of a world war was only a matter of months away. As it turned out, the interval was six months. Until then our side had not speculated on the possibility of the Spanish Civil War's merging with a general conflict; nor had we maneuvered to provoke such an outcome. To the contrary, we had sat by patiently as the cruel farce of "Non-Intervention" developed and showed that the Western democracies were unwilling or unable effectively to check the advance of fascism. (Did one not hear a rising chorus in France uttering the slogan: "Rather Hitler than the Popular Front"?) We could have gambled on a world war, provoking incidents to hasten its advent.

We refused to do so. At the League of Nations, as Foreign Minister of Spain, I repeatedly denounced the blatant violations of the Non-Intervention Pact. Then in that same forum Prime Minister Negrín announced the voluntary withdrawal of the International Brigades, in the hope that at last the Non-Intervention Committee would put an end to the massive military assistance Hitler and Mussolini gave the forces of General Franco. Before he died Negrín told me that the unilateral withdrawal of the International Brigades had been a mistake on his part, for had we kept them in Spain our fighting capacity on the Catalonian front would have been enhanced.

But in February, 1939, world war—I stressed—was inevitable and near at hand. Consequently, it was our duty to prolong our resistance in the central zone until it broke out. So when the Cabinet finally voted unanimously to return to the central zone, Negrín and I felt there was not a moment to lose in implementing the decision. Two hours after the session ended, the two of us, under assumed names, left for Alicante on an Air France plane that flew over Franco territory and landed in that coastal city. We were aided in our departure by the head of the French airline, a supporter of the Spanish Republic, who realized that a Fascist victory in Spain would threaten France's security. Without his intervention we could not have left in so brief a time.

Our arrival in Alicante was like a bombshell to the defeatists in the central zone, who for a long time had urged an end to the struggle, as British and American agents stood by and counted the hours before the war would terminate. We knew when we landed in Alicante that some of the Republican leaders, military as well as civilian, would spread slanders concerning our arrival. But our hopes lay in the mass of the soldiers who, commanded by loyal officers, heeded the call to return to the central zone from France, where they had been evacuated with the Catalonian army. We were confident they would follow the new orders dictated by the new course of the war, so Negrín and I immediately undertook the task of reviving their fighting spirit. A few days later the other members of the Republican government arrived in Alicante. For its part, defeatism was also active. Then at the beginning of March, 1939, there was a second coup against the Republic: General Segismundo Casado, in command of the Madrid forces, turned out to be a second Franco.

Elsewhere° I have dealt in detail with the question of whether we could have effectively resisted in the central zone until the outbreak of World War II. What happened subsequently in the resistance movements against Hitler's armies in the various nations of Europe proves that our idea was not farfetched. We could have resisted in the central zone: I believe I have argued this point convincingly, and will not return to it again. But just think how important it might have been if the Spanish Republican Army in the central zone, resorting to guerrilla tactics, had become a constituent part of the Allied armies in September, 1939. If we had succeeded—and those of us who advocated continuing the war in the central zone did what we could to bring it about—the outcome might have been quite different. Not only might we have saved the Spanish Republic; not only might we have spared Spain thirty years of the Franco regime; but the spirit of revolutionary socialism epitomized in our slogan "To resist is to win!" might have affected the over-all European situation at the end of World War II.

It was this policy of "To resist is to win!" which links the Spanish Civil War of the 1930's with the new period of active struggle against the Franco dictatorship that opened in 1967, and which guarantees its strength and continuity. Just as in February, 1939, the dividing line now is between those who want to continue the struggle and the liquidators; between those who assert that only an active policy, resorting to all means of struggle including mass violence against the violence of the Franco regime, can lead to the liberation of Spain, and those who favor an evolutionary policy, "national reconciliation," "the inevitability of gradualness." The so-called "hard line"—I prefer to call it the realistic line—is opposed to an opportunistic "realism" of surrender.

Until recently the story of those Spaniards who fought on the Allied side in World War II had not been told. Recently, however, a Spanish journalist working in France, Alberto Hernández, a Socialist active in the French Resistance movement during World War II, has written a monograph sketching the main outlines of that story. It is the history of the Spanish guerrillas who continued the war against fascism and for democracy, even though betrayed and abandoned by

° In *The Last Optimist* (New York: The Viking Press, 1950).

the Western democracies. Spanish Republicans fought against the Nazis in the Norwegian port of Narvik in 1940; they fought in the Maginot Line, even after Marshal Pétain's capitulation, and forced the Marshal to issue a special cease-fire order; they were in Africa, in Chad and the Libyan desert, at Stalingrad, and in the Pacific. Five hundred Spanish parachutists came down over the island of Crete, only seventeen of whom escaped with their lives. There were some 1,500 Spaniards in the Tunisian campaign, with 500 casualties. There were Spaniards in the French, Belgian, and Italian Resistance movements. On the Eastern Front an entire company of Spanish soldiers attacked the Germans to the cry of "Just like at the Ebro!" thus commemorating one of the outstanding victories of the Spanish Republican Army in the Spanish Civil War. The extraordinary thing is that this fighting spirit remained alive in the concentration camps organized by the French government to "maintain order" among the Spanish Republican soldiers. Early in 1939, after the fall of Catalonia, over 500,000 Spaniards took refuge in France from the Franco regime which the Western governments lost no time in recognizing diplomatically. The concentration camps that were then set up were a dishonor to France and would have turned others, less politically aware, into enemies of France. The Spaniards overcame their resentment and, when World War II came, offered to die for the very country that had treated them so shabbily. In the French concentration camps, despite all the difficulties, the Spanish refugees kept their political organization intact. After the surrender of Marshal Pétain, the political organization changed into a paramilitary one operating against the German armies. A network of small guerrilla groups was established in southern France, especially in the Pyrenees region. French writers of the postwar period have offered some revealing statistics regarding the number of Spaniards in the French Resistance movement. Thus Marc Edouard, in a documented study of the so-called "Hundred Days of the Red Republic of the Maquis," speaks of "more than 6,000 Spanish guerrillas meeting in Bordeaux" in the first days after the Liberation. Putting figures together, one arrives at an estimate of 70,000 Spanish Republican volunteers during the years 1942–1944.

From the outset the Spaniards faced the problem of arming themselves on their own. The air drops went to the French

Resistance movement. The Spanish guerrillas got their first sticks of dynamite with the aid of Republican refugees who worked in mines and quarries. By their ingenuity and initiative in manufacturing bombs, they recalled the first days of July, 1936, when the masses responded to the Franco uprising. The guerrillas obtained their first arms by seizing them from German army patrols and the French Fascist police, using old pistols, sometimes lacking even ammunition. One night, for example, a group of Spanish guerrillas located in Saint Paul de Jarrat took advantage of an evening of entertainment in a popular local café. A group of French gendarmes were there drinking and enjoying the show. Utilizing one of their members who had a good singing voice, the Spaniards distracted the gendarmes sufficiently to snatch away their weapons, a military operation executed between stanzas of "La Paloma" and other popular Spanish songs.

A similar spirit has been manifested within Spain in the current period. During the first months of 1968 the fight against the Franco regime took on a distinctly violent character, yet little in the over-all world picture seemed to presage it. The Spanish Left was in a state of utter confusion. There was no effective international action against the continuation of the "scorched earth" policy practiced by the U.S. forces in Vietnam; Fascist coups were being launched in several countries, such as Greece; the United Nations revealed itself as helpless to stop aggression; and quarrels within the Socialist camp had demoralized many of its adherents. All sorts of new intellectual theories were evolved to account for this feeling of impotence, while the reactionaries had a field day, confident that the Left was in a state of virtual collapse.

But not all the Left conceded defeat. A good many looked to those places where new fighting forces were regrouping, and in Europe one of those places was Spain. So, once again, as thirty years before, interest in the developing struggles within Spain extended across continents. The revival of militancy in the students' movement and the increasingly effective leadership of the Workers' Commissions have done much to clear the political air inside Spain. No longer is it necessary to argue endlessly with those who continue to have illusions about the gradual evolution of the regime toward democracy or those who, in the face of all realities, sing the praises of "national reconciliation." One fact dominates the current Spanish scene, and its importance must not be underestimated: the correct political line has finally been found. It has taken a long time; the efforts and sacrifices have been many. But the period of doubting is over. More and more Spaniards—especially among the youth—are listening to those who assert that there is only one way out for Spain: a revolutionary way.

9

THE GUERRILLAS
Latin America, Asia, and Africa

Since 1960 guerrilla activity has been the most popular and widespread form of revolutionary struggle in Spanish- and Portuguese-speaking America. The *guerrillero*—guerrilla fighter—is deeply rooted in Spanish tradition; and after 1962 he assumed unprecedented political significance in the Western Hemisphere. Indeed, the past decade may well be called the decade of the guerrillas. Their activities vary greatly, from Venezuela to Colombia, from Peru to Guatemala and the rest of Central America. But their object is the same: to put an end to the age-old rule of the privileged castes, the big landowners, and the foreign corporations in collusion with the local capitalists and bureaucrats—in a word, to eliminate human exploitation.

In some countries it has not been very difficult for the guerrillas to win over the peasants. In Peru, for example, the peasants in the Andes regions are essentially revolutionary, and there, in 1965, the Peruvian guerrillas won notable victories under the slogan "The land or death. We shall win." The second part, ". . . or death. We shall win," reminds one of the Cuban Revolution. Nevertheless, although Fidel Castro did exert some influence on the revolutionary movement in Peru, it was not as great as the U.S. Latin American experts in Washington claim. The names of the Peruvian guerrillas have a decidedly native ring: Tupac Amaru, Pumacahua, Pachacutec; and as far back as 1781, Tupac Amaru, who claimed descent from the

Incas, challenged the Spanish authorities. His feats have not been forgotten on the high altiplano of the Andes.

The President of Peru in the early 1960's, Belaúnde Terry, realized that he had to do something to avert a large-scale peasant uprising. So on August 10, 1963, his government announced the forcible expropriation of 78,000 hectares of land in the districts of Junín and Pasco. It was a limited reform, the original plan having been truncated because of opposition in parliament by the reactionary A.P.R.A. Party and the supporters of former President Odría. One of the guerrilla leaders, Luís de la Puente, declared that he was ready to take direct action because Belaúnde Terry's government had failed to keep its promises, especially with regard to agrarian reform.

The guerrillas of Latin America were systematically denounced as Communists by their respective governments, a charge that was much too general, and in some instances wide of the mark. As a matter of fact, in some of the countries involved, the official Communist parties were not happy at the appearance of the guerrillas. Thus in Venezuela, in 1964, some of the leaders of the Communist Party of Venezuela, asserting that guerrilla activity was at an end, insisted on a return to normalcy. Wherever the guerrillas were not under Communist control or were under the influence of non-Communist revolutionary movements, the official Communist leadership viewed them with suspicion.

The Latin American Communist parties, except for the special case of the Dominican Republic, shared Moscow's viewpoint concerning peaceful coexistence. Many of them envisaged a parliamentary solution; and this led occasionally to sharp confrontations with the guerrillas. The clash was unusually sharp in Venezuela, where, just prior to a meeting of the Organization of American States, the leadership of the Venezuelan Communist Party expelled Douglas Bravo, a Communist guerrilla leader who had risked his life to come down from the mountains to Caracas and argue his case with the Party Central Committee. Bravo, unable to convince his comrades, returned to his guerrilla comrades in the mountains to continue the fight. In March, 1967, his expulsion from the Party was made public; and on that occasion Fidel Castro went out of his way in one of his speeches to pay Bravo a warm tribute and sharply attacked the Venezuelan Communist leaders as defeatists.

During 1965 and 1966 and well into 1968, guerrillas fought in the mountains of Colombia, Guatemala, Peru, and Venezuela. In some places they were crushed by the government forces, which resorted at times to the use of planes and large numbers of soldiers. Officially the revolts were proclaimed dead, but several months or a year later new outbreaks would occur. The important thing was that revolts had occurred; and the teachings of Ernesto "Che" Guevara were gaining wider influence among the revolutionary elites on the American continent. Some of the more serious commentators spoke of "the forward surge of Latin America."

What all these movements had in common was the will to carry out the revolution by armed force. Often the idea of national planning based on the immediate needs of the Indian and mestizo masses, as in the case of Peru, was combined with the evocation of a glorious past—in order to emphasize their feeling of independence toward the United States, which, by contrast, was the natural ally of the exploiting classes. In Peru there was a veritable cult of Mariategui, author of *El hombre matinal* (*The Morning Man*). To José Carlos Mariategui, influenced in contradictory fashion by Georges Sorel and Nietzsche, the man of the morning was the man of the revolution. But Mariategui, for all his intellectual complexities, was not alienated from the masses. His confidence in the awakening of the masses and the role of the villages inspired the Peruvian guerrillas that came after him.

Every six months one government or another in Latin America announced that the guerrillas were liquidated, yet it was not long before the guerrillas again made their presence felt. At the end of March, 1967, Venezuelan artillery had to be used against a group of guerrilla fighters in the Bachiller Mountains. At the same time a state of emergency was decreed in Bolivia, a country in which guerrillas seemed previously unknown, and the Bolivian air force had to intervene. Bolivian President Barrientos, on the radio, accused "international Communism," and General Jorge Belhonte, head of the armed forces, asserted that the subversive movement had been organized by Che Guevara, who, he claimed, had twice visited Bolivia illegally.

In Guatemala two movements, the MR-13 (Revolutionary Movement of the 13th of November) and F.A.R. (Rebel Armed Forces), supported the guerrillas as part of an active opposition. F.A.R. considered it indispensable to collaborate with a section of the middle class in order to build a mass movement. To them, the enemy of the Guatemalan people was the triple alliance of U.S. imperialists, native militarists, and the wealthy upper class; and in view of the upper-class opposition to any peaceful evolution toward a better society, F.A.R. judged that recourse to violence, though regrettable, was necessary. In Guatemala the most favorable terrain for the guerrillas was of course the mountains, but on one condition: that the terrain was not too densely populated. In his book on guerrilla fighting—which the Guatemalans took very much to heart—Che Guevara said that an excess of population was a disadvantage, especially in the initial phase of guerrilla activity. It is interesting to note that in the regions where the Guatemalan guerrillas operated, the peasants came to them for advice and help in solving their problems. The fact that the guerrilla forces included students and intellectuals enhanced their standing. Moreover, some of them were active in the fight against illiteracy, teaching the peasants and their fellow guerrillas how to read and write. Much has been written about the apathy of the Latin American peasant; but many of the peasants who joined the Guatemalan guerrillas had to be "calmed down" rather than aroused. They had to be taught to see the struggle in its historical perspective, and not merely as "machete strategy."

As the war in Vietnam unfolded and the thrust of U.S. power came more and more to the fore, the importance of the guerrillas and the revolutionary movements in the rest of the Western Hemisphere increased. One of the most potentially promising was the A.P. (Popular Action) in Brazil; another was the E.L.N. (Army of National Liberation) in Colombia. They moved more and more to the Left, looking increasingly toward Cuba as their main source of inspiration. They viewed the revolution as "a matter for all Latin America" and not an exclusively national problem. In the words of Luben Petkoff, one of the top leaders of the F.A.L.N. (Armed Forces of National Liberation) in Venezuela: "We do not look upon the liberation of Venezuela as the liberation of the country in which we were born. When we speak of liberating Venezuela, we mean liberating all Latin America. We do not recognize boundaries in Latin America. Our boundaries are ideological. We interpret international solidarity in a genuinely revolutionary sense. We have enlisted in the fight against imperialism so long as it exists. We will not lay down our arms until imperialism, specifically North American imperialism, has been rendered helpless."

Guerrillas dominate the Latin American revolution—a revolution that will develop in the coming decades with ups and downs, with periods of relative calm and of great ferment, but a revolution that nothing can hold back.

The masses of Latin America had the Sierra Maestra encounter of 1957 as their backdrop when they entered upon the stage of world history. The victory of the powerful guerrilla movement in eastern Cuba, composed of peasants, students, young intellectuals, and workers, challenged many of the traditional ideas of the left-wing parties that had pinned their main hopes on a coalition of their leaders. The idea of a coalition made up of the Socialist and Communist parties and the left-wing Catholics proceeding along a democratic and parliamentary path to the seizure of power was challenged by a revolutionary strategy drawing much from the lessons of the Chinese Revolution. Indeed, for a considerable length of time in Latin America this strategy bore a single name: Cuba.

The Guatemalan guerrillas were inspired in part by the Cuban example, but they had their own native roots. The most dynamic revolutionary groups in Guatemala came to realize that the reforms undertaken by their most socially advanced governments—that of Juan José Arévalo, which succeeded the Ubico dictatorship when the latter was overthrown by a student revolt in 1944, and that of Jacobo Arbenz in 1950—had not succeeded. The Arbenz government, enjoying the firm support of the peasants, clashed with the United Fruit Company, the U.S. corporation long accustomed to dictating the law in Central America, when it sought to implement its election promise of widespread agrarian reform. The moment agrarian reform involved the land owned by the United Fruit Company, the Arbenz government was doomed by the U.S. government. An officer named Castillo Armas was hand-picked by Washington to stage a *coup d'état*.

In the history of the march of socialism in Latin America, the Guatemalan experience must be noted as evidence of the complete disillusionment of the most active elements of the people with reformist solutions. This disappointment made them especially receptive to the appeal of revolutionary socialism, with guerrillas as its most effective instrument of struggle. And the guerrilla leaders saw their function as just that: to mobilize the peasant masses disillusioned by the failure of reforms. Undoubtedly, the democratic governments had been sincere in their efforts to achieve such reforms; but in practice they had been unable to carry them out or effectively defend them against the combined opposition of U.S. business interests and home-grown domestic capitalists. The Guatemalan revolution must therefore be viewed as a long-term process. It is not a series of heroic but futile actions in a given space of time, with interludes of repression forced by the reactionaries and U.S. intervention; but armed insurrection sustained and constantly renewed by the guerrillas whatever the political situation of the moment. The first Guatemalan guerrillas liked to quote a passage taken from the writings of Mao Tse-tung, in which the Chinese leader said: "Some confused comrades think that the task of the Red Army, like that of the White Army, is simply to fight. They do not understand that the Chinese Red Army is an armed force created to further the revolution. Today especially [Mao's words were written in 1929] the Red Army must not limit itself to fighting: besides doing that and destroying the armed forces of the enemy, it has to carry out political work: propaganda among the masses, organization of the masses, helping them to establish revolutionary power. Unless these tasks are included in its activities, unless these goals are set, the fighting loses its meaning and the Red Army its *raison d'être.*"

An outstanding Guatemalan guerrilla leader, Antonio Yon Sosa, national head of the MR-13, has related his experiences as follows: "Conversations guerrillas have had with the peasants confirm the state of mind of the people bound to the land who have high hopes of making it theirs. This land here—one of them told the guerrillas— was distributed. Then came 'liberation' and again they took it away from us. That land over there was not distributed. It's the best land, it belongs to the rich—they didn't touch it." Here, in simple but eloquent terms, is expressed the prevailing sentiment of the Latin American peasants toward agrarian reform of the moderate type. And it also explains why John Kennedy's famous "Alliance for Progress" program aroused more skepticism than enthusiasm among those who in theory were its beneficiaries. "In the time of Don Jacobo [President Arbenz]," another peasant commented, "all we wanted was arms. We can't fight only with machetes. They didn't give us any and so Don Jacobo was overthrown. Had we been given arms, they wouldn't have got rid of him." Guerrillas and peasants agreed on this one point: the counter-revolution of 1954, attributed to the C.I.A., won because the people were not armed.

The MR-13 grew out of an attempted military uprising against the Ydígoras government, as corrupt and authoritarian as that of Ubico, and so subservient to the United States that it turned Guatemala into a training camp for mercenaries recruited to fight against the Cuba of Fidel Castro. Once the coup foundered, a group of leftist officers sought refuge in Honduras and El Salvador, then returned to Guatemala as soon as possible, where they made contact with other elements in the opposition, the Communists of the P.G.T. (Guatemalan Labor Party) and the students. From this coalition the F.A.R. was born. In February, 1962, the fight was renewed and brought to the mountains. Sent by Yon Sosa, the men of the "Guerrilla Movement Alejandro de León of the 13th of November" went into the Sierra de las Minas. Alejandro de León, on his return to Guatemala, had been hounded by the police and had died under police bullets. In the course of the struggle the MR-13 became radicalized. An anti-feudal revolution of a predominantly democratic type was no longer its goal. The enemy was far more powerful and was capable of a far wider range of activity than the Guatemalan reactionaries. The fight of the MR-13 acquired world-wide significance, assuming the proportions of an anti-imperialist and anti-capitalist revolution. In short, a Socialist revolution.

The guerrillas inspired confidence in the peasants by the forthrightness of their language and their resolute fighting spirit. They were not people who talked only about things the peasant knew all his life from daily experience; they also had guns in their hands. For the peasants this was a guarantee that they would not be forsaken. When they left one village and went to another, after having united the peasants around a single concrete political task, the comradeship forged during days of discussion and teaching was sealed by a promise to be back. "*Hasta pronto*" was the magic phrase. At the same time the guerrillas appealed to the soldiers with speeches like this one: "Soldier, refuse to fire on your peasant brothers. Refuse to torture them and loot their villages. Support the organization of peasant committees in the villages. Support the confiscation of land. Join the peasant militias." The peasant committees were organized under the guidance of the guerrillas, but in accordance with local conditions in each village. The whole village then proceeded to appoint its committee. Generally there were three members: the military representative, the civilian representative, and the person who served as liaison with committees from other villages. The committees undertook to organize their own militia, which cooperated closely with the guerrillas but retained its own initiative as the "armed expression" of the village. By helping the guerrillas and cooperating with them, the peasants acquired military experience and an awareness that they were part of the armed struggle for liberation.

If the MR-13 had had decisive influence on the voting at the Tricontinental Conference of Havana in 1966, specifically on the question of peaceful coexistence, the outcome there would have been quite different. Even so, approval of the highly controversial resolution was obtained by a majority of only thirty-one votes, with many significant abstentions. This was a reflection of the sharp controversy that had for some time divided Latin America with regard to two diametrically opposed orientations: peaceful coexistence and Socialist world revolution. The MR-13 accused the Soviets of trying to slow down the revolutionary movements of Africa, Asia, and Latin America because Moscow felt that their activities acted as road blocks in the pursuit of its international policies.

The revolt in the Peruvian Andes also took the form of guerrilla fighting. In April, 1965, the guerrilla leader Pachacutec of the M.I.R., who had set up a base in the valley of Convención, in Cuzco province, announced to the Peruvian people that he had begun an armed struggle, and one of its chief revolutionary aims was "free land for the peasants." These magic words were enough to assure the M.I.R. guerrillas of initial successes. The resort to tactics of insurrection resulted, as we have said, from general skepticism concerning the possibilities of peaceful democratic evolution. The Peruvian peasant does not vote. This explains why, for example, in the 1962 election the three candidates of the Left received altogether some 50,000 votes out of a total vote of 1,800,000. To the 5,000,000 Peruvian Indians the results were a foregone conclusion. As one Peruvian guerrilla leader told me: "The fate of the guerrillas has its ups and downs. But even in our worst moments, when it looks as though we are about to disappear for good, the surviving remnant, however diminished in numbers, remains here as an example and a regrouping center for the future. That's the power of the maquis. Its potentialities do not die while the national regime continues to govern by means of constant repression. Even if they are forced to retire, the M.I.R. guerrillas will have accomplished more than thirty years of verbal propaganda by other parties of the Left."

At the end of 1965 other guerrillas, not affiliated with the M.I.R., made their appearance. One, for example, bearing the name of Javier Heraud, allied itself with one of the two Communist parties. (In Peru, as in other parts of Latin America, the Communist movement has two wings: one pro-Soviet, the other pro-Chinese.)

Politically, the crisis in the middle-class parties and the absorption of Haya de la Torre's A.P.R.A. movement by the government apparatus, begun in 1945 under President Bustamante Rivero and completed under Presidents Odría and Prado, favored the growth of the M.I.R. The peasants moved into action by appropriating farms in the mountain region; the metalworkers occupied the mines; the agricultural trade unions of Cuzco inscribed on their banners: "Land or death." Thus the M.I.R. impelled the governing class of Peru to "modernize," and to adopt sweeping reforms.

The guerrilla movement has attracted many intellectuals. Inevitably, the guerrillas have been criticized by the orthodox Communists, who, quoting Lenin, declare that nothing is further from Marxism than the attempt to foist on the masses forms of struggle arbitrarily devised by intellectual adventurists. But the guerrillas retort that reality, not a taste for adventure, imposes these forms of struggle. In the guerrilla movement they see a mobile strategic force that is politically and militarily autonomous, that does not depend on orders from the cities, where the leaders are inclined to be more timorous, and that acts in accordance with the diverse circumstances of mountain struggle. Advocates of guerrilla warfare are convinced that, just as in Cuba, the rebel army will be the center around which the revolutionary party will unite; *it* will give birth to the party, not vice versa.

As seen from Havana, the Latin American revolution is a "must," but a revolution based more on the guerrillas than on the existing political parties. In the middle of 1967 the eventual "reappearance" of Che Guevara at the head of an insurrectional movement was considered certain by many in the Cuban capital. His popularity had not diminished. His famous letter to Fidel Castro, lofty in its revolutionary aims and effectively written in Che's personal style, was reprinted on posters throughout Cuba. The alleged differences between Fidel and Che were ridiculed, and emphasis was placed on "the Cuban way to socialism." A leading slogan then was: "Neither Moscow nor Peking, but Havana."

Most of those who have studied the Cuban Revolution on the spot, from its origins to the present day, agree on one thing: Without Fidel Castro's "adventurism" there would have been no Cuban Revolution. Fidel himself, in his important speech of July 26, 1966, stated that at the beginning of the armed struggle in Cuba no more than twenty others believed in it. He went on: "We would have been lost, if in order to make a Socialist revolution we had to dedicate ourselves first to teaching socialism and Marxism and then to making the revolution afterward." And he concluded: "To believe that consciousness must precede the struggle is a mistake."

Three facts in the last few years confirm Cuba's determination not to yield to its critics in the matter of "the necessity of revolution in Latin America." They were cited in an excellent analysis of the Cuban Revolution by the French journalist Marcel Niedergang that served as a prelude to the Inter-American Conference of heads of state at Punta del Este in April, 1967:

1. Fidel Castro's challenge to the leadership of the Communist parties in Latin America, who, from 1966 on, criticized "petty-bourgeois adventurism" and "mistakes committed by advocates of armed revolution."

2. The appraisal in the Cuban press, especially in *Granma*, organ of the Cuban Communist Party, and *Verde Olivo*, a publication of the Cuban armed forces, of military actions carried out by revolutionary leaders in some Latin American countries in conflict with the

Communist leaders or the non-Communist Left—for example, the M.I.R. in Venezuela, which had simply renounced armed struggle as the main form of struggle.

3. The pre-eminent role accorded Havana at Punta del Este, despite the absence of Major Che Guevara.

Although he was absent, his slightest declaration found a response in Cuba and the communications media of the Left forces in the world. In the middle of April, 1967, a message was published in Havana, under Che Guevara's signature, asking the peoples of the "Third World" "not only to send their best wishes to the fighters of Vietnam but also to share their risks." The message contained a criticism of the solidarity demonstrations in "the progressive world" staged by advocates of peaceful coexistence. In that connection Guevara evoked "the bitter irony the gladiators in the Roman circus felt when cheered by the plebeian spectators." He urged revolution-aries everywhere and above all in the Americas to "follow the road of Vietnam," suggesting that "armed groups form coordinating commit-tees to make it more difficult for Yankee imperialism to enforce its repression."

The Bolivian guerrillas, who were quite active at that time, frequently referred to Guevara's book, *Memoirs of the Revolutionary War*. That they had learned its lessons well is shown by the British journalist Murray Sayle of the London *Times*, who for four days participated in an anti-guerrilla operation carried out by the Bolivian army. "The Bolivian rebels are specialists in guerrilla warfare," wrote the British journalist, who found a photograph of Che Guevara and a speech by North Vietnam's General Giap translated into Spanish in one of the positions abandoned by the guerrillas.

Another of the many signs of recent changes in Latin America has been the presence of revolutionary priests. In general, the Catholic hierarchy has been on the side of the ruling classes against the people; but in the lower ranks there have been quite a few priests who have refused to be drawn into the anti-Communist campaign. "A Che Guevara in a cassock"—this was a description applied to the Colombian priest Camilo Torres. Born in Bogotá in 1929, he came from a wealthy upper-class Colombian family. He studied at the Catholic University of Louvain, in Belgium, and on his return to

Colombia held the chair of sociology at the National University. In 1962 the Colombian Ministry of Education, like its French counterpart in May, 1968, clashed openly with the students. Father Torres took the side of the students and was forced to resign from his post. Then he began a political career that made him famous throughout the Americas.

His evolution was swift. He saw only one way out for the peoples of Latin America, especially his own people: armed struggle for the conquest of power. Not satisfied with preaching, he moved into action and joined a guerrilla group. When on February 15, 1966, he lost his life in a clash with the Colombian army, the news shook all Colombia. By his courage in rejecting the time-worn anti-Communist slanders of the Colombian Right, who accused him of being a "fellow traveler," "crypto-Communist," and the like, Father Torres won the respect and affection of the Colombian masses. He told his listeners openly that as a Colombian, a sociologist, a Christian, and a priest, he was a revolutionary. As a Colombian, because he could no longer remain aloof from the struggles of his people. As a sociologist, because his scientific study of reality had brought him to the conclusion that the present society could not be changed without a revolution. As a Christian and a priest, because by supporting the people's revolutionary cause and defending social justice, he felt that he was fulfilling his duty and carrying out his mission of practicing human brotherhood in action. Father Torres believed that central social and economic planning offered the only real solution to the problems of poverty and human exploitation; and was the only effective way of defeating the alliance between the big financiers and landowners. Planning was essential; if the Marxists offered the best guarantee of planning concrete measures for the people's welfare, one could not be anti-Marxist in the name of the Christian ideal. Indeed, in such a case the true Christian must collaborate with the Marxists.

Everywhere in Latin America Father Torres' ideas made headway among the "new guerrilla priests." Even some of the higher clergy were attracted, such as Monsignor Camara, archbishop of Recife and Olinda, in Brazil. In Peru, some fifty young priests published a book denouncing "the chronic situation of injustice, oppression, and stagnation" in their land. An Argentine priest, Juan García Elorrio,

general secretary of the "Latin American Camilo Torres Association," asserted that it was the duty of every Christian "to be a
revolutionary." The same note was struck in Mexico, Bolivia, and the
Dominican Republic. Indeed, in the folklore of Latin America two
names are now linked: Camilo Torres and Che Guevara.

The theme of guerrilla action was vigorously discussed at the
Havana Tricontinental Congress, January 3–10, 1966, at which the
revolutionary movements of Africa and Asia were also represented.
Once the conference was over, rumors spread that the Latin
American guerrilla groups were dissatisfied, feeling that they had not
been well represented by the delegates from the official Latin
American Communist parties, who were pro-Soviet, whereas some of
the most active guerrilla forces in Latin America at that time—
1966—were sympathetic to Peking's policies. This, for example, was
the case of the MR-13 in Guatemala, which we have described
above. From the outset these Guatemalan guerrillas challenged
accepted leftist dogmas and fought openly and proudly for the
Socialist revolution. They proposed: expulsion of the imperialists;
expropriation without indemnification of their landholdings and of
the big capitalist enterprises; expropriation without payment of the
native landowners; distribution of land to the peasants; a minimum
wage for workers and a sliding scale of salaries; one national union of
workers; worker control over production; democratic rights and
freedoms for the Guatemalan people: free press, free assembly, the
right to organize; arming the population and dissolving the army of
the dictatorship; an end to police crimes and tortures; abrogation of
all military or any other treaties with imperialism; establishment of a
workers' and peasants' government. As is evident, this broad
program was clearly revolutionary.

This first Tricontinental Conference had come into being because
the revolutionary forces in Africa, Asia, and Latin America were able
to agree that many of the difficulties they faced in their struggles
could be overcome if they formed a common front against imperialism. But the first session convened without one of its animators, the
dynamic Moroccan leader Ahmed Ben Barka. He had presided over
the preliminary international conference held in Cairo in September,
1965. The reactionaries, aware of the capabilities of this leader of the
Moroccan opposition, moved quickly to eliminate him, and Ben

Barka fell victim to a kidnapping plot hatched by the Moroccan government and venal officers of the French police. When news of his tragic disappearance became known, many connected it with his vigorous efforts on behalf of the Tricontinental Conference.

The Latin American delegates at Havana evoked Simón Bolívar's speech at the Congress of Panama: "Solidarity, defense, unity of the Latin American republics, not to fight or conquer anyone, not to wage war, but to defend themselves against common dangers; to win respect for their sovereignty, to resolve their differences by conciliation, and to fight for their progress and prosperity." Among the Latin American groups represented were: the F.R.A.P. of Chile; the Communist Party of Cuba; the Armed Forces of Liberation from Guatemala; the Movement of National Liberation from Mexico; the F.I.D.E.L. from Uruguay; and the Front of National Liberation from Venezuela. Over-all, the Africans, Asians, and Latin Americans participating in the Havana Conference came from almost as many nations as there are members of the United Nations, thus representing a goodly percentage of the world's population.

The movements represented at this Congress were, as noted, diverse and in varying stages of development. Some advocated free enterprise and property rights; others were frankly oriented toward socialism. Nevertheless, there were strong bonds of unity among them, a unity that was strengthened by the events then occurring in Vietnam and the Dominican Republic. For their part, the imperialists realized how dangerous it would be if the Africans, Asians, and Latin Americans achieved solidarity. For years the Latin Americans had been moving in an anti-imperialist direction. Among other things, this was one of the major effects of the Cuban Revolution. The Latin American Conference for National Sovereignty, Emancipation, and Peace, held in Mexico in March, 1961, heard Mexico's great President, Lázaro Cárdenas, say: "To accept isolation among our own peoples, possessing the same history and united by blood and language, would be a serious mistake, as serious as remaining aloof from developments on the other continents, when it is clear that our problems are not foreign to world developments. A lasting peace is bound up with the liberation of colonial territories, absolute respect for national sovereignty, and consolidation of the economic emancipation of humanity. The majority of humanity belongs to this group of peoples—the underdeveloped nations. It comprises many peoples of Africa, Asia, the Near and Middle East, and Latin America."

The peoples of Africa and Asia had also prepared for this broad movement of revolutionary solidarity. At Cairo, in December, 1957, the First Solidarity Conference of the Afro-Asian peoples had taken place; it was followed by three others, the last one in Ghana in May, 1965. And in the ensuing years the combined action of the peoples and movements that met in Havana, for the first Tricontinental Conference, was to leave its mark on world events.

At the Conference itself, the chief topic of discussion was not even on the agenda. It was the question: Where is Che Guevara? Ever since he had quit the Cuban government, the question had been echoed by millions of Latin Americans. As for Guevara himself, he had outlined his revolutionary views in the Uruguayan magazine *Marcha*: "We have not sufficiently understood the need to create the new man—not the one who represents the ideas of the nineteenth century, nor the one who represents the ideas of our sick and decadent century. We must create the man of the twenty-first century, even though he is still a subjective and undefined dream." Then he wrote of the first heroic epoch of the Cuban Revolution: "From the ideological point of view, one of our basic tasks is to find the formula by which we can perpetuate this heroic attitude in daily life." Hence the importance of properly choosing the instrument for mobilizing the masses—an instrument which, without disdaining the proper use of material incentives, is essentially moral in nature. So Guevara, though absent from this first Tricontinental Conference at Havana, profoundly influenced the thinking of many of the delegates who were looking for a clear political line to unite the peoples of Asia, Africa, and Latin America.

To many the news that Guevara had fallen at the hands of the Bolivian army came as a tragic shock. Hitherto they had known Bolivia only for its tin, the fabulous fortune of the Patiño family, and its picturesque mountainous sites that had begun to attract tourists. But Bolivia was also a center of guerrilla activity. Suddenly, therefore, this country that had always been looked upon as one of those most dependent on the U.S. economy, was thrust in the vanguard of the anti-imperialist struggle. Within a few months the new guerrilla front opened in the Andes had become a serious effort at revolution. One of the U.S. "advisers" sent to La Paz confessed his surprise, in an interview granted the French journalist Marcel Niedergang, at "the highly developed technique of camouflage" displayed by the rebel Bolivian guerrillas and their ability to melt away into their surroundings, "resembling what we are now witnessing in Vietnam."

The guerrillas had not chosen their zone of activity by chance or merely in view of the advantages of the terrain, but with an eye to the future and to bigger operations. From Nancahuazu, the guerrilla center, they could, if their position was consolidated, pour out in three decisive stages: on the eastern plain by way of Camiri; through the valleys of Cochabamba; and through the passes of the altiplano. And their ultimate hope was to form three columns that would march in parallel fashion on the capital, La Paz. Everything in the operation bespoke far more than a spirit of adventurism.

Proof of how decisive the actions of a few individuals can be—and in direct line of descent from the Cuban Revolution—is the example of the Perero brothers in the armed struggle in Bolivia. They first appeared in the neighborhood of Nancahuazu as buyers of a livestock ranch. Friendly, open, they soon won the good will of all the local inhabitants. The livestock that came out of their ranch, however, were not llamas but guerrillas. The Perero brothers had set up a training camp (later uncovered by the Bolivian army and razed). In 1965, as members of an extreme leftist group, they decided to join the pro-Chinese Communist group led by Oscar Zamora, one-time general secretary of the International Union of Students with headquarters in Prague. As one of the Perero brothers told a foreign correspondent: "We decided to make an insurrection. In Latin America the only way out is by armed struggle." The Bolivian guerrillas were able to adapt themselves to places completely uninhabitable for others; and indeed, this was their strength.

It cannot be sufficiently stressed—at the risk of sounding monotonous—that the guerrillas of Latin America must be viewed in their historical perspective. Let us suppose that when this book appears the guerrilla movement in Latin America seems quiescent. (In the summer of 1968, for example, there were many reports in the U.S. press about the fading away of the guerrilla movement in Colombia.)

Yet I am confident that in a year, or two, or five, there will be a resurgence of guerrilla activity throughout Latin America; for that is the pattern of the struggle there.

The Havana Conference of the O.L.A.S. (Latin American Organization of Solidarity) in August, 1967, confirmed the many-sidedness of the Socialist movement and the extension of its operating range. An event of signal importance, it provided the revolutionary movements of Latin America with a coordinating organization they had hitherto lacked. The feeling that henceforth they could count on one another would undoubtedly encourage them to overcome the hardships inherent in guerrilla warfare. With convincing authority Fidel Castro discouraged a demonstrative public rejection of the policy of peaceful coexistence as advocated by the Soviet Union, but in the more restricted confines of the committees there were numerous critiques of that policy. The immediate target was the Communist Party of Venezuela, because of the repercussions of the Douglas Bravo affair.

Douglas Bravo, head of the F.A.L.N., had broken with the Communist Party of Venezuela (C.P.V.) and had spent many months in Caracas working intensively among the Venezuelan youth. This activity met with the disapproval of his former comrades in the Political Bureau of the C.P.V., to which he had belonged and in which he had defended the line of armed combat. Now at the O.L.A.S. Conference in Havana this viewpoint carried the day, and the main resolution adopted indicated that armed combat was the chief method of making the revolution. Significantly, the Conference chose one of the guerrilla leaders, Major Néstor Valle of Guatemala, to read its conclusions. After evoking Latin America's past, from the time of colonial emancipation in the nineteenth century, it asserted that "U.S. imperialism is the worst enemy of humanity." Counsels of moderation offered by Soviet Prime Minister Kosygin, who went quickly to Havana after his Glassboro, New Jersey, meeting with President Lyndon B. Johnson, did not seem to convince the delegates. Nor did they cause the Cuban leaders to soft-pedal their remarks, for in his closing address Fidel Castro harshly attacked the activities of the C.I.A. and criticized the "rightist leadership" of the Communist Party of Venezuela. He further declared that throughout the Conference there had been a clear and unmistakable dividing line between "those who want to make the revolution and those who want to slow it down."

If Castro took particular pains not to give Moscow any excuse for halting vitally necessary economic aid to Cuba, some of the other Cuban speakers did not feel obliged to soften their language. Thus the head of the Cuban delegation, Armando Hart, supported by a majority of the gathering, sharply assailed the policy of peaceful coexistence. Everything that happened at the 1967 Havana Conference has important implications for the future; for there the bases were laid for the future activities of the revolutionary forces in Latin America, and their strategy and tactics were outlined.

Observers emphasized the skill displayed by Rodney Arismendi, general secretary of the Communist Party of Uruguay, in avoiding too sharp a break between the various forces among the Latin American Left. But throughout the entire Conference advocates of the policy of peaceful coexistence were kept on the defensive. The dominant tendency was that henceforth revolutionary movements had to depend primarily on themselves, and not on the Socialist countries. Various speakers appealed to the U.S.S.R. not to hold back the activities of the revolutionary parties in Latin America. As for the United States, all they could expect from that quarter was unrelenting hostility. It was clear from the evidence: whether in Guatemala, Brazil, Argentina, the Dominican Republic, or Bolivia, attempts at bourgeois democracy had led to military coups backed by Washington.

Another important aspect of the Havana Conference was the way in which Vietnam and the O.L.A.S. were defined as two fronts of the same battle, thus giving an international dimension to the struggle of the Latin American guerrillas—now their interests and solidarity extended to other, far-off lands as well as to their comrades in the Americas. It was this feature of the Conference that worried the United States the most. James Reston wrote in *The New York Times* that U.S. government leaders had hoped that the victorious defense of South Vietnam would make the Communists renounce wars of national liberation; but they had been wrong. One had only to look at the Havana Conference: Vietnam had become the key to the new peripheral strategy and its possibility of victory. Che Guevara's last message: "We must create two, three, many Vietnams!" had been heeded. That was why he had been named honorary chairman of the Conference, and his portrait dominated the hall, along with that of Simón Bolívar, the Liberator. Arismendi, the Uruguayan Communist leader, proposed a compromise between the two main lines of thought at the gathering to the effect that: "Armed combat is a higher form of struggle." That is, armed conflict was not the only way. But it was thenceforth that the Conference gained momentum as one speaker after another addressed the delegates.

For two weeks the Havana Solidarity Conference discussed the best ways of mobilizing, organizing, and connecting the revolutionary struggles against imperialism in Africa, Asia, and Latin America. In itself such a meeting ninety miles from U.S. shores, coinciding with escalation of the war in Vietnam, was a noteworthy event, despite many contradictions and weaknesses revealed in the course of the debates. Apart from the resolutions adopted, the significant fact was that the Conference responded most warmly to those revolutionary movements most actively engaged in guerrilla fighting or similar modes of struggle against imperialism. This over-all sentiment pervaded the various liberation movements on the three continents. Aware that the fate of the liberation movement in Angola and Mozambique was closely linked to that of like-minded movements in Asia and Latin America, they realized the need for solidarity, for mutual aid in propaganda, money, and arms. Hence, too, the realization that the march of socialism in the underdeveloped countries depended equally on the success of the guerrillas in the Portuguese colonies in Africa, in the former Belgian Congo (Zaïre), and on the battlefields of Vietnam.

The most notable speeches at the Conference were realistic and constructive. There was no wild-eyed optimism: the revolution was not for tomorrow. But the revolutionary road had been opened. And in the 1970's the imperialists would find it much more difficult to maintain their positions of power than in the preceding decade.

Not so long ago I spoke with one of the most intelligent of the Dominicans living in exile in Paris. Here is how he summed up his situation, which applies similarly to many other Latin American revolutionaries as well: "To me as a man of the extreme Left, Juan

Bosch is simply a well-intentioned liberal. But he is a Dominican patriot who refuses to be a tool of Washington, like so many other so-called Latin American statesmen. That's enough for me to support him. A man like that, honest and independent, who cannot be bought by dollars, can be persuaded to pass a series of reforms on behalf of the masses. He's much better than Betancourt in Venezuela, who started as a Communist, then defected, and now hates everything genuinely left-wing. Or than a Figueres in Costa Rica, who poses as a Socialist. In many countries of Latin America, when a man like Juan Bosch appears, we have to support him. To vow that one can only support a hundred per cent leftist means letting the reactionaries stay in power for a good long time."

At that time—1965—the problem of U.S. relations with Latin America was in the forefront of attention. It was just before the Inter-American Conference at Rio de Janeiro, at which the U.S. State Department tried hard to appear well disposed toward reforms and democracy in Latin America. But U.S. military intervention in the Dominican Republic in that same year did little to ease the task of the State Department spokesmen. Washington's sole argument was to depict Juan Bosch as a puppet of the Communists; but Bosch had defined his own position, when, on preparing to assume the presidency of the Dominican Republic, he declared: "I don't think we have to imitate the example of Fidel Castro in the Dominican Republic. We have an immense task ahead of us: to institute economic and social reforms, and restore civil liberties after thirty years of the Trujillo dictatorship." Bosch was elected President by 62 per cent of the voters.

But before his plan to draw away from the United States could materialize, the effects of American military intervention into Dominican affairs could be felt. The Rio de Janeiro meeting of the O.A.S. was one of the stormiest ever held. Even a government like that of Venezuela, usually so quick to align its inter-American policies with those of the United States, protested this time against U.S. intervention. The Peruvian parliament went much further, denouncing the United States as an aggressor. In the months to come the landing of U.S. marines in the Dominican Republic aroused anger and indignation throughout a Latin America already disturbed by the U.S. role in Vietnam. And the Latin Americans felt that if the

United States were successful in Vietnam, they themselves would be the first to suffer the consequences. Fidel Castro put it in these words: "If the United States is allowed to destroy North Vietnam, it will attack Cuba." So in the streets of Latin America there were mingled cries of: "Marines, out of Santo Domingo! Americans, out of Vietnam!"

When in 1965 the United States intervened in the Dominican Republic against Juan Bosch on behalf of General Elías Wessin y Wessin, one of the "strong men" of the Trujillo regime, Washington dropped all its liberal pretenses of the Alliance for Progress and the Rooseveltian "Good Neighbor" policy. The intervention, prompted mainly by the fear that the new government in Santo Domingo might bring Cuba back into the family of Latin American nations, meant a return to the policy of the "big stick," and an abandonment of more or less liberal regimes in favor of those able "to maintain law and order." This "law and order" meant reactionary and usually militarist dictatorships.

Meanwhile ferment increased throughout Latin America. The landing of four hundred U.S. marines at Santo Domingo on April 29, 1965, on orders of President Lyndon Johnson "to protect the lives of U.S. citizens" was denounced by all the democratic forces of Latin America. It was compared with a similar action several decades earlier in Nicaragua, against the people's movement of General Augusto Sandino. As the marines landed in Santo Domingo, followers of former President Juan Bosch, deposed in 1963 by a U.S.-backed military coup, fought courageously in the streets against the counter-revolutionary forces of Air Force General Wessin y Wessin. It was the latter who had appealed to the United States for help, thus affording President Johnson a ready pretext to send the marines and some warships. The four hundred U.S. marines soon became four thousand, and began to fire at the Dominican people.

Juan Bosch himself, as we have seen, was not an extreme leftist. He was a genuine liberal, but Washington disliked and distrusted him. During the few months of his presidency he had initiated a series of reforms highly displeasing to U.S. corporate investors. Moreover, he was suspected of pro-Castro sympathies. At that time, I heard it frequently stated in the corridors of the United Nations that from the viewpoint of public interest the most one could hope for in various Latin American nations was a liberal of the Juan Bosch type, desirous of social reforms and following a policy independent of the United States. For even that would have represented a big step forward in Latin America's relations with Washington.

In the 1960's, however, military coups which for a quarter of a century had served to underpin U.S. influence in Latin America began to lose their effectiveness. In Brazil the military coup of April 1, 1964, which toppled President João Goulart from power and with him the first reform government the country had had, was unable to hold back the revolutionary wave. Some 2,500 Brazilians, stripped of their civil rights and threatened with imprisonment, left the country. Among the exiles were outstanding members of Brazil's intelligentsia: writer-economist Josué de Castro, famous for his world campaign against hunger, Celso Furtado, architect Oscar Niemeyer, Governors Miguel Arraes and Brizola, and the man Washington feared most, Francisco Julião.

Grandson of a big landowner, trained for the law and eventually for a political career in which he was expected to rapidly climb the ladder of advancement and wealth, Francisco Julião moved in the opposite direction. He used his talents as a writer and speaker to serve the people. He himself has told how, at the age of eighteen, on reading Engels' *Anti-Dühring*, he became a Marxist. As time went on, Julião became the leading spirit in the Peasant Leagues. His ideas on how to win the peasantry to the revolution were original: he considered it more important to educate politically the tenant farmers rather than the farmworkers (peons). The peons would come later, during the second revolutionary stage, but for the moment Julião felt that they were too closely bound to the routines that enslaved them, lacking self-esteem and class-consciousness. So he believed he had to begin with the tenant farmers. "The tenant farmers," Julião said, "who till the worst lands of the big landowners and always pay excessive rent—in money, services, or kind—are easier to organize. They have some security, some savings, and an awareness of the value of their work: the field they rent is always less than the area they could cultivate. If we could promise them the land as their property, we would enlist them as soldiers in the revolution. Through them we could attack the weakest link in the system."

In 1968 the Peasant Leagues spread throughout Brazil and were supported by the students and the writers, who composed a kind of folk poetry on their behalf, very simple and very popular verses but with decidedly revolutionary content. The Leagues began to arm themselves, because Julião favored direct action and opposed peaceful coexistence with the bourgeoisie. He denounced the "progressive" laws as dead letters. The laws that really prevailed were those of the estate-owners. He considered Goulart's government weak, doomed to defeat at the hands of U.S. and Brazilian big business whenever it sought to translate propaganda into acts. Julião was harsh and intractable toward the other elements of the Left—especially rigid and intransigent toward the Communists, with whom he clashed.

"Castelo Branco," Julião would say, "rendered the revolution a great service when he dissolved the political parties. The parliament, castrated, is subservient to the military. More than ever, elections are a farce. But at least they no longer fool anybody. 'Democracy' such as we had with Kubitschek and Goulart is over and done with. True liberation is forged in much harsher struggles. The party we want is a mass party with a revolutionary orientation." Comments like these led people to characterize Julião as impatient and "pro-Chinese." But judging from his own statements, he was not impatient: "Our revolution will be a long, a very long process. Intervention by the United States will be inevitable. But when the Brazilian people rises up against the oligarchy, North American imperialism will crumble in ruins over the whole continent. It will react as it has reacted in Vietnam; only here it will need five times more forces than in Vietnam. The liberation of Latin America began in Cuba and is continuing in Vietnam; each time it will grow bloodier and bloodier. We know that we'll receive no help. We don't count on it. We'll capture our arms from the enemy."

In exile Julião had an ally: Father Lage, a priest with an interesting political past. In France, Father Lage had been a "worker-priest" and he had been sentenced to twenty-eight years in prison for his efforts on behalf of the workers. In Brazil he was not the only example of a priest taking the people's side. But whereas most social-minded Latin American priests espoused social reforms, particularly agrarian reform and greater social equality, and rejected

Marxism, socialism, and Communism, Father Francisco Lage called himself a Socialist and a revolutionary. "The people," Lage wrote, "are far more radical than all those who call themselves radicals. They don't accept the idea of agrarian reform. When you talk to them about it, they raise their rifles and shout: 'Land, land!' That is, they don't want an individual distribution of plots of uncultivated land; they want all the big estates to belong to those who worked them. In essence, collectivization of the large landholdings."

One of the most interesting and valuable studies of the Mexican Revolution is that by Jesús Silva Herzog, editor of the outstanding Latin American publication *Cuadernos Americanos.* In it Silva Herzog emphasizes that to Francisco L. Madero, a wealthy man from the northern part of the country and the first liberal candidate to challenge General Porfirio Díaz, who had been Mexico's dictator-president for thirty years, the essential task was to transform Mexican political institutions. Madero summed this up in a dual formula: effective voting and no re-election to the presidency. Today this still remains the bedrock premise of Mexican politics.

In 1910 Díaz's opponents were not overly concerned about economic and social problems, nor were they receptive to the idea of class struggle. Silva Herzog relates how once at a public meeting, when asked why he didn't share his money with the poor if he felt so deeply about them, Madero retorted: "The people do not demand bread, they demand freedom." But the people did demand bread and the peasants demanded land. From the outset the masses were more concerned with improving their living conditions than with perfecting the governmental system and instituting pure democracy. A better life: that was the heart of the matter in the Mexican Revolution.

The revolutionary upsurge soon went far beyond the initial aims of its original leaders and left them behind. There ensued instead an open struggle of the poor against the rich, of peasants against landlords. "The socializing spirit of the Revolution was born of the anguish of the hungry and desperate masses." For Mexico this was a decisive step forward, even though there were numerous subsequent retreats, in its march to socialism. And among the leaders of the first period of the Revolution there was one, Emiliano Zapata, who immediately sensed the urgency and intensity of the agrarian question. When the Mexican constitution of 1917 was ratified, it proclaimed the principle that the subsoil belonged to the nation and established the principle of land distribution to the people through indemnification. Years later, in the 1930's, President Lázaro Cárdenas carried forward those principles by giving a new and vigorous impetus to agrarian reform. General Cárdenas instituted land distribution on a virtually unprecedented scale. But it was not only the peasants who benefited from his presidency, a landmark in the history of modern Mexico and one that aroused strong sympathy and hope in the rest of Latin America; Cárdenas was also the friend of the organized industrial workers. Moreover, he was forthright and unshakable in his defense of Mexican national sovereignty and independence. Thus he challenged the international oil combines, expropriated their holdings, and proved that Mexico could get along very well without them.

His foreign policy was exemplary. From the opening shots he realized what the Spanish Civil War was: the first battle in the world war waged by international fascism on Spanish soil. Impressed by the valor and determination of the Spanish people, the Mexican President gave the Spanish Republicans his unconditional support, and Cárdenas became a heroic figure to the Spanish people. His support of the Spanish Republic, undeviating and uncompromising, was so strong that no succeeding Mexican president has since dared to alter it, despite frequent suggestions from influential Mexican quarters and despite constant pressure from the United States. A change in Mexico's thirty-year-old policy toward Franco would have been looked upon as Washington's reward to the Spanish dictator. If the law of no re-election had not been in effect in Mexico, Lázaro Cárdenas' second term of office, with the valuable experience of the first term behind him, would have had far-reaching positive results for the future of Mexico and all Latin America.

The full thrust of the African Revolution was felt in the United Nations itself in the debates touched off by the tragic events in the Congo in 1964. One of the sources of these events was Madrid, Spain, where agents of the colonialists, terrified by the progress of the African Revolution in the former Belgian colony of the Congo, sought out Moïse Tshombe. Under the protective wing of Francisco Franco, one after another of the defeated leaders of world reaction had gathered in the Spanish capital, awaiting the hour of return to their respective lands. One such was Moïse Tshombe, in whom the colonialists saw their "man of destiny" and, conveniently forgetting that he had been the first separatist in the Congo, brought him to Léopoldville and installed him there as head of a national government.

In international affairs one often forgets the origin of problems that later develop into serious conflicts; hence the confusion in the minds of those who judge the course of events solely from the headlines of the daily press or the television screen. The origin of the Congo conflict in 1964, which turned against the West and hastened the revolutionary process in Africa, may be found in the transfer of Tshombe from Madrid to Léopoldville. For from that moment on two things became clear: the international companies with mining interests in the Congo were determined to regain their power there; and the naming of Tshombe as Prime Minister of the Congo would have vast and dramatic consequences throughout Africa. After all, he was "the man of the West," and considered by most Africans the assassin of Patrice Lumumba, the hero of the African masses. This was the "storm over Africa," reminiscent of an earlier "storm over Asia" made famous by Soviet director Pudovkin's film of that name.

In the course of the 1960's two political storms raged violently and concurrently—in Africa and in Asia. They may be summed up in two names: the Congo and Vietnam. Efforts by the former colonial powers to regain their lost influence by utilizing subtler forms of neo-colonialism only served to strengthen the movement toward African unity. The Conference of African States held in Cairo a few months before Tshombe was installed as Prime Minister in Léopold-ville, showed that to the majority of the African leaders Moïse Tshombe was an "outlaw." At that time an African delegate to the United Nations told me in Geneva: "It's quite natural for Tshombe to use mercenaries. He's one himself, a mercenary paid by the Belgians and Americans." At Cairo, Tshombe was repudiated, suffering the humiliating experience of being branded as anti-African.

Yet Washington insisted on supporting Tshombe, against the will and sentiment of the majority of the African states. Part of this support was the so-called "humanitarian operation" over Stanleyville. It was easy to predict that the combined Belgo-American attack against the supporters of Lumumba, who had made Stanleyville their capital, would be in the name of a humanitarian ransom operation. But this served to give unusual dimensions to the conflict between the United States and the African states. And indeed, African unity began to take shape around the Congo conflict. Speaking with African delegates in the corridors of the United Nations, I could gauge the intensity of their emotions. African unity had been a dream, a long-term aspiration, but at the various Conferences of the African States commencing in 1962, the difficulties of converting this dream into a reality had become clear. The events in the Congo during the 1960's, however, gave a decided impetus to the idea of unity. In the United Nations, for example, the most militant of the African states—the Congo Republic (Brazzaville), Guinea, Mali, Ghana, and Algeria—formed an impressive vanguard; and the 1964–1965 session of the world organization was highlighted by the revolt of the African states against the Western powers, a forerunner of events to come in Africa. As I recall the debates over the Congo question in the Security Council, they impress me as striking evidence of the change in the international picture brought about by the emergence of new revolutionary forces. Delegates from the United States, Belgium, and the United Kingdom turned pale and found it hard to restrain their anger at the spectacle of the Minister of Foreign Affairs from a tiny African state—the Congo Republic (Brazzaville)—dealing with them as an equal as he enumerated his charges against the spokesmen of the Great Powers.

Some of those African states were among the poorest members of the United Nations. They could have used U.S. financial aid; nevertheless, they behaved with self-assurance, unafraid of reprisals from those who possessed great wealth and managed the fund for underdeveloped nations. In truth, the shadow of China loomed over this historic debate. When the first Chinese teams of experts arrived in some of the African states, the Americans joked about it; later, they learned to take the phenomenon seriously. The then Secretary General of the United Nations, U Thant, was not exaggerating when he called the Charter of the Organization of African Unity, drawn up in Addis Ababa, Ethiopia, "one of the historic documents of this century."

Of course, Africa has a long way to go. It is a continent in which the working class is still virtually nonexistent as a class. The big problem of tribalism has to be met and overcome: up to now, an African's tribe has been his motherland. Moreover, the African nations must avoid "the easy solution," a military coup or renewed dependence on the Big Powers. Perhaps that is why the African Revolution is so little understood by the many Western intellectuals and political leaders who are often heard complaining that many of the African governments and leaders with the broadest influence over the African masses do not behave according to the classical concepts of democracy or fail to respond to appeals from the "democratic" countries to imitate their methods of government. A refreshing contrast is offered by the noted French writer Jean-Paul Sartre, who, in his study of Patrice Lumumba, provides a valuable insight into the essence of the African Revolution. The political evolution of that outstanding African leader, whose assassination has not dissipated his influence either in his own country or in the rest of Africa, is in itself of considerable interest. It illuminates many things that may seem obscure to those unable or unwilling to assess long-term trends in African society—the ascendancy of an African working class and the general rise of African socialism.

Lumumba began his political career as a believer in nonviolence. The movement he created, the National Congolese Movement, repeatedly asserted, despite frequent provocations by its opponents, that it would not deviate from its pacifist way. In fact, at one point Lumumba dismayed some of his supporters when, appearing before a Belgian audience in Brussels, he expressed himself in tones they considered too kindly and conciliatory. Yet at the proper moment he could be tough. Thus, replying to Belgian King Baudouin on June 30, 1960, Lumumba evoked "what our fate has been in eighty years of colonial rule. . . . Our wounds are too fresh and too painful for us to wipe them from our memory." He soon found himself at odds with the black petty bourgeoisie, eager to obtain for itself the best advantages colonization could still offer. But those who, taking the Belgian authorities' promise of eventual equality at face value, went to work for the colonial administration, whether in the private or public sector of the economy, soon found that they never rose above very minor and subordinate posts. Lumumba himself was tempted to enter the postal service; but he held back in time. This personal experience brought him closer to the working class, and he began to denounce "the back-breaking work performed at wages that don't provide enough food to keep one from going hungry, that don't provide decent clothing and housing, that don't allow one to educate one's children." He learned the fundamental lesson that "within the colonial system no profound reforms are realizable." Promises of reform were dust tossed in the eyes of a working class that was beginning to grow aware of its exploitation.

Four years before the Congo attained independence, Patrice Lumumba was the idol of the masses in Stanleyville. They were still largely inchoate, a proletariat in the making but still unorganized; and a peasantry groping for a way in which to voice its elementary demands. Lumumba discerned the situation clearly. As a native son of the Congo, he was distressed and tormented by the horrible conditions in his country; but he was also a fighter for a free Africa. His speech at the Accra Conference, where he asserted that the dissensions delaying the true liberation of his country were the same as those perpetuating African separatism, was proof of this. The radicalization of his political thinking was therefore merely a matter of time, and in his evolution he came to deserve Sartre's description of him as the "black Robespierre."

Together with Lumumba, Frantz Fanon embodies the revolutionary spirit of Africa. His voice was raised against the hypocritical paternalism of the colonialists. Independence was not a favor one begged for; it was a right that the "wretched of the earth" (the title of his best book) forcibly took from the imperialists and exploiters. He did not expend his energies in complaining about injustice; he preferred to devote them to the task of enlisting the people in the struggle. When he denounced the tactics of the colonialists and neo-colonialists, he did not preach or moralize; he sought rather to give the peoples of the Third World new weapons. For he saw the Third World as a heterogeneous composite of peoples vacillating and groping their way to the future. Some of them were still enslaved; others had won only the shadow of independence; still others, more politicized, were more alert to the danger of a new imperialist infiltration or open aggression. Fanon felt that the masses were held back by the dead weight of submission they had for so long accepted—this was true above all for the weak industrial proletariat. But there was also the peasantry—and they, if properly led, would respond to the call for insurrection. Their potential for triumphing over obstacles would be demonstrated to the extent that the "wretched of the earth" learned how to unite among themselves. It was an arduous undertaking, and Fanon insisted that there be no illusions on that score. Colonialism, momentarily defeated, could change its tactics. Imperialist aggression assumed various forms, especially the protective guise of liberalism or economic and financial infiltration. Neo-colonialism was more subtle and cunning than naked out-and-out colonial domination. To fight for total liberation demanded a far-reaching effort; to achieve success required the joint exertions of the victims of colonialism, old and new, on the three continents of Africa, Asia, and Latin America.

Fanon therefore called for concerted action by the exploited masses of those three continents, counting mainly on the peasantry. In the final analysis the peasants were the genuinely revolutionary element in those places, despite their seeming lethargy and submissiveness. But first they had to be aroused and mobilized. "The peasant," wrote Fanon, "has nothing to lose and everything to gain. The peasant, the classless one, is the hungry and exploited one; he discovers more quickly than anyone else that only violence pays." Basically he had nothing against the industrial proletariat. At the same time he could not forget that a section of the European working class—not to mention the working class in the United States—had remained insensitive to colonialism, and had often for purely selfish motives taken a stand against the native workers in the colonies. In Fanon, the man of action took precedence over the theoretician.

Frantz Fanon, born in Martinique in 1925, studied medicine and psychiatry in France, and then worked in an Algerian hospital during the rebellion there. He joined the Algerian liberation movement, the N.L.F. (National Liberation Front), where he began his real political career, and he quickly became one of the most powerful leaders of African nationalism. He was a keen thinker, but, as we have stressed, above all a man of action. His brief service in the diplomatic corps did not soften him, as it has so many others. Named by the Algerian government-in-exile to its embassy in Accra, Ghana, Fanon spent less time issuing propaganda statements than in acquiring arms for the N.L.F. and shipping them by way of Mali. He became acquainted with Patrice Lumumba and immediately felt great admiration for the Congolese leader. Lumumba's assassination in 1961 came as a terrible shock to Fanon and spurred his efforts to continue the struggle, yet he himself was not destined to outlive Lumumba for very long. At the end of 1961, at the age of thirty-six, Fanon died of leukemia. His death was a tragedy for the whole African movement.

The divisions in the Socialist camp saddened but did not demoralize Fanon, because he foresaw the eventual need of a second revolution to guarantee the achievements of the first Socialist Revolution in 1917; and in the Moscow-Peking controversy that developed before his death, Fanon took a pro-Peking position. A convinced Marxist, he nevertheless did not accept some of the thinking of the official Western Communist parties regarding the natural solidarity between the European proletariat and the working people in the colonies. Instead, he claimed, the European worker benefited from colonial exploitation and so was not overly interested in fighting against it.

Completely committed to the cause of the disinherited millions in the colonies, Fanon rejected the systematic condemnation of violence involved in the theory of peaceful coexistence. He was a partisan of violence; in his view it was the only way to transform former slaves into complete human beings, fully equal to their former slavemasters, in the course of the decolonizing process. It was not merely a question of formally gaining national independence with a national flag and anthem of their own. He saw clearly the dangers of neo-colonialism, with the middle classes in the newly independent nations still courting the good will and financial support of the former colonial powers, instead of relying on the masses to impel the revolution forward. Though that might mean painful sacrifices for a time, ultimately it would assure genuine independence based on economic independence.

He learned much from the example of the Congo and the evolution in Lumumba's thinking. "Purifying" violence was not something to which he was temperamentally inclined, for Fanon had seen more than enough terror applied by the French authorities to members of the Algerian N.L.F. to glorify it. What he strove for basically was the creation of a new type of human being.

On many occasions Amilcar Cabral—assassinated in January, 1973—articulated the viewpoint of the peoples and nationalist organizations in the Portuguese African colonies, stressing above all the importance of the "weapon of theory." Proceeding from the idea that class struggle is the motive force in history, he emphasized that every liberation movement must adapt itself to local and national circumstances. Both factors, theory and a feel for the immediate reality at hand, must be combined. To Cabral, ideological weakness —and in some cases complete lack of ideology—was one of the chief shortcomings of some of the liberation movements struggling against imperialism.

As leader of the P.A.I.G.C. (African Party for the Independence of Guinea and Cape Verde), Cabral considered distinctive forms of imperialist domination to be:

1. Direct domination, with political power exercised by outside elements. This is classical colonialism—or colonialism pure and simple.

2. Indirect domination, with political power exercised wholly or in part by native-born agents—usually referred to as neo-colonialism.

In the first case, the social structure of the dominated people, at whatever stage we study it, may undergo the following consequences: (a) complete destruction, generally accompanied by an immediate or rapid liquidation of the native population; replacement of the latter by an alien population; (b) partial destruction, generally accompanied by the consolidation of a considerable portion of the alien population; (c) apparent conservation, but with the native population confined to special zones or reserves and usually deprived of chances for a livelihood; large-scale introduction of an alien stock.

Facts, Cabral asserted, make it unnecessary for us to show that violence is the essential instrument of imperialist rule. If one accepts the premise that liberation is a revolution that does not end with the mere acquisition of a national flag or anthem, then one must conclude that victory is impossible without the use of liberating violence.

From 1965 to 1966, there was a series of military coups in Africa:

in the Congo (Léopoldville), Dahomey, the Central African Republic, Upper Volta, Nigeria, and Ghana. Colonels and generals, sometimes aided by the "services" of the former colonial powers, clashed with the new political forces that had come to power after independence. In many cases the army seized control without much difficulty; and so began an era of neo-colonialism, in which the regimes sought to compensate for the lack of a popular base by loans and other forms of financial aid from international financial circles.

In Ghana, an army of little more than 10,000 shattered Kwame Nkrumah's party with its 100,000 members and 2,000,000 supporters—a political force that had seemed the most formidable in black Africa. "Moderate" Nigeria and "revolutionary" Ghana, as they were classified in the Afro-Asian group of nations in the United Nations, suffered the same fate. In general the prevailing characteristic of all these military coups was a swing to the Right. This was all to the liking of the United States, which was engaged in a general offensive to strengthen its position throughout black Africa. It made no secret of its aims: an unrelenting fight against Communism; control and exploitation of markets that seemed unusually promising; control of the sources of raw materials. American penetration of Africa proceeded in all directions: in mining, American capital was invested in mines already intensively exploited as well as others that held the promise of high profits; a similar situation prevailed in banking, airlines, and oil distribution. While the First National City Bank and the Allen group acquired the shares of the former French banks in that region, Pan American World Airways extended its communications network throughout Africa.

If one bears in mind that until recently U.S. foreign trade represented only 5 per cent of its total trade, and that U.S. trade with *all* of Africa, including the Union of South Africa, represented only 5 per cent of that 5 per cent, one has an idea of the startling increase in U.S. business dealings with Africa—one more manifestation of the global mission the United States has set itself.

That there have been cases in which a Great Power, interested in exploiting the resources of a newly independent African nation, has given it economic aid even if its regime was not politically palatable does not contradict what I have written above. This was a way of keeping the regime economically viable until an opportunity arose for a *coup d'état* when the more amenable colonels or generals could take over and steer the country away from genuine independence and socialism. It was this danger of remaining at the mercy of the Great Powers that impelled Nkrumah to develop his thesis concerning African socialism. Along with Lumumba and the Algerian Ben Bella (despite his shortcomings as an administrator), Nkrumah was one of the few African leaders with a Socialist vision of Africa's future. He claimed that "Nkrumahism," based on scientific socialism, possessed universal validity. Not content with defining general aims and principles, he sought the intellectual instrument that would enable the new African nations to attain those objectives on a solid basis, impervious to all harmful outside interference. Nkrumah rejected the "plurality of socialisms": the existence on the African continent of an "Arab socialism" *à la* Nasser, or of an "African socialism" of some other predominantly national type, clashed with his over-all concept of a strong and united Africa.

Even though he annoyed many other African leaders by insisting that he was the only one capable of guiding African unity, on the economic level Nkrumah advocated policies which the technical organs of the United Nations found to be constructive in spirit and realistically feasible. On the matter of Inter-African economic integration, the United Nations Conference for Trade and Development, which grew out of the 1964 Conference for Development, declared that Nkrumah was right. Africa's inter-regional trade reaches a scant 7 per cent or 8 per cent (approximately $450,-000,000) of the total trade volume of the continent. In addition to the many national boundaries, there are the commercial ties with and economic dependence on the industrialized nations, some of them—such as the United States—disposing of tremendous sums of capital. Hence it was difficult for the developing countries to accept Nkrumah's ideas.

Let us look at Africa's imports from abroad: textiles, roughly $900,000,000 annually; wheat, $160,000,000; shoes, $70,000,000; meat, $50–$60,000,000; vegetables, $30,000,000; fish, $20,000,000; and fruits, $13,000,000. Even without increasing production, imports could be reduced and payments more nearly balanced if Nkrumah's ideas on inter-African economic cooperation had been taken into consideration. There are real possibilities for the establishment of an African Common Market. Furthermore, there is the possibility of native exploitation and refining of oil, which by the 1970's could well assure the African countries of some 40,000,000 metric tons of oil. But, as Nkrumah indicated, integration first by zones and then on a continental scale is the only way to an African socialism capable of effectively resisting the pressures, maneuvers, and plots of those interests that for so long made Africa a base for capitalist exploitation and colonial domination.

Thus, a dispassionate study of the situation in Africa shows how realistic Nkrumah's Socialist visions were.

The peoples of Africa and Latin America, seeking to liberate themselves, can learn much from Hanoi. In many respects the Vietnam War, like the Spanish Civil War thirty years ago, has stirred the conscience of the world and offered a challenge to the world Socialist movement—and the two conflicts have common traits that have not been adequately explored.

From the Vietnam War a great figure emerged—Ho Chi Minh. And he had the good fortune to have as biographer a brilliant French writer and authority on Asian affairs, Jean Lacouture. When the Vietnam War reached its climax, its outstanding leader had more than half a century of revolutionary struggle behind him. Known by various names—Nguyen Tat Thanh (his original name), Ba, Nguyen Ai Quoc, Vuong, Line, he finally entered history as Ho Chi Minh.

The unbelievable courage of the Vietnamese people, which electrified the world in the 1960's and 1970's, is rooted in a combination and fusion of two elements: heroism and revolution. Theirs was not only a patriotic war; it was a political war as well. The Vietnamese people resisted the global thrust of U.S. militarism as the Spanish people resisted international fascism in the 1930's. Their resolute fight attained epic proportions, as they defied the mightiest military machine built by the wealthiest and most highly industrial-ized nation on earth. One is reminded of the tattered French revolutionary army at Valmy forcing the model Prussian army to retreat—a revolutionary event that Goethe dimly grasped. Ho Chi Minh embodied this heroism of the Vietnamese people.

Ho Chi Minh's political genius was fully revealed after World War

II. He developed his strategy on the basis of two solid Leninist principles: "the favorable moment" and "the main enemy." His first reaction after 1945 was disappointment that France continued to support "the band of French colonialists draping themselves beneath the tricolor that symbolizes liberty, equality, and fraternity to deprive us of our territory and oppress our people." Thus, twenty years before confronting a much stronger power, Ho sounded the keynote of Vietnamese determination: "Our entire people has only one will and one heart: to fight against French colonialism." His words presaged Dien Bien Phu for the French.

The last time I was with Ho Chi Minh was when we traveled together by air from Peking to Moscow for the Twenty-second Congress of the Soviet Communist Party, he as an invited delegate, I as a journalist. Unusually young-looking for his years—was it not Malatesta who said, "Age doesn't exist, it's merely a prejudice"?— Ho remained friendly and serene during one of the most terrible periods of the Vietnam War. Everyone who visited him in Hanoi confirmed this point.

His early years had been adventurous. When still very young, he signed on as a cabin boy on the steamship line plying between Haiphong and Marseilles. Later in France he knew hard times as an exile, as he took all sorts of odd jobs and wrote from time to time in the French Socialist and Communist press. Most of the French people he knew were Socialists and Communists: the latter attracted him more, especially Paul Vaillant-Couturier, whom he admired for his personal style and magnetism. In Ho's own words: "In the beginning it was patriotism and not Communism that made me believe in Lenin and the Third International. Little by little, proceeding step by step, combining the study of Marxism-Leninism with practical work in the course of the struggle, I came to believe that only socialism and Communism can free the oppressed and the workers of the world." In an article entitled "The Road That Has Led Me to Leninism," which appeared on the occasion of his seventieth birthday, Ho Chi Minh describes the impression made on him by "Lenin's theses" while he was working in Paris as a sketcher of "Chinese antiques" manufactured by a French firm. At that time he was still a member of the French Socialist Party, mainly because of its sympathy for the oppressed peoples. But "Lenin's theses" went beyond sympathy; they got to the very heart of the problem—and Ho was convinced that they offered the only sure way to liberation. In the ensuing years Ho divided his time between propaganda and organizing activities. In 1928 he participated in a Congress against Imperialism in Brussels, together with Madame Sun Yat-sen of China and Jawaharlal Nehru of India. Later, dressed as a Buddhist monk, he converted young bonzes in Thailand to the struggle for the independence of all Southeast Asia. Imprisoned on numerous occasions, he utilized his time in jail to organize, agitate, and write. Released from prison in 1943, he immediately plunged into the fight against Japanese aggression and laid plans for a free Republic of Vietnam.

Among his many talents were those of a negotiator. Time and again he demonstrated this skill in his extraordinary efforts to consolidate the independence of his country, threatened by the forces of General Jacques Leclerc—a general from a country Ho had loved so much. Twenty years later, as the Vietnam War escalated, one wonders what would have happened if Ho had succeeded in 1945 in establishing cordial relations with the representatives of the United States, making use of professed U.S. anti-colonial sentiments at that time against the French intervention. But this was not to be. Twenty years later the enemies were Johnson and Nixon; General Charles de Gaulle was a friend.

Madeleine Riffaud, the French journalist who created something of a stir in 1967 with her account of the days she spent with the Vietcong (National Liberation Front), has told how during the First Indochinese War she discovered that the Viet Minh fighters were poets. She fell in love with their poetry. Ho Chi Minh, too, was a poet; he gave a lyrical, and at the same time a very realistic, dimension to the resistance movement. There was indeed much poetry in those Vietnamese—men, women, children—who at night rebuilt bridges and roads destroyed by U.S. planes. In one of the documentary films produced on the spot, one sees the smiling face of a Vietnamese woman night worker: she is young, graceful, and smiling. Her whole being is like a poem. The Vietnamese people have exhibited a greatness for all humanity to see. In the midst of napalm and bombings of schools and hospitals, they have continued to build socialism among the "scorched earth" and the ruins. The spirit of the people is summed up in the plans prepared by engineers and architects for rebuilding Hanoi and Haiphong in the event of their total destruction by U.S. bombs. At times Ho would shudder at the thought of the Socialist efforts of twenty years subjected to the relentless bombing of the strongest air power in the world. But then he would smile: the Socialist idea was indestructible. Every statement he made during the most terrible days of the escalated air war was serene—worthy of inclusion in all anthologies of the resistance movement.

Along with the Chinese Revolution, the Vietnam War—the resistance and national liberation movement of the Vietnamese people led by "Uncle Ho"—is one of the great events of the second half of the twentieth century. To the masses of the world Ho Chi Minh and General Giap have represented the victory of militant socialism over discredited bureaucratic socialism. To many it has become clear: the future lies only with revolutionary socialism.

Ho Chi Minh showed his flexibility and diplomatic dexterity in maintaining warm relations with both Moscow and Peking at a time when differences between the two capitals foreshadowed a momentous rupture. The same was true of his relations with the ruling group in Hanoi, which includes several outstanding personalities in their own right. One of them, Truong Chinh, was a highly respected intellectual who for a long time was general secretary of the Communist Party of Indochina. Truong looked to China as the guide of the world Socialist movement; and his influence on the Vietcong forces has been very great, since he is the author of a kind of handbook for the guerrilla fighters, *La Résistance vaincra* (*The Resistance Will Win*). In the Political Bureau of the Communist Party of North Vietnam, others who lean to the Chinese view include Le Duc Tho, long an outstanding resistance leader in the south and the brilliant negotiator of the cease-fire of January, 1973; Nguyen Duy Trinh, who has served as Minister of Foreign Affairs; Hoang Quoc Vicet, head of the trade unions; and To Huu, one of the finest poets in Vietnam. In the other camp—partisans of the U.S.S.R.—are General Giap, who enjoys enormous prestige among the people; Prime Minister Pham Van Dong; Interior Minister Ung Van Khiem; and the economist Le Than Nghi. Ho Chi Minh worked skillfully with both of these trends, avoiding any clashes that would have

jeopardized much-needed aid from both China and the Soviet Union.
In his efforts he was seconded by one of the most capable persons in
the leadership: Le Duan, the general secretary of the Communist
Party.

The advance of socialism in various forms in the most diverse areas
on earth during the second half of the 1960's provoked a series of
military coups and countermeasures of all kinds. Alarmed at the way
in which, despite dissensions and difficulties, mainly economic in
nature, the Socialist and near-Socialist nations exerted an ever
stronger pull on other nations, the reactionary forces looked to the
armed forces for salvation. It was the sword against the idea.
Intelligence services of the imperialist powers—in the forefront the
American C.I.A.—courted ambitious army officers and put lavish
financial resources at their disposal. Deposed or persecuted former
heads of state have frequently attested personally and publicly to this
state of affairs.

The African continent was shaken by a series of coups in 1966. It
was as if the fall of Ben Bella in Algeria served as a signal to generals
and colonels in various African nations to enter openly into the game
of subversion at the invitation of foreign intelligence services.
Evidently the United States had decided to exploit the economic
difficulties in several of the newly independent nations; and to
thwart any serious attempts to overcome these difficulties by moving
more quickly toward socialism, the Americans encouraged military
dictatorships they could easily manipulate.

Of all the African *coups d'état*, that in Ghana caused the most
alarm in the progressive African states. The toppling of Kwame
Nkrumah, the Socialist-minded leader of Ghana, by army and police
officers, reverberated in Guinea, Mali, and other like-minded states.
In fact, Guinea's president, Sékou Touré, defied conventional
diplomacy and offered to share his powers with the Ghanaian
president. And in Asia, President Sukarno in Indonesia was ousted by
the military, in a coup accompanied by a bloodbath almost
unprecedented in this era of widespread, large-scale violence.

The term "socialism" has been greatly broadened since the end of
World War II. For one thing, the anti-colonial revolution has

brought new political forces and personalities into play. Take, for example, the case of Arab socialism. During the 1960's its strongest center was in Egypt, where President Nasser, whatever one's opinion of his policies and character, was undeniably the most progressive individual in the Egyptian regime.

Arab socialism, as interpreted in Egypt, was quite different from Marxian socialism. There were three basic differences between the two: First, under Nasser only a part—albeit the greater part—of the Egyptian economy was socialized. This included foreign trade, basic industries, banks, and large department stores. By contrast, three-fourths of small business and industry remained in the free sector. Socialization was not applied in the countryside, although efforts were stepped up to broaden the system of cooperatives. A very sharp controversy erupted among the Socialist-oriented Egyptian intellectuals as to whether the socialized sector should be enlarged or not, and a number of curious concepts resulted, some of them difficult to defend from a strictly Marxist point of view. One of these held that socialism was completely compatible with the maintenance of private production.

The second general difference between Egyptian socialism and Marxism is the attitude toward religious matters. In general, the former emphasized that socialism was not synonymous with atheism: a Socialist can claim to be neutral on that score or even accept and observe traditional religious practices. Many of the most orthodox Egyptian Marxists held socialism and religion to be entirely compatible. Of course, in the same breath they stressed that Islam represented a progressive force in the fight against imperialist rule and for the independence of the Arab states.

The third basic difference revolves around the question: How does one arrive at socialism? By the dictatorship of the proletariat or by democratic means? To this the leaders of Arab socialism replied that the problem was not urgent as far as Egypt was concerned. They felt that it would be urgent when Egypt had become industrialized, with a working class—an industrial proletariat—in the vanguard. Meanwhile, these spokesmen of Arab socialism continued, they had to work toward their goal by collaborating as closely as possible with the workers, the peasants, the intelligentsia, and the "national bourgeoisie." In their view, this model held equally for the rest of Africa and the Middle East.

These views are held by a small but compact group within the broad party of the Arab Socialist Union whose most important function is to create cadres that combine professional ability with Socialist thinking. Only by increasing the number of these cadres from a few thousand to tens of thousands can the government be propelled along the path of long-range planning and a Socialist economy. With due regard for differences in time, social milieu, and technical training, these Arab Socialists remind one somewhat of the early British Fabians, with their faith in "permeation" and the gradual spread of the Socialist idea. Whether they will achieve similar successes in the contemporary Arab world, with its complexities and its many storms and stresses, is another matter.

10

THE
CHINESE REVOLUTION

In the years ahead a fuller and more accurate assessment of China's contribution to socialism will emerge. Few revolutions of the scope of the Chinese Revolution have been less understood; and among those who have understood it the least have been some of the "experts," the Chinese specialists from abroad.

I do not pretend to be an expert on anything; yet I am proud of having clearly grasped what has happened in China. Ever since my first visit to that country—in 1957—I have been thoroughly convinced that the Chinese Revolution will succeed. What makes it an unprecedented event in world history is the vastness of the area in which it occurred and the appeal it has had for the disadvantaged nations of the world. My faith in the success of the Chinese Revolution was based on two factors: the outstanding intelligence of its leaders, Mao Tse-tung and Chou En-lai, and the genuineness of its popular support. It was not a revolution "on command"; it was deeply felt by the Chinese masses. The overwhelming majority of the Chinese people identified with the Revolution because it gave them enough food to eat for the first time, freed them from epidemics, gave them a sense of their own dignity. Its leaders had faith in the masses, in their ability to solve the complicated problems of agriculture, and to change from unskilled workers into expert technicians. The leaders did not have to impose discipline or love of work on the led, for these traits came from the very heart of a people determined to make China a great revolutionary nation.

Now, in 1973, it is easy to sing the praises of China, for within one year China won three major victories: it entered the United Nations, received the visit of President Nixon in Peking at the request and initiative of the President himself, and concluded an agreement with Japan normalizing relations between the two countries. *Alles rennt nach China* (Everything's running toward China): that was a headline in the German-language Swiss press commenting on the arrival in Peking, on the same day, of the Minister of Foreign Affairs of West Germany, the Italian Minister of Foreign Trade, the Mexican Minister of Trade, and an Argentine delegation. Today China's international authority and popularity is a fact. Yet in the course of its twenty-four-year existence the Chinese Revolution has been often and severely put to the test. It has had ranged against it—for basically different reasons—the two most powerful nations on earth, the United States and the Soviet Union.

The Chinese leaders have been criticized by some "perfectionists" of the Left, unable to distinguish between revolutionary emotionalism and revolutionary policy. The same thing happened in Russia at the beginning of the October Revolution. Lenin was bitterly criticized by some of his closest comrades for having signed the 1918 Treaty of Brest-Litovsk, which ended the war for Russia on terms imposed by the German generals. The Left Bolsheviks of those days thought in the romantic terms of the French Revolution, of Robespierre and the Jacobins with their ragged people's army defeating the disciplined Prussian forces at Valmy. Seeking to emulate their French predecessors, they wanted to reject General Hoffmann's *Diktat*. But to Lenin the essential thing was to save the Russian Revolution; and by thus yielding and signing the ignoble Brest-Litovsk Treaty, Lenin demonstrated his full measure as a farsighted revolutionary.

None of the concessions recently made by China—if such they were—compare in seriousness with Lenin's action at Brest-Litovsk. The China that received President Nixon—one of the reproaches leveled by the "purists" of the Left—was as revolutionary after that curious event as it had been before. There were no concessions on matters of principle; but there was revolutionary flexibility, with a well-defined goal of putting an end to the "encirclement" threatening the Chinese Revolution. The astonishing achievements of the People's Republic of China in its twenty-four years of existence—in agriculture, industry, oil production, and nuclear weaponry—found parallels in the domain of diplomacy. While writing the final pages of this book, I heard one of the ablest diplomats in the Western world say: "Militarily it is difficult to defeat China; but diplomatically China is unbeatable."

On the occasion of the twenty-third anniversary of the founding of the People's Republic of China, an article appeared jointly in the newspaper of the Chinese Communist Party and that of the army. Commenting on the recent diplomatic successes, the article declared: "China has not changed. It has remained faithful to its principles. Only it has learned how to behave with the necessary flexibility and self-control. In the center of the Chinese view of the world we see revolutionary struggles in Indochina, in the Middle East, Africa, and Latin America, the growing influence of nations of the 'Third World,' and the struggle of small and medium-sized states against the power politics of the superpowers." This is an affirmation of what China's role on the international scene will be in the remaining years of this decade. The awakening Third World will find support and guidance in China, with the small states receiving the same equality as the large ones. A trifling incident attests to this: in October, 1972, a delegation from one of the tiniest sovereign states on earth, the Republic of San Marino, visited Peking, where it was received with the same honors as had been accorded President Richard Nixon.

China is now firmly established within its borders and on the international scene. As evidence of its vitality I am giving in the pages that follow some impressions of my stay in China during the Cultural Revolution, where I was one of the few foreigners afforded an opportunity to follow events from close at hand. My account may have some historical value in itself and permit us to anticipate the future. Now that it has emerged safely and with renewed strength from its Cultural Revolution, China cannot be destroyed—by anyone or anything.

It was the winter of 1957, and as I flew out of Ulan Bator, capital of Outer Mongolia and the last stop on my way, I had the feeling of entering a country whose success or failure would vitally determine the future of world socialism. The landscape below me was awesome. After we left Irkutsk, there was the huge expanse of Lake Baikal, then the endless mountains of Outer Mongolia. From time to time we saw from the air barely perceptible signs of life below. We wondered how the inhabitants of the region lived during that season of the year when everything seemed buried beneath the snow. On our arrival at Peking, that city too was enveloped in snow. On my first visit, and on every visit thereafter, Peking has lived up to its reputation as a beautiful city. Eagerly I observed the countless details in which the old intermingled with the new.

After liberation, general planning became a feature of Chinese life. Specifically, in urban affairs the rule adopted was that nothing that might spoil a city's basic character would be allowed. It was projected that by 1969—that is, on the twentieth anniversary of the victory of the Revolution—Peking would have expanded considerably. Special attention was given to tree planting, not only in order to enhance the city's attractiveness but also to lessen the effects of the fierce winds that at certain times of the year blow in from the desert. Tien An Men Square and the "Boulevard of Long and Peaceful Life" began to outshine the Champs-Elysées in Paris.

It was only eight years after liberation, yet one felt the rhythm of the New China. The general rule seemed to be: "Stand on our own feet"—which meant resolutely tackling the job of changing a backward country into one of the most advanced in the world. The first new children's hospital we visited was only two-thirds built, yet in the finished sections services were operating as if the whole structure had been completed. A national agricultural exhibition—the first of its kind in China—was inaugurated a few days after my arrival. China's millennial history—as everyone knows—is essentially the history of its countryside. Traditionally Chinese emperors would come during the winter solstice to the Temple of Heaven—a marvel of beauty—to sacrifice to heaven and pray for good crops. But the Revolution gave the Chinese people something more realistic than prayers: an agrarian reform designed to improve once and for all the lot of the Chinese peasant.

Twenty years before taking power, Mao Tse-tung focused his interest on the Chinese countryside. Even before liberation, agrarian reform had been instituted, albeit in a limited and rudimentary form, in areas occupied by the Chinese Red Army. But now, after liberation, it was being vigorously implemented. Land distribution during the first years after liberation would have been merely a passing phase, similar to many such episodes under the "social-minded" emperors, had not the Socialist regime proceeded systematically by stages, forming cooperatives on a wide scale and orienting them toward eventual collectivization.

As Mao Tse-tung recalls in his writings on the agrarian question, long before the establishment of the People's Republic his party had encouraged the peasants to organize mutual-aid groups, which were the forerunners of agrarian reform. The 1950 law included a series of measures designed to avoid any unnecessary haste that might alienate the peasants from the Revolution. At the outset lands belonging to the rich peasants, whose past did not warrant expropriation, were left untouched except for the large areas that remained uncultivated. The agrarian reform was thus applied gradually, without forcing the pace, and bearing in mind that it was not enough to parcel out land regardless of the economic situation in the countryside. Moreover, a paramount concern in any land distribution was that farm production be maintained at the level required by the needs of the entire Chinese people.

The first type of "mutual-aid teams"—the initial stage in the agrarian reform—had a seasonal character, and these teams were adapted to the seasons of the year and the state of the crops. The second type that replaced them was the permanent or all-season mutual-aid team, functioning the whole year round. Experience showed that after a year of working together, discussing problems day by day and seeing with their own eyes that work in common produced far more crops than working on one's own, the spirit of association spread and was consolidated. Moreover, the mutual-aid teams were a good school for educating personnel for the future cooperatives. And, in fact, the next step was the creation of farm cooperatives of producers. This phase began cautiously: some twenty families and twenty hectares per cooperative were the prevailing unit. These were modestly called semi-Socialist, inasmuch as the cooperative did not yet own land; only the form of labor had been socialized.

In the period 1951–1955, the mutual-aid teams by vote of their members turned into producers' cooperatives. The next step, the collective farm, marked a decisive turn toward socialized agriculture. Nevertheless, the government took care to avoid any peasant discontent at this significant change by making such associations voluntary; the peasant was free to join the collective farm or to quit it. Parallel with the development of the cooperatives went the education of technical experts who could help the peasants solve their problems. In 1957, besides the Peking University of Agronomy there were seven regional institutes for farm research and five institutes for specialized research. An institute for plants and crops was about to open, and there were some hundred and seventy research stations and experimental farms run by the various provinces and autonomous regions.

Eight years after the victory of the Revolution, the Chinese countryside had changed more profoundly than in the previous two thousand years. Hundreds of millions of peasants had changed their methods of work; individually and collectively they were transformed. Everywhere agrarian reform, as it improved the peasants' conditions, also increased their demands. Freed of the staggering burden of high interest payments to the moneylenders, well fed, no longer barefoot and in rags but well clothed and shod, they yearned now for manufactured goods. Multiply this by hundreds of millions and one has a cycle involving agriculture, light industry, and heavy industry, with the cooperatives requiring tractors and farm implements.

Before going to Shenyang, which I used as a base from which to visit the big steel factories and blast furnaces of Anshan as well as the coal mines and oil refineries of Fushun, I stopped off for a few days in Changchun. This is a charming city of parks and gardens, as its Chinese name signifies: "eternal spring." If Anshan was the "steel city," Changchun was "the auto city." The Chinese were determined to build cars rivaling the finest foreign makes and surpassing them in design, drawing on their time-honored tradition of craftsmanship and their sense of the artistic. I confirmed that this feeling was still very much alive when I visited the rug factory in Tientsin, where the colorful display was a delight to behold.

In Changchun, at the Geological Institute, I heard the story of the first teams that went out to K'oramai (Karamai) in Sinkiang province to search for oil. Many foreign experts were skeptical about these explorations, but before long China was producing oil in impressive and increasing quantities. It was another example of the spirit that infused the Chinese Revolution. The initial teams sent to K'oramai worked under the most wretched conditions. The desert winds threatened their temporary installations; the water was so bad that only terrible thirst made one drink it; swarms of flies and mosquitoes forced workers on the job to cover themselves from head to foot, despite the blazing heat. Only a people like the Chinese could thus challenge nature in order to make their country self-sufficient in oil. The victory at K'oramai, turning a desert waste into an oil center working at capacity, justified the optimism of the professors and students at the Geological Institute regarding the impressive subsoil resources of their country that awaited exploitation, and was a striking example of Chinese self-reliance.

In various interviews with ministers and experts involved in planning, I was able to discern what had guided their thinking in drawing up their First Five-Year Plan and how they envisaged China's economic future, with a stable currency and a constant effort to insure a proper balance among agriculture, industry, and foreign trade. Thanks to the efforts made under the First Five-Year Plan, the basic industries had been strengthened: metals, electric power, fuel, machinery, and chemical products—with particular stress on abundant supplies for the countryside.

The successes achieved did not blind the Chinese leaders to their shortcomings. Expressions such as "shortages," "backward nation" often came from the lips of those with whom I spoke, whether cabinet minister, factory director, or managing committee of a farm cooperative. But situated and explained in their proper context, these obstacles did not affect the confidence with which the Chinese proposed to solve their problems. Stabilizing the currency had been one of the outstanding achievements, as I realized when I spoke with the authorities in Shanghai. That city had for years been the stamping ground of the foreigners in China—the best and the worst of them. Shanghai's history was a textbook illustration of China's domination by the foreign powers, a sordid history of exploitation and hypocrisy—especially the latter, because in one breath the foreign governments spoke of saving China for the Free World while they kept Chinese boys in the textile mills under conditions that violated the most elementary conditions of humanity and Chinese girls were forced into the same position or driven into prostitution. Meanwhile the mill owners prayed to God and relied on the forces of "law and order." Certain houses of ill fame enjoyed special notoriety as the meeting places for specialists in kidnapping, which flourished in Shanghai in the 1930's and 1940's on an unprecedented scale. For protection, affluent Chinese surrounded themselves with bodyguards, often recruited from the city's underworld and therefore affording only relative security. Kidnapping for ransom went on so frequently that only when a wealthy cotton millionaire like Li Tsao-ming or someone equally powerful was involved was there any general outcry. Li was notorious because, among other things, he had negotiated the $30,000,000 loan to induce Chiang Kai-shek to break with the Communists. His ransom was set at several million dollars, and the episode heightened Li's prestige among his foreign associates.

Under Chiang Kai-shek opium was prohibited in China, but only for those who did not have enough money with which to buy it on the illegal market. Thus in Shanghai, a city corrupt to the core, most of the opium consumed found its way across the Yangtze River. The commanding officers of the military garrisons stationed along the river shared the proceeds of this contraband traffic. But rather than dwell on the many aspects of Shanghai's history, let me concentrate on the years immediately preceding the Communists' entry into the city and then show by contrast what happened afterward. There was, for example, the currency problem. Every hour the money fell in value, until one had to pay 11,000,000 Chinese dollars (in Shanghai in those years English was the language used in business) for 100 U.S. dollars. Who benefited from this monetary chaos? Foreigners and Chinese nationals associated with them. When Shanghai was liberated in May, 1949, the new money introduced by the crumbling Chiang Kai-shek regime—the so-called gold yuan—

had fallen from an initial four-to-one ratio with respect to the U.S. dollar to several million to one. People preferred a handful of rice to a whole pile of yuan!

The entry of the Communists into Shanghai put an end to this era of sordid corruption and chaotic turbulence. How the Communists behaved when they took Shanghai is of considerable historical significance because it foreshadowed what the Red Army would be like in the Chinese Revolution. Gaining the confidence and trust of the people, it really became a People's Army. An Associated Press dispatch sent from Shanghai on May 26, 1949, and printed in various U.S. newspapers, related: "The behavior of the Communist troops here explains why they are winning the war. . . . The Communists have made a good first impression in Shanghai." An anti-Communist merchant recounted how he saw a Communist soldier eating a bowl of dry rice. A "coolie" offered him a cup of boiling water, which to a poor Chinese was a substitute for tea. The soldier declined his offer, explaining to those present that the People's Army of Liberation never took anything from the public. Other Communist soldiers refused the offer of beds, preferring to sleep on the pavement. Again they said that they did not want anyone to make sacrifices for them.

In 1957 I visited many educational centers, from grade schools to the most highly specialized advanced research institutes. Since so much has been written abroad about the successful fight against illiteracy in China, I prefer to talk about the Institute of Nationalities. (As a Spaniard, I was personally interested in this problem since my own country faces serious problems of regionalism, especially in Catalonia and the Basque region, problems that have intensified under the Franco dictatorship.) To give one an idea of the diversity of the Institute: seventeen languages are taught in its Language Department, and sometimes a student from a minority people has to begin by learning his own language, which he has known only in rudimentary fashion. At the Institute he is given a thorough grounding because after leaving it he will assume a leadership role among his own people. Thus a Hui (Chinese Moslem) woman, formerly a student at the Nationalities Institute, had been elected mayor of Yangchow in Kiangsu province.

The Common Program adopted after liberation proclaimed the

unity of all the national minorities. Some 35,000,000 of these were given the same status as the majority Han (racially Chinese) people and allowed to develop their own culture autonomously. The largest autonomous region was the Chuang region in western Kwangsi with a population of 8,000,000; but the oldest in point of time was Inner Mongolia, situated in the extreme north of China. Respect for national minorities was such that if, for example, a Miao appeared before a Chinese court, the authorities had to provide an interpreter in his language so that he could be sure his statements were being correctly transcribed. This detail impressed me more than the fact that at the Institute every minority had its own place of worship and special eating places where its favorite regional dishes were served.

Of the interviews I had during my first visit to China, three seem most memorable to me: with Premier Chou En-lai, with Kuo Mo-jo, president of the Academy of Sciences, and with Marshal Li Chi-shen, who died a few years later. All dwelt on themes that helped me understand the course of the Chinese Revolution. Chou En-lai in particular impressed me as one of the capable and imaginative statesmen of our time, and had China not been the object of such slander and misrepresentation, he would quickly have been recognized as such. Even some of China's most outspoken adversaries have frequently praised his diplomatic skill. At the Bandung Conference in 1955 he was a central figure; at Geneva he diplayed both strength and subtlety in his reasoning.

As we spoke, I noticed his penetrating glance, his expressive hands, and his firm tone of voice free of bitterness or arrogance. As early as 1957, Chou En-lai could give me an explanation of United States policies that was equally valid fifteen years later. He asserted that the United States had allowed itself to be dragged into a situation in which it could make neither war nor peace; in short, it could not win either a military or a diplomatic victory. Chou saw the reason for this in the defeat suffered by the U.S. armed forces in Korea, a humiliation that one day would have to be avenged. The American military leaders would demand this and would therefore be ready for any type of adventurism. Having struck in one spot and failed, they refused to look deeply into the causes of the failure and change their policies accordingly; so they would then strike elsewhere, convinced that the strongest power on earth could impose its "leadership," even though the peoples it claimed to save for democracy rejected the U.S. offer. Chou discussed U.S. policy toward Peking in sober tones: for a country that prided itself on its common sense, U.S. policies seemed to make no sense: "Not long ago Eisenhower told one of his most distinguished visitors that the U.S. refusal to recognize China was not logical. But, apparently, the Americans mean to continue to be illogical." Eisenhower explained the seeming illogic by claiming that the United States could easily forget the consequences of World War II but not those of the Korean War. When he heard that, Premier Chou En-lai declared (he could not help smiling): "The American President is right about that, because the United States was a winner in World War II but lost the Korean War."

Chou analyzed the causes of international tension, without resorting to clichés. He spoke of the way in which some countries worshipped the dollar, which often made them support Washington against their own interests and feelings, and then found themselves in a position of subservience, seeking loans from Washington to solve their economic difficulties rather than pursuing a vigorous policy of national planning. Hence the United States could play the master, as at the United Nations, where so many nations reluctantly voted with the United States. We spoke of China and the United Nations. "Our position on this question is set," the Premier asserted. "We will never enter the United Nations so long as the representatives of Chiang Kai-shek are in the organization. And this applies to the specialized agencies as well. Recently, as a matter of fact, there have been approaches along those lines. We have let it be known that our attitude has not changed. The Chinese people would not stand for it. We have counted and still count on the support of the people, without which what we have done could never have happened. But they would never allow us to propose the concept of 'two Chinas.' Furthermore, if we did we would ill serve the cause of peace. We would introduce one more confusing factor into an already extremely confused international situation. Ours is not the case of one of those divided nations which, looking toward reunification, agrees to send a representative or observer to international bodies where the other part of the country in question is represented. The attempt 'to create two Chinas' will never succeed. Outside the United Nations we are

doing what we can on behalf of peace and international cooperation." It was quite clear that China was not going to give anyone an
excuse to attack it; at the same time the fate of anyone insane enough
to do so was not enviable.

With Kuo Mo-jo, a scholar and man of wide erudition, I was able
to discuss some of the noted literary and artistic figures in China's
past. During the great dynasties of the Tang (618–907), the Sung
(960–1126 and 1127–1279), and the Ming (1368–1643), some of the
emperors had been excellent poets as well as statesmen. Mao
Tse-tung, the present-day leader of the Chinese Revolution, is in that
long tradition. But Kuo preferred to talk about "the big cultural fact"
that had involved hundreds of millions of Chinese in intellectual
activities hitherto reserved for a privileged handful—a mandarinate.
"The road to literary progress in China," said Kuo Mo-jo, "is open.
Before liberation all our thoughts were concentrated on the struggle.
It completely absorbed us. Today we can again write novels and
plays. Yet even in the midst of the strife, literature was not
neglected. In 1942, at the Yenan Literary Forum held in the then
liberated areas, Mao Tse-tung discoursed on the principles and ideals
with which the artists and writers of the liberated China should be
imbued. Today in China we have all the conditions for a literary
rebirth. But this calls for sustained work: to be a writer it is not
enough to have correct feelings and attitudes. Of course, one's life
must have substance and content; but there is also the problem of
craft. Our young writers want to broaden their horizons. After
liberation, for instance, all of Shakespeare's works were translated
into Chinese. And many of us have studied *Don Quixote*, that
masterpiece of human wisdom."

Another question that came up during my interview with Kuo
Mo-jo was the attitude of the Chinese intellectuals toward the
regime. Western publications had carried articles by writers who had
visited China and returned home describing dissatisfaction and even
opposition among the Chinese intellectuals. To this Kuo replied: "In
no way do we wish to stifle creativity. But China does not have so
many genuine intellectuals that it can afford to have them lose
themselves in sterile and negative activities instead of serving the
people and the national rebirth. During the last few years the great
majority of Chinese intellectuals have revised many of their former

ideas, not under pressure from anyone but impressed by what the people have been able to accomplish in the eight years since liberation. They have clearly seen the shortcomings of the old society and have accepted the superiority of the new Socialist system."

Kuo gave me some intimate details about Mao Tse-tung, with whom he had long been associated. He referred to the famous meeting of February, 1957, in which Mao gave his much-discussed speech "On Contradictions." Considered a notable event in the history of the Chinese Communist movement, it had been preceded by a series of meetings—first with leaders of the National Congress whom Mao had addressed for four hours, then with Communist and non-Communist writers and intellectuals, and later at various places throughout the country. Kuo Mo-jo had attended one such meeting. "I only wish," said Kuo, "that many of our opponents could have heard Chairman Mao. They would have had before them a Communist, but also a leader with farsighted vision. Mao spoke of the contradictions still prevalent in China: To shut one's eyes to them would be a serious mistake. He spoke with such frankness that some of his listeners were undoubtedly disconcerted. But I was not; for I have always felt that one of Mao's chief qualities is that of a teacher, and I believe he will go down in history as a teacher—with a capital 'T.' He impressed me with his insistence on critical discussion—not only on the part of his supporters but also those who disagreed."

Answering a question I asked concerning the non-Communist parties in the government—a situation generally viewed with considerable skepticism abroad—Kuo Mo-jo insisted that one of Mao Tse-tung's outstanding traits was his ability to combine firmness of principle with great flexibility in order to cope with unexpected situations. He realized the need to win the overwhelming majority of the Chinese people to the cause of the Revolution: although the country had many centuries of great culture behind it, its present political backwardness was undeniable. "The problem of a broad democratic base," Kuo stated, "is crucial in guaranteeing victory for the Revolution. Marxism is the basic philosophy and the Communist Party is the leading party in China; but non-Communists are not excluded from participating in the government."

Time and again he returned to the wrong image of Mao Tse-tung many outside China have: "You have seen Chairman Mao. He is the soul of simplicity. When he launches a new idea, his first concern is to explain it to the masses. Explain it, not impose it. When the movement for farm collectivization reached its peak in 1955, Chairman Mao traveled throughout the country, talking direction to the peasants and discussing with them, ready to revise his own ideas if contact with the realities of farm life warranted it."

Kuo Mo-jo felt that one of the main cultural achievements of the Revolution was the opening of the universities to the people. Previously enrollment had been limited to children of the rich, but now, within less than ten years, China had millions of trained experts and technicians; and, above all, hundreds of millions of Chinese able to read and write. In 1957 there was still no talk of China's acquiring nuclear weapons; but my Chinese interlocutor was convinced that with the popularization of science among the masses China would train scientists capable of astonishing breakthroughs in science and technology.

My conversation with Marshal Li Chi-shen gave me an insight into an earlier phase of the Chinese Revolution: the so-called democratic revolution preceding the Socialist Revolution. Marshal Li had been a comrade-in-arms of Chiang Kai-shek and in 1957 was the leader of the Kuomintang Revolutionary Committee, one of the non-Communist parties in the government coalition. I visited him in his house, filled with mementos of Dr. Sun Yat-sen. "The Kuomintang Revolutionary Committee," the Marshal explained to me, "is a party that follows the policies and principles of Dr. Sun Yat-sen, the founder of the Chinese Republic. He was a man beloved by the masses. You should have seen them at his funeral procession in 1925 on the streets of Peking! From the beginning Sun Yat-sen realized that the Manchu monarchy could not be changed into a constitutional monarchy, as some of our Chinese reformers then thought. Only when the people assumed power could China regain her independence and rebuild itself. He was a patriot and a revolutionary. Our reverence for him has not lessened." In fact, a few days later I attended a commemorative gathering in which Sun Yat-sen's memory was extolled by all the leaders of the democratic parties. Marshal Li told me in detail how the coalition government functioned. "Today the government of China is a united-front government. My party is part of it. We have three ministers in the government: Posts and Telegraphs, Textiles, and Overseas Chinese. Two of the provincial governors are members of our Kuomintang Revolutionary Committee. You told me that you have attended sessions of the Consultative Assembly and have visited parliament, so you know that our party is represented in both bodies. Also in the provincial congresses and local organizations." At that time the Kuomintang Revolutionary Committee was the most important but not the only non-Communist Party with ministers in the Cabinet. There was also the Democratic League and others. Having them in the Cabinet was in line with Mao's thinking: "One has to be able to criticize. If not, centers of dissension and misunderstanding are formed. People must be given the chance to say what is on their minds."

Mao's speech of February, 1957, was such an unusually impressive analysis of the Chinese Revolution that the London *Times* of June 20, 1957, printed the full text. Commenting on it editorially, the *Times* observed that it "was an example of realism, patience, persuasion, and flexibility." It was an appeal for greater freedom of expression. Indeed, the idea of involving non-Communists in the government had long been held and often reiterated by Mao in the years before victory, as a glance at his writings will show.

My third visit to China took place a year after Mao Tse-tung launched the Cultural Revolution. I had followed in the world press and on the radio the reactions outside China to this vast and virtually unprecedented social upheaval. Remembering the early years of the Russian Revolution and the fantastic distortions of events there, I am convinced that the world hostility that greeted China during its Cultural Revolution was even greater than the Soviets experienced in the 1920's. Now, in addition to hostility from the capitalist world, China received critical treatment from the Soviet Union and the Socialist countries allied with it. To progressive-minded readers, the critical comments in *Pravda* and the Communist press in France, Italy, and Latin America proved much more painful and disconcerting.

In general the two main sources of news about China during this period were Hong Kong and Tokyo. Hong Kong had long been a center for foreign correspondents denied entry into China by the

Peking government. Separated by only a few miles from a land they could not penetrate, the correspondents were bound to feel resentment, and so they read and interpreted the Chinese press in a tendentious manner, playing up all sorts of items of gossip and sensationalism from ill-disposed foreign visitors returning home from China by way of Hong Kong. Tokyo competed with the British colony in spreading rumors and lurid reports about China. The Japanese correspondents stationed in Peking read Chinese fluently, and to them the wall posters and drawings, still visible on Peking's walls when I arrived there, were a ready source of information they could interpret at will. The writings on the wall were a grab bag of comment, in which provocateurs and those genuinely opposed to the Cultural Revolution uninhibitedly attacked leading political figures. All the Japanese correspondents had to do to discredit the Cultural Revolution and give the impression of a China in chaos was to translate the texts of these wall posters and phone or cable them abroad.

The Peking government took no measures against the Japanese journalists stationed in China. Only when Japanese Premier Sato went to Taiwan and publicly supported Chiang Kai-shek were credentials withdrawn from three Japanese newspapermen, but four others remained to transmit all the gossip circulating in Western diplomatic circles in Peking. Chinese officials commented: "If they want to discredit themselves and their papers by announcing every week that the Cultural Revolution is a failure and Mao Tse-tung's star is in decline, let them make themselves as ridiculous as they please." One incident, involving the representative of the Yugoslav News Agency, deserves mention: The correspondent had cabled a story about an alleged meeting of the Central Committee of the Communist Party of China in which "Mao Tse-tung has been placed in a minority." Pure invention! The correspondent was asked to leave China and his agency invited to send a replacement.

Personally, I found all doors open to me. I was given a very able Spanish translator, Tang Ming-sin, who had accompanied me on my previous visit to China in 1961; and I had direct conversations in English or French with Chinese or foreign observers concerning the various phases and aspects of the "Great Proletarian Cultural Revolution." The kind of interviews I had in China in the autumn of

1967 were quite different from those I had had on my two previous visits, when I had "interviewed" ministers in various political and economic bureaus. This time I talked with the main actors in the Cultural Revolution: proletarian revolutionaries; Red Guards; members of the armed forces and the newly formed revolutionary committees who combined the functions of government and party as they took over power in province after province. I was fortunate enough to be received by Chairman Mao and to renew an old friendship with Premier Chou En-lai; but my real interviews were with peasants, young workers at the head of the new factory committees, and young soldiers. It is through these interviews that I shall try to give as clear and straightforward a picture as I can of the Cultural Revolution, which, except in a few notable instances, has been so poorly presented to the outside world.

One point must be stressed from the start: What happened at the precise moment in the second half of 1966 when the Cultural Revolution and the activities of the "Red Guards" began in China must be seen in relation to the development of U.S. foreign policy. It was then that the Vietnam War was unleashed in all its fury. Vietnam appeared to be merely the first stage in U.S. global policy; a chance, if not an excuse, for the United States to lay the basis for a strategy designed to achieve world mastery. At that very moment the Chinese decided to follow a path that was bound to be unpopular abroad, yet they went ahead despite the harm it might bring to their prestige in the world, the loss of sympathy among the progressive movements in other countries. Undaunted, the Chinese displayed a militancy that shocked and scandalized many; but it served notice on the world that here was a country of 700,000,000 ready to challenge U.S. pretensions to world domination.

To convince everyone of the seriousness of their intentions, even though in the process they might risk a U.S. nuclear attack and jeopardize the achievements of seventeen years of tremendous efforts and sacrifices, the Chinese did not hesitate to bring millions of young people out on the streets of China in a first wave of assaults on what they labeled "revisionism." The real target was the Soviet Union, which, in their view, did not dare confront the United States even though it was in a better position militarily to do so. Whoever does not grasp that the main motive behind the Cultural Revolution and the stormy demonstrations of the Red Guards was to prove that China would stop at nothing in its determination to check the United States, has failed to understand what happened in China in 1966. One Western writer, I believe, did understand it: K. S. Karol, in his thoughtful book, *China: The Other Communism* (1968). Karol asserts that the "Great Cultural Revolution" had no historical precedent, that its origins and pattern were difficult to explain. But he insists that the West is in error if it believes that such a movement, visibly inspired from above and with limited goals that could have been attained in other, less spectacular ways, lacked genuine broad-based support. There was nothing artificial about it; quite the contrary, it evoked impressive enthusiasm from those who led it—in the first place, the Red Guards. In China, Karol points out, the masses did not have to be whipped up by reiterated appeals to their revolutionary duty for them to manifest their will.

Another valuable eyewitness account is in a book by the Italian Alessandro Casella, author of many volumes of reportage on the Far East, in which he relates a conversation he held with Red Guards in Canton. His interlocutors, who told him their life histories, included: Lu Chung-wei, a fifteen-year-old Red Guard from central China; Yang Chu-tung, a few years older; and Sze Wan-wei, a young woman of eighteen from Canton. Lu Chung-wei, who bore the brunt of the conversation, explained to the Italian journalist how the Red Guards had formed. He himself was a student in High School No. 3, in the city of Anhwei (Hopei province). His father was a soldier, his mother a housewife. "The thing started in Peking," the fifteen-year-old Red Guard began. "In the spring of 1966 the students in the high school attached to the University of Hsin-Hua formed a battalion of Red Guards, and on August 18 they were received by Chairman Mao, who wore a Red Guard armband for the occasion. The news spread throughout the country, by radio and television. On August 19 a group of Red Guards formed spontaneously within my school."

"How did that happen?"

"At first a small group of politically active students formed themselves into a Red Guard. The other students, to become Red Guards, had to become candidates and be voted on by this group."

"Could everyone be elected a Red Guard?"

"No. You had to belong to one of the five pure classes [working class, small peasantry, soldiers, cadres, and revolutionary martyrs]. In very exceptional cases a bourgeois student would be accepted if he could prove he had renounced his class origins. Actually, only forty per cent of the students are Red Guards. The others are 'revolutionary students' who enjoy the same advantages as the Red Guards but cannot wear the armband."

"And what role did the Party play in creating the Red Guards?"

"The idea of the Red Guards came from the people. The Party had nothing to do with it."

A few days after the Red Guards were formed, Lu Chung-wei became a candidate. Since he came from a "pure" class, he had no trouble getting elected. Some time later, his comrade Yang Chu-tung asked the Red Guards group at school to allow him and Lu Chung-wei to leave for Peking, Shanghai, and Canton in order to establish "revolutionary contacts" with other students. His proposal was accepted. After waiting two days at the Anhwei station, the two youths took a train to Canton, where they were helped by a Red Guard reception committee.

"Why the Red Guards?"

"To protect Chairman Mao and the Central Committee of the Communist Party."

"Protect them from whom?"

All three, including the young woman Sze Wan-wei, replied to the question as follows: "There is a small group in power that has taken the capitalist road and is opposed to Mao. Mao has taught us that the armed enemy has been beaten, but that now we must fight against the unarmed enemy trying to re-establish a bourgeois society in China. How shall we fight? In the ideological field. For more than ten years now they have been telling us at school to concentrate on intellectual work. The students thought only of studying, passing their exams, entering a university and finishing with good marks, then making money. They did not think of serving the people and the country."

"How do you intend to correct that?"

"By following the road outlined by Mao's Thought."

"Are there many reactionaries?"

"No, there are very few real reactionaries. The others are persons who haven't understood. They have to be shown their mistakes, and if they persist in them, they have to be denounced."

"And if they persist in their mistakes?"

"Then we'll destroy them!" Here they burst out laughing and added: "Ideologically, of course."

In reply to a question about Chou En-lai they answered that he was a true Socialist and followed Mao. As for other former leaders accused during the Cultural Revolution, the proper authorities would decide whether they should keep or lose their jobs.

"What do you think of the United States?"

"The U.S. imperialists are world enemy Number One. China cannot be intimidated. If they invade us, we'll crush them. But the Chinese people are friends of the American people forever, just as the Russian people are friends of the Chinese people despite the revisionists."

So much for Casella's reportage. Now for our own impressions.

In preparation for a face-to-face encounter with the peasants, I visited an exhibition of clay sculptures on peasant life before the Liberation. Young and old artists were represented, exhibiting life-size figures that depicted with grim realism the lot of the peasants in feudal and colonial China. Here, for example, was the sinister Liu-tse, the despotic landlord from Shi Chuan, whose figure dominated the first in a series of scenes covering a large exhibition hall. His family owned 200,000 *mu* (about 25,000 acres), and he himself 12,000 *mu*. The exhibition bore the title "The Pavilion Where Taxes Were Collected" and it was held in a Peking building to which peasants used to be summoned when they had violated a contract. Yet it was the landlords who unilaterally stipulated the contract conditions and arbitrarily decided whether or not it was being fulfilled. The peasants called Liu "the living monster of hell," a title that had a special meaning for contemporary Chinese since they used the terms "monsters and demons" to characterize those who sabotaged the Cultural Revolution. More than a hundred families of poor peasants lived and toiled on Liu's land, which contained twenty-eight private houses for his family, his "overseers of the whip," and his "private police." The police possessed 10,000 guns with which to snuff out any attempt at rebellion; nevertheless, there were such attempts. At the outset a few peasants were kept in cages and tortured as an example to the rest. The overseers would accuse the peasants of stealing grain paid as taxes which they themselves had filched and would then beat them with steel-pointed whips. Likewise, if any peasant protested against fraudulent grain weighing by Liu's lackeys, he was punished by whipping, confinement to a cage, or abduction of a daughter if she was considered sufficiently attractive to the master. Clay figures alternated with written documents that attested to the numerous abuses. One of the documents was a bill of sale for a poor peasant's son. The peasant had given up everything he owned, even his few chickens, to pay his taxes, but the landlord claimed he still owed some arrears; so the peasant's son was sold as a mercenary for the landlord's army. Young peasant wives paid a different kind of tribute. Landlords took special delight in drinking their milk after they had just given birth to a child. From the fifth section of the exhibition on, one saw examples of past peasant rebelliousness. This hall had a quotation, in large letters, from Chairman Mao: "There may be thousands of principles. But only one prevails—the principle of rebellion." Thus an old farmer rebelled when called upon to sell his only granddaughter as a servant to the master. An old peasant woman flung herself against the bars of the jail cage, exclaiming: "Someday this cage will be smashed!" Then, in the final section, there were graphic scenes of peasants marching triumphantly toward liberation.

From the clay figures of the exhibition hall we went among living human beings, spending four days and nights with the peasants in the village of Shashiyu, in the Tsun Hua district of Hopei province, about three and a half hours by car from Peking. This was one of the thousands of People's Communes so often reported in the foreign press as having been liquidated. We slept at the house of one of the leaders of the fifteen production brigades in the commune. His wife served us meals as tasty as any we had in our Peking hotel, and husband, wife, and daughter all overwhelmed us with their kindness and generosity. Peasants old and young came to the house to see us: the children sang for us a song that was then very popular in China: "Steering Depends on the Helmsman." We held hour-long conversations with the peasants and, reconstructing the lives of the old people, we understood the meaning of the phrase that came often to their lips: "If we're living today the way we are, if we have this or that, we owe it to Chairman Mao."

Our host told us of his life before the Revolution. "Deep down I was probably a revolutionary when I had to eat roots while the landlord was living in luxury. But I was a revolutionary asleep until one day a soldier in the People's Army handed me a leaflet explaining how peasants organized their lives in the areas occupied by the Communists."

"What happened to the local landlord?" I asked him.

"He's here, working in the commune. He has no political rights. But he's eating, which wasn't the case with us when we worked under him."

He told about the exactions of moneylending, whereby to borrow a hundred kilograms of grain they had to pay fifty kilos in interest. He started to work when he was ten years old, but now he took pride in the commune to which he belonged. Talking with him and the other peasants between sips of green tea and munching apples and nuts, we heard the whole story of developments for the past eighteen years—in which barren, rocky soil had been made into green and fertile earth. Production increased as the peasants became increasingly motivated. In 1949 they produced 40 kilos of grain per *mu;* in 1957, when they became a superior-type cooperative, production increased fivefold to 198.5 kilos per *mu.* But under the People's Commune the figure rose to 300 kilos and they hoped to raise it even higher under the impetus of the Cultural Revolution. That was why Chairman Mao's appeal to "commit yourself to the Revolution and promote production" had found a ready response in the countryside. Every house in the commune we visited had a portrait of Mao on the wall. Skeptics and opponents may call it an "icon," but one prays to an icon. The peasants did not pray to Mao; they heeded his advice.

Here let me tell the story of the commune's shepherdess as she related it to me. She was an attractive young woman who had joined the commune like so many others—intellectuals, students, soldiers— to lend the peasants a hand at sowing and harvest times. Although she was studying for a profession, she became very fond of farm life and decided to remain on the commune. One job was open, that of taking care of the livestock. She tried her hand at it several times, but failed. The donkey ran away; the cows were improperly milked; even the pigs proved recalcitrant. Disheartened, she was ready to leave the commune and return to school when she remembered what Chairman Mao had written in one of his three articles on "Serving the People": rereading it, she mustered new courage and stayed on. Now she was a very efficient shepherdess in charge of a well-kept and prosperous barnyard.

Another favorite passage of Mao's among the peasants was the one about "the old fool." I heard it several times in the commune, once in front of a large tract of land covered with corn and fruit trees that had formerly been rocky wasteland. Mao wrote: "There's an old Chinese tale called 'the old fool who removed mountains.' It tells about an old man who lived a long time ago in the north of China and was called the old fool of the northern mountains. His house looked south facing the two high mountains, Taiyang and Wangtu, that obstructed his view. The old fool decided to persuade his sons to remove the two mountains with picks and spades. Another elder known as the old wise man saw this and said with a laugh: 'What foolishness! It's absolutely impossible for the few of you to remove such high mountains!' The old fool replied: 'After I die my children will survive me; when they die, my grandchildren will remain and then their children and the children of their children, and so on indefinitely. Although those mountains are very high they do not grow, and every spadeful we remove makes them smaller. So why shouldn't we be able to remove them?' So after answering the old wise man's skeptical sally, the old fool kept on digging day after day. Moved by this, God sent two angels down to earth who removed both mountains. Today two high mountains weigh down the Chinese people: one is called imperialism and the other feudalism. The Communist Party of China has for a long time decided to eliminate them. We have to stick to our decision and work without stopping; we too will succeed in moving God. Our God is none other than the broad masses of China. If they rise up and dig alongside us, why won't we be able to eliminate those mountains?" So Mao ended his parable.

Mao's story about the old fool stirred the people into action. I could see this plainly as I mingled with them. There were no mountains they could not remove, and no force could hold them back. I was convinced that once the Cultural Revolution was over and the hundreds of millions of Chinese resumed their everyday work, the country would take a great leap forward, especially in the decade of the 1970's.

This commune we visited, Shashiyu, was one of the communes that had had to struggle hardest against the hostile elements of nature. So here we could plainly see evidence of how the Cultural Revolution had improved their work. As the commune developed, the government had loaned them 180,000 kilograms of grain until the production brigade to which our host belonged could become self-sufficient; and now they were able to sell the government 210,000 kilos of grain. "Why this change?" our Chinese friend commented. "The earth is the same as before. But the peasants have changed. Now we believe in ourselves, in our ability to produce more for our country and ourselves. Did you hear the song our young peasant women just sang: 'The sky is high, the earth is vast, but our affection for Chairman Mao is much greater.' 'Affection,' that's the word. Before Liberation I was one of the few in this village who could read and write. Today in our commune all our children can read and write. Two of them are doctors, with university degrees. The doors of the universities have been opened to poor peasants. Production has increased; so has the peasant's well-being. This house is mine. I built it with what I saved from my earnings. This production brigade numbers 112 families: 84 of them were poor peasants; 24, middle peasants; three were landlords; and one the son of rich peasants." My host then took us to visit one of the other houses, where one of his contemporaries sang songs of the old days. That night we heard the song: "To us the land is like pearls; only the rich own it. Water is like oil that trickles away. For us there are stones on which we sleep and roots with which we fill our stomach. In winter we have no cotton clothing to protect us against the cold." When the song was over, a young peasant woman pointed to the pile of blankets on her bed.

When we left the commune, a sizable group gathered to bid us bon voyage: Yen Lan-chu, our host during the stay; the commune's doctor, Yiao We, who had come to take our blood pressure to see if we were in condition to climb the nearby hills; and many neighbors and their children. All were smiling and invited us to visit them again on our next trip to China. "By then," Yen told us, "we'll be still further along. China is going forward all the time; never again will it go backward. Tell that to all the peoples outside China. If they don't believe it now, some one day they'll believe it."

As a going-away present they gave us a few pieces of local rock artistically sculptured and mounted on wooden bases, reminding us that the chief source of pride for the commune members was that they had transformed a rocky cliff into a terrain yielding corn and fruit trees. A few months previously Premier Chou En-lai had visited them to congratulate them for having completed an emergency irrigation system as a precaution against natural calamities. A group known as the "young women of iron" had helped build the reservoir by carting earth from over a hundred miles away. For ten days and nights they hiked and carried soil, singing and waving red flags. Now one could see greenery and the beginnings of a forest where once had stood a barren cliff.

The next agricultural commune we visited, Chie Ming, had also made tremendous advances in productivity. Chie Ming was famous on two accounts: its managing director, Wuan Kuo-fan, was a member of the national parliament, and it had a live "three-legged donkey." On the wall in the director's office there was a picture of Mao conversing with Wuan Kuo-fan. Wuan spoke to us logically and concisely, and supplied impressive statistics: his commune, compared with others in the region, was a small one, consisting of 340 families—20,000 inhabitants in all; but, large or small, the communes had brought economic progress to the countryside which would not have occurred if the agrarian program had remained at the stage of cooperatives. "The higher-type cooperatives," commented Wuan Kuo-fan, "fulfilled their tasks. They were a big step forward from the primitive cooperatives of the first years after Liberation. In them the peasants felt protected against the return of the state of affairs that existed in China only twenty years ago, when peasants worked from sun-up to nightfall and slept little because of the wolves. The higher-type cooperative was good, but it wasn't enough. Take water, for instance, the basic problem in backward farm regions. With the lower-type cooperative the problem began to be solved; with the higher-type cooperative another step forward was taken. But only when twenty villages merged into this commune could we solve the water problem once and for all." At the same time the commune had encouraged reforestation, and three million pine trees had been planted on the hitherto barren, unproductive hills. "We are creating groves and livestock," the commune leader told us. "Before we only had a three-legged donkey; now we have a hundred head of livestock. Before only ten pigs; now four hundred. Every family has at least two pigs."

Wuan Kuo-fan took us to see the "three-legged donkey," which got its name because it served several villages at the same time. "It has done its duty," he said with a smile. "It's very old but we keep it here as a symbol of the change from the starvation economy of the past to the growing well-being of the present." The commune had its own exhibition of the history of Chinese peasant life. Wall posters, made popular by the Cultural Revolution, were much in evidence: the peasants moved easily from hoe to paintbrush, and the exhibition itself was well arranged and brightly colored. The first part depicted peasant life before Liberation, centering on the life of a peasant woman who had formerly lived in a hovel but now owned a house of her own and had money in the commune's bank. The second part gave a graphic description of an attempt by a reactionary group in the commune to take over leadership. This occurred on January 30, 1967, when, in Wuan Kuo-fan's words, the "counter-revolutionary forces of economism" took the offensive against the Cultural Revolution. Here was evidence that even in a commune considered won over to Mao's ideas, which proudly displayed seven autographed letters from Chairman Mao, the old reactionary ideas died hard. So serious was the situation judged that on February 4 Chou En-lai personally visited the commune with instructions from Chairman Mao. We saw several photographs of Chou with Wuan Kuo-fan. The "enemy agents" were isolated and made to undergo a long process of political re-education, after which their opposition collapsed.

Despite these internal disturbances, production in this commune increased during the first year of the Cultural Revolution and a further rise was foreseen in the next planning period. Wuan explained the planning process to us in detail. It went from below to those on top, in line with the principle of inner democracy, in which authority resided in the masses. Every production brigade presents its draft of a plan, which is submitted to members of the commune as a whole, so that every member has an idea of what is proposed and can express his or her opinion. Wuan felt that his commune was superior to the Soviet-type of collective farm: "It's hard to find a peasant who isn't satisfied with the commune. The commune is the peasants' idea; it's a bridge to enable us to pass from socialism to Communism. The system has swept over the whole country. Even in Tibet they are beginning to organize communes." Before we left Wuan and his commune, they proudly showed us one of the fourteen tractors they now possessed. As they said goodbye they sent good wishes to the Spanish peasants in their fight for liberation and gave us an ample supply of chestnuts, of which their commune produces more than a million kilograms per year, for our journey.

After an extensive visit to the communes in northern China, in which we singled out those in which "the victory over nature" had been most arduous, we visited two other communes near Peking and one on the outskirts of Shanghai, all of them interesting for diverse reasons. The Commune of Chinese-Albanian Friendship about fifteen miles from Peking was formed from the merger of three higher-type cooperatives: it has 5,700 families, about 25,000 persons occupying an area of 3,800 hectares. It is highly mechanized and produces cereals, livestock, and other farm produce. This commune cultivates a type of horse ideal for work in the fields, and its duck production is enormous. During the past year the commune sold the government 41,000 ducks; this year the figure would reach 45,000. (The Western press made much of the fact that one of the victims of the Cultural Revolution was the famous Peking restaurant "The Pressed Duck." A few days later we ate there. What had happened was that the one-time luxury restaurant was now a popular-priced restaurant, but the ducks—which came from the commune we visited—were just as tasty as before.) This commune is modest compared with many others in China, yet 80 per cent of its land has been adequately irrigated; it has six barns with 2,500 milk cows, 600 horses, and 14,000 hogs. Agricultural machinery is, of course, very important; but more important still is the social and cultural life of the commune's inhabitants: 6,000 of its children are in school; it has six polyclinics, with a medical staff numbering forty, a film group, and five radio stations.

The People's Commune "North Bridge" in the Shanghai region

was particularly interesting because of its paramilitary aspects. Remember that toward the end of 1967 the U.S. escalation of the war in Vietnam made many fear that the war would soon spread to China. This commune has its own small-scale blast furnaces, a workshop for farm implements and furniture, and a shopping area where all sorts of things are for sale, many of them made in the commune. In short, it is self-sufficient, capable of resisting and surviving in the event of a major war. Many Chinese communes in the countryside are similarly prepared, for contrary to most of the world's political leaders, Mao Tse-tung has not played on fears of a nuclear war but has instead inculcated in the Chinese people faith in their own strength—in Chinese: *tzu-li keng-sheng,* meaning "self-reliance." Many abroad have made fun of the Chinese expression "The most powerful atom bomb is Chairman Mao's Thought"—but it has been the key to over-all Chinese policy. There is no secret about China's ability to produce the hydrogen bomb; in fact, twice I saw a film devoted to that subject, in which the narrator stressed that nuclear energy will be used for the Chinese people and for all peoples fighting for liberation. In the film I saw human beings and farm animals emerging unharmed from the shelters and caves assigned to them in an area rather close to a nuclear explosion. And safeguards were taken to protect the nearby plant life from the danger of radiation. It is not that the Chinese take the bomb lightly; but they are reacting to what they call the atomic blackmail of the superpowers.

I recall that at the conclusion of one of my lectures in Peking I expressed the hope that China would not be attacked, whereupon my words were greeted with a polite smile. Several days later a young Spanish woman, daughter of an exiled Spanish political leader, came to see us at the Peking Hotel. I had known her in Geneva as a very intelligent young person but not overly interested in politics. Now, however, after two years in China, she spoke Chinese, dressed in Chinese style, and identified completely with the Chinese students with whom she lived. To her I repeated the same hope that China would not be attacked. She replied: "By whom? The Americans?— Let them come! Let them come!" She seemed to reflect the general attitude of self-confidence of the young Chinese with whom she associated.

The directives of the Central Committee were clear: "The masses must assert what is right, and correct what is wrong, in order, little by little, to achieve unanimity. The facts must be discussed and people convinced by reasoning—that is how debate has to be carried on. Coercion must not be used against the minority that supports different viewpoints." That the young people who went out in the streets in support of the Cultural Revolution committed excesses goes without saying. One cannot expect the movements of millions of youths passionately committed to a cause to behave like a well-trained ballet. Yet Western journalists cabling from Peking have informed us that, for example, during a five-hour parade past the Soviet Embassy organized by the "Red Guards," not a single chandelier was broken or a single ink bottle tossed against the Embassy walls. True, there were nasty incidents at the demonstration in front of the British Embassy, but some evidence seems to point to instigation by *agents provocateurs.*

The campaign against the Soviet Union followed an uneven course. There were moments when the Chinese hoped, however transitorily, that the differences in the camp of the Socialist giants could be smoothed over, as in November, 1964, when Chou En-lai went to Moscow after Khrushchev's fall to discuss major issues. The Soviets said afterward that the visit failed because Chou En-lai had asked the impossible: that the U.S.S.R. should publicly retract all its mistakes, with the Chinese defining and listing what those mistakes were. But Peking, on the other hand, asserted that the attempt at reconciliation failed because the Russians stubbornly insisted on placing the issue of peaceful coexistence above all others. The Chinese Communists' intransigence and refusal to compromise on this point reminded me to some extent of Lenin's attitude during World War I.

In 1966 people of the Left who were more sympathetic to Peking than Moscow and who were against the policy of peaceful coexistence advised the Chinese Communists to be more flexible. The Chinese reply recalled Lenin's answer to the centrists in the Second International who had urged him not to vex the right-wing Socialist leaders but to win them over by practicing a little diplomacy. The Chinese reacted as Lenin had, decades previously: "Nothing and no one can be gained by confusion," even though they realized that in the short run they would be the losers. On the eve of the Twenty-third Congress of the Soviet Communist Party, Moscow had the support of the majority of the world's Communists, at least the official leadership of the parties, in the Sino-Soviet dispute. The French and Spanish Communist parties took a distinctly anti-Chinese position; the Romanians opposed any move that might lead to a break with the Chinese Party; the Italian Communists, still under Togliatti's able guidance, adopted a middle-of-the-road position of flexibility. But Mao in 1966, like Lenin in 1916, thought more of the future than of the tactical needs of the moment, and was content to let the Russians have their short-term successes. He was confident that the course of the Vietnam War, the drive of the U.S. imperialists to extend their military and economic influence everywhere, and the logic of the movements of national liberation would prove Peking right.

"I was with the Russian Revolution when it was a revolution. Now I'm with the Chinese Revolution because it still is a revolution." I heard these words on the night of January 12, 1967, uttered by a participant in a round-table conference organized by the Swiss radio network in Paris. The speaker was not a famous name; but he sounded very sure of himself as he confronted various well-known personalities of the French Left. When the broadcast was over, I jotted down his words, for they impressed me as historically significant.

Around this time I spent a whole week listening to accounts of China on various radio stations broadcasting in all the languages I know. For most of them Tokyo was the main source of information, since Japanese journalists in Peking constituted the majority of the shrunken corps of foreign correspondents stationed in the Chinese capital. Whatever their feelings about events there, they could not complain about Chinese censorship. One of them told how one of his outgoing telegrams was held up. But he was able to phone its entire contents to his editor in Tokyo. He was not expelled; his journalist's credentials were not suspended for a single day. Yet at that very moment the world press presented a picture of China as totally isolated from the outside world and bordering on a state of chaos. And, at the same time, Chairman Mao's *Little Red Book* appeared in Europe in an Italian translation to which the leading newspapers of

Italy—*Il Giorno, La Stampa, La Gazetta del Popolo, Il Resto del Carlino*, and others—devoted long, analytical articles. Everywhere interest in China was mounting; and attempts to isolate the People's Republic as if it were some contagious disease were foredoomed to failure, from whatever quarter they arose.

In the Great Proletarian Cultural Revolution the young people of China spoke out. During 1965 the League of Communist Youth assumed the task of involving *all* the young people of China, not only the activists, in matters of domestic and foreign policy. These efforts were preparatory, as it were, to the organization of the Red Guards, and May 4, 1966, Youth Day, seemed to crown these efforts: after two years of ideological preparation the Red Guards appeared at Tsinghua University in Peking. Then, on August 18, 1966, following a plenary session of the Central Committee of the Communist Party, a million Red Guards publicly rallying around Chairman Mao were given official status as an organization. Obviously, therefore, this was no spontaneous youth outburst exploited by one section of the Party against another and jeopardizing the very Revolution they were pledged to uphold. It was the end result of a process two years in the making and guided by the Party leadership. As one Western journalist who was on the spot commented on his return from Peking, "It was certainly a well-controlled violence."

In the first year of the Cultural Revolution a hundred million copies of Mao's *Little Red Book* were published. His three main articles, "Serving the People," "In Memory of Norman Bethune," and "The Foolish Old Man Who Removed the Mountains," were widely read and discussed in the factories, at the universities, and in the People's Communes, with special hours set aside for this purpose. Mao's *Little Red Book* is a distillation of much that he has written and spoken since the founding of the Chinese Communist Party in 1921. As I went about the country, I noticed that every meeting or work session began with a reading from the *Little Red Book*. Certain of Chairman Mao's statements recurred with great frequency, and I took notes on these, some of which I am here reproducing as freely translated:

The nuclear power that guides our cause is the Communist Party of China. The theoretical base that guides our thinking is Marxism.

Classes struggle: some classes emerge victorious, others are eliminated. Such is history—the history of civilization—during the past thousands of years. To interpret history from this point of view is historical materialism; to uphold the opposing point of view is historical idealism.   •

Making a revolution is not like painting a picture or making an embroidery; it cannot be polite, quiet, subtle, placid, courteous, moderate, and magnanimous. A revolution is an insurrection, an act of violence by which one class overthrows another.

All Communists must understand this truth: "Power grows out of a gun."

All reactionaries are paper tigers. They may seem fearful but in reality they are not so powerful. Seen in perspective, the people, not the reactionaries, are really powerful.

Revolutionary war is the war of the masses and can only be won by mobilizing the masses and relying on them.

What is the real iron wall? The masses, the millions upon millions of human beings who genuinely support the revolution. That is the real iron wall which no force whatever can smash.

Without a people's army the people will have nothing.

Beware of arrogance. That is a basic problem for every leader and it is also an important condition for maintaining unity. No one should be arrogant, not even those who have achieved big successes in their work or have not committed any mistakes.

The people, and the people alone, are the motive power that makes world history.

We must be modest and prudent. We must guard against conceit and impulsiveness and serve the Chinese people with all our heart.

To acquire a real understanding of Marxism, one must not only learn it from books but above all through class struggle, through practical work and intimate contact with the masses of workers and peasants. If besides reading Marxist books our intellectuals get some understanding of Marxism through their contacts with the workers and peasants and from their practical work, we will all speak the same language. We will not only speak the common language of patriotism and the Socialist system, we will also be able to speak the common language of the Communist view of the world.

The central task and the highest form of every revolution is the taking of power.

These are but a few of the quotations from Chairman Mao's Thought that inspired the Chinese masses during the Cultural Revolution. Their strength lies in their clarity and simplicity of formulation, making them accessible to every worker and peasant. They represent Marxism as applied to every domain of politics, philosophy, economics, and military science. The Chinese are convinced that the Vietnam War has confirmed the correctness of Mao's views on military strategy: the revolutionary approach to war, which stresses above all the human element. "Weapons," Mao writes, "are an important factor in war, but they are not decisive. The decisive factor is man and not things." Class divisions lend a distinctive character to armed struggle in that they create an insuperable antagonism between the revolutionary and the counter-revolutionary forces, whether in conflicts on a national or an international scale. Under those conditions victory can only come as a result of a prolonged struggle, in which the masses have been mobilized and given a political consciousness superior to that of the enemy. This is Mao's theory of prolonged warfare which rose out of the long struggle of the Chinese people: eight years of war against Japan and three years against the Kuomintang.

In the great public debate unleashed by the Cultural Revolution, the *dazibaos*—wall posters written in large letters—gave millions of Chinese the opportunity to express themselves freely on a wide variety of themes. No one was prevented from expressing his opinion directly, even about the highest authorities of the Party and the government. It was, as one Western scholar puts it, a "volcanic mass movement," an explosion of public opinion, a vast national debate involving two different courses—"two political lines"—to follow. Most serious observers of the Chinese scene agree that in this plebiscite Chairman Mao was overwhelmingly supported. Furthermore, it was essentially a movement from below, even though at times it took on aspects of the "cult of personality," revealing many instances of idolization, even sanctification of Chairman Mao. Nevertheless, despite numerous verbal and physical excesses, the fact remains that in the Cultural Revolution the vast majority of the Chinese people showed their affection and respect for Chairman Mao.

The first *dazibao* was placed on a wall at Peking University in June, 1966. It is now shown at the Red Guard Exhibition, where I had its text translated for me. After it was put up, it was reproduced in the press at Mao's express recommendation, thus assuring it immediately of the widest publicity. The style is simple and straightforward, but severe against "persons with power inside the Party who follow the capitalist path." Its appearance came two weeks after the May 16 statement of the Central Committee of the Communist Party; so the opposition to Mao's Thought now knew what was in store for them.

That during the first year of the Cultural Revolution the struggle among the students was violent and protracted we learned from the lips of some of the principals when we visited the Institute of Geology of Peking University. Red Guard Rojo Nie-chen, one of the student leaders of the Institute, explained to us why he and his comrades had been from the outset on the side of the Cultural Revolution. The first reason, he said, was that Chairman Mao led it, because to him "Mao Tse-tung is the greatest leader in world Marxism-Leninism. And we are Marxist-Leninists, that is, against U.S. imperialism and Soviet revisionism. And it was Chairman Mao who led the Democratic Revolution and then the Socialist Revolution to victory. By saving the Chinese Revolution from following the capitalist path, he has saved the World Revolution."

After these introductory remarks, Nie-chen told us what had happened in the "Red East," as the revolutionary section of the Institute of Geology was called. Agents of the opposition had infiltrated the Institute and were setting groups of students against one another. "We felt it was a life-and-death question for the future of the Chinese Revolution. Abroad you probably don't realize that for us 1966 was a decisive turning point. Counter-revolutionary elements had grown strong everywhere within the Party, at the University as well. Then on June 1, 1966, a historic document drawn up under Chairman Mao's guidance was approved. The Great Cultural Revolution was under way. In our Institute, as well as throughout the country, there was a struggle between two political lines. The Red Guards won, but the counter-revolutionaries did not give up. They sent a large group—'work brigades'—into our Institute to defeat us." Later, I often heard mention of these "work brigades"—in reality, "shock brigades"—when I visited the factories and port of Shanghai.

Another student took up the story: "Taking advantage of Chairman Mao's absence from Peking, the counter-revolutionaries tried to throttle the Cultural Revolution. In the Institute we reacted strongly, demanding the expulsion of the 'work brigades.' But they went over to the offensive; and we had twenty days of utter disorder and terror. To sow confusion they labeled us and the professors who supported us as the counter-revolutionaries. It's an old tactic: waving the red flag to fight against the red flag. Finally, Chairman Mao returned to Peking and decided that the 'work brigades' had to be withdrawn. So now we can resume our professional activity and follow the genuinely revolutionary line."

The internal fight must have lasted a good many months, for it was only on April 3, 1967, that the Revolutionary Committee of the Institute was established. In speaking with these students and many other young people, I realized how much the Cultural Revolution motivated them and spurred them to concrete achievements, so that in such a spirit these future geologists would leave the Institute and go into different parts of their country to discover new sources of oil and various mineral resources. A last-year student told me that Soviet experts had been very skeptical about China's oil possibilities, yet from year to year oil production in China has increased and important new sources have been discovered; and now China is producing various types of gasoline for civilian and military use. Once the decision was made to become self-sufficient in fuel resources, imports were curtailed. My student informant went on: "We have succeeded in stabilizing production; we have discovered new theories unknown to the capitalist world. We have beaten one record in drilling wells. We already have refineries functioning at capacity. They can go on ignoring China as an oil producer, as they do in lots of other respects. We don't care. We're saving a good many surprises for the high-and-mighty industrialized powers. Like when we exploded the 'H' bomb."

The task of the *dazibaos* was always to convince and not to kill. By physically crushing one's opponents, one accomplishes nothing; their wrong ideology would survive any futile "purges." Minds and consciences had to be "purged," as the very important declaration of August 8, 1966, explained: "We must apply the method of convincing by facts and rely on reasoning. We must not use coercion to suppress the minority that has different points of view. The minority must be protected because sometimes the truth is on its side. Even if its positions are wrong, it must be allowed to defend them and to present its opinions."

Fourteen months later, on my next visit to China, Chou En-lai returned to this same theme. Speaking in Wuhan, where some of the most violent encounters between opposing groups had occurred, the Prime Minister declared: "The current Great Cultural Revolution is a mass movement, a general examination and rigorous test of cadres at all levels. The truth is, the cadres are good or relatively good. As for those who have committed mistakes, even serious mistakes, most of them can correct their mistakes after being re-educated. We believe that after being criticized by the masses many of the cadres can and should be rehabilitated." This has always been Mao's position as well as that of his closest collaborators. The fact that in the clash between opposing factions some blood was spilled does not refute the policy of "convince, not kill." In June, 1968, in a generally unsympathetic article on the status of the Cultural Revolution appearing in *The New York Times*, it was acknowledged that not a single opponent of the Revolution, including the most stubborn and highly placed, had been arrested or put to death.

My contacts with students in the specialized institutes fulfilled a double role: I was able to broaden my personal knowledge of the Red Guards, who played a very important part in these schools of higher learning, and at the same time I noted some of the implications of the Cultural Revolution for the future of education in China at all levels. This point was one of the most widely debated abroad, inasmuch as the closing down of the primary and secondary schools for such a long period of time had left the impression of irreparable damage to the Chinese educational system. Thus, at the University of Medical Science in Peking, I was received with much interest and enthusiasm. In the course of a discussion with a dozen or so students, most of them wearing Red Guard armbands, I mentioned Dr. Norman Bethune, who had been in Spain during our Civil War before going to China. One of the students quoted Chairman Mao's comments: "The spirit of Comrade Bethune, his complete dedication to others without the least concern for himself, was expressed in his infinite feeling of responsibility for his work and his infinite love for his comrades and the people. We must all learn from his absolute disinterestedness." Summarizing the results of our discussion, the students asserted that by entering fully into the life of the masses, they received a "general education" that made up for any delays they might have suffered in their "specialized education." As a young woman Red Guard who acted as unofficial chairwoman of our encounter exclaimed: "Now we really know our people!" Another student, from a family of poor peasants, who had recently entered the school said: "All things considered, the losses have been minimal, the gains very great. I'm not talking only about our cases, children of poor peasants who previously could scarcely dream of being admitted here and getting a degree. It's the whole atmosphere of the school that has changed. Now there's a greater desire to work, not just to get a privileged job but to be able to serve the people better."

I recalled to the students what my old friend Professor Wu Hoau-hsing, director of the Peking Cancer Institute, had told me a few days before. Since the students knew his work, they were interested in hearing his opinion about recent progress made by Chinese medicine and future prospects for workers in the medical sciences. (In a previous book on China, I have written how I met Professor Wu during a trip on the Yangtze River journeying from Chungking to Wuhan, and how he helped us retrieve a film from the famous gorges of that river.) Professor Wu embodies devotion to his people: like other Chinese scientists and technical experts educated abroad, he had returned to China, giving up a comfortable existence for double the amount of work and less monetary reward. When I first met him he was, although not a Party member, enthusiastic about Mao's "immense personality," to use his own words. The hard years 1966 and 1967 had not caused him to change his mind; on the contrary, now he admired Chairman Mao even more. In fluent French, Professor Wu described to me how the big ideological shock had brought about better results in his profession. In medicine and general scientific research there was a renewed effort to contribute to the general welfare. Individual Chinese redoubled their energies in trying to become new persons. Professor Wu, who had just returned from a scientific mission in Switzerland, told me amusing anecdotes concerning the West's ignorance about China; on the other hand, he was impressed by the interest shown by his Swiss colleagues in the medical work being done in China. His Cancer Institute had expanded since 1961, when I first visited it, and now some of the equipment bore comparison with that in the most highly industrialized nations of the West. Much of the machinery was made in China, in accordance with the above-mentioned principle of "walking on one's own two feet." The Institute had a good record for curing cancer of the womb: almost 100 per cent in first-stage cases. Emphasis was on preventive medicine for all diseases, and Chinese medical scientists rejected out of hand any defeatist attitude toward old age, which in China was not a barrier to continuing working if a person wished to. At the same time they opposed using human beings as guinea pigs in experiments for trying out new cures. "Only socialized medicine can answer the needs of the people," Professor Wu asserted with a vigorous nod of his head.

In China the cost of medical care and drugs is minimal: eyeglasses are three yuan, less than $1.50; an office consultation about ten cents; an X-ray, fifty cents. For the most serious operation—heart surgery, for instance—a doctor can ask no more than thirty yuan, about $15.00. The Red Guard we met at the Medical School told us what had happened among the student body: "Our university was founded in 1959. Actually, from the beginning there were two opposing points of view: those who favored purely professional training above everything else and those who tried to make our doctors serve the people. The 'Chinese Khrushchev' introduced a course of eight-year study, aiming at a reduced and exclusive student body. It would have meant a minority of privileged students taking all the time they wanted to complete their training. As one of our comrades has told you, there wouldn't have been a single spot for sons and daughters of poor peasants like himself. But those were just the ones best able to 'go to the countryside,' as Chairman Mao recommended. They knew about the lack of medical care in the farm areas; they knew the conditions under which their parents and grandparents had lived. So we Red Guards rebelled. We wanted the doors of the universities opened to peasants' children and volunteered ourselves to go to the countryside. But some of our comrades have just returned from the country; they can tell us the story in their own words." One of the group referred to began: "The Minister of Health was following a policy of separation from the masses, neglect of the countryside. We saw this with our own eyes as we walked for miles in the country, stopping at remote villages and living with the peasants and participating in their work. We were part of the masses and went to the masses. We gave medical assistance where it was needed; at times we performed emergency surgical operations. The mistakes of the past, when doctors preferred to remain in the city, have to be corrected. That's part of the Cultural Revolution applied to our Medical School. We haven't decided as yet how many years a medical student should study, but in any case not eight years. That's a lot, and it's not in line with the acute need for medical personnel in the Chinese countryside, which we students saw with our own eyes during our 'Long March.' "

Everyone knows about the Chinese Communists' historic Long March in 1934, one of the great stories of the Chinese Revolution. Contemporary Chinese literature abounds in stories and anecdotes about it. Each time that I have visited China I have heard impressive new details, and have always come away with the feeling that here was a historic lesson in the way in which one outwits and defeats an enemy far superior in manpower and armament. From 1966 on, Chinese youth engaged in the Cultural Revolution sought to relive the epic of the Long March by hiking over the entire country in every direction, undaunted by mountains, rivers, or other natural obstacles. Our student-informant went on: "This contact with the masses protects us against any temptation to arrogance. It's an antidote to intellectualism and the tendency to worship technology above everything. We want good technicians, of course, but on condition that they are good revolutionaries. . . . The peasants call us soldiers without uniform in the People's Liberation Army."

As I left the Medical School, one of the students said to me: "When the Spanish people need us, we too will go to Spain, like Norman Bethune." Listening to these highly motivated and political-minded young people, I recalled what a vital part Chinese youth have played in the twentieth century. *Youth* was the name of the magazine founded in 1915 by the intellectuals of Peking in their campaign against the Confucius-dominated society and for a new China. The famous student demonstration of March 4, 1919, in Peking was followed by similar outpourings of students in Shanghai. I have seen eloquent photographs of the clashes between the students and the Chinese police as well as the police of the foreign occupying powers. In China the university youth have been the shock troops in every new movement of liberation. Mao Tse-tung, even before he was a Marxist, took part in the work of the "Society for the Study of New Men." He founded the magazine *Hsiang-kang* and, having studied journalism at the university, took charge of student publications while he earned his living first in a Shanghai laundry, then as a bookkeeper. Of the twelve founders of the Chinese Communist Party, Mao was the only one of peasant origin and, at the same time, one of those most closely in contact with the student movement.

For centuries the Chinese peasantry existed in abject poverty and misery, victimized in turn by the feudal lords, then the warlords, and more recently the foreign companies who behaved as though China belonged to them. And, of course, the Imperial Court acted in complicity with the imperialists' interests. Even during the period of the Dowager Empress Tzu Hsi, a forcible and forbidding woman with a reputation for hating foreigners, the imperialists dominated, and China was squeezed like a lemon between its foreign and domestic rulers. Nevertheless, from time to time the people, particularly the peasantry, rose up and challenged their overlords in a thousand-year-old struggle, crowned by the historic victory of the Chinese Revolution in 1949. Then, under Mao, came the Agrarian Reform—so profound and far-ranging a reform that henceforth the Chinese peasants, through their People's Communes, became key factors in the great national upsurge.

The Church too had joined with capitalism and colonialism to exploit the Chinese peasants. Its methods were subtler, more concealed, but no less iniquitous. Much has been written about foreign missionaries and their civilizing work in Asia. Undeniably they showed persistence and, in individual instances, capacity for self-sacrifice and compassion. How else could they have penetrated the entire country, even virtually inaccessible Tibet? But their business was of this world as well as the next. All the treaties imposed on China from abroad, with the complicity of the Manchu emperors, from the Opium War in 1841 on, contained clauses favoring the missionaries. Inevitably, therefore, the missionaries appeared in the eyes of the Chinese people as allies of the exploiters of their land, their railroads, and their customs' revenues. This accounts for the scant popularity of the missionaries when the Revolution broke out.

China was the key to the missionaries' penetration of Asia. The world possesses a wealth of data revealing how the Roman Catholic bishops, exploiting the combination of poverty, flood, and drought, purchased whole villages. Moving from one place to another on their litters, borne by eight men, the bishops became great experts on land questions—but in order to appropriate it, not to see to it that it was more fairly distributed. They enjoyed the same diplomatic immunity as ambassadors; hence they were the targets of the same peasant hostility as were the representatives of the foreign powers, one of which placed a sign at the entrance to its Concession (occupation zone) in Shanghai: "Chinese and dogs not admitted." Indeed, in the several times I have visited China since the Revolution, I have marveled at how little resentment is felt toward foreigners, including the Japanese, who for so many decades behaved toward the Chinese in a way that shames the human species. No, in general the missionaries were far from the saintly people the West has sought to make of them. So it is not surprising that as early as 1885 the uprisings in Szechwan province, the main base of missionary uprisings, took on an anti-clerical, anti-Catholic character.

In a sense, the Chinese Communist Party considers itself the heirs of the Taipings vis-à-vis the peasants (the Taiping Rebellion lasted from 1850 to 1864). Before political parties existed in China the peasants formed secret societies in many parts of the country, some of them dating back to the eighteenth century. Many Chinese writers have stressed the peasants' ability to meet secretly and form these united action groups, which bore many names, some of them colorful: the Big Brothers of Szechwan, the Celestial Bamboo and the White Lotus sects, the Red Spear and Big Sword societies in northern China, and—at the dawn of the twentieth century—the

Righteous Fists, or Boxers, who made the Boxer Rebellion. All of them grew out of the interconnected evils of hunger, floods, and imperialist intervention; and all contributed to the development of the Chinese Revolution, which came to a climax in the mid-twentieth century.

The peasants' lot seemed a matter of total unconcern to generation after generation of rulers, except that now and then some individual in authority showed impressive initiative. Thus on my first visit to China I had admired the waterworks constructed two thousand years before by the engineer Li Ping, whose statue stands near the site of his achievements. He had succeeded in separating the waters of the mighty Yangtze River—the Son of the Ocean—and utilized them to such advantage that the region became the best rice producer in the country. Since rice was the staple article of the Chinese diet, one can readily see what a tremendous accomplishment this must have been. Yet apart from a few individual instances of this type and some concern for the problem on the part of a few enlightened emperors, the fate of the Chinese peasant could not have been more tragic. Even the Ming Dynasty, so creative in other fields of human endeavor, left the peasants in a terrible state of wretchedness when it passed from the scene in the seventeenth century.

Poverty sowed death among the peasant population but at the same time kept alive in them a spirit of revolt that bided its time and waited for the favorable moment to explode. In his military writings, Mao Tse-tung evokes the spirit of these peasant revolts—a knowledge of which aided him during his revolutionary campaigns and especially on the famous Communist Long March. The Chinese Communists learned how to treat the peasants as allies instead of as enemies, as had traditionally been the case in Chinese villages, where the people were wont to tremble every time a body of soldiers drew near.

The Brotherhoods, too, had a long tradition of struggle. The Kelao Brotherhood, for example, had fought against the Manchus for three hundred years; and, unwavering in its hatred of the foreign dynasty, tried to assassinate the Manchu Empress in 1901 when she returned to Peking from a visit to Siam. The Brotherhoods, excellent guerrilla fighters as well as skillful smugglers, were without peer in obtaining arms. Later they received help from the students, who, despite primitive methods, became specialists in making bombs and played an effective part in the revolts of 1908, 1909, 1910, and 1911, until the Chinese monarchy was toppled and the first Chinese Republic was proclaimed.

The extent of peasant exploitation can perhaps best be shown by the fact that even their excrement was taken from them. Before the development of chemical fertilizers, human excrement was the chief source of land fertilization; and the take-over of public toilets was included among the items of organized looting. A popular saying confirmed the practice: "They rob you of your sweat, your breath, your saliva, your work, your woman, and your shit." The item "your woman" referred to the fact that frequently a peasant had to lease or sell his wife; and during famine periods the sale of daughters was widespread. Accounts of the period tell of the painful discussions within family groups—one of the decisive arguments for sending off a daughter to a rich family, with or without pay, was that at least there she would be assured of having enough to eat. This situation of long-endured suffering and pent-up hatred often—as we have mentioned above—gave peasant revolts in China an unexampled ferocity. Frequently, too, the reprisals were terrible, in which the armies of the foreign occupying powers joined with the native soldiery. In 1900, after a peasant uprising in which a few foreigners were among the victims, Peking was sacked by Western troops aided by the Japanese. Fifty thousand persons were slain by French, British, and German soldiers, who also raped any woman they encountered on the way. In a few cases, those who were about to be slaughtered had just been baptized by the missionaries, who were happy to ease their passage to heaven. The sack of Peking was intended as a lesson the peasants would never forget. But less than two years later the rebellions began again—with this difference, that now they broke out every six months instead of every year. No amount of repression could quell the rebellious spirit of the Chinese peasants, especially now that they felt that the fall of the Manchus was at hand and had found a leader in Dr. Sun Yat-sen, "the father of the Revolution."

Visiting the Historical Museum in Peking, I saw how almost invariably peasant revolts accompanied each change of dynasty in China, evidence of the centuries-long struggle to break the bonds of feudal serfdom. Now as I spoke with the peasants, lived with them, ate with them, and slept in their houses, the theoretical lessons of the museum were embodied in unforgettably live human beings.

With intelligent planning and a strong will socialism can triumph in the most unsuspected places, as it did on the "roof of the world"—in the Tibetan land of lamas that extends amid well-nigh inaccessible mountains from northern India to Burma, a plateau with an average altitude of 13,000 feet, and to the north of Tibet a vast desert with one of the most forbidding climates on earth. When the Chinese Revolution occurred, Tibet was a land enveloped in legend and mystery, one of the least likely of places to be socialized, its people in many respects still living as though in the Middle Ages. When the forces of the Chinese Red Army entered the capital city of Lhasa on September 9, 1951, they were ceremoniously received by the Dalai Lama in accordance with the "treaty for the peaceful liberation of Tibet." Serfdom was still the prevailing institution in Tibet; so, taking into account these deep-rooted feudal traditions, the Chinese government proceeded with unusual caution, and five years later, in view of Tibetan resistance to its socializing measures, decided to suspend all reforms in basic social structure until 1962. I was in Peking in 1957 when this decree was made public, and I discussed it with young Tibetans of both sexes, students at the Nationalities Institute, who were preparing for the time when Tibet would evolve toward socialism.

But the Tibetan feudal society, dominated by big landlords and the Church hierarchy, who thought they could nip in the bud any social change that menaced their privileges, was not allowed to stand intact. This was a challenge to the rest of the Chinese Revolution; and the Peking government, disregarding the resistance of the wealthy, proceeded to introduce "democratic reforms" it deemed indispensable to help the Tibetan people overcome the despotic rule of the big landowners, the nobility, and the monasteries. Basing itself on the mass of serfs, who represented nine-tenths of Tibet's population, the Chinese government proceeded boldly to do away with slavery and prepared the ground for the building of socialism. The "three antis" were introduced: against rebellion, against forced labor, against slavery, along with the "two minuses": reduction of taxes on farm work and reduction of interest on debts.

A broad educational campaign prepared the peasants for an agrarian reform, a campaign in which every effort was made to destroy prejudices that had survived for centuries. Thus the inhabitants' religion condemned the use of insecticides and deep plowing because these might disturb the earth spirits, and in most parts of Tibet farm work was being done with the same implements as those used during the Middle Ages. Then the freed serfs had to be regrouped in suitable economic units so that the agrarian reform did not remain merely on paper. Plows were modernized and enough of them distributed so that every family in the now regrouped teams of mutual aid had eight different farm implements at its disposal. Consequently, the cultivated area increased rapidly to 40,000 hectares, which meant a 34 per cent increase in the amount of grain for every inhabitant of the region. Farm experts were sent in and a start was made in scientific cultivation of the land. The yield was such that even the most skeptical were convinced: in six years total production of cereals was almost 50 per cent higher. Similar results were forthcoming with the livestock. The shepherds who from time immemorial had relied on prayers to combat foot-and-mouth disease among the cattle now began to be persuaded of the usefulness of veterinarians.

The liberated serf and shepherd encouraged by the lower death rate among their livestock knew that now their families could go to the fifteen modern hospitals and 149 health centers and clinics scattered throughout Tibet. They saw roads being built that put an end to an isolation they had previously considered as natural as being born and dying. Four main highways were constructed: from Sikang to Tibet, more than 1,200 miles long, approaching Lhasa from the east; from Tsinghai to Tibet, a hundred miles shorter than the preceding one, coming from the north; from Sinkiang to Tibet, coming from the west; and Yatung road, coming from India. In addition, there was the railway that linked Lhasa with the interior of China and the Peking–Lhasa air route.

Industrialization proceeded slowly but surely, adapted to the most pressing needs of the moment: repair of farm implements and trucks and manufacture of consumers' goods, with women joining the work force in increasing numbers as they were won over to the goal of building socialism. Without entering into detail, one may say that this was a transformation virtually unprecedented in history and proof that a land even on the lowest level of underdevelopment can solve its problems if it succeeds in releasing the creative capacity of the masses of its inhabitants.

Everywhere I went in China I had conversations: in the communes, in the universities and research centers, in the factories, and at all social levels. As on no previous visit to China, this time I felt I had made close contact with the Chinese people, and when I left their country it was with a vision of a China that would maintain itself and go forward for many years to come. Whatever I learned about China made me feel privileged; but it also made me feel obligated to report my experiences in a clear and accurate way.

There was, for example, the question of China's relations with the outside world. The presence in Peking during my stay there of two high-ranking delegations—one from Pakistan and the other from the Congo (Brazzaville)—showed me that in the midst of the upheavals of the Cultural Revolution, China's foreign policy continued along the lines of collaboration with countries with different social and political systems, on the basis of equality, reciprocity, and independence. I was present at a state banquet on the eve of the Chinese national holiday at which Premier Chou En-lai dwelt on those points. It was a farewell banquet for the mission from the Congo (Brazzaville), and the head of the mission, Prime Minister Ambroise Noumazalay, said in his opening remarks: "We are happy to see that the People's Republic of China understands the policy of nonalignment consistently followed by my country. The People's Republic of China helps us without the haggling that characterizes imperialism, colonialism, and neo-colonialism; which means that it shows great understanding and brotherhood, and has full respect for our dignity and sovereignty." Chou En-lai replied to his words: "When they refer to aid our Congolese friends invariably express pleasure toward China. This makes us feel somewhat concerned. Chairman Mao has taught us: 'China must make a relatively large contribution to humanity. But for a long time our share has been very much reduced. This concerns us. As a people who have achieved victory in our Revolution, we must help those who are still fighting for their liberation. This is our internationalist duty.' The Chinese people will always follow this advice of Chairman Mao. In any case, the help is mutual."

"The kind of aid we get from China is characterized by its economic disinterestedness"—we heard many Asians and Africans comment in this vein at the Peking Hotel, where they ate at tables near ours. At that time the Chinese capital was host to Tanzania's Agriculture Minister, Amir Jamal, who was quite pleased with China's contribution to the building of the 1,200-kilometer railroad from Tanzania to Zambia. The Yemeni representative was equally pleased with the help the Chinese gave in building the cotton textile combine at Sanaa. Starting in 1970, the Chinese envisaged increasing assistance to the developing nations as their own economy improved; and the policies followed in the Congo (Brazzaville) and Tanzania would, it was hoped, be extended to other nations of Asia and Africa. All the aid, whether in the form of technical experts, credits, or interest-free loans, was given on the basis of the Eight Principles of Aid as formulated by Chou En-lai in 1963.

As China increases aid to the developing nations, so does its foreign trade increase—both things go hand in hand. But during the long period of China's exploitation, when its artistic treasures were looted, its foreign trade was manipulated by the Great Powers, as I was reminded during conversations in which my interlocutors quoted precise statistics to reinforce their point. The foreign powers, taking advantage of the "unequal treaties," controlled customs duties; 80 per cent of Chinese imports and 70 per cent of exports were in the hands of foreign companies, backed by the privileges of extraterritoriality and "gunboat diplomacy." Silk, a classical source of Chinese wealth, and tea were greedily coveted by the Japanese and British; even Chinese agricultural production was sold by methods devised by outside consortiums who vied with one another in trying to enrich themselves at the expense of the Chinese people. Coal, iron, and all the other natural resources were similarly exploited, and if a few Chinese did participate in the operation it was simply to placate and/or bribe the governing authorities.

The Revolution freed China's foreign trade, and within a few years it rose from $1.5 billion in 1952 to $5 billion in 1966. It rose still further in 1967 and 1968, so that China was no longer faced with a situation in which whatever trade balance it enjoyed had to be used to pay off the interest on debts owed the foreign powers and the monopolies established inside China. Today China has no foreign debt outstanding—including none to the U.S.S.R., which has been repaid in full for all the loans it advanced. Its budget is balanced; and commodity prices remain stable, showing if anything a tendency to go down, as we could see for ourselves when we visited the markets and large department stores in Peking and Shanghai.

I cannot stress too strongly the fact that, boycotted by the United States, shaken by the Cultural Revolution, and no longer enjoying economic collaboration with the Soviet Union, China resolved to tackle on its own many of the problems that beset even prosperous industrialized nations. Its example was not lost on the other peoples of Asia, particularly India, which played host in 1968 in New Delhi to a conference of the "Third World" nations and could offer them nothing tangible in the way of aid. But to these other peoples China stood out as the nation that within twenty years had started from scratch, had stood "on its own two feet," without foreign loans or investments, and had successfully gone forward.

At the permanent Industrial Exhibition in Shanghai, a kind of showcase display of the best of the Canton International Fair, I held extensive talks with experts who gave me projections of China's industrial production and its effect on foreign trade. Progress was apparent in everything related to farm machinery, inasmuch as agriculture is a constant in the Chinese economy. As a result, harvests improved constantly: in 1967 grain harvests reached 230,000,000 tons, not counting the grain reserved for production teams. With new techniques and mechanized farming, in many regions of China grain production jumped from the pre-Liberation figure of 30 kilograms per *mu* to 500; and in the case of cotton, to more than 50 kilograms per *mu*. The number of tractors under the system of People's Communes multiplied eighteenfold; for when Washington's trade boycott put an end to the importation of farm tractors from the United States, a simple solution was found: they were built in China.

So it was this mass participation, of both peasants and workers, that gave such an impetus to the nation's economy. How often in the countryside we heard comments like the following: "We don't count our hours of work, because we're working for the progress of the commune. We're not being forced to act by anyone. Each and every member of the commune, by means of our regular meetings, can decide the work program for each year. But it's only rarely that someone wants to work less. By fulfilling the goals in our plan each member of the commune improves his personal well-being as well as the commune's prosperity. Once we overcome natural calamities and provided we maintain this revolutionary spirit of 'serving the people,' the 'great leap forward' made by agriculture in recent years will be extended to all the People's Communes in the years to come. No, the Chinese people are never going to know hunger again." To be sure, there remained the danger of drought and of floods, which in 1968 and again in 1972 menaced the crop harvest; but not to the extent of creating famine such as in neighboring India.

We heard the same kind of comments in the factories: "Maybe some foreign visitors consider our system of requiring the workers to participate in all decisions concerning production a waste of time. But the facts show just the opposite: the practice of 'three-cornered' discussions has resulted in quantitative and qualitative progress. Those who take part in these discussions are administrative personnel or Party representatives, engineers and technical experts, and the workers. Thus the workers do not feel themselves merely cogs in the production process but masters of their own fate; they do not look on the machine as reducing them to the condition of automatons, robots, but as instruments to be used and improved for the betterment of all. Hence the increase in the number of inventions, with the workers demonstrating their inventive and creative skills, which is now one of the distinctive traits of our factories and which has been tremendously stimulated by the Cultural Revolution. Already it has led to a lessening in production costs and will enable our country to expand its exports. On the other hand, these 'three-cornered' discussions prevent bureaucratic highhandedness and dictation by the professional elites. The engineer and worker discuss with each other and exchange views on an equal basis. This is revolutionary democracy in action, the 'mass line' translated from theory into practice."

Most Westerners—and even some persons in the Soviet Union—were taken by surprise at China's rapid progress in developing its atomic-energy program. But they had paid insufficient attention to the strong emphasis placed on scientific research when China's First Five-Year Plan was initiated. At that time a twelve-year plan was formulated to study long-range projects, including the development of automation and the use of nuclear energy for peaceful purposes. Chou En-lai had indicated that by 1970, the last year of the Third Five-Year Plan, Chinese science should reach levels favorably comparing with the most advanced in the world. At the Physicists' Congress held in Peking in 1966, I could see that Chou's forecast had not been lightly made, for by then China was producing scientists capable of building nuclear bombs and would soon have scientists able to carry out space exploration. As one of these scientists, who one day may receive a Nobel Prize if the Committee deems "Red China" worthy of receiving one, told me: "Contrary to what many abroad think, the Cultural Revolution, far from slowing down the rate of scientific research, has actually quickened it noticeably." And an economics expert in Shanghai said to me: "The solution lies in Chairman Mao's Thought, which teaches us that with revolutionary determination all difficulties can be overcome. We must not hope for anything from outside aid, but must rely on the creative power of our own people. Facts and figures speak for themselves: at the annual Canton Fair we can offer thirty thousand articles for export. Here, for instance"—the economist pointed to a roomful of new products —"you can see what China is doing in the way of steel smelting. We have big centers of metallurgical production at Anshan, Shanghai, Peking, and Wuhan, some of which you have personally visited, and where we have introduced uniquely Chinese techniques, such as sending oxygen into the summit of the revolving furnace. We make all the equipment for large power plants such as the one on the Hsinan River; we make buses, railway locomotives, even airplanes and ocean liners, things that the China of twenty years ago could never have dreamed of producing. And what are twenty years in the history of China? Right now, as we're going through this exhibition, China is in the second year of its Third Five-Year Plan. Come back again when the plan has ended. You'll see a lot more progress. And in many cases what we have made has been with inferior-quality machinery. The small hen has laid big eggs."

Everywhere I went I sensed this feeling of confidence in China's future; and this it is, I am certain, that keeps the Chinese Revolution to its ever bold and youthful course.

On my 1966 visit to China I had ample opportunity to study the Sino-Soviet conflict on the spot, and since it is a matter of such overriding importance to the future of world relations as well as to the march of socialism, I must now dwell on it at some length. There is such massive documentation on this question that whole volumes could be written about it. Here, however, let me limit myself to a brief résumé of the highlights of the controversy.

When I was in China in 1961, I did not hear a single criticism of the Soviet Union. On the contrary, when I saw the train linking northern and southern China pass over the Wuhan Bridge across the Yangtze River, I recalled that on my previous visit (in 1957) the bridge had almost been finished. The Chinese head conductor then had launched into warm praise of the contribution of the Soviet engineers; and this despite the fact that for two years relations between Moscow and Peking had been steadily deteriorating. The Chinese claimed that the Russians unilaterally broke the 1957 agreement by which the Soviet Union had promised to deliver to China prototypes of nuclear weapons; they also insisted that in 1960 Khrushchev had unilaterally decided to end the agreement concerning Soviet economic aid to China. At a time when China was undergoing the worst series of natural calamities in over a century—floods, drought, extremes of climate—Soviet engineers and technical experts were recalled to Moscow overnight, with orders to take back with them sketches and plans affecting about a hundred and fifty industrial projects then under way. This was a terrible blow to the Chinese economy, already so hard hit in its agricultural production, and it was only by deciding "to stand on their own two feet" that the Chinese people, so long inured to hardships, were able to make a striking recovery within two years.

But neither the question of nuclear weapons nor the withdrawal of the technical experts, though both issues were deeply resented by the Chinese, was the real cause of the conflict. Nor was it rival territorial claims, about which so much has been written and spoken. The basic issue was a broad disagreement as to the best way of serving the revolutionary cause, of opposing the global expansionism of U.S. imperialism, and consequently involved the prospects for peaceful coexistence, which for Khrushchev and indeed all his successors has been the keystone of Soviet foreign policy. This disagreement was restrained and kept muted for quite some time, but it really burst out into the open with the Twentieth Congress of the Soviet Communist Party, at which Khrushchev launched a violent attack against Stalin in his famous "secret report" that shook the entire world Communist progressive movement. Thereupon the great Soviet leader, admired for twenty-five years, was now presented, by the very ones who had previously extolled him, as a dictator madly lusting for power, a criminal, a despoiler of Lenin's heritage, a mediocre statesman, and a lamentable military strategist and leader.

The Chinese, who had no reason to be overfond of Stalin, since he had never shown any fervent belief in the success of their revolution, felt that the unleashing of this furious anti-Stalin campaign, to a chorus of approval from many foreign Communist parties that had hitherto been completely pro-Stalin, would create tremendous confusion in the ranks of the working class, weaken the Communist movement, and give all their enemies cause for encouragement and glee. Here we cannot enter into a detailed analysis of the charges against Stalin contained in Khrushchev's "secret report," but it is obvious that by its very nature it created a situation that emboldened the most aggressive forces in world imperialism and ushered in a period of revolutionary retreat which assumed various forms. Between the Twentieth and Twenty-second Congresses of the Soviet Communist Party, there were frequent communications between Moscow and Peking, while the Peking *People's Daily* and the Moscow *Pravda* hurled polemics at each other. The Sino-Soviet conflict then took a turn for the worse at the end of 1959, after Khrushchev, in a speech ostensibly attacking Trotsky, indirectly but unmistakably assailed the Chinese; and the Seventh Congress of the Hungarian Communist Party, at the beginning of December, 1959, was praised by the Soviet leader for having criticized the People's Communes and the "great leap forward" in a disdainful rather than comradely spirit.

The anti-Chinese offensive began to take shape. On April 16, 1960, on the occasion of the ninetieth anniversary of Lenin's birth, the

Chinese replied in their magazine *Red Flag*, in a lengthy article entitled "Long Live Leninism!" which is essential reading for a serious study of the Sino-Soviet conflict. Describing the strength of the Socialist camp, the article rejects the policy of seeking at all costs to come to an understanding with the United States. In the words of the article: "New Socialist countries have been born. The Socialist camp, with the Soviet Union at its head, occupies a quarter of the territory of the world's population. The colonial system of imperialism has begun and is continuing to disintegrate. Naturally, the struggle has its ups and downs, but taking everything into account, the Liberation movements are broadening. A great new era is opening up before us."

The section devoted to the main question of war and peace presents the Chinese position as it has been and as it will continue to be, if I may judge from my most recent visit there. Imperialism, say the Chinese, is as threatening and aggressive as ever, and the only way of limiting its thrusts is by mobilizing all the material and moral forces capable of winning if they learn how to attack. For the Socialist countries it is not a question of indulging in adventures, but of coldly examining all the possibilities of enemy aggression, including the most ferocious—so that, when the appropriate moment comes, they can properly reply and win. And that is the only way of preventing a third world war.

Meanwhile the controversy intensified in the decade following the appearance of the article in *Red Flag*, and China was widely portrayed as belligerent, adventurist, chauvinist, a disturber of the peace, and the like; but the premises contained in that article and, more important, the Chinese government's observance of them, remain unchanged. The Declaration of the eighty-one Communist parties that met in November, 1960, seemed to point to an improvement in Sino-Soviet relations. But new events disturbed these favorable portents, the most important of which was the Twenty-second Congress of the Soviet Communist Party, held in October, 1961. In Moscow at the time, I heard Khrushchev's main speech from the foreign press box and clearly noted the reaction of the Chinese delegation headed by Chou En-lai to the violent attacks directed at the Albanian Labor Party. In the corridors of the Congress, an independent observer commented to me that during the preceding year the Albanians had supported the positions of the Communist Party of China. Henceforth, at successive Communist Party congresses in various countries after 1962, it was clear that Albania had become the target of attacks that were really aimed at Peking. But as one of the most capable leaders of the Italian Communist Party stated in December, 1962: "A Party like ours does not have to say Albania when it means China."

In the exchange of letters between the Chinese and Soviet Communist parties during 1962–1963, there were moments when it seemed as if the conflict might be resolved. One such occasion was when the Central Committee of the Soviet Communist Party, on February 21, 1963, expressed the belief that "the difficulties through which the Communist movement is passing are temporary in nature and can be overcome," and the Central Committee of the Communist Party of China replied on March 9 in the most cordial terms, agreeing with those sentiments. But then, in July of the same year, the signing of the Moscow Treaty on nuclear testing widened the rift considerably. Moscow hailed the treaty as "a great victory for peace," whereas Peking denounced it as a "big fraud and a move designed to disorient the peoples of the entire world." Moreover, Moscow especially resented the fact that Peking recalled that two years previously, on September 9, 1961, Khrushchev had replied to a similar Anglo-American proposal to ban nuclear testing in the atmosphere by characterizing it as "a trick which the Soviet government could not and would never tolerate."

Then came the Cuban missile crisis of 1962; and the controversy boiled up again. "The Soviet leaders claim," the Chinese asserted, "that we are opposed to the withdrawal of the missiles and that we do not want the Soviet Union to try to avoid a nuclear war. Wrong! We never approved the sending of the missiles in the first place, hence we do not oppose their withdrawal. What we are firmly opposed to is that you should accept absurd and humiliating conditions imposed by U.S. imperialism." Numerous articles on the Chinese side could be cited that are severely critical of peaceful coexistence and warn of the danger of creating illusions about negotiations, "thus paralyzing, as Khrushchev does, the peoples' will to fight." Moscow replied with the "Suslov Report," in which Mikhail Suslov, the outstanding theoretician in the Soviet Communist Party, accused China of advocating revolution through war and defended the policy of peaceful coexistence as practiced by Moscow. Nonetheless, despite attacks and counterattacks, every now and then there appeared a ray of hope that the conflict would be resolved. On the occasion of Khrushchev's seventieth birthday, the Chinese Communist Party sent congratulations couched in these terms: "The differences that exist between us are only temporary. In the event of a world war our two parties, our two countries, and our two peoples would stand side by side against our common enemy. Let the imperialists and the reactionaries tremble at our unity!"

Two significant events then occurred scarcely hours apart: Khrushchev's fall from power and the explosion by China of its first atomic bomb. The Chinese leaders saw in Khrushchev's fall a chance to smooth over Sino-Soviet differences, and Premier Chou En-lai traveled to Moscow to this end. But neither side modified its basic position, and the rift continues to the time of this writing, with serious, unpredictable, and incalculable consequences for the march of socialism.

When an opportunity arose for me to visit one of China's military installations, I accepted with alacrity. My visit to the headquarters of the 5th Tank Company of the Chi Nan military command more than fulfilled my expectations, for if I had previously had any doubts concerning the democratic nature of the People's Army of Liberation, that day's visit totally erased them from my mind.

In a large, neatly kept soldiers' dormitory, seated around tables bunched together, we met with the officers and soldiers of the company together with the company cook, who, as we shall see, played a prominent part in our discussion and deserves a vivid full-length sketch on his own. We did not begin our questions until each soldier present identified himself by rank and serial number, thus enabling everyone to participate in the discussion without asking permission of his superior officer. First a tankman spoke at some length, stressing that political understanding had to be rated above all other attributes. Professional military ability and discipline were very important things, but they derived from a clear political line. "And a clear, correct line," he added, "means Mao's Thought."

All of those present were familiar with Mao's principal writings, and study of them was an important item in the daily routine of this tank company. One of Mao's most popular works in the armed forces is his "On Prolonged War," written in 1938, in which he deals with mistaken methods that provoke tensions between officers and soldiers and between soldiers and the people. To Mao, the fundamental question is the need for an attitude of respect toward the soldiers and the people, and from this attitude flows the appropriate policies and methods to be adopted toward the masses. Political work in the army is based on three main principles: first, unity between officers and soldiers; second, unity between the army and the people; and third, disintegration of the enemy forces.

An officer present entered into a detailed analysis of the question of "chaos," commenting as follows: "Abroad they claim that the Cultural Revolution has made China a prey to violence and chaos, and that we are sinking deeper and deeper into that chaos. Those who say that lack imagination to visualize what would have happened without the Cultural Revolution, and if 'the Number One' [i.e., Liu Shao-chi] had taken the country, as he had already begun to, along the road of revisionism and capitalism. For the masses in this country are profoundly revolutionary, as has been shown since the Cultural Revolution began, and they would not have put up with any turn to the Right. They would have fought as the Chinese people know how to fight, and then there really would have been violence and chaos. There would have been a new and second civil war."

There was a lull in the conversation around the table as we looked at the pictures hanging on the large wall. Painted by the men of the 5th Company, they helped convey to us the way in which the army viewed the problems of the Cultural Revolution and the outside world. Some of the murals consisted of a series of scenes relating to Vietnam and the Liberation movements in Asia, Africa, and Latin America. At the entrance to the room there was a double arch, on it a legend in two languages, Chinese and Spanish, greeting the present writer as "the veteran fighter for the Liberation of Spain." Numerous questions were put to me concerning the struggle inside Spain and the state of the workers' and students' movements. The soldiers were amazed, and rightly so, that for so long the main parties in the anti-Franco opposition had neglected the peasantry, potentially a significant revolutionary force in Spain inasmuch as that country is, like China, predominantly agricultural.

Another wrong attitude toward China, the soldiers asserted, is to view it as a nationalistic Big Power, concerned only with safeguarding its own tremendous future and basically indifferent to Liberation movements in other parts of the world. Indeed, they stressed, just the opposite is true. As a matter of fact, at the Peking Hotel I spent much time talking with Africans, Asians, and Latin Americans who personally attested to the proletarian internationalism they encountered in present-day China. Since this will be one of the fundamental elements on the world scene in the years immediately ahead, and is a factor of extraordinary importance for the future development of the left-wing parties in the world, it foredooms, in my opinion, any attempt to expel China from the Communist or Socialist—or whatever one chooses to call it—family of peoples.

A soldier then spoke of all the hundreds of millions of human beings in the world still living in an enslaved condition. "The decolonization that followed World War II," he pointed out, "still needs to be carried out in fact. For instance, I call the peoples of Latin America colonized because they are still economically in the hands of U.S. big capital. I think Chairman Mao points the way to their liberation." Then, opening a book of Mao's quotations, he read: " 'On what does our policy rely? We must rely on our own power, and that means we must strengthen ourselves by our own efforts.' " He read on: " 'We believe in relying on our own strength. We hope to obtain foreign aid, but we must not depend on it. We have faith in our own strength, in the creative power of our entire people.' " And the soldier concluded: "He's right to rely on the army. We soldiers get up every morning and shout: 'Long live Chairman Mao!' We are patriots and revolutionaries, but we are also internationalist fighters. The Spanish people can count on us. All the peoples of the world who fight against imperialism and revisionism can count on us. And we are friends of the Soviet people who produced the great Lenin."

An officer then dealt with the subject of a people's war: "The success of a people's war depends entirely on the soldiers' level of political consciousness—whether it be an ordinary private or the

commanding general of a division. What matters is the revolutioniza-
tion of the army. We proved it in our war against Japan and against
the Kuomintang counter-revolutionaries. At all times the Japanese
and the Kuomintang were superior to us in arms and men, yet
eventually we defeated them. Today the Vietnamese are proving this
as they face the powerful U.S. war machine. A revolutionary army
cannot be decisively defeated. Even if decimated, it regroups and
rises up again." Several other officers and men expanded on this
broad theme, and one soldier declared: "China has put an end to
nuclear blackmail. Even before we had the atomic bomb, we were
prepared to fight against any enemy who might attack us. In the
resistance war against Japan, the Chinese people fought without any
modern weapons. Now we have the atomic bomb and will produce
as many as we need to be a nuclear power. But without having the
bomb, and facing an enemy that has the most modern weapons and
all the bombs imaginable, the Vietnamese people have kept at bay
the U.S. army, technologically the most advanced army on earth."
An officer went on from there: "That's of tremendous revolutionary
importance. It should greatly encourage all revolutionary peoples.
Doesn't Chairman Mao say: 'Weapons are important, but the people
are the decisive factor.' This has freed the peoples of a sense of
helplessness. I'm sure you Spaniards have people in Spain who would
like to fight against Franco, but defeatist and revisionist leaders
discourage them by saying: 'What can we do against Franco's
powerful army backed by the Americans?' So have faith in the
people; develop the armed struggle and don't give the enemy a
breathing spell."

Now it was the company cook who spoke up. He told us that he
had been a good tankman but that one day he had the unlucky idea
of cooking a dish from his own province. The dish met with such
success in the company that he was named company cook. At first he
considered it a demotion, but then he recalled that Mao had written
about serving the people: one could serve the people whether in the
highest posts of the government and Party or in the seemingly
lowliest jobs. This applied to generals as well as cooks; and so he
quickly grew reconciled to his fate. When my wife expressed the
desire to taste the dish he had made, he answered: "Why don't you
stay and eat with us, and I'll make it." The whole room applauded

loudly. When he extended his invitation to us, the company cook did not have to consult anyone or ask anyone's permission. We heard some of the soldiers murmur: "The People's Liberation Army is not like any other army in the world," and we began to realize why.

Having visited People's Communes, military bases, and universities, we decided to see some factories. At Furnace No. 1 in Chi Nan, I got a preview of what China's industrial development would be like once the mass enthusiasm released during the big upheaval of the Cultural Revolution was fully brought to bear on every domain of the country's economy. We were received at the plant entrance by the "revolutionary rebels" in charge of the factory, two young male workers and a young female worker, representatives of the Committee that "had taken power and expelled the 'advocates of economism.'" For we must not forget, they insisted, that in a Socialist society there is still class struggle; indeed, the factory we were about to visit was proof of that. They stressed that the road taken by Furnace No. 1 was the one that all Chinese industry would follow in the future: "The road of confronting all difficulties with a revolutionary will to overcome them through the creative initiative of the masses. The masses can do it all." In support of their viewpoint they pointed to the impressive number of technical innovations introduced by the workers. "Previously, a few engineers and technicians with their titles and degrees refused to admit that the workers were capable of inventing anything they themselves had not thought of. Now we'll visit the workshops and you'll see for yourselves what the workers have done." They proceeded to show us a furnace with improvements suggested by a workers' team that made it superior in quality to one imported from Switzerland. "The Cultural Revolution," they continued, as we wandered about the factory, "has not affected work here unfavorably; just the opposite. It has doubled the will to improve, to work more and better so that one day revolutionary China will be on the same level as the most industrialized nations in the world. In the Third Five-Year Plan now under way, there will be a 60 per cent increase in production."

"And aside from factory production, are the workers improving their personal conditions?" we asked.

"The income each worker receives has doubled during the

change-over in this factory. The workers pay no direct taxes; 4 per cent of their wages is enough to pay for their rent and electricity; medical care and education of their children are free. But the study of Chairman Mao's works prevents them from beginning to think in a bourgeois way. His last directive to fight against selfishness has been enthusiastically received in this factory. It means a fight against dull routines, a fight against defeatism, a working class constantly progressing. Here the Cultural Revolution has triumphed 100 per cent. And forever."

That last phrase—"and forever"—is worth remembering. It set me to thinking about all the speculations outside China that once Mao Tse-tung disappears his successors will slow down the Revolution. The imprint of the Revolution that began in 1966 is so strong that much time will have to pass before it is effaced; indeed, it has been so profound that even now most people are unaware of its depth.

One of the areas in which the Cultural Revolution gave rise to the liveliest controversy, inside as well as outside China, was the field of literature and art. In Peking I found some persons "resuscitated" or actively functioning whom the foreign press had described as "liquidated": among them was Kuo Mo-jo, head of the Academy of Sciences and one of China's outstanding intellectuals with a world-wide reputation, whose alleged "purge" had been widely commented on in Western literary circles. I saw him at various official receptions and found that he was still head of the Academy and a member of the Parliament; in fact, he had just received the Vietnamese delegation that had come to celebrate the Chinese national holiday and he was a vigorous spokesman of his people in condemning the war in Vietnam. Despite what Western intellectuals may think, some of China's best writers have supported the Cultural Revolution, as evidenced by Han Suyin's recent books *China in the Year 2001* (1967) and *The Morning Deluge* (1972), in which the author of the novel *A Many-Splendored Thing* (1952) and the autobiographical *The Crippled Tree* (1965), *A Mortal Flower* (1966), and *Birdless Summer* (1968) offers a passionate defense of Mao Tse-tung's China. Her credibility as an interpreter is enhanced by the fact that, born in Peking of a Chinese father and a Belgian mother, she has never belonged to the Chinese Communist Party.

She travels constantly to and from China; and no one who has seen and heard her on American, French, or Swiss television will easily forget her vibrant and persuasive voice.

Han Suyin has analyzed the background as well as the future of the Cultural Revolution, presenting it not as a passing phase but as arising out of the very origins of the Chinese Revolution—from the period of "Red bases" in 1927 followed by the Long March in 1934, with Mao Tse-tung seeking constantly to transform the Chinese nation from a feudal state to a China based on atomic energy and remolded, Socialist-minded human beings. His goal has been the formation of the new human being who combines theory with practice, the revolutionary whose thought and behavior are completely committed to the cause of the Revolution.

Why did Mao Tse-tung succeed in the Cultural Revolution? For the same reason that he emerged victorious from all the inner-party struggles of the Chinese Communist Party and the Chinese revolutionary movement in general: because for more than forty years he has formulated and defended the "correct line." In the final analysis the reason for his success is that he identifies with the Chinese people in a way that is not elsewhere to be found in relations between those who govern and those who are governed. His strength lies in the masses, in his frequently reiterated appeals to "rely on the masses," to "base oneself on the masses," to merge with them and learn from them.

Mao's literary style, discerningly analyzed by Han Suyin, offers the key to the popularity of his writings, the reason that his *Little Red Book* has been read and committed to memory by hundreds of millions of people. It is a unique phenomenon and, as such, one that has baffled foreign observers who fail to realize that, as we have sought to establish, in China the "cult of personality" has been entirely different from its appearance elsewhere and has sprung up spontaneously from the masses. They have identified so closely with Mao's Thought that the "cult" will continue long after Mao himself has departed from the scene. All of Mao's writings and speeches, Han Suyin observes, have the ring of peasant realism; they are direct, concrete, focused on essentials, disregarding non-essentials. His similes and metaphors combine the spirit of peasant folk songs with the verses of the classical poets, and show how the latter derive from the former. The quality of his poetry is its universality, with an imaginative surge that is the mark of the creative individual. His way of thinking is practical, without opening any gap between word and deed, thought and action. Free from abstract theorizing, Mao believes that the function of philosophy is not to interpret the world but to change it. The Cultural Revolution is summed up right there. To change the world and to change human beings means concentrating on education, with a view to creating a new, revolutionary generation. Hence, the emphasis placed on the youth. In Mao's own words: "The world is yours as it is ours, but in the final analysis the world is yours. You young people, full of vigor and vitality, are in the prime of life, like the sun in the sky at eight or nine in the morning. All our hope reposes in you."

To prepare the Red Guards—the young revolutionary workers and peasants who tomorrow will take over—meant eliminating everything that could confuse them. This was as true of the myth of the Party's infallibility as of the myth of beauty as it had been idealized on stage and screen, with emperors portrayed as heroes and concubines or court ladies of past eras held up for admiration to a people summoned to build, create, and fight. Diatribes against that kind of idealized art appeared frequently on the wall posters of the Cultural Revolution.

For my own part, I had many talks with young stage and film directors, actors and actresses, concerning the effects of the Cultural Revolution on the arts, especially in the theater, cinema, and ballet. A day or so before, I had seen *Red Detachment of Women*, a revolutionary ballet in three acts and six scenes created and performed by the Ballet Company of Workers, Peasants, and Soldiers under the personal direction of Chiang Ching, Mao's wife. Its theme reflects the orientation of the new revolutionary art of the theater growing out of the Cultural Revolution—an art inspired by the life of the masses, with the people as hero. The first scene takes its theme from a quotation by Mao: "At bottom, all the truths of Marxism can be summed up in a single sentence: 'Rebellion is justified.'" The story runs as follows: Wu Ching-hua, daughter of poor peasants, has been shut up in the prison of a despotic landlord, Nan Pa-tien, Lord of the South. Since she has refused to become his slave, Liu Szu, Nan Pa-tien's lackey, is ordered to sell her. She manages to escape from her prison and meets Hung Chang-ching, an officer of the Red Army, who, hearing of her misfortune, shows her the road to a place where she can enlist. Arriving at the Red base camp, she finds everyone in the midst of celebrating the founding of the "Red Detachment of Women." She is warmly received by the soldiers and peasants, who tell her that the only way to conquer the three mountains that weigh down upon the Chinese people—imperialism, feudalism, and bureaucratic capitalism—is to take arms in her hands and follow the Communist Party in its making of the Revolution. Pretending to be a rich Chinese overseas merchant who has just returned from abroad to visit his relatives, Hung Chang-ching, the Red Army officer, penetrates the inner sanctum where the tyrannical Nan Pa-tien is celebrating his birthday. That night Wu Ching-hua, the escaped slave, also enters the house. When she sees the landlord all her hatred wells up again; she fires her gun, but the shot only wounds him. Meanwhile, her premature action causes the Red Army officer's plan to miscarry. Red Army soldiers enter the house, but Nan Pa-tien manages to escape through a tunnel. The soldiers open the grain storehouses and distribute food to the poor peasants—it is one of the gayest scenes in the ballet. The young Wu Ching-hua—and how marvelously the ballerina dances her part!—learns from the Party that making the Revolution is not a matter of personal revenge, that it can only be made by freeing all the working people of the world and eliminating all the reactionaries. In the final scenes the People's War triumphs, and the liberated area increases constantly. Wu Ching-hua, now a Party member and model fighter in the Red Detachment of Women, takes over the post of her rescuer, who has died heroically. The finale was a dazzling display of ballet steps, waving flags, light, color, and movement, bringing the entire audience to its feet with stormy applause.

We also saw *The Red Lantern*, a Peking revolutionary opera, the theme of which is the anti-Japanese war of resistance as it affects three generations of railroad workers who fight against the invaders. Li Tieh-mei, interpreted by a well-known young actress who was a Red Guard, inherits the red lantern and swears to be a worthy successor of her revolutionary forebears. Another Peking work we saw was *Shachiapang*, dealing with eighteen wounded soldiers of the

New Fourth Army who distinguish themselves by feats of heroism. Others included *The Raid Against the White Tiger Regiment* and *The Capture of the Bandits' Fortress*, rich in intrigue and humor; and the jewel of the new revolutionary theater, *The Young Woman with White Hair*, a ballet describing the fight of the Chinese peasants under Communist leadership against the landlords.

As a prelude to our conversation in the film studio in which we had gathered, we were shown a movie, *The City of Eternal Light*, which, after the screening, one of the film workers described as "eternal darkness." This was one of the productions that had been denounced by Chiang Ching and her associates in their campaign for clarity in art and literature. The film we saw dealt with the conversion to socialism of a well-known former capitalist in Shanghai, Kuo Lin-shan. By chance I had visited one of his large estates on a previous trip to China and had talked with his servants, who were far more skeptical about his alleged generosity than the film was. Kuo's house was sumptuous, furnished with beautifully colored rugs made in Tientsin that were prize articles of export; the women in Kuo's family were clad in precious silks and wore resplendent jade and coral necklaces. To the young film-makers the setting was virtually an act of provocation. As one of them told us: "Its production was not an accident, no mere whim of an esthete fascinated by brilliant and sensual settings. It was not a criticism but a glorification of the ideas of 'Number One' [Liu Shao-chi], who, contrary to Chairman Mao, claims that the class struggle is no longer a problem. When it was produced in 1957, it immediately provoked a series of adverse criticisms from the revolutionary elements in the film studios. On the other hand, the Vice-Minister of Culture, Shia Ye, a supporter of 'Number One,' defended it. Even during its filming," the young film-maker went on, "there were serious incidents, and for a while the shooting had to be suspended because of objections from the workers. Then the producers and the film director, who was a former Kuomintang general, made certain revisions; but they did not change the essential point, which runs counter to Mao's theory about class struggle, even in a Socialist society. You know what Mao says: 'Classes struggle; some classes emerge victorious, others are eliminated. That is the history of civilization for the past thousands of years. In a class society every person exists as a member of a definite class, and all ideas—without exception—bear their class stamp.' And so the film was finally finished."

But it was another motion picture, *The Intimate History of the Ching Court*, that really unleashed the storm. "Since it has been shown throughout the country," Mao Tse-tung wrote in a letter, "the film *Intimate History of the Ching Court* has not yet been criticized and repudiated; in fact, it has been called patriotic, although in reality it is a film that betrays our country." The controversy provoked by the publication of Mao's letter pitted Chiang Ching, his wife and at that time member of a committee in charge of cinema work, against high officials from the Propaganda Department of the Central Committee of the Party. The chief spokesman for the latter group was Ju, then assistant head of the Department, who, supported by the most highly placed officials, defended "the progressive and patriotic character of the film" and refused to permit public discussion of the affair. *The Intimate History* deals with an ostensibly historical subject, the Reform movement of 1898 and the struggles of the anti-Manchu movement during the last years of the Ching dynasty against the Dowager Empress Tzu Hsi, as violent in her anti-revolutionary sentiments as in her love bouts. In front of the Summer Palace she had built, there was a lake; and on my first visit to China I had heard the tale of the young warriors specially picked by the ruler for a night's pleasure and then hurled into the lake to silence them forever. Chiang Ching, in her critique of the film, accused it of portraying the Chinese as panic-stricken before the imperialist aggression of the so-called "allied forces of eight Powers" —to wit, Great Britain, the United States, Germany, France, Italy, Russia, Japan, and Austria-Hungary. Instead of showing any genuinely patriotic spirit of militancy against imperialism, it depicted prostration before the foreigners' "irresistible" force. Su Ching-cheng, a high-ranking Mandarin, breaks down and weeps when he sees the imperialists advance, failing to display even a shadow of resistance.

The precursors of the Cultural Revolution were also indignant at the glorification of Chen Fei, the Emperor Kuang Hsu's concubine and the agent of imperialism in the film, who in order "patriotically" to save a corrupt and decadent dynasty, exclaims as she welcomes the aggressors: "I am sure that the foreign powers will not harm Your Majesty, but on the contrary will help you to strengthen the throne." One of the charges against Liu Shao-chi was that he had concealed the fact that such a film was being made on the eve of China's Liberation and had lent his authority to its being subsequently exhibited. And he did this despite its wrong interpretation of the Yigetnan movement—an important movement that attested to the revolutionary spirit of the Chinese people, with eight hundred secret meeting places in the city of Peking alone.

The attack against reactionary cinema was extended to all the performing arts, revolutionizing the Peking Opera and the Ballet. This was accomplished, not by harming the techniques of operas that enjoyed widespread popularity because of the charm of their music and dancing, but simply by changing their content and characters. Instead of romantic episodes there were themes of struggle; instead of emperors and Court beauties there were workers and peasants, singers and dancers proudly raising their Red Guard armbands across the entire stage, and transforming every simulated attack on imperialism into a dazzling kaleidoscope of movement and color.

At the Yenan "literary forum," in 1942, Mao Tse-tung had posed the central question: art and literature for whom? For Marxists, particularly for Lenin, this question had long since found an answer. As early as 1905 Lenin had insisted that literature and art "must serve the millions and tens of millions of working people." Obviously there was another kind of literature for the exploiters: in China this was the art and literature of the feudal era. In Yenan, Mao praised Lu Hsun, whose essays and novels enjoyed renewed and even greater popularity during the Cultural Revolution because of his keen critique of the advocates of "art for art's sake."

One of the members of the Revolutionary Committee in the film studio we visited summed up his thinking as follows: "We feel that the ideas expressed by Chairman Mao in Yenan twenty-five years ago are still valid and are our guide. In the years ahead they will enable us to produce stage and screen works that are not only more useful for the revolutionary education of the masses but superior in form and content to what was seen on the Chinese screen before the

Cultural Revolution. I do not recall ever seeing the entire personnel of the Peking Opera and the film studios work with the enthusiasm they have today."

On my several trips to China, Shanghai was one of the cities I eagerly looked forward to visiting, for it was there more than anywhere else that I saw evidence of the past behavior of the imperialist powers toward a China humiliated and disarmed by the last dynasty that governed it, the Manchus. There I could see—in 1957, only eight years after Liberation—the giant leap forward to a better life for the masses, in contrast to the time when children ten to twelve years old, if they were not killed off in early infancy because there was no food for them, worked in Japanese or British textile factories under conditions of unspeakable exploitation. There too, speaking with the authorities and some of the older residents of Shanghai, I learned about the crime gangs, the profitable kidnappings for ransom, the extremes of luxury and misery, and the many human vices that attracted to the city all those in search of new sensations and the most exotic perversions, the pick of the international riffraff—themes dealt with in countless pornographic novels and films with an Oriental flavor. But there also I found the whole record of the heroic years of struggle for a New China: the first decisive revolutionary steps by Mao Tse-tung and Chou En-lai; and before them, the untiring democratic efforts of Dr. Sun Yat-sen, highly respected by the Chinese Communists—although not one of them—even during the upheaval of the Cultural Revolution.

Arriving at the Shanghai airport, we were greeted by lovely-looking Chinese youngsters, smiling and cheering; and I remembered photographs of the adolescent boys and girls imprisoned twelve and fourteen hours a day in the old Shanghai in the foreign-owned factories and workshops. Landing at Shanghai, we made our first contact with the Cultural Revolution; then a year later, on our departure from China, we were given an enthusiastic send-off by a dozen Red Guards, with flags and musical instruments, impressing on us that we should never forget we were leaving behind "a youth determined to carry high the banner of revolutionary socialism" whatever course the rest of the world might take.

But victory had been won only after a very real and very hard fight, as we learned in conversations with the Shanghai dockworkers who had taken so active a part in it. This proved to be one of the most interesting discussions we had during our stay: it concerned the various episodes of the Cultural Revolution and its future fate. Our dockworker informants did not seek in the least to hide the seriousness of what had occurred during "the January storm." The port of Shanghai, vital center of China's foreign trade, had been picked by those opposed to the policies of Mao and the Red Guards to deal a mortal blow to the Cultural Revolution. Tens of thousands of "ill-informed workers, influenced by the Chinese Khrushchev," were brought to Shanghai in trucks, and there were violent, bloody clashes in the city, especially in the harbor district. When we visited this section, the partisans of Mao had won all along the line; they received us and explained in some detail the battle they had waged against a tenacious opposition. The port of Shanghai had returned to normal again, except that now work was proceeding with greater enthusiasm than ever, while railway traffic was beginning to recover from the chaos it had suffered during the months in which the Red Guards had seized trains by force so as to be able to travel from one end of China to the other without paying any fare, as they spread the gospel of Chairman Mao's Thought. They did this not in a spirit of juvenile adventurism or rootlessness but as part of an ideological crusade. At the same time, they had done everything possible to prevent the rolling stock from damage. In any case, it was astonishing that the trains on the most heavily traveled lines were still running. This was so primarily because Premier Chou En-lai had intervened and had seen to it that the essential services functioned; he had also re-established unity among the various factions of the railway work force. It was a veritable "battle of the rails" that Chou had won, in the face of many obstacles and provocations. On November 25, 1967, Chou En-lai in a speech to the railway workers spoke of the government's "uneasiness" at the state of the railroads, so vital a factor in the country's industrial and economic development. In the months thereafter the victory was consolidated by the formation of a "grand alliance of the revolutionary workers of the railway services" on a national scale. And now that unity had been restored among the railwaymen, a better distribution of commodities would result, to the benefit of all.

Little by little things returned to normal in the way anticipated by Mao when he originally launched the idea of the grand revolutionary alliance and the triple alliance. Along with grave incidents, there were also all kinds of odd and amusing anecdotes connected with the struggle; and the dockworkers told us a few of these stories. Some of the foreign sea captains, for example, tried to take advantage of the turbulence in China to reveal their deep-seated arrogance and hostility. One British sea captain, entering port flying the Chinese flag upside down, waxed sarcastic when he saw groups of longshoremen reading Mao's *Little Red Book* in their rest periods between loading and unloading cargo. The Briton in question was called aside by the longshoremen and reminded that Shanghai was no longer the city of yore when British warships imposed their commands by cannon fire and protected the opium trade; and that until the Chinese flag was flown right side up and the captain personally apologized to the workers, not a single sack would be unloaded from his ship. The dispute went on for several days, but ended with the British captain according full satisfaction to the dockworkers; and when the British ship began its return voyage home, there were mutual toasts for the friendship of the two peoples and the crew received several copies of Chairman Mao's *Little Red Book* in English translation.

At the piers I saw boats from many nations—Dutch, British, French, Japanese—being loaded; and the warehouses had been greatly enlarged since my previous visit—all signs of China's abiding faith in the future of its foreign trade.

Undoubtedly, however, the most complete version of what happened during the "January storm" was the one I received from my fellow journalists of Shanghai, with whom I held many hours of discussion. Here let me try to summarize our conversations. The fight to re-establish the correct revolutionary line at the newspaper *Wen Hwei* (meaning "flower of literature and art") was of overriding importance because it went far beyond the editorial offices of the publication itself and influenced the whole struggle in Shanghai. The two main centers of resistance to the Cultural Revolution—though there were many others of lesser significance—were Wuhan, where an army general, annoyed by the presence of Red Guards, assailed

Mao and created a serious crisis, and Shanghai, where the supporters of "China's Khrushchev" mobilized all their forces to attempt to gain control of the city.

The critical moment at *Wen Hwei* (founded in 1938) came on January 3, 1967, when members of the editorial staff, backed by the Shanghai authorities, published a series of reportages and articles assailing the Party, socialism, and Chairman Mao's Thought. "There-fore, we revolutionary journalists found it necessary to confront this negative attitude and unmask those who falsely hoisted the red flag. We were aided by the fact that Chairman Mao himself had criticized the stand taken by our publication during the past few months. As a matter of fact, during 1961–1962, the publication's policy had been openly counter-revolutionary although veiled at times in revolution-ary language. A new editor-in-chief, expressly sent in by 'China's Khrushchev,' had taken charge of this 'two-faced operation.' On November 10, 1965, *Wen Hwei* carried an article by Chairman Mao that encouraged his supporters to continue to fight against the position of our editor-in-chief and his accomplices." In view of the appearance of this article months before the Cultural Revolution, it is clear that the struggle was an old one; and here let me quote one of the journalists on the staff of *Wen Hwei*: "You can see that the Cultural Revolution was not a whim of Mao's, but a healthy and indispensable revolutionary counteraction."

In Shanghai itself the fight intensified: on one side Mao's supporters, on the other the Mayor of Shanghai, Dzao Di-chiu, and the Party Secretary Cheng Pe-shen, "agents" of Liu Shao-chi in Shanghai. Mao's article was published in *Wen Hwei* at a time when he happened to be in Shanghai, and that was one of the reasons it appeared; but when he left the city, Liu's supporters returned to the attack. Then, in January, 1967, the moment of crisis came and Mao's supporters had to get control of the newspaper. But this was no easy matter, our Chinese colleagues assured us, because Liu's people had called them "the counter-revolutionaries." So they had had only one recourse: go to the masses. They called a meeting of ten thousand persons, including printers, the personnel of other publications, and all workers in the graphic-arts field, to explain the situation. At that crucial moment only eight editors were left on the paper to carry on the fight; but they all swore to continue, no matter what the outcome. In the second half of December, these eight revolutionary editors held meetings with their friends on seven nights in succession—meetings that lasted from seven in the evening until two in the morning, discussing how to take power, first on the newspaper and then in all Shanghai. "On the night of January 3, we went into action. It was the first case of taking power in the city. On January 4, we brought out a new publication that carried the following declaration: 'Mao Tse-tung's Thought is our weapon. We consider the spreading and defense of that Thought the highest task of our paper.' It was like a breath of fresh air. That same January 4 we received a message from the masses of Shanghai which read: 'Teach us how to act, remember what Chairman Mao said: "Keep up your courage, dare to struggle, defy difficulties, and advance in waves." ' And that's how the revolutionary masses advanced in the January storm. Around that slogan we organized interviews and reportages; we created a popular base to support our fight against economism."

My Shanghai journalist acquaintances acknowledged that it had been a hard struggle, involving extremely violent clashes and encounters, "but we never forgot that our goal was not to eliminate the enemy physically but to win them over to the correct line. That's how we broadened our campaign and won over many previous dissenters." Next we discussed the current situation at the paper; previously, its columns had been open solely to intellectuals and technocrats; now it was a genuine mass publication: "At present, peasants, workers, soldiers write for it. The spirit of true China has entered it. We've added Red Guards to our editorial staff. One worker, when his day's work is done, regularly comes to our office to help us. And in the midst of our congratulatory messages we received a note from Chairman Mao warning the new publication to avoid the dangers of 'becoming conceited or over-hasty.' "

Not only has the newspaper's circulation increased, my informant continued; its contents have become more interesting, "because there is a great creative capacity in the masses, and you should see how well simple people can express themselves." And that was how we made the acquaintance of the illiterate woman of Shanghai, with whom I spent an entire morning. She was a peasant woman from the interior who could neither read nor write but who had become a highly effective propagandist for Mao's Thought, excerpts of which she had someone read to her and which she in turn commented on in her drawings. Some of these sketches appeared in the Peking *People's Daily*, and my wife and I were given copies of them. As we proceeded from her earliest to her more recent sketches, we were struck by the gradual improvement in drawing and content. But one had to hear her own explanation of them to appreciate the success she had with a growing audience, from Shanghai and the nearby provinces, that came to listen to her. Her conception of Chairman Mao's Thought was in direct relation to what he had done for the Chinese people. She began with a graphic evocation of her life before Liberation. We had heard numerous similar stories in the People's Communes, but this account from the illiterate Shanghai woman struck us with unusual force because, as the woman herself said, to illustrate Chairman Mao's Thought in sketches she had "to have her ideas in good order" before putting them on the large blackboard perched on the raised platform from which she was talking. The general theme of her illustrated lectures was: "What country people owe Chairman Mao."

"Just as everything that helped me see clearly came through my eyes and made me draw," she said, "so my drawings enter into the masses who come to hear me. I can see that from the questions they ask me. If I have to show how the People's Commune has solved the farm question, I draw the life of the peasants before Liberation, then under the first cooperatives, under the higher-type cooperatives, and today in the People's Communes. I watch my audience and discover the points I have to emphasize, and then I make new sketches." She then told of her interview with Chairman Mao, who had invited her to visit him in Peking. "He treated us all as equals. I was so impressed my hands were shaking, and I spilled some tea from my cup on his jacket. He smiled and went on talking. They put me up in a room near his; and before I went to bed Chou En-lai came in to see whether I was all right and if the mattress was comfortable." (I thought of the "Kang" bed, hard as cement, on which my wife Luisa and I slept in the People's Commune of Shashiyu.)

The illiterate woman of Shanghai helped me to gain an insight into the future of the Cultural Revolution. The mistake many foreigners make—I cannot insist too often on this—when they try to assess the importance of the Cultural Revolution, is to see it exclusively as a factional fight—Mao Tse-tung versus Liu Shao-chi—and fail to realize that essentially it brought the Chinese masses into the Revolution in an active, not a manipulated, way, as participants committed—*engagés,* to use the French term—to the fight to keep China in a revolution that would not adjust to the "inevitable demands of bourgeoisification" as the years elapsed. In some ways the Cultural Revolution in 1966–1970 did stand out in distinct contrast to the years immediately preceding it. But its revolutionary impact on the Chinese earth has been too profound for me to imagine that at some future date a retreat from socialism as conceived by Mao Tse-tung will set in.

As if to bear this out, our visit to the Red Guards Exhibition in Peking proved to be one of the highlights of our stay. We spent several days at this exhibition, trudging dozens of kilometers as we went through the various pavilions accompanied by enthusiastic young Red Guards. Its full title is: "Exhibition of the Revolutionary Rebellion of the Red Guards," with emphasis on the words "Revolutionary Rebellion," reflecting the will of the Chinese youth to keep the Revolution clean and incorruptible and a guide to the rest of the peoples of the world. This reference to "the peoples of the world" was constantly on the Red Guards' lips.

In the very first pavilion, where the initial theme was "The Four Old Ones and the Four New Ones," numerous pictures and documents depicted "China's Khrushchev" as attempting, in our guide's words, "by every means to replace the dictatorship of the proletariat with a return to the bourgeoisie." The salient dates were illustrated by posters and photographs, the latter extremely interesting in their profusion of detail, giving the impression of a motion picture of the Chinese youth in action.

The dates stand out: *May 16, 1966.* A directive from the Central Committee of the Communist Party of China to all regional bureaus, provincial, municipal, and autonomous-region committees of the Party, to all committees and departments of the Central Committee, as well as to all leaders in state institutions, mass organizations, and the political department of the People's Liberation Army. The communication warns that bourgeois representatives have infiltrated the Party, the government, the army, and various cultural fields; they are counter-revolutionary revisionists bidding for power who will turn the proletarian dictatorship into a bourgeois dictatorship if they are allowed to do so: "Some of these persons have been exposed, but others have not. Still others, we are confident, will recognize their mistakes and continue the Party line. . . . Party committees at all levels must give full attention to this."

May 29, 1966. Appearance of the first Red Guards at the high school affiliated with Tsinhua University. A letter of warm support to them from Mao Tse-tung. The legend noting this event runs: "Angry outcries increase. The headquarters of the counter-revolution is located."

June 8, 1966. A serious clash at Peking University, pitting students and teachers who support Mao against partisans of "Number One," Liu Shao-chi, who has sent in one of his famous "Work Brigades" in order to "re-establish order"; but Liu's group is crushed. Liu characterizes the situation at the university as "counter-revolutionary chaos"; Mao calls it "magnificent."

I saw that incident dramatized by one of the new theater groups, and lovely young Red Guards celebrated victory in a spirited finale of dancing in which the audience wildly cheered every victory of the masses and sang, as the play ended, the popular "Steering Depends on the Helmsman." In one scene a portion of the "Work Brigade" realizes its mistakes and goes over to the side of those fighting for the Cultural Revolution; and the stormy applause that greeted this scene seemed to confirm the correctness of the tactics of winning over the enemy—not destroying and killing them. As our guide explained, the fact that there was violence and that those guilty of assassination were executed did not vitiate the basic principle.

August 5, 1966. Mao writes his historic wall poster—*dazibao*—calling on the masses who are still on the margin of the struggle to "bombard the General Headquarters"; he reveals to them the existence of "two lines" and urges them to join one or the other group. Meanwhile, as the General Headquarters is "identified," counteractions multiply. Liu Shao-chi's wife, whose beauty and elegance provide a field day for the popular caricaturists, visits the various centers of higher education in order to defend her husband's line. A mural at the exhibition shows "Number One's" wife engaged in her "monstrous activity," attacking the student Kue Ta Fu, a Red

Guard hero and subsequently a member of the Peking Revolutionary Committee. One photograph depicts revolutionary students locked up in a hall after the "Work Brigade" has invaded the university; they are wounding each other and writing with one another's blood on the walls: "We shall fight until death for Chairman Mao's correct line."

August 18, 1966. The order goes out to destroy the "Four Old Ones" and promote the "Four New Ones." The Red Guards respond by covering the walls of the city with posters denouncing the "Four Old Ones." "In a short while," the young Red Guard guide told us, "the Four Old Ones were finished, because from the beginning we had the masses on our side: peasants, workers, and soldiers. Together, we crushed all the elements in the Party who followed the capitalist path." That same August 18 was a great day for the Red Guards, for Mao Tse-tung greeted a million of them gathered on Peking's Tien An Men Square.

"China's Khrushchev" and his wife were pictured at the exhibition in a series of caricatures similar to those we saw in the streets of Peking. " 'Number One's' father," commented another Red Guard who accompanied us, "came from a very bourgeois family and his wife was like a high-society lady in her tastes and preferences. You can see that from the way she behaved during the official visit to Indonesia." Another photograph showed "Number One" embracing Nikita Khrushchev.

The exhibition was replete with examples of the campaign against the "Four Old Ones." One poster portrayed Confucius as the "ancestor of all the reactionaries"; and another, "Number One" as an apologist for Confucius. There were letters written by Red Guards which stated that the true works of art should be protected but insisted that they should not be utilized "for glorification of feudalism." The same held true for Confucius. "Let historians of Chinese civilization allot him the role he deserves in the realm of ideas. But let no one use any of the Four Old Ones against the Four New Ones in the political domain, or use Confucius' reactionary thinking against Mao Tse-tung's revolutionary Thought."

A long horizontal showcase placed in the center of one of the halls was crowded with artistic treasures saved by the Red Guards during the most turbulent days in the summer of 1966. We gazed admiringly at this collection of inestimable worth, and paused for an unusually long time at one piece of marvelously carved jade that had escaped the greediness of foreign collectors. The showcase also displayed quantities of gems, pearls, turquoises, corals, and all the other precious stones found in China as well as centuries-old books and pictures. Besides the artistic treasures there were objects attesting to the cunning of the reactionaries who hoped for the return of "better times." Uncovered in their homes and now on public display were shares in British companies dating to before Liberation, Belgian railway bonds, and many similar objects that had been concealed in expectation of the "day when Chiang Kai-shek would return." "They can keep waiting," one of our young Guards remarked with a smile. Property deeds had been found in the unlikeliest places, the preferred hiding place being chairs with false bottoms. In other houses there were secret lists of those who were to be executed when the "Lord of Formosa" returned in triumph, and a large quantity of weapons—"in order to assassinate the leaders of our country," the legend ran.

Here was some of the evidence of the scope and depth of the opposition to Mao and the violence of the struggle between "the two lines" of Mao Tse-tung and Liu Shao-chi. Even some of the "pro-Chinese" groups abroad, above all in Western Europe, thought that Liu would win out over Mao; but Mao's victory, consolidated in the course of 1968, did much to correct widespread mistakes in the evaluation of the Cultural Revolution.

A curious sidelight was the way in which the exhibition noted the changes in the names of the Peking streets from the start of the Cultural Revolution to the present. The change that created the most stir involved the street on which the Soviet Embassy was located— an embassy large enough to house a staff of over a thousand persons at its peak but now reduced to about two hundred. Originally the street was named "The Tail of the Coat"; then, to satisfy their Soviet allies, the name was changed to "Full Pride"; but now, under the Cultural Revolution, it was called "Avenue of Anti-Revisionism." Moreover, many poems were on display at the exhibition, proof of the latent literary ability of peasants, workers, and soldiers. A few stanzas of several poems were translated for us as well as a few paragraphs from a recent novel written by an ordinary soldier that was enjoying widespread popularity. To a foreign observer, whether well or ill disposed toward China, all this may seem naïve or childish; but in the reality of present-day China all these things are seen in quite a different light.

Our visit to the Red Guards Exhibition, which lasted several days, was occasionally interrupted by intervals of tea drinking as we sat around a large table and continued our animated conversation with our Red Guard guides. Occasionally other companions of theirs came up and joined us; and so we had the advantage of direct contact with representatives of Chinese youth, who smiled contagiously but were also deeply serious in their passion about the problems of socialism. Nothing is a substitute for these firsthand personal experiences—not even the most thoroughgoing or profound volumes I have read that are part of the vast existing literature on the Chinese Revolution.

I early came to the conclusion that the best contribution I could make to a correct understanding of the Chinese Revolution was, if possible, to let the Chinese speak for themselves, and to reproduce faithfully what they said to me. So I held conversations with peasants, workers, soldiers, Red Guards, students, professionals, as well as old Chinese friends of former years; and I note these conversations as documentary material for future historians as well as for the insights they have given me at the present time. One series of colloquies stands out: it was with a group of military-political experts, including Sun Hun-wen, who personally participated in China's revolutionary wars. For four entire afternoons I listened to a group of these military-political experts talk, taking down enough notes to fill a volume. Here let me sum up the essence of what they said.

Liberation of oppressed peoples is impossible without armed struggle. "In a class society, revolutions and revolutionary wars are inevitable; without them it is impossible to achieve leaps in social development and to overthrow the reactionary ruling classes so that the people can win power" (Mao Tse-tung). The exploiting reactionary class will never willingly give up its positions; so the people have to resort to violence to achieve liberation.

One must rely on the masses. Again a quotation from Mao: "What is the true wall of iron? The masses, the millions upon millions of human beings who support the Revolution with total sincerity. That is the true wall of iron which no force can break. The counter-revolution will not succeed in dividing us; on the contrary, we shall destroy it. Uniting millions of human beings around the revolutionary government, and developing our revolutionary war, we shall crush every counter-revolution and take power throughout all of China." One of our interlocutors interjected that what was valid for China is valid for other countries; hence for Spain too.

The revolutionary forces are like a tree that grows only from deep roots. Limited activities, distributing underground literature, sabotage, are not enough. Armed struggle is the only way. To go forward victoriously, the masses must be united—above all, the peasants.

To take power is the main objective; and then to consolidate it. It is not easy to take power, nor is it easy to consolidate it. The way in which the Cultural Revolution was conducted corresponds to the universal law on the seizure and consolidation of power as expressed by Chairman Mao—a law that is the essence of Marxism-Leninism. It involves the destruction of the old state apparatus and is a question of revolution, not reform.

"One has to pay the price for armed struggle." This question arose more than once in our discussion with the military-political experts. The philosophy of "survival," by which one must above all "prevent loss of life" and "prevent the human race from disappearing," must be subjected to a rigorous, dispassionate analysis. Temporary sufferings will be later compensated for when the people enjoy a life worth living. Either one wants liberation or does not want it—the choice has to be made.

All preparatory work in the pre-revolutionary stage must be done with a view to armed struggle. Here were passed in review a series of heroic exploits during the 1920's and 1930's in China: actions by the Shanghai students, strikes by workers in key cities. But all of these important actions were taken without the help of the peasants; hence the revolutionary movements were isolated and defeated.

After the failure of the first revolutionary war, Mao Tse-tung drew the necessary conclusions. And the experts stressed that Mao always saw clearly the primacy of the peasant question: "Our Party, until it finally achieved the correct line based on Chairman Mao's viewpoint, went through a difficult period of apprenticeship. But the success of the 'revolts of the autumn harvests' brought theory in line with practice, and thereafter the road was clearly indicated." In the final analysis this means giving the countryside precedence over the city, surrounding the city from the liberated countryside. But one must begin with the countryside, without of course neglecting political work in the city.

At this point I objected: "But in the October Revolution of 1917, Lenin led the struggle from the city."

"No doubt, but the circumstances of the Russian Revolution are quite special. When the October Revolution broke out, the Russian bourgeoisie was very weak, and the Czarist army, routed, was in full disintegration. On the other hand, the capitalist countries hostile to the Russian Revolution were too much absorbed in their own war to fight against it, and so they could not intervene from the moment the Revolution began. Intervention occurred after the Russian Revolution was victorious. That's why," Sun Hun-wen repeated, "Russia is a special case."

So our discussion reverted to China's experience. On October 23, 1927, the peasant forces sent by Mao reached Sinkiang mountain. Their retreat had been forced by the failure of the first revolutionary war, but at the same time it was an offensive: they attacked the enemy's weak side and ushered in a new stage and a new method of struggle: "establishing a rural base," and proceeding later from that base to attack the cities. "This was a very important contribution to Marxism-Leninism by Mao Tse-tung."

Then there followed discussion of the thesis that armed conflict must begin in the countryside, from which I excerpt here only the main points: In the city the struggle is harder because there the enemy is in control. The city is the political center, the place where the old apparatus of the counter-revolutionary state is in the most favorable position to counterattack. To begin the fight in the city, above all in a predominantly agrarian country, means to neglect the revolutionary element par excellence, the peasantry; it means facilitating the enemy's repressive operations, because in the city the enemy's concentrated actions of repression can be carried out more quickly than in the countryside. Thus, in rural areas, unlike urban ones, one can find places from which to launch offensives that prevent one's forces from being isolated and defeated. Revolutionary action acquires mobility, a capacity for initiative, a freedom to choose the moment to attack and to retreat that is denied one in the city.

This is not a revolutionary romanticizing of the peasant; it is the correct revolutionary military strategy. Enemy tanks find it difficult to operate in the countryside, but guerrillas have their two feet on which they can advance and, if necessary, withdraw. Hence one of the preconditions for success in a prolonged war is to avoid engaging the enemy in places where one is weaker. Establishing the struggle in the countryside means initially strengthening the revolutionary forces; moreover, it means attracting the working-class forces to their side because the latter know that when they move into action they can count on solid support from the countryside. Thus the worker-peasant front becomes an operative reality. Then and only then can the armed struggle be unleashed without the enemy's being in a position to easily end it; and the longer it continues, the greater are its possibilities for spreading and for resulting in victories.

But an organization—a party—is essential. Otherwise such activities, however heroic, remain disorganized and so prove sooner or later to be sterile.

We then turned to a consideration of the Democratic Revolution (the phase that corresponds, for example, to the present state of affairs in Spain). The Democratic Revolution is by no means the Socialist Revolution and has limited aims; but even so, the bourgeoisie is inadequate for assuring its victory. The bourgeoisie is incapable of making the Revolution; hence the United Front must be placed under the leadership of the working class, with close worker-peasant unity as the basis for a revolutionary policy of the masses. This unity must be intensified under a system of democratic centralism, in which one must avoid the tendency of destroying democracy but must not fall into the error of "ultra-democracy." Without political theory no victory is possible; but a political theory that is not applied is useless.

In the period of the Democratic Revolution one must unite with all those who want to make the Revolution. But this process of unification can succeed only if it has at its disposal a force of its own resolved to fight until final victory; a force that refuses to accept compromises or a so-called "half victory." The enemy will always take advantage of such "half victories" to regroup and counterattack. Moreover, unity must be forged in the midst of struggle. Struggle without unity is wrong; unity without struggle is equally wrong. And one must never take one's desires for reality. The policies of the United Front must always be based on a concrete situation. And one must never forget that the bourgeoisie can participate in the Democratic Revolution but it cannot and must not lead it. This theme came up time and again.

So from these and many other conversations I drew my conclusions as to what course China would follow in the years ahead. Victory for Mao Tse-tung's line seemed assured for a long time to come. Of course, there would be periods of struggle and consolidation: on the one hand, Mao's opponents would never acknowledge themselves beaten; on the other hand, Mao would use each new victory to strengthen the revolutionary triple alliance of masses, Party cadres, and army. Many of the Party officials who for a year and a half had been hostile to Mao's line or who had left their Party posts during the clash between "the two lines," were now won over to the Cultural Revolution; and Liu Shao-chi's line was increasingly weakened and isolated.

Having successfully survived this major test, China could now direct its tremendous energies toward developing its industry, agriculture, and foreign trade, without retreating an inch in its ideological concepts and its revolutionary mission in the world. Consequently, I understood the sense of calm that governed China's leaders as they viewed the world scene. Their country had broken out of its commercial and diplomatic isolation, and they were confident that any attempts to isolate them from the masses of the world would fail dismally. In all this there was also the renowned Chinese patience, the ability to wait as long as necessary for the facts to decide who had been right.

My conversations in my Peking hotel room with these seasoned military-political experts, lasting many hours, would alone have justified my third trip to China. In the midst of the Cultural Revolution, at a time when the outside world asserted that all criticism had been muted and all free discussion killed in China, here I was, a non-Chinese and a non-Communist, engaged in a completely free give-and-take of ideas with responsible Chinese officials. More-over, I asked questions which could scarcely have been posed or answered in another capital of the Socialist world.

I left China with the feeling that this might be my last visit there. There is a Chinese proverb that says: "There is no three without four," and I do remember having been in Peking at the same time as that great American W. E. B. Du Bois, who was then ninety years old. It is indeed a rejuvenating experience to travel in China and to witness the enthusiasm of its people, the ardor of its youth. Nevertheless, I wondered whether I would return.

In any event, I considered myself fortunate indeed to have been in China at the height of the Cultural Revolution and, as a writer on international affairs, in a position to tell the truth as I saw it no matter how unpopular it might be. For it was not popular in the West—even in many left-wing circles—to hear it said that the Chinese Revolution was not going to lose its vitality, not even after the disappearance of its central figure, Mao Tse-tung. And that having stood the test of that vast upheaval, the Cultural Revolution, which was like several earthquakes all in one, China would overcome all its difficulties.

Together with the Russian Revolution of 1917, the Chinese Revolution has left its mark on an entire century. Just as the Russian Revolution in its great period of upsurge was ill understood and presented falsely, so the Chinese Revolution—and the Cultural Revolution within it—has been woefully misunderstood. Those who refuse to face the facts and indulge in wishful thinking have missed its historical significance. But however much they talk about "the chaos in China," and however long the Cultural Revolution continues, and whatever harsh and even violent clashes may recur between the two opposing lines of Mao and his opponents, China is now a great revolutionary force for socialism in the world—and becoming more so, each new day of its existence.

11

SOCIALISM IN THE 1970's

The world has emerged from the "Cold War" period that followed World War II, in which the Great Powers strove for world leadership. There is now an unmistakable desire on the part of many peoples to rid themselves of every kind of foreign domination and an unshakable resolve to assert their national independence. This is the outstanding and distinctive feature of our present-day world: thrusts toward world hegemony are met by counterthrusts of independence. As a result, we have a very complex international situation, with a good deal of confused thinking in the camp of socialism. The danger is that many, because they do not understand what is going on, will fall victim to skepticism and cynicism and thereby play into the hands of the reactionary, anti-Socialist forces.

Year after year U.S. imperialism continued its brutal assault against the people of Vietnam. Washington's insane policy—under three successive Presidents: Kennedy, Johnson, and Nixon—also stemmed from confused thinking and a profound lack of understanding on the part of United States generals, diplomats, and political leaders. They just did not understand the nature of a popular revolutionary war, a war in which a small people's will to struggle, to win, and if need be to die, doomed the efforts of the strongest military, industrial, and financial power on earth: the United States of America. In theory the United States was "unbeatable"; in practice, after an agreement was finally arrived at in the winter of 1973, it had lost the war.

But since the war in Vietnam took so long to be brought to an end, and since Czechoslovakia's independence was reduced to a mere fiction in 1968 by a Soviet show of force, many feel that to go on talking about socialism and revolution seems to be complicity in a falsehood. Consequently, they succumb readily to disillusionment and despair. They begin to feel that nothing—whether the Russian Revolution, the Chinese Revolution, the Tupamaros' struggle in Uruguay, the liberation struggles in Africa, the underground fight in Spain—nothing whatever merits the confidence of workers, students, intellectuals, or the masses in general. As a result, during the past few years confusion has grown in the ranks of the left-wing movements of the world, weakening and at times demoralizing them to the advantage of the reactionary forces. The source of this confusion lies primarily in the fact that political parties which once enjoyed the confidence of the masses have been somewhat discredited. They are suspected of being attracted more by pursuit of power than by the Revolution, and in countries with parliamentary regimes of being interested solely in winning elections and thus putting their own people in the seat of government.

Has there been a downgrading of militancy, forcing a split in left-wing parties with those of their members who are not prepared to give up a revolutionary line? So *gauchisme*, or "ultra-leftism," was born. The French term is perhaps the best way of describing the many dissident groups that have broken away from the major parties and movements of the Left—the Communists, Socialists, anarchists —and then in turn have split into even smaller groups, all of which quarrel stridently and bitterly among themselves and add to the general confusion. Free of the tight discipline of an established left-wing party, each *gauchiste* group claims to be the sole represent-ative of genuinely revolutionary ideology, strategy, and tactics.

One must really have a Marxist training and an abiding faith in the revolutionary capacity of the masses not to be discouraged by this lack of unity and understanding among the various leftist groups and sects that ransack the vocabulary to find distinctive names and symbols for themselves. But despite the bewildering and often exasperating proliferation of such groups, especially to those accustomed to thinking in terms of a single unified Communist or Socialist party, or a more or less united anarchist movement, one must not view these splits as definitive. Indeed, such a viewpoint would be extremely harmful to the cause of socialism. For just let the reactionaries threaten and the "grouplets" immediately take steps to unite, as was the case in France, for example, in the spring of 1972 when a worker in the Renault factory was killed by an employee of the management. Quickly all the constituent elements of the revolutionary Left, including Trotskyists, Maoists, and others, set up a united front to protest the slaying. This tendency to close ranks whenever there is a provocation from the Right can be confirmed in various parts of the world.

There is no reason, therefore, from the revolutionary and Socialist point of view—using "Socialist" in its broadest sense—to consider *gauchisme* a bad thing *per se*. To begin with, *gauchisme* is inevitable. If parties and movements in which revolutionary hopes have been placed become "bourgeoisified," to use a favorite current expression, what alternative presents itself to their former members or sympathizers who refuse to give up their revolutionary aims? Either they go into retirement and stay at home, or they split off and set up a separate group. True, *gauchisme* made terrible mistakes at the outset, and it was never sufficiently understood by those members of the traditional parties of the Left who condemned out of hand any dissidence. Another element of confusion to some—likewise deriving from the complex international situation, although it is a much more transitory thing—is the reactivation of China's foreign policy after the Cultural Revolution. As a result, the bipolar hegemony of the two superpowers has now become at the very least a triangular relationship, and this has had very serious, very important implications for the future of socialism.

It is from this angle—the ending of bipolar politics—that one must view President Nixon's visit to Peking in 1972. Remember that the visit came at the request of Nixon, not of Peking; and this put the Chinese leaders in a favorable position to end any efforts at

U.S.-Soviet joint control without themselves making any concessions in the realm of principles. Former Premier Pierre Mendès-France, who was in China after Nixon's visit, has commented publicly that China sacrificed neither its ideology nor its interests as a major power. The fact that China has now fully entered upon the international scene with its ideology intact and a profound belief in equal rights for all nations large and small, is something of extraordinary significance. In the words of Cambodian Prince Sihanouk, who has lived in political exile in China for several years and seen China from the inside, "the Third World nations, both those inside and outside the United Nations, have in China a nation that 'will never sell them out.'" Not once during Nixon's visit to Peking did I hear a single expression of misgivings from the North Vietnamese participants in the Paris peace talks with the United States—and particularly not from Madame Binh, the able Foreign Minister of the National Liberation Front, who does not mince her words—that Nixon's visit to the Chinese capital might change China's attitude toward the Vietnam War one iota.

A good many confused or pessimistic leftists, looking for an alibi to cover up their own political weariness or inactivity, put forth the argument that at bottom all nations are alike, all of them care only about their national interests, and all leaders are solely after power. But let them apply these ideas to concrete situations in the world today to see how wrong they are.

Undeniably the present world situation is complex, and even the so-called "experts" and "pundits" in international affairs frequently go wrong in their appraisals and predictions. Why then should one be puzzled if young workers or students cannot see clearly what is happening in Asia, Latin America, the Middle East, or Spain? But their lack of understanding is no excuse for a totally negative, destructive attitude—as, for example, that socialism has no future whatsoever.

Let us take the case of the Spanish Communist Party, now split, with one section headed by Santiago Carrillo and La Pasionaria, and the other led by General Enrique Lister, neither one of which has succeeded in winning over the Spanish youth. The Spanish Socialist

Party (Partido Socialista Obrero Español) is divided into a bureaucratic section, the Social Democrats in exile (known as the Toulouse Socialists because their headquarters are in that French city), and the Socialists inside Spain, who are militant and have an entirely different position from the right-wing Socialists. Spanish youth, who are the best hope for a truly democratic Spain, are eager to fight against the Franco dictatorship by means of specific actions in the factories, fields, and universities, but they do not find the old-line parties of the Left, the Socialists and the Communists, sufficiently responsive to their attitude. Nevertheless, whatever disillusionment they feel does not make them passive. On the contrary, they have formed new Socialist-oriented organizations that carry out an open fight against Spain's repressive regime. Here I am neither flattering the youth nor blaming them for the splits in the Left; but it is a fact that in Spain, as elsewhere, the youth constitute the fighting vanguard, and they are the ones who will win in Spain. Not to understand this means not to see the basic core of truth in a very complicated situation.

Attracted by a revolutionary program, many of these young people, some of them dissidents from the old-line parties of the Left, others members of no party, have swelled the ranks of the F.R.A.P. (Revolutionary Anti-Fascist and Patriotic Front), a broad movement that seeks to unite all revolutionary groups. Its very existence is proof that it is wrong to characterize the Spanish youth of today as apolitical. No, they are not disillusioned with politics, but what they reject is a kind of politics that pretends to speak for them and manipulates them for narrow partisan purposes, and which they no longer believe capable of leading to a Socialist revolution. Militant, dynamic, they have formed action groups on all the continents, and they represent a rejuvenating force, not a disturbing element, for socialism; not a step backward but a forward leap toward socialism.

If I seem to harp on Spain so much, it is not simply because I am Spanish but because in the present situation Spain is objectively the country in Western Europe with perhaps the greatest promise in the not-too-distant future of promoting a Socialist resurgence that is bound to affect the rest of Europe and Latin America as well.

In some countries in Western Europe—in France and Italy, in any case—the Right has temporarily gained some ground in the world-wide battle between the forces of Left and Right. But the Left has responded with vigor. In France the Communists and Socialists agreed on a common program for the national elections of March, 1973, the political significance of which is obviously far-reaching; and the two parties did well at the polls. For the first time since the 1930's a Popular Front government has a chance to take power in France and spur working-class unity. Although France is not on the threshold of a new May–June, 1968, neither is the French Right finding it so easy to govern the country in the face of rising social tensions and heightened political awareness on the part of the Left. In Italy the Socialists have left the government and have adopted a more militant stance in opposition. The Italian trade-union federations are uniting, not into one organically fused movement, but sufficiently at least to press for the legitimate demands of the Italian working class. Talk of a Fascist peril is increasing in Italy, but should the Italian Neo-Fascists take to the streets, the Socialist-Communist forces would respond far more resolutely than when Mussolini staged his March on Rome in 1922.

European socialism has been heartened by strong voices from the north. Scandinavian socialism may seem relatively mild and evolutionary, but in Sweden Olof Palme has proved that one can be a prime minister and still remain a Socialist. Sensitive to the changes on the world scene, aware of the new correlation of forces and the new phenomenon of small nations challenging the Great Powers, Palme has been neither confused nor defeatist and has remained a farsighted Socialist. As Prime Minister of Sweden, Palme has not been ruffled by Washington's lively displeasure and has personally led demonstrations against the massive U.S. air assault on North Vietnam. At the World Conference on the Environment, the Swedish delegation declared categorically that it was useless to speak of protecting the environment when in Vietnam the environment was being subjected to large-scale destruction with the earth scorched and the vital dikes threatened. The Swedish Socialist statesman did not mind being a lone condemnatory voice in official circles in Western Europe. While some of the most eminent Socialists in and out of government kept silent, Palme spoke out clearly, without empty rhetoric, in a way that reminded one of Jean

Jaurès. He has explained how right after World War II he was obsessed by the problems of the Third World and how, at that time, he was looked upon as mad when he proposed that every industrialized nation devote 1 per cent of its gross national product to aid for underdeveloped countries. Olof Palme did not take refuge in a comfortable position of above-the-battle neutrality, because he insisted that neutrality did not mean isolation or abstention. Instead, he declared bluntly: "A United States military victory in Vietnam would be its greatest humiliation" and, on another occasion, "I will not consent to my country being humiliated" by President Nixon. Palme felt that the greatest humiliation of all would be a victory against a small people won by unrestricted use of U.S. air power.

From the official Communist camp, the head of the Romanian Communist Party, Nicolae Ceausescu, an independent-minded leader, rendered an equally valuable service to the Socialist cause when he asserted his country's fierce desire for independence after Soviet tanks entered Czechoslovakia in 1968. At the time a rumor went the rounds that Ceausescu had told Leonid Brezhnev that undoubtedly Soviet troops could reach Bucharest, but that it would cost them at least twenty thousand lives. True or not, the story illustrates the climate of resistance to any foreign intervention that Ceausescu had created in his land. Speaking for more than six hours on July 19, 1972, to the National Conference of the Romanian Communist Party before 2,200 delegates and 500 guests, the Romanian leader dwelt at length on his country's domestic and foreign policy. In that connection he announced the establishment of a Ministry of Development designed to raise the Romanian standard of living within two decades to such an extent as to prove that socialism meant not poverty but more authentic and more lasting prosperity than free enterprise could provide. Ceausescu also called for a genuinely independent foreign policy and the creation of a supranational organization in the Balkan area which, though it might be viewed with disfavor by the Great Powers, "would be an organization for the closest economic cooperation among the nations in the region." He also urged that the Balkans be converted into a demilitarized and atom-free zone. Finally, he reiterated his key point: the absolute right of each nation to achieve socialism along the road it chooses.

Minority groups, no matter how small, have their place and the right to defend their viewpoint, as Jean-Paul Sartre has tirelessly proclaimed. That is why the militant French writer and thinker has paid tribute to such "grouplets" as the animators of true socialism, for, according to Sartre, they fill the vacuum left by parties that have moved away from the Revolution. Some intellectuals, dashed in their hopes of this or that revolution, or this or that political party, have quit the struggle and make sport of Sartre's *engagement*. But that noted intellectual is an impressive living example of one who refuses to give up the fight for socialism as he sees it. A Nobel Prize winner who refused to accept the prize on principle, an intellectual whom French President Charles de Gaulle addressed as *"mon cher maître,"* Sartre has sponsored radical and extremist groups with which he did not fully agree but which he felt served the cause of revolution.

As the last quarter of our century draws near and historical changes occur with dizzying rapidity, one change seems to me sensational: the attitude of the young people in the United States. Here was a nation that by virtue of its power, position, history, and traditions seemed destined to remain "uninfected" by the universal challenge to the established order; yet in a few years the young people of America have changed all that. They have refused to accept the explanations of the Vietnam War given them by the Establishment; they have rejected a society based on wealth and racial discrimination and have only contempt for reactionary, anti-Socialist, and anti-Communist leaders in the working class, such as A.F.L.–C.I.O. president George Meany.

Of course, when one speaks about the new United States, the "other" America, one must omit the conservative forces, including the trade-union leadership. For things have really developed in that country in a topsy-turvy fashion. The sons and daughters of the affluent no longer accept their parents' affluent, racist society in which they have grown up because it violates their deepest sense of ethics and social justice. On the other hand, many workers have become "bourgeoisified." No greater indictment can be made of labor leaders such as Meany than that they have been unable or unwilling to educate the working class politically, to "politicize" their union members. Instead they have bent all their energies toward a "pork chop" policy of making money and have vociferously supported their government as it rained death over Vietnam. And that is why the labor movement in the United States has alienated such broad sections of the international labor movement, in which it had figured as an unrespected exception.

But the young people who campaigned in the presidential election for Eugene McCarthy in 1968 and for George McGovern in 1972 have given a powerful impetus to the movement for change. Their activity is not just a passing phenomenon, for while their movement will undoubtedly have its ups and downs—as in the anti-Vietnam and peace actions that spanned so many years—the process itself is irreversible and represents one of the many complexities in the current world situation. Many have failed to understand this because they do not realize the deep-seated nature of the changes occurring in the United States. Millions of high school and university students have contributed significantly to this process, so that now even some of the trade-union leaders are beginning to take note of it. Hitherto only a few heads of small, local unions have fought consistently against racism at home and the Vietnam War abroad. War veterans —the Vietnam Veterans against the War—and older ex-soldiers such as the Veterans of the Abraham Lincoln Brigade who fought in the Spanish Civil War have taken a similar stand. But now some of the leaders of the largest trade unions in the country are beginning to have second thoughts about the selfish, narrow, shortsighted, and reactionary direction of the American labor movement.

Every time in recent years I have attended a session of the General Assembly of the United Nations in New York City, I have been struck by the international repercussions of what is happening inside the United States. And whenever I have spent time with young people there, I have come away encouraged by their attitudes: they have asked me questions about the activities of the anti-Franco students in Spain; they read widely about world affairs, showing familiarity with books which were previously studied only by scholars and specialists; and they have manifested a deep desire to bring about a United States known for the quality of its life and the greatness of its spirit, not by the amount of destruction wreaked by its B-52 bombers.

The Cuban Revolution of 1959, led by two remarkable individuals, Fidel Castro and the late Ernesto "Che" Guevara, opened a new period of history in the Western Hemisphere. Following in their wake, Salvador Allende in Chile sought to give a new, powerful impetus to the advance of socialism in Latin America.

The Chilean "experiment" was exciting in itself, and Dr. Allende combined steadfast loyalty to his Socialist ideals with great political skill. Without the latter he would have found it difficult to undo the intrigues of the dual opposition to his regime: the opposition within Chile from all the special interests who felt threatened and the opposition from the United States, which from the outset manifested its hostility toward Allende's policy of nationalization. Despite this twofold opposition, President Allende succeeded in one year alone—1971—in nationalizing Chile's copper industry, taking over the banks, expropriating 1,378 landed estates, increasing the consumption of blue-collar and white-collar workers by 12 per cent, and expanding housing at a faster rate than ever before.

It goes without saying that neither the domestic opposition, led chiefly by the Christian Democratic Party that preceded Allende's government coalition, nor the United States could tolerate the idea that such an experiment in "socialism through democracy" could succeed, inasmuch as Allende's success would transform the situation in Latin America and give the march toward socialism irresistible momentum in that entire area. So no efforts were spared to topple Allende. These attempts reached a high point with the truckers' strike in October, 1972, supported by all the elements the right-wing and extreme right-wing opposition could mobilize. It was a political strike with the aim of paralyzing the nation, and Salvador Allende emerged temporarily victorious from what had been the sternest test in his presidential career. He won because at that time he had on his side the bulk of the working class and the army.

Whereas in Brazil the United States used the Brazilian army to stage a coup and do away with the progressive though weak and vacillating government of President João Goulart, in Chile matters were different. There the army had always been on the side of the lawfully constituted government; and that was one of the reasons why Allende always took pains to remain within the framework of legality. Unable, therefore, to utilize the Chilean army against

Allende, the U.S. government tried a more indirect method: a world boycott of Chile's copper, the chief source of its national wealth. Simultaneously with the above-mentioned assault launched by the Christian Democrats in October, 1972, against the Allende government, the U.S. Braden-Kennecott copper interests sued in the courts of Paris and Rotterdam to have all Chilean copper destined for Europe confiscated. Dr. Allende, proceeding calmly but with determination, thwarted this dual maneuver of the Chilean opposition and the U.S. economic saboteurs. He still seemed to have the army on his side, as well as the overwhelming majority of the workers behind him. Not a single factory closed its doors; the railways, seaports, mines, and public utilities functioned normally. Workers and students—Party and non-Party members alike—volunteered to distribute food to the population.

Allende's enemies—in Chile the wealthy residents of Barrio Alto, where they have their expensive villas, and in international financial circles those who grew panicky at the thought that Allende's experiment might succeed—were confident that inflation and economic crisis would throttle this attempt to achieve socialism through democratic means. So whereas Brazil's military regime received at least $456,000,000 in 1971 from international financial institutions, Allende's Chile received barely $55,000,000. But in the words of Allende's Minister of Economy, Carlos Matus: "To us the crisis is the solution. . . . If the previous government had been in the situation in which we found ourselves, it would long since have fallen. . . . You see, there remains the fundamental fact that in spite of everything most Chilean workers live better today than two years ago."

Dr. Allende was not easily provoked or intimidated, because he realized that in the final analysis his strength lay in the confidence the masses had in him. He resisted suggestions from the M.I.R.—the movement of the extreme Left—that he deal more harshly with the right-wing opposition. Nevertheless, he continued to maintain good relations with the M.I.R., which during the October, 1972, crisis backed him completely. He was a legalist, but he was also a man of action. A ranking official of the Chilean government who was close to Allende told me in 1972 that the President would patiently exhaust every effort to pursue a democratic, constitutional path. But if the opposition tried to abuse his patience and resorted to violence, he would reply with violence—even if it meant arming the workers of Chile. Events tragically belied these hopes. The army brusquely shed its neutrality, and in September, 1973, leaders of Chile's armed forces staged a well-planned, forcible coup similar in some respects to the July, 1936, Fascist uprising in Spain. Blood flowed freely. Allende himself met a tragic death in his presidential palace. Counter-revolution triumphed in Chile—for how long it is impossible to say. But the overturn was a shattering blow to those who believed that in Allende's Chile a peaceful, democratic way to socialism was possible. Many now pointed to the example of Castro's revolution in Cuba as the way out for the peoples of Latin America.

As socialism develops in the world, Africa presents one of its least understood stages and is an added source of confusion in the camp of the Left. Nevertheless, a close study of the various currents at work in independent Africa shows that, despite all the obstacles to the formation of a united African front, the decade of the 1970's offers increasingly favorable prospects for the advance of socialism there.

Thus far the newly independent nations of Africa have followed a long, hard road, punctuated by frequent military coups and neo-colonial intrigues. At the outset the main goal was national independence, a complete break with the imperialist ruling powers. This independence bore the imprint of democratic intentions and respect for elementary human rights as well as a vague awareness that the newly liberated nations should come to an understanding among themselves in order to resist the pressures of the colonialists, who were thinking up new, indirect ways to exploit them. Political thinking in the newly independent nations was directed, albeit slowly and cautiously, toward socialism. And the initial promoter of African unity was the great Afro-American writer and thinker Dr. W. E. B. Du Bois, a man I was privileged to know well. (I shall never forget having dinner in his house: Du Bois was then almost ninety yet ate and drank much more than I did. The following year Du Bois went to China, and then to Ghana, where he remained until his death, at ninety-five, working on his monumental African Encyclopedia.)

Du Bois was a lifelong Socialist in the fullest sense of the term, and when toward the end of his life he joined the Communist Party of the United States, it was a meaningful act of solidarity toward the American Communists, who were victims of Senator Joseph McCarthy and the ensuing "McCarthyism." Through Du Bois' eyes I perceived the future in store for the African nations at a time when many were disoriented by the cliché that those nations were not yet ready for independence, a thesis dear to the heart of neo-colonialists of every stripe. I have also discussed this problem with Gabriel d'Arboussier, whom I knew in France and who, in Dakar, has specialized in the study of Marxism and social classes in Africa. D'Arboussier was convinced that in Africa the facts "incontrovertibly supported the scientific theory of Marxism," and that one of the reasons for the slowness of the African countries to become genuine masters of their own destiny was their pronounced economic backwardness and the existence of a still very weak working class.

Africa's advance toward socialism must be visualized in terms of both this factor and Lenin's theory on the national and colonial question. Lenin, it will be recalled, insisted that so long as foreign domination remains, class conflicts within the colonial community are attenuated by the very demands of the fight for independence. To shake off the colonial yoke all must unite. But at the same time Lenin asserted that it was the inescapable duty of the working class in the dominating imperialist powers to recognize without reservation and by its deeds the right of the dominated and colonized peoples to their independence.

The original concept of independence has been replaced by the more precise and more militant term "genuine independence," a concept brilliantly analyzed by Amilcar Cabral. Cabral, assassinated in Conakry, Guinea, in late January, 1973, was one of the great African leaders and, according to Basil Davidson, the noted British writer on African affairs, a worthy successor to Patrice Lumumba and Frantz Fanon. In Cabral's words: "Though the struggle for independence is our main preoccupation, we must not shut our eyes to problems that go beyond our liberation struggle and bear on the future of our peoples, their economic, social, and cultural evolution along the road of progress." In his memorable speech to the Tricontinental Congress of Havana in 1966, Cabral branded as adversaries not only those still illegally occupying African territories but also U.S. imperialism and those Africans who still believed in compromise and accommodation with their former racist oppressors. In this respect the Ninth Conference of the Organization of African Unity (O.A.N.), held in Addis Ababa, Ethiopia, in June, 1971, constituted a victory for the progressive forces, who rejected a "dialogue" with the Republic of South Africa as proposed by Ivory Coast President Félix Houphouët-Boigny at the Fifth Congress of the United Party of the Ivory Coast. By a vote of 27 to 6, with 5 abstentions, the delegates at Addis Ababa condemned *apartheid* and white-minority rule in South Africa. The Tenth Conference, assembled in Rabat, Morocco, in 1972, reaffirmed this position.

It was a salutary controversy, because no matter how annoying it was to Socialist-oriented Africans even to discuss "dialogue" with South Africa, the debate clearly revealed once again that the touchstone of one's desire for African independence is one's attitude toward *apartheid*, Portugal's colonial policy, and every other manifestation of colonialism and neo-colonialism on that continent. Thus, because South Africa is a relatively wealthy nation, rich in gold, diamonds, platinum, and uranium, some Western powers which claim to be democratic have courted it assiduously—a scandal similar to the "appeasement" of Hitler's Germany in the 1930's. The racist regime of South Africa is becoming, if anything, more oppressive and tyrannical. One of the leaders of the South African resistance movement, Tombo, who lives in exile in Tanzania, is a friend of mine and I see him whenever he comes through Paris; from Tombo I get a detailed account of the daily persecutions, violations of human rights, and breaches of the United Nations Charter in South Africa.

The guerrilla warfare in the Portuguese African colonies points up theories of armed struggle, revolutionary internationalism, and solidarity in battle. The three African countries that constitute the rearguard of the fighting front against Portugal—Guinea, Tanzania, and Zambia—are themselves in the vanguard of the advance of socialism in Africa. The struggle against colonialism goes hand in hand with a constant effort to lay the basis for the socialism of tomorrow. As Amilcar Cabral stated: "The biggest success in our struggle is not that we have been able to win victories over the Portuguese colonialists, but that on the territory we control we have created a new social and cultural life even while we have been fighting. . . . We have conquered more than two-thirds of our national territory without forgetting that national liberation, the fight against colonialism, the realization of progress, and the attainment of independence will all be devoid of meaning to the people unless they bring a real improvement in their existence." In short, unless socialism is achieved.

To the powerful Socialist forces in the Soviet Union and China, to the resurgent Socialist forces in Europe, we must add those of tomorrow in Africa, Asia, and Latin America. Although, I reiterate, the current world situation is complex and at times seems confused, it must not be allowed to obscure from us the living reality of a socialism that increasingly provides an answer to the peoples' demands for peace, social justice, an end to racism, and a world in which each nation, big or small, enjoys equal rights in playing the part history allots it. There is no reason whatever to be dismayed or demoralized by the contradictions and cross currents on the present world scene. On the one hand, world reaction is fighting to survive; on the other, socialism is gaining the upper hand, offering humanity a genuine reason and hope to live. The masses with their revolutionary potential and their creative capacity will guarantee the future of socialism.

INDEX